Power Plays and Pulpits

Telford's Century in Scotland 1750 – 1850

John L. Millar

All rights reserved

No part of this publication may be reproduced, stored in a retrieval system, or transmitted in any form by any means, electronic, mechanical, photocopying, recording or otherwise, without the prior permission of The Handsel Press Ltd

British Library Cataloguing in Publication Data:
a catalogue record for this publication
is available from the British Library

ISBN 978-1-912052-88-2

© John L. Millar 2024

The right of John L. Millar to be identified
as the author of this work has been asserted by him
in accordance with the Copyright, Designs and Patents Act 1988

Typeset in 11pt Minion Pro at Haddington, Scotland

Printed by Helix Binders, Grangemouth

Cover design by Laura Millar

Contents

Acknowledgments and Author's Note	iv
Foreword by the Revd Dr John L. Bell	vi
Introduction	1
Essay 1: The Changing Face of Scotland	4
Essay 2: Perennial Poverty in the Highlands and Islands	17
Essay 3: The Clearances and the Consequences	40
Essay 4: Facing the Difficulties	63
Essay 5: Moderates and Evangelicals: the Battle for the Soul of the Church	91
Essay 6: 'Education, Salvation and Damnation'	120
Colour Section: Parliamentary Churches Today / Maps of Areas Before and After the Clearances / Location of Parliamentary Churches / Telford's Drawings of Church and Manse	
Essay 7: The Distinctive Religious Spirituality of the Highlander	156
Essay 8: The Kirk's Growing Pains	191
Essay 9: Planting New Churches: the Kirk's Highland Ambitions	226
Essay 10: The Parliamentary Churches and the Disruption	264
Epilogue	273
Appendix 1: Glossary	274
Appendix 2: Current Status	278
Appendix 3: Proprietors	281
Appendix 4: First Ministers of Parliamentary Churches	286
Appendix 5: Post-Disruption	289
Bibliography	291

Acknowledgements

The idea for writing this book was sparked by visits to see my dear friend and colleague Revd Valerie Watson. At the time, Valerie was minister on the beautiful Inner Hebridean island of Islay and one of her three congregations worshipped in a Telford church in Portnahaven. Before commencing my visits to see Valerie I knew nothing about the Parliamentary Churches or, indeed, much about the Kirk's history in the period which this book covers. These decades of unrest were certainly not covered in the Ecclesiastical History syllabus in the Faculty of Divinity. We were too busy learning about Athanasius and the Council of Nicea with not much focus on what was happening in Scotland.

I was enchanted by Portnahaven church and resolved to learn more about its history. In short order, a book was born. Valerie insists she only provided some useful background information but Valerie's contributions to the final draft of this book, now a series of essays, is much much more. Her first love is Scottish history and I learned so much from her. Thank you, Valerie.

Without the support of so many people it is doubtful if this book would have got over the line. The personal effects of Covid got in the way on two occasions and, additionally, friends and family encouraged me to keep going in the face of other recurring illnesses.

Copyright acknowledgment to the National Library of Scotland and others is in the colour section in the middle of the book.

I specifically thank my son Ally who gave prompt and expert IT support from Latvia when needed. Also, Ally, as a professional writer, immediately offered himself also as editor-in-chief and the final narratives are so much the better for his expertise and assistance. Thank you, too, to his super-creative wife Laura for designing the front cover. I thank John Bell whom I have known from university days and is a close friend. John willingly and immediately agreed to write the foreword. His encouragement over the four years of research and writing has been immense.

My dear friend Fiona Hunter is a cartographer and undertook to provide the maps which give insight and clarity to the situation in the north and west. Thank you so much, Fiona.

Revd Dr Jock Stein at Handsel Press provided much-needed advice and direction. Thank you, Jock.

Finally, to my beleaguered wife Sandie who has been a virtual book-widow for these past four years. However, throughout that time, she has been nothing but encouraging and supportive, indulging me often when the lure of the study pulled me away, even in the middle of the night. For her patience, understanding and forbearance I can only offer my heartfelt and undying love and thanks. If this book is for anyone, it is for Sandie.

June 2024

Author's note

John Millar is a retired Church of Scotland minister who served in parishes in Glasgow and Lochaber. He is married to Sandie, a retired head teacher, and lives in the west-end of Glasgow. John is a composer of hymns and choral anthems, a keen student of British and American politics, an over-ambitious cook, a passable piano-player and in total love with his wife, children and grand-children. He is one who needs to know more, but ought to know better. He especially supports the work of ReviveMS, a charity focusing on those who suffer from multiple sclerosis and their carers.

Foreword

Recent years have seen the unveiling of aspects of Scotland's history not usually taught in schools. These range from the drowning or burning of women considered to be witches, through active engagement in the operation of slave plantations, to the wilful clearances of native peoples from their land to make way for sheep.

Such aspects of the nation's past occasionally hit the headlines, and the engagement of people of Christian faith with such enterprises cannot be ignored. Less commonly recognised are realities such as the 'Highland Problem', the 'Royal Bounty Provision', the 'Parliamentary Churches' and the influence that British notables such as Thomas Telford, Lord Liverpool and Viscount Melbourne had in the reshaping of civic and religious life in Scotland.

The nation has a long pedigree of a geographical and cultural divide between the predominately affluent English-speaking East and South including the Central Belt, and the more impoverished and Gaelic-speaking North and West.

This collection of essays sheds light on discriminatory practices, Protestant colonising endeavours and ecclesiastical myopia which may be fairly attributed to the 'Established' Church of Scotland from the 17th to the 19th centuries, with regard to the Highlands and Islands.

Here we have an amazing treasury of insights into the relationship between Presbyterianism and Parliament, the impoverishment of Highland peoples and their pastors, and the long-running battles between Moderates and Evangelicals in their wisdom and ignorance as regards how best to offer the services of religion to people whose rural or island life, language and culture, bore little resemblance to that of their ecclesiastical and feudal overseers.

In the past, many Church of Scotland ministers functioned as diarists of land and people, providing information to the compilers of the nation's Statistical Accounts. John Millar, the author of this book, offers us not only factual information regarding ministry in the Highlands and Islands, but also insights into the largely unknown effects of religious and political oversight on some of the most impoverished ministers and congregations in Scotland's past.

It is a great, informative and disturbing read.

John L. Bell

Introduction

The year 2024 is the two-hundredth anniversary of the passing into law of the Highland Churches Act. This Act of Parliament was specifically legislated to facilitate the building of 'Additional Churches in the Highlands and Islands of Scotland' and brought into being what became known as 'Parliamentary Churches'.

The Church of Scotland had long since recognised the need to provide an extended missionary presence across the vast swathes of the inhospitable landscapes of the north and west. It was not uncommon for clergy, working on their own, to be expected to minister to, and meet the needs of widely-scattered communities in parishes up to 60 miles long and 40 miles wide. Some people in the remotest parts never saw their minister from one year to the next.

Such a necessary increase in ministers and buildings was beyond the finances of the local and national Church and, after a similar scheme had been approved for the Church of England, the General Assembly of the Church of Scotland petitioned the Government for financial assistance. This first overture was in the Parliamentary session 1817-1818. The following six years saw the Kirk prosecute its case in the face of formidable opposition, both from English MPs and from dissenting congregations within Scotland who opposed close Church-State relations. It took a further six years to bring the project to completion. The thorny matter of the Kirk's relationship to the State, in terms of both government and the Scottish legal system, was both unclear and confused, and in the main, untested.

When the Highland Churches Bill was finally enacted, the renowned Scottish engineer Thomas Telford was appointed to oversee the project. He was given a budget of £50,000 with strict conditions attached. 32 churches with manses were to be erected at an expenditure of no more than £1,500 per site. The Government would bear stipend costs of £120 per annum per charge. Dissenters continued to voice their disapproval of the Kirk being in any way 'indebted' to the State. By the time the build-work was completed, Telford, conscious of the authority under which he had been appointed, had submitted seven progress reports directly to the Lords of the Treasury. Only as a courtesy did successive General Assemblies receive these reports. This was very definitely a British Government project.

The General Assemblies of 1699 and 1700 had offered encouragement and advice to local Highland presbyteries to build more churches and even earlier commissions had recognised the pressing need for new buildings and the redrawing of parish boundaries. 125 years later the Parliamentary Churches scheme was the Kirk's first serious and co-ordinated attempt to implement what became known as 'Church Extension', a systematic plan which envisaged an increase both in the number of church buildings and in the number of parishes. The Church Extension scheme was later adopted with success in the more populous regions of the central belt and this movement, centralised through the work of a General Assembly committee and galvanised by the redoubtable Dr Thomas Chalmers, drove the church forward especially in the 1830s. The 'organic' growth in the number of churches had already been a feature for decades where congregations had outgrown buildings and erected new places of worship but there had been little of this planned church growth in the north and west.

By the time the Parliamentary Churches were up and running, the Kirk was in a ferment of theological, doctrinal and constitutional dispute, a period which became known as the 'ten years' conflict'. By the end of the 1830s schism seemed inevitable and culminated in The Disruption of 1843, where one third of ministers abandoned the Kirk to form the Free Church. Many kirks across the north and west including some Parliamentary Churches were vacated as ministers led congregations out of the Church of Scotland.

During those years of conflict the Kirk was forced to self-examine what its purpose was, its place in society, its relationship with the levers of Government, its obligations to the civil law and by no means least, how best to serve its people. The Highland Churches Act had a troublesome conception and the Parliamentary Churches themselves a challenging birth and infancy but which gave them, their ministers and congregations a prominent role in the calamitous events leading to 1843.

This book comprises a series of essays which attempts to set out the historical, economic, social and theological contexts of the times within which the Parliamentary Churches were established and the particular challenges the Kirk faced across the Highlands and Islands, from within and without. As Great Britain prepared itself for a long period of Victorian prosperity, the situation north of the Highland line was to remain relatively untouched by such aspirations.

Introduction

The Church of Scotland has long regarded itself as being a 'broad' church, able to accommodate the widely-held differing theological perspectives of the conservative and the liberal. Herein lies its strength ... and its weakness. As the Kirk struggled to hold together the views of the right and of the left, it became increasingly obvious throughout the 1830s and early 1840s that matters would reach breaking point.

During this brief but dramatic moment in time, the Church of Scotland faced challenges and change so significant that its trajectory would be realigned entirely. Although the essays which focus on the Parliamentary Churches conclude the book, this is a story with a broader context: of where the Scottish nation was in the late 18th and early 19th centuries; of the differences between the Highlands and Lowlands in terms of language, culture, history, geography and spirituality; of the theological stresses and strains felt within the Kirk itself; of the constitutional issue of 'Church and State'; of the difficult relationship with successive Governments and the Kirk's attempts, over 20 years, to secure a measure of state funding; of the arguments relating to the competing claims of civil and ecclesiastical law; and lastly, how the Kirk, over successive decades, attempted to find solutions to the 'Highland Problem'.

Although the Parliamentary Churches were caught up in the tumult of the times, they remained a bold enterprise which altered the parochial landscape of the north and west, thus changing the face of the Kirk forever. The coming of the Parliamentary Churches was one such 'solution' and whose model, it was hoped, would be rolled out across the nation. But it was not to be and perhaps this was a missed opportunity.

At present, despite the momentous changes affecting the Kirk across the entire country, the Parliamentary Churches have their honourable place among the Kirks of Scotland. As buildings, the legacy of these Telford churches is secure, at a time when Scotland herself is still engaged in working out its place, as a people and a nation, part of a United Kingdom and the wider world.

Essay One

The Changing Face of Scotland

'In most respects, indeed, the Scotland of 1800, unlike that of 1707, was abreast of contemporary progress . . . the Scottish banks, with their deposits and cash-credits were all along a boon to industrialists, merchants, farmers and fishermen.'

Rait and Pryde, *Scotland*

Economic Change

In *A History of Scotland* Rosalind Mitchison remarks:[1] 'Scotland packed into about 30 years of crowded development between 1750 and 1780 the economic growth that in England had spread itself over two centuries.' That rapid rate continued for several more generations. Mitchison hails the great Scottish economic boom, highlighting that industrialisation was not only creating wealth for some, but also bringing in its wake a new level of poverty for others. However, outside the cities there existed 'another' Scotland in the main untouched by increases in trade and commerce. The Highlands and Islands remained a world apart, facing their own challenges and problems, but they too would experience change of a different kind.

In 1785 New Lanark was established – an early form of urban planning centred around water-powered mills and workers' housing. The 'father of civil engineering' John Smeaton completed the Forth & Clyde canal in 1790 – a route for sea-going vessels across the 'waist' of Scotland from the Firth of Clyde to the Firth of Forth. Both James Watt and Thomas Telford became two of the chief agents of the industrial revolution. Watt's development of the steam engine drove forward the exploitation of the Scottish coalfields and powered much of Scottish industry while Telford made his mark as a builder of bridges, canals, roads and harbours. Trade with the West Indies grew from the exporting of cheap cloth for slaves in return for the highly profitable commodities of tobacco, cotton and sugar.

---

1 Rosalind Mitchison, *A History of Scotland,* second edn, 345.

Essay 1: The Changing Face of Scotland

Daniel Weir, writing in 1829 his *History of the Town of Greenock*, reported that

> in Spring 1816, the first ship from Scotland for the East Indies sailed from Greenock. This vessel, the *Earl of Buckinghamshire, Captain Christian*, of 600 tons register, was soon followed by others, and the tonnage now embarked in the trade is very considerable . . . It is to be hoped, that, ere long, the trade to China will also be thrown open to the country at large; petitions to the legislature, to this effect, having lately flowed from every corner of the kingdom'.[2]

Economic change was under way, and Scotland was beginning to make headway towards a modern industrial society. It had started in cottages and village smithies and workshops – iron work, spinning and weaving, distilling, tile-making, rope and box and brickmaking. Once steam technology had advanced sufficiently to power machines that would produce materials in bulk, industry came to town. The development of the iron trade was rapid: in 1827 the entire production of Great Britain was 690,000 tons, Scotland contributing 36,000 tons. 20 years later Scotland alone produced 690,000 tons. Exports multiplied nine-fold in 50 years. The production of printed cotton cloth, produced by cylinder and invented by Thomas Bell, rose in Scotland every year from 1818 when 46,565 bales were produced to 1834 when the number of bales rose to 95,603.

Coal was the power that fuelled the large works that mushroomed across the middle of Scotland – along the line of the coal field that stretched from Ayr to Fife, down the coastlines and along large rivers with tall cranes and cables, in growing towns with massive mills. Daniel Gray in *A Life of Industry: the Photography of John R. Hume* takes us into the large engineering enterprises that proliferated throughout the 19th century:

> Ironworks, steelworks and collieries seem now mystical and mythical beasts from a distant age. They are fierce and yet magnificent, their scale making us gulp. Perhaps we may imagine the way they shook the senses; piercing ears, singeing nostrils, drying mouths. How the heat must have swarmed, and how the grime must have gathered in the hair, nails and crows' feet of men. Those men filed along precarious edges and climbed improvised ladders . . . and underground miners shared

---
2 Daniel Weir, *History of the Town of Greenock, 1829*, 31.

a bond that was mightier than the machines which powered their industry. Communities were built on their drudgery.[3]

A huge increase in productive capacity fed the fast-growing population of Scotland; in 1750 the population was around 1,265,000; by 1801 the population was over 1,600,000, and by 1831 it was well over 2 million: an unprecedented rate of growth. Industry came to town, and the people followed. Greenock was one such town that experienced an influx of workers from the Highlands and Islands. In the 1790s the Highland population in the town represented a third of the total. Wealthy Highland inhabitants raised by voluntary subscription the sum of £1500, and erected a 'large, elegant and commodious Gaelic chapel, and endowed it with £100 per annum'. Their choice of minister was quite clear: he must be of the Established Church and one who would be able to preach both in Gaelic and in English.

From early 17th century it was recorded that Greenock consisted of a single row of thatched cottages with the beginning of a herring industry. By 1795 Greenock possessed only a rope work, a few factories and two sugar houses but by this time workers from the Highlands and Islands were appearing in numbers. Greenock was expanding rapidly. By 1845 the list included wool, flax and cotton mills, grain and rice mills, sugar refineries, tanneries, potteries, breweries, a distillery, cooperage, paper and chemical works. Besides these, there were seven shipbuilding companies and four boatbuilders, along with foundries, chain and anchor works. The poet John Davidson wrote of Greenock:

> This grey town . . . that pipes the morning up before the lark
> with shrieking steam, and from a hundred stalks
> lacquers the sooty sky; where hammers clang
> on iron hulls, and cranes in harbours creak,
> rattle and swing whole cargoes on their necks.[4]

Urban Migration

The town population quadrupled in the last quarter of the 18th century: it subsequently rose from 17,458 in 1801 to 36,000 in 1845. A footnote in the 1845 Statistical Account for Glasgow recalls the status of mineworkers in times past:[5]

---

3 Daniel Gray, *A Life of Industry: The Photography of John R Hume*, 45.
4 John Davidson, *Greenock: A Ballad in Blank Verse*, 1894.
5 *The Statistical Accounts of Scotland 1845: Rutherglen, County of Lanark*, vol. VI, 378.

> It is a curious fact, which we believe is not generally known, that, previous to the year 1775, all colliers and other persons employed in coal works in Scotland, were, by the common law of the land, in a state of slavery. They and their wives and children, if they had assisted for a certain period at a coal work, became the property of the coal master, and were transferable with the coal work, in the same manner as the slaves on a West Indian estate were till lately held to be property, and transferred on a sale of the estate.

Hugh Miller noted that the emancipating act in 1775 had fallen short, and a second act was passed in 1799 because 'many colliers and coal bearers still continue in a state of bondage.'[6] Miller discovered that this slavery had not derived from the ancient times of general serfship, but to have originated in comparatively modern acts of the Scottish Parliament and in decisions of the Court of Session – in acts of Parliament in which the poor ignorant subterranean men of the country were, of course, wholly unrepresented, and in decisions of a Court in which no agent of theirs ever made appearance in their behalf. In Airdrie the only industries at the end of the 18th century were farming and weaving: all the farmers owned their small farms, 207 of them, and the weaving industry employed 227 children who flowered muslin with the tambour-needle.

Across the Lowlands the practice of combining small farms into a large farm was widespread. Numbers made superfluous by this measure flocked into towns, where with difficulty they earned a scanty subsistence. Between 1755 and 1831 the population of Lanarkshire grew from 82,000 to 317,000, most of them in towns, and the population of Glasgow and the suburbs grew from 62,000 in 1791, to 147,000 in 1821 to 202,000 in 1831. Foreign trade, notably the importation of sugar, cotton and rum from the West Indies grew exponentially, bringing great wealth especially to the Glasgow area.

Coal works and iron works and greatly increased demand for weavers for the Glasgow manufactures accounted for the progressive increase in population in Airdrie in the following 30 years from 4,500 to nearly 10,000. The Statistical Account for Kirkcaldy in 1845 describes the difficulty linen manufacturers had in expanding their businesses as they had to provide houses for their weavers. Linen output was in direct proportion to the number of weavers the trade could accommodate.

---

6 Hugh Miller, *My School and Schoolmasters*, 302 fn.

Matters improved around 1845 however as 'weavers now find houses for themselves and seek after manufacturers who are willing to employ them.'[7] Businesses were growing, and in 1845 the gross value of linen manufacture in the town reached £80,000 per year (over £8m in today's terms). In addition to home trade with Scotland and England, these linens found markets in Canada, the United States, South America, the West Indies and Australia, further fuelling the Atlantic trade. In the report citing Hamilton for the same year, males employed in manufacture totalled 1257, all but 122 of them living in the town. The minister added to his report to the New Statistical Account:[8] 'This is a manufacturing population, a great proportion of whom are doomed to damp shops, stooping postures, meager fare and long hours.'

The prosperity of the towns was felt by few, and increasing squalor and disease pervaded the overcrowded streets and houses. In 1845, of the 202,426 residents in Glasgow, 5006 were paupers, i.e. those officially in receipt of poor relief – 'one pauper for every 40.43 persons.' Tight-knit rows of tenements with no sanitation or fresh air were built closer and closer together. In 1818 the population of the greater Glasgow area was afflicted by typhus fever. Voluntary contributions were raised of over £6,600, a temporary fever hospital treated over 1900 patients. In 1833, the 'year of the cholera' carried off large numbers, especially women. Friedrich Engels, German philosopher, political theorist and factory owner, wrote of Glasgow in 1844:[9] 'I have seen wretchedness in some of its worst phases, both here and on the Continent, but until I visited the wynds of Glasgow, I did not believe that so much crime, misery and disease could exist in any civilised country'. Industrial innovation developed nearly a century ahead of concern for the health and safety of workers and the education of children. John Davidson painted a similar picture of Greenock:

> This grey town . . .
> Where men sweat gold that others hoard or spend,
> And lurk like vermin in their narrow streets.

Women also found work in the towns. Archibald Buchanan of Catrine was one of the earliest pupils of the industrialist and mill owner Richard Arkwright who had invented a simplified type of spinning machine, the 'jenny'. Around 1795, Buchanan refitted the mills of James Finlay

---

7 *The Statistical Accounts of Scotland 1845: Kirkcaldy, County of Fife*, vol. IX, 753.
8 *The Statistical Accounts of Scotland 1845: Hamilton, County of Lanark*, vol. VI, 277.
9 Friedrich Engels, *Condition of the Working Class in England*, 50.

and Company at Ballindalloch in Stirlingshire with very light mule jennies thus dispensing with the need to employ men as spinners. Young women were immediately engaged for the work. These he found 'more easily directed than the men, more in attendance to their work, and more cleanly and tidy in the keeping of their machines and contented with much smaller wages. This system has from time to time been partially adopted at other works in Scotland and England; but men are still most generally employed.'[10]

The Old Statistical Account for Glasgow reports that 'Delinquents are often little advanced above childhood, and yet a healthy child of 7 or 8 years, or at most of 10 years of age, can now earn a very decent subsistence from some of the numerous manufactures established among us.'[11]

Intellectual Change

The middle to the end of the 18th century was a time of far-reaching social and intellectual change. The Enlightenment had fostered lively debates in the universities and city clubs over law, government and economics. A growing interest in science and medicine began to have their impact upon society. With the abolition of the slave trade in 1807 came a new and enlightened attitude towards humanity by some, but slaveholding underlay the highly profitable trade from which Scotland had benefited for decades. Opposition led to the creation of Emancipation Societies in Glasgow, Edinburgh and Paisley in 1833.

Jean-Baptiste Say, a liberal French economist in favour of competition, free trade and lifting restraints on business, visited Glasgow around 1830. He sat down in the classroom chair which had been used by Dr Adam Smith, and after a short prayer, said with great fervour, 'Lord, let now thy servant depart in peace.'[12] This liberal pursuit of arts and science was largely restricted to members of the professions and some landowners, but the new wealthy classes were becoming more enlightened about their democratic rights. As their wealth increased the existing political structure seemed to many to be unjust and corrupt. In 1831, the year before the Great Reform Act, one Englishman in 30 was enfranchised yet it was true for only one Scotsman in 600.

---

10 *The Statistical Accounts of Scotland 1845: Glasgow, County of Lanark*, vol. VI, 143.
11 *The Statistical Accounts of Scotland 1793: Glasgow, County of Lanark*, vol. V, 535.
12 *The Statistical Accounts of Scotland 1835: Glasgow, County of Lanark*, vol. VI, 139 fn.

Scotland was proud of its educational reputation, although a concern is voiced in the Statistical Account of 1845: 'That the schoolmaster has been successfully abroad, there can be no doubt; and that the working-classes are becoming more intelligent, every good man must observe with delight; but they are as yet in the transition state, at the point when a 'little learning is a dangerous thing.'[13]

There was concern that educational standards were dropping, even towards the end of the 18th century: in the County of Orkney and Shetland, in the parish of Bressay, Burra and Quarff, the minister lamented that the education of youth was not more attended to[14]: 'The people discover a quickness of apprehension and an aptness to learn which deserve to be encouraged. Many of the young men go abroad, and such of them as have got a decent education rise to prominence.' In Old Monklands in 1793 the public school at the parish church where the salary, £5 11s. 1½d, contributed to by more than 100 heritors,

> is scarcely worth collecting. The schoolmaster is also precentor and session clerk. The emoluments of these offices, though trifling, are better than the salary, but the whole is so shameful a pittance in such a wealthy parish; and it is a disgrace to the country, that such a useful body of men are, in Scotland, so poorly provided for, and calls loudly for redress.[15]

The Revd Lachlan McLachlan, the parish minister of Craignish in the Presbytery of Inveraray, complained in the same year:

> The school salary amounts to about £20 per annum, a miserable allowance to a man of genius for employing his time and talents in qualifying a rising generation to fill up the vacant stations in society with honour. What a reproach to the people of Scotland! At this rate, the ages of darkness will again commence, and Scotland will, ere long, be as remarkable for wealth and ignorance as it was formerly for poverty and learning.[16]

By 1836, little had improved. According to the reports of the government sponsored 'Commission for Religious Instruction' as drawn up by ministers, there was clear reluctance to improve the lot of school-

---

13 *The Statistical Accounts of Scotland 1845: Glasgow, County of Lanark*, vol. VI, 155.
14 *The Statistical Accounts of Scotland 1794: Bressay, Burra and Quarff*, vol. X, 200.
15 *The Statistical Accounts of Scotland 1793: Old Monklands*, vol. VII, 273.
16 *The Statistical Accounts of Scotland 1793: Parish of Craignish, Presbytery of Inveraray*, vol. VII, 443.

masters in every area of the land. In the north and west especially, poor salaries and irregular payments were common complaints. Mr McLachlan was prescient in linking wealth and ignorance for it was not just a plea for improved salaries for teachers but a concern for society's values as a whole.

The authors of the Glasgow contribution to the New Statistical Account of Scotland, drawn up in 1835 by the Principal of the Glasgow College, the Very Revd Duncan Macfarlane, D.D. and by James Cleland, LL.D., Statistician, Member of the Society of Civil Engineers, attested to the multiplication of newspapers and publications which found a growing readership: the *Glasgow Courant* in 1715; the *Journal* in 1729; the *Chronicle* in 1775; the *Mercury* in 1779; the *Advertiser* in 1783 (which changed its name in 1804 to the *Herald*); the *Courier* in 1791; the *Clyde Commercial Advertiser* in 1805; the *Caledonia* in 1807; the *Sentinel* in 1809; a second *Chronicle* in 1811; the *Scotsman* in 1812; the *Packet* in 1813; a second *Sentinel* in 1821; the *Free Press* in 1823; the *Scots Times* in 1825; the *Evening Post* in 1827; the *Trades' Advocate* in 1829; the *Liberator* in 1831; the *Scottish Guardian* and the *Argus* in 1832; and the *Weekly Reporter* in 1834. In 1840 there were 20 newspapers being published weekly in Glasgow alone. The Glasgow Report declared that book societies had been established,[17] 'conducted on a plan similar to that of circulating libraries, with this difference, that the books belong to the readers themselves, who are chiefly of the working classes'. There was a growing appetite for education and information among the working classes.

Change and Hardship

David Hume in his political essays had pointed out that the value of anything depends on the amount of labour needed to produce it – a thought which was to give the working man a new notion of his own importance in the scheme of things. In cities, towns and in some areas of rural Scotland there were sporadic protests about an unjust society. After the peace of 1815 there were periods of bad trade. While industrial expansion soon began again, recurring periods of unemployment arose from the fluctuations of the trade cycle. After 1820, increasing squalor and disease intensified the insecurity of life for the poorest section of the working population. The Napoleonic war had ended in 1815 but the peace had had two serious consequences: it had brought hardship especially to the rural labourers, two-thirds

---

17 *The Statistical Accounts of Scotland 1845: Glasgow, County of Lanark,* vol. VI, 183.

of the entire male population still being employed on the land; the demand for some goods had suddenly plummeted. Scotland shared in the general unrest and discontent of the years 1817-22. In 1819 high levels of unemployment were the cause of great distress. Economic hardship and injustice brought a new element into the rumbling undercurrent of Scottish radicalism. The 'Radical War' of 1820 failed; treason trials were held in the counties of Ayr, Renfrew, Dunbarton, Lanark and Stirling; three leaders were executed and about twenty men were transported to Australia. The militia in Greenock fired on the crowd and killed eight people, including an eight-year-old child. A week of strikes particularly among the weaving communities where it was estimated that 60,000 had stopped work, weapons taken up but above all, a threat to establish a 'Provisional Government' was quickly and violently put down by government forces. However, it indicated a new if tentative solidarity of purpose among the working classes.

The article for Glasgow in the New Statistical Account touched on the issue of unemployment and the city's handling of protests:

> When thousands of workers paraded the streets demanding employment or bread, upwards of 600 persons were almost instantly employed at spade work or breaking up stones for the roads. The magistrates employed upwards of 340 weavers at spade work in the Green, nearly the whole of whom remained for four months... and not one of them left their work to attend public meetings in the Green although thousands marched past them with radical ensigns, accompanied by well-dressed females carrying caps of liberty.[18]

They added that the distress continued during the greater part of 1820, and distributions of clothing, meal and coals were given to those who could not find work. And a similar period of unemployment occurred in 1826 and again public assistance was given, for a year and a half.

Power Inequalities

Various expedients were resorted to by several of the trades, with a view to raise or maintain their wages, such as long apprenticeships. In highly critical terms *The Statistical Accounts of 1845* refers to the development of trades unions,

> many of them having rules and practices surpassing the closest corporations, and outvieing the fiercest tyranny of the darkest

---

18 *The Statistical Accounts of Scotland 1845: Glasgow, County of Lanark*, vol. VI, 121.

ages; and it is strange, that, although these unions have in most of the trades been successively overthrown, still new unions urge the hopeless combat. It bespeaks deplorable ignorance in the mass of the operatives, who have so allowed themselves to be led by a few designing and selfish knaves; and submit to be urged by the violent wrong-headed fools of their order – a class to be found in all communities.[19]

The Account also reported on continuing unemployment which hit all connected with the shawl trade and weavers of all descriptions. Many of the most respectable firms stopped payment. And two savings banks, 'planned and puffed into repute' not by designing and selfish knaves of the lower order but by the magistrates of Paisley, closed their doors.[20] The corporation of Paisley had debts which exceeded the income of the burgh and was declared bankrupt.

The 1832 Reform Act did little more than partially extend the franchise within the propertied classes. The urban and rural elites shared a common faith in property ownership as the best guarantee of political stability. They were politically conservative but economic radicals in their development of capitalism. They removed from the statute book laws such as controls on wages and prices, accelerating the dominance of market forces. The old political order emerged from this early phase of Scottish industrialisation largely unscathed. The power of the landed classes had been modified but not toppled, and it would be another 50-plus years before the old political order began to shift significantly.

The political order of Scotland may have remained unscathed, the power of the landed classes may have survived for another generation or two, but the Church of Scotland entered a century of social and spiritual uncertainty and conflict.

Within the ministry of the Church of Scotland theological and social conflict was evidenced at the meetings of the General Assembly throughout the 1820s: the long-established dominance of the Moderate wing was facing an energetic, more disputatious Evangelical wing. There was an acute shortage of parish ministers: the towns were hugely overcrowded, and the city churches severely under-resourced to meet the needs of a rapidly expanding population. Many of the middle class were Seceders, leaving parish churches and taking their wealth with

---

19 *The Statistical Accounts of Scotland 1845: Glasgow, County of Lanark*, vol. VI, 155.
20 *The Statistical Accounts of Scotland 1845: County of Renfrew*, vol. VII, 554.

them, leaving congregations unable to support a minister. In some areas of the towns and cities barely one person in 20 had any church connection. [21] 'No religious instruction and no desire for it' was Hugh Miller's comment on the lack of religious commitment he encountered among working men in Edinburgh, which he attributed to 'the cold, elegant, unpopular Moderatism'; humbler people had been lost to the Church during the course of the two preceding generations. And the church lagged behind the realities of life in the cities and large towns of Scotland.

The population of greater Glasgow in 1791 was 62,000, served by eight city parish churches plus two on the edge of the city, and three chapels-of-ease. By 1831, the population had risen to 202,000. At that time the Presbytery of Glasgow had ten city ministers and 12 in surrounding parishes. In 1834, 13 chapels-of-ease ministers were raised to the status of parish ministers, bringing the clerical members of Glasgow Presbytery to 35. In 1845 Edinburgh Presbytery recorded 17 city churches and eight outlying parishes, serving a population of 160,000, rising to 190,000 in 1851.

Challenge to the Church

Following the quotation of an embarrassingly fulsome appreciation of the clergy of Scotland in 1808 by Lord President Hope, the Lord Justice-Clerk: 'Where has there been since the world began such a body of clergy in point of virtue, learning, piety, and a faithful discharge of their parochial duties? The clergy of Scotland, I am proud to say, have never been equalled by the clergy of any nation upon earth.'[22] The ministers of Glasgow in their report in 1845[23] speak a little defensively of 'the present overgrown state of the parishes' making full ministerial visitation next to impossible. They recited the laborious duties of a city parish minister, preaching two sermons every Sunday, as well as occasional charity and missionary sermons, running classes for the youth, visiting the sick, assisting the kirk-session in the distribution of the poors' funds, superintending the parish schools and sharing the management of benevolent institutions with the magistrates, as well as their attendance at funerals, kirk-sessions, presbyteries, synods, and general assemblies, and, at best, partial ministerial visitations to the families of their parishioners.

---

21 Hugh Miller, *My Schools and Schoolmasters*, 306.
22 *The Statistical Accounts of Scotland 1845: Glasgow, County of Lanark*, vol. VI, 190.
23 *The Statistical Accounts of Scotland 1845: Glasgow, County of Lanark*, vol. VI, 191.

In 1826 the Glasgow City Mission was established to address 'the total inability of the clergymen of the city to attend to the religious wants of a numerous class of the community, many of whom have no desire for religious instruction.'[24] There were too few churches, so missionaries visited the poor in their own houses, with a view to increasing their knowledge of evangelical truth. By 1831, 20 licentiates or students of divinity worked full-time in the City Mission, and by the following year there was one missionary in every parish, two in the largest parishes.

A report in 1791[25] lists 'dissenting denominations' in Glasgow – two Burgher and one Anti-Burgher, an English chapel and a congregation of Independents, one or two for Anabaptists, one for Glassites, a large Methodist meetinghouse and two congregations of the Relief, 'and a Popish meeting which is conducted with such discretion, that it cannot give the slightest cause of offence'. A less grudging acceptance of Roman Catholics is evident in the efforts of industrialists, who were suffering skill shortages, to attract Highlanders to their factories rather than emigrate to America, by promising security to Roman Catholic Highlanders in the exercise of their religion. This had some success. The increased numbers of Catholics 50 years later, however, owed much to the arrival of Irish workers; by 1841 almost a quarter of the people of the western Lowlands had Irish roots, most being Catholic although a minority were Ulster Presbyterians, and their ancient rivalries migrated with them. But the long debate in Scotland on popery, and home-grown anti-Catholicism, was evident in the years before and after the passing of the Catholic Emancipation Act in 1829. In the Church of Scotland, it was part of the greater conflict of traditional and liberal beliefs.

The Church had long held the view that 'the system of popery was contrary to the Word of God and fraught with superstition'. These words appear in the Glasgow Petition opposing Catholic emancipation, but they echo the language of Acts of the Scottish Parliament in the 17th century such as the Act of 1696:[26] 'Papists employing Protestant servants who by writing, speaking or otherwise debauch and pervert any of his majesty's Protestant subjects to the errors and superstitions of popery, shall be held, proceeded against and punished as a trafficking papist'.

They also echo reports to the General Assembly throughout most of the 18th century. In 1725, the annual King's Bounty of £1000 was

---

24 *The Statistical Accounts of Scotland 1845: Glasgow, County of Lanark*, vol. VI, 193.

25 *The Statistical Account of Scotland 1793: Glasgow, County of Lanark*, vol. V, 518.

26 Act anent Protestant servants in Popish families, 9th October 1696, Records of the Parliaments of Scotland to 1707 (RPS/1696/9/146).

dedicated to 'the Reformation of the Highlands and Islands, for promoting knowledge of true religion and for suppressing popery and profaneness.' And most influential of all within the Church of Scotland, the Westminster Confession of Faith; drawn up in 1646, became the principal subordinate standard of doctrine in the Church of Scotland. Ministers and elders were required to 'sign the Formula' on ordination – an acceptance of the Westminster Confession as a confession of their own faith. It defines the Pope as the Antichrist, and the mass as idolatry.

But the language of General Assembly reports had begun to change subtly from the 1780s onwards. The King's Bounty is directed to 'promoting religious knowledge', with no specific reference to suppression of popery. The concern about Catholicism as a threat to the Protestant succession, half a century and more after the last Jacobite uprising, seemed to diminish. The liberal, Moderate culture of the Church of Scotland sought to mollify the vehemence of the old documents and it was the opposing Evangelical wing which sought to recover and strengthen the Church's Reformation credentials. But it was Revd J. Wylie of Carluke in addressing the Synod of Glasgow and Ayr who asserted that toleration was of the very essence of Christianity, and as Christian ministers and elders it became them to 'adopt the language of peace and goodwill to all brother Christians.'[27]

However, many ministers could not reconcile their spiritual and legal commitment to the Westminster Confession with the Emancipation Bill. And people in the streets demonstrated that loyalty to past generations who had struggled to establish and to re-establish Presbyterianism was not held lightly, and the indigenous anti-Catholicism had not disappeared; emotional meetings were held, handbills proliferated, protests continued until the Act received consent. But the arguments did not end as splits among Presbyterians widened. The issue of toleration for Roman Catholics, after all, was only one sliver of a splintering Church.

---

27 *Glasgow Herald,* 14th March 1829.

Essay Two

Perennial Poverty in the Highlands and Islands

As the Church of Scotland emerged from the 18th century into the 19th, it had been an institution fraught with tensions for several decades. This in an already divided nation wrestling with competing larger notions of romantic nationalism and British loyalty, and between patriotism and parochialism. This cultural bifurcation further extended across geography, history and crucially language. From the end of the 18th century issues of industry and land management were to play increasingly pivotal roles in the economy of the Highlands. While there was no such 'Highland line' in terms of delineation on a map dividing Scotland, there was a clear recognition that the far north (and not *that* far north) was a different place.

> For that is the mark of the Scots of all classes: that he stands in an attitude towards the past unthinkable to Englishmen, and remembers and cherishes the memory of his forebears, good or bad; and there burns alive in him a sense of identity with the dead even to the twentieth generation.
>
> Robert Louis Stevenson, *Weir of Hermiston*

A Different Country

In *Letters from a Gentleman in the North of Scotland to His Friend in London*, related by Edmund Burt in the late 1720s (and not printed until 1754), Captain Burt commented that 'The Highlands are but little known even to the inhabitants of the low country of Scotland . . . But to the people of England, excepting some few, and those chiefly the soldiery, the Highlands are hardly known at all.'[1]

The Government, whether in Edinburgh until 1707 or in London thereafter, were of the opinion that the Highlands of Scotland were a problem. The 'Problem' for the Government varied through the

---

1 Edmond Burt, *Letters from a Gentleman in the North of Scotland*, Letter I, 4.

years and down the centuries – warring clans, lawlessness, Jacobitism, Catholicism, non-payment of taxes, history of rebellion, an uncharted landscape. The Highlands and Islands were considered a single entity – an uncivilised, dangerous place where it was a struggle to survive. There were long spells of 'quiet times' in between, and in troubled times often the troubles were limited to a small area, but the attitude towards the Highlands and Islands seems consistently one of suspicion and distrust and even contempt.

The north-west Highlands and Islands were defined in terms of 'otherness' from a centralising government which placed increasing importance on cultural homogeneity. The Highlands were viewed as peripheral in all aspects – political and social, cultural and linguistic and especially religious. This marginalising of the north-west Highlands and Islands was exacerbated by the remoteness of the land until well into the mid-19th century. The Highlands and Islands were commented on disparagingly by visitors and travellers; they weren't even considered picturesque.

Burt's Letters long pre-date the romanticism which the Victorians found in the grandeur and majesty of the Highlands; for Burt it is a 'disagreeable' landscape of 'huge naked rocks', 'of monstrous excrescences', 'the hills a gloomy brown and a dirty purple'.[2] Sir Walter Scott had not yet 'sold' the noble savage in his majestic mountains to readers in the south. Martin Martin, in his *Description of the Western Islands of Scotland*, notes that foreigners sailing through the Western Isles,

> have been tempted from the sight of so many wild hills that seem to be covered all over with heath, and faced with high rocks, to imagine that the inhabitants, as well as the places of their residence, are barbarous . . . but the lion is not so fierce as he is painted, neither are the people described here so barbarous as the world imagines. The inhabitants have humanity and use strangers hospitably and charitably.[3]

Those in later generations, however, who followed Burt into the Highlands from the industrialised and prosperous south were struck by the degree of difference from their own lifestyle. To the town-dweller in the south of Scotland the Highlands may as well have been a different country. Those living south of the border had simply no

---

2 Edmond Burt, *Letters from a Gentleman in the North of Scotland*, Letter X, 282-5.
3 Martin Martin, *Description of the Western Islands of Scotland*, 345.

regard for Scotland at all. Only when it suited did the Government turn its mind to Scotland, and especially the Highlands and Islands, as a legitimate and convenient recruiting ground for the Services.

English perceptions of just what lay beyond the Cheviot Hills would have been coloured by the writings of the English radical John Wilkes in his widely-circulated volumes and disparagingly titled 'The North Briton'. Resistant to any promotion of the idea of Scottish *nationhood*, Wilkes, writing between 1762 and 1771, was critical of all things Scottish. A thoroughly biased publication promoted a picture of Scots and Scotland as impoverished, starving, venal wretches dressed in tartan rags. Wilkes was vehemently opposed to any Scottish influence in Parliament or Court. For Wilkes, Scotland or 'North Briton' as he liked to call it, was at best little more than an administrative outpost served by Parliament, or at worst, a mere colony to be held at arms-length for fear of cultural contamination.

Dorothy Wordsworth undertook a 'Tour Made in Scotland' in 1803 but ventured only as far as Glencoe and Killiecrankie. The suggestion is that poor roads prevented her from travelling further. As Dorothy Wordsworth was completing her tour, Thomas Telford, having been commissioned by the Government two years previously, had already undertaken his first surveys to improve General Wade's military road network across the Highlands. Telford would oversee an extensive programme of construction and reconstruction of roads, bridges, harbours and the costly building of the Caledonian Canal.

The Feeble Highlander

> *It is a fact that morally and intellectually the Highlanders are an inferior race to the Lowland Saxon.*
>
> The *Scotsman* 1846

The failed Jacobite risings of 1715 and 1719, culminating in the events of 1746 at Culloden, had identified the despised Highlander as a dangerous insurrectionist who needed to be brought to heel and whose military potential needed to be neutralised once and for all. The British Government achieved this largely by undermining the cultural and social identity of the Highland people. 'Southern' authority had to be imposed in order to make the economic gains in the Highlands that had been achieved throughout the Empire. There was a surplus of monetary wealth searching for suitable investment opportunities. Eyes were trained on the potential of the north and west but before the expected returns could be generated it was necessary to destroy the Highland threat to the new social and economic order by eradicating 'Celtic barbarism' and civilising the Highlands.

James Loch, Edinburgh lawyer and head administrator of the Sutherland Estates was reported to have said that he would 'never be satisfied until the Gaelic language and the Gaelic people would be extirpated root and branch from the Sutherland Estate; yes, from the Highlands of Scotland'.[4] There existed the traditional perception of Highland culture which tended to dismiss the Celt generally as intrinsically inferior to the superior Anglo-Saxon. These same commentators looked to the day when the Gaelic language, seen to be a brake on progress, would be wholly supplanted by English. Then, and only then, might the Highlander enjoy the same economic prosperity from the fruits of trade and industry as the city-dwellers.

In 1820 James Loch wrote a detailed account of the situation across the county.[5] It has proved a valuable insight to the mindset of those who would exercise a governing authority over a powerless and captive population who lived at the whim of their superiors, and mainly at the margins of subsistence. Loch did not hold back when describing the improvements under the Sutherlands. In his report, he was fulsome in his praise for the new infrastructures in the county: roads, bridges, harbours built; a new post office and mail link established and various inns as rest-stops for horses and coachmen constructed; brickworks and farm steadings created; a vibrant export market for wool, fish and mutton established and 'the English language made the language of the county'. Loch, an Edinburgh-born barrister and later MP showed his contempt for the Highlander, aligning himself more with the educated and culturally sophisticated Southerner. He joined many others by repeating the outworn trope which considered the Celt as an inferior breed: 'A hardy but not industrious race of people', and again, 'Impatient of regular and constant work, all the heavy labour was abandoned to the women, who were employed occasionally, even in dragging the harrow to cover the seed; the great proportion of [the men's] time when not in the pursuit of game or of illegal distillation, were spent in indolence and sloth'.

---

4 Alexander MacKenzie, *History of the Highland Clearances*, 122.

5 James Loch, *An Account of the Improvements of the Estates of the Marquis of Stafford in the Counties of Salop and Stafford and on the Estate of Sutherland*, 1820.

His comment underlined a prejudice held by many that the Highlander was his own worst enemy: 'No country of Europe at any period in its history, ever presented more formidable obstacles to the improvement of a people arising out of the prejudices and feelings of the people themselves'. Either Loch was ignorant of, or held little regard for the cultural differences and nuances of those whose traditions and heritage came from north of the Highland line. He condemns the Highlander for refusing to welcome and embrace the Sutherlands' 'tireless efforts to raise them from such a state of continual poverty and occasional want; to supply them with the means, and to create in them the habits of industry [which] was, and is, the bounden duty of the owners of every such property'. Loch surmised that there may have been organised active resistance:

> However, many [natives] have constantly been the willing instruments of those who have from time to time endeavoured to disturb the progress of those arrangements which have been so steadily pursued by Lord and Lady Stafford for the improvement of their estate and the benefit of the people.

In his report Loch sets out the reasons for clearance:

> It is well known that the borders of the two kingdoms were inhabited by a numerous population, who, in their pursuits, manners and general structure of society, bore a considerable resemblance to that which existed in the Highlands of Scotland. When the union of the crowns, and those subsequent transactions which arose out of that event, rendered the maintenance of that irregular population not only unnecessary, but a burden to the proprietor to whom the land belonged, the people were removed, and the mountains were covered with sheep. Taking this example as their guide, experience had still further proved, that the central and western Highlands of Scotland were equally well calculated for the same end.

The inference is clear however: had the Highlander been more prepared to embrace and adopt the new improvements under the patronage of the Sutherlands, as Loch saw it, the human catastrophe wrought by the Clearances for which the Duke and Duchess are best known would not have impacted so severely, if at all. While a success in terms of economics and business, the blame for the human failure of the Clearances was laid, not at the feet of a rapacious and profit-driven landlord, but firmly at the feet of an uncooperative and ungrateful people who clearly did not know what was good for them. As a result, the forced evictions from the Straths of Kildonan, Strathbrora and Strathnaver and their townships and crofts were advanced with terrifying efficiency. Removal notices were routinely drawn up by sheriffs and Justices of the Peace and issued to parish ministers across the county with reference to the particular area earmarked for community removal. These notices were either posted on church doors or read out often by reluctant ministers, both Evangelical and Moderate, from the pulpit who nevertheless were obliged to remind congregations of the necessity to obey the law and to remove themselves quietly and with no trouble. As the Marchioness's chief agent, Loch's aim was clear: to shepherd the people off the land and control the lives of the 'ignorant and credulous people' to the extent that at one time the young among them had to go to his agents for permission to marry.

Comparisons between those who lived above and below the 'Highland line' were too readily made. The Southerner was industrious, ambitious, enterprising and ready and willing to embrace the new working practices in the growing urban conurbations. By contrast, the Highlander was seen to be indolent, ill-educated with an easy acceptance to receive charity while resistant to improving his lot by embracing economic and industrial change. This skewed vision regarded the Highlander living uneasily on the margins of economic viability, utilizing a language inaccessible to those beyond his kith and kin and infected with a lingering pre-Reformation legacy of Catholicism. Ministers in the Evangelical Party would go on to claim that this jaundiced view was the root cause of the idleness displayed by Moderate ministers from the more liberal wing of the Kirk who served in the Highlands or came from there. Since the post-Culloden years, the perception had taken root: the Highlander could not be improved (despite the Kirk's efforts) and Celtic inadequacy was the root cause of his own fecklessness and Highland economic failure.

Thomas Telford Steps into the Picture

Had you seen these roads before they were made,
you would lift up your hands and bless General Wade.

Major William Caulfield, inspector of military highways.

Although his biographical details are scant, Edmund Burt is believed to have been an engineer working under command of General Wade on the construction of roads and bridges in the Highlands. Between 1723 and 1740 General Wade built nearly 250 miles of military roads, the first metalled roads built in the Highlands. But these were laid following the Jacobite Uprising in 1715 and were located, not for trade, but to suit military purposes of stationing soldiers in the Highlands to suppress any signs of rebellion. That probably accounts for the comments in the Statistical Account of the Revd Roderick Morison of Kintail Parish in Wester Ross: 'Till of late, the people of Kintail as well as other Highlanders had a strong aversion to roads. The more inaccessible, the more secure, was their maxim'.[6] But most longed for road improvements. In his report for the 1793 Statistical Account of Scotland, the minister of Glenorchy and Inishail hoped for improvements from

> the present incommodious acclivities and descents of roads in the parish: The great military road from Stirling to Tyndrum and Inveraray passes through the parish from one extremity almost to the other, as does also, for many miles, the military road from Tyndrum to Fort William. In the original formation of these roads, the obvious and proper line has not always been selected. The traveller often feels, to his cost, that the road was brought to the gravel, and not the gravel to the road.[7]

At the end of the 18th century there were 800 miles of roads, many of them ill-constructed, most of them in poor repair and some no longer usable. New road building came by an unlikely back door; by way of fish. The British Society for extending the Fisheries and improving the Sea-Coasts of this Kingdom (in short, The British Fisheries Society) had long expressed concern about the rapid depopulation of parts of the Highlands and in particular the impoverishment of the population who were dependent on fishing on the west coast of Scotland; they asked the Government to undertake extensive improvements to the harbours, and to address their concerns about social dislocation.

Thomas Telford was a friend of Sir John Sinclair, Caithness landowner and Trustee of the Board for the Improvement of Fisheries and Manufactures. Sir John had requested of Telford several reports for the Fisheries Society. Pultneytown, in Caithness, immediately south of

---

6 *The Statistical Accounts of Scotland 1793: Kintail, County of Ross and Cromarty*, vol. VI, 244.

7 *The Statistical Accounts of Scotland 1793: Glenorchy and Inishail County of Argyll*, vol. VIII, 345.

the Wick River, was laid out by Thomas Telford in 1786 and was so successful it became known as 'Herringopolis' with the harbour so full of fishing boats that you could walk across it without touching water.

Telford shared his views with Sir John on the necessity also for road improvements. The minister of Halkirk Parish, where Sir John was Patron, reported in 1797 that by Sir John's example and encouragement, the whole county was 'animated and heartily engaged in making, repairing and improving roads, which proved to be a great advantage. They are tolerable now for more than half of the year.'[8] He added, 'It is regrettable that hitherto the results have been very far short of their laudable exertions'. Telford's reports for the Fisheries Board on harbours and roads eventually moved the Government to action.

In July 1801 Telford received a request from Nicholas Vansittart, Joint Secretary to the Treasury, to proceed with the improvements to the roads and harbours of the Highlands including establishing safe and convenient access from the mainland to the Islands; detailed instructions on the work to be done would follow. By the time the instructions arrived in September, Telford had virtually completed the first survey. He was helped to a degree by a succession of reports in previous years on the state of the fisheries and the roads in the Highlands and Islands. By then, many individuals and institutions had taken an interest in how best to improve trade and industry in the Highlands: one by John Knox in 1784 in a volume entitled *A View of the British Empire, more especially Scotland, with some proposals for the improvement of that country, the extension of its fisheries, and the relief of the People*; the same year Professor John Anderson of Glasgow University had produced a similar report on the Hebrides and the Aberdeen Highlands. The Highland Society of Scotland, formed in 1784, continually urged the House of Commons to pursue these matters. In 1789 the MP for Skibo, George Dempster, secured Prime Minister Pitt's promise to set up a survey of Highland roads. In 1799 Colonel Anstruther, Superintendent of the Military roads in the Highlands, wrote a report[9] on the counties north of the Caledonian Glen, where internal communication was difficult and dangerous to life and limb and where any communication with the southern counties

---

8 *The Statistical Accounts of Scotland 1797: Halkirk, County of Caithness*, vol. XIX, 11.

9 Quoted in *Commissioners of Highland Roads and Bridges, Fourteenth Report*, 1828.

was impracticable, and thus, Anstruther concluded, the Highlands remained isolated, receiving no benefits from the rapid advances in the south. Telford backed up these earnest pleas with authoritative technical surveys.

When Sir John Sinclair compiled the Statistical Accounts of Scotland, his express purpose was to ascertain the state of Scottish society (see Appendix One). The original questionnaire which he sent out in 1790 to the Church of Scotland clergy required from each of them a lengthy, highly detailed survey of their parishes and districts: the size and nature of the population, its age-spread in terms of the respective occupations, social status, race and creed of their parishioners; the resources and output of each district, its acreage distinguishing waste, arable and pasture, the quantity of its vegetable products, the number and kind of its livestock, its manufactures and mineral deposits; the financial state of the inhabitants, the respective rent of land, houses, fishings, etc., the wages received by different kinds of workmen, the number of paupers and the sum contributed for their maintenance; and finally the state of the communications. It is noteworthy that communications was the final item, because in the response which Telford gave to the Treasury, communications took first place.

'If I rightly comprehend the subject,' he wrote in response to the invitation to undertake the survey, 'their Lordships' aims are directed to four great national objects, viz – First – rendering more perfect the communications between the different districts of England, Scotland and Ireland'.[10] The second, third and fourth were, respectively: the improving of the Fisheries, improved intercourse with northern parts of Europe and providing naval protection for the Fisheries. Telford knew that access to the markets in the south was critical for growing prosperity but in the current state of roads and bridges, the road south was entirely beyond reach for many areas of Highlands and Islands. Improvement to communication was the key.

The Commissioners for Highland Roads and Bridges were appointed and required to report on an annual basis to Parliament. The Government advertised in Edinburgh and Glasgow newspapers, inviting applications for financial assistance from proprietors who were interested in improving local roads, harbours and bridges. On receipt of an application, Telford would make a preliminary survey and

---

10 Letter to Nicholas Vansittart October 1801, quoted in Sir Alexander Gibb, *The Story of Telford*, 64.

provide an estimate of the cost, one half of which would be provided by the Government, and the other half to be deposited in the Bank of Scotland by local landowners.

The Second Report was submitted by February 1803. Telford admitted to anxiety about how the Report would be received: 'I have endeavoured to make the northern proprietors sensible of their own interests, and to convince Government and the public that the nation at large is deeply interested in the proposed improvements.'[11] In that Report he explained that the military roads were in the wrong place, inaccessible, inconveniently steep and rendered of limited use by the lack of bridges over the principal rivers. But these were not the areas worst served: the most isolated areas where no military roads had been built by Wade were vast; they included

> the wide and extensive country . . . comprising the Counties of Ross, Cromarty, Sutherland, and Caithness, with the greater part of Inverness-shire and the whole of the Western Islands, intersected by arms of the sea, dangerous ferries, deep and rapid rivers, and innumerable lesser streams subject to frequent and sudden floods, without the accommodation of bridges, piers or other facilities.

He recommended considerable improvements in the lines of communication by land and sea between north and south and across the land. Telford considered an extensive road and bridge-building programme to gain access to the remotest parts, principally routes westwards from Fort William to Arisaig, to Lochalsh and the Hebrides. A canal through the Great Glen to unite east and west fishing grounds was proposed with new routes connecting with Skye and the Hebrides. In the far north new routes were planned linking Inverness with Caithness and Sutherland and new roads via Dingwall and Wick to connect with small ports in the north such as Tongue and Thurso. It was an immense civil engineering undertaking.

The Commissioners finally reported to Parliament in 1828 that they had 'succeeded in effecting a change in the state of the Highlands perhaps unparalleled in a similar space of time in the history of any country.'[12] The improvements were lauded in the General Observations

---

11 *Letter to Andrew Little,* February 1803 – quoted in Sir Alexander Gibb, *The Story of Telford,* 71.

12 Quoted in *Commissioners of Highland Roads and Bridges, Fourteenth Report,* 1828.

on Sutherland in the New Statistical Accounts of Scotland:[13] 'Before the year 1811 there were no formed roads within the county, but in that year the first Parliamentary roads were completed, and since then the rapidity with which the whole county has been opened up and intersected by leading lines and cross-branches of excellent roads, and all necessary bridges, is one of the most remarkable events in the annals of northern improvements.' Such achievements throughout the north-west Highlands and some islands owed a great deal to Thomas Telford.

First Migrations and the Highland Economy

Not only was Thomas Telford commissioned to design and oversee the completion of these infrastructure projects which improved hugely communications across the north and west, he was also asked to comment on the state of the Highland economy.[14] In this matter, at least, he presented his 1803 report 'with no small degree of hesitation' because, on the causes of the rapid depopulation of parts of the Highlands, he had reached two conclusions which he knew would not be agreeable to Parliament or proprietors. The first ran against the prevailing principle of *laissez-faire*. Landowners and Parliamentarians – and Telford himself – shared a common faith in property ownership as the best guarantee of political stability. However, Telford introduced a note of caution:

> As the evil at present seems to arise chiefly from the conduct of landowners in changing the economy of their estates [the Clearances], it may be questioned whether government can with justice interfere, or whether any essential benefits are likely to arise from this interference.[15]

He was clearly reluctant to advocate Government intervention. Telford strongly advocated a more flexible approach and concluded by advising that 'where such a numerous body of the people are deeply interested, it is the duty of government to consider it as an extraordinary case, and one of those occasions which justifies them in departing a little from the maxims of general policy.'

---

13 *The Statistical Accounts of Scotland 1843: General Observations on Sutherland*, vol. XV, 218.

14 Thomas Telford, *Letter to Andrew Little*, 1803.

15 Thomas Telford, *Survey and Report of the Coasts and Central Highlands of Scotland*, 1803.

He recommended that 'regulations should be made to prevent landowners from lessening the population upon their estates below a given proportion.' The best information he had procured on emigration levels was that about 3000 persons had left the Highlands in 1802, prior to his reporting, and he believed that three times that number would be leaving in the current year. The real objective of the Passengers Vessels Act of 1803 was to substantially increase the cost of passage and to deter future emigrants. This was finally repealed in 1826. The other conclusion that Telford offered was that although there were some unimportant collateral causes of emigration, the most common form of 'improvement' was by landowners converting large districts of the country into extensive sheep-walks. This required far fewer people to maintain the same tract of country; the people employed for this were experienced sheep farmers encouraged to come up from the south of Scotland thus displacing the local people, leading some to emigrate. The new Highland situation brought Telford, the Government and the powerful landowning lobby into direct confrontation.

Telford had also been asked to address concerns about dislocation of people. L.T.C. Rolt, in his biography of Telford, comments: 'One of Telford's wide terms of reference was to investigate the causes of emigration from the Highlands, although one might think that these would be obvious enough even to the most boneheaded government official.'[16] Telford insisted that improved communications, by means of roads and bridges, were essential; 'and for this reason I have said that if these conveniences had been sooner introduced into the Highlands, it is possible this emigration might not have taken place, at least to the present extent.'[17] It was not until Telford and the Commissioners for Highland Roads and Bridges accepted the responsibility in 1803 that the work of construction was taken seriously in hand.

The speed with which the Government took action on Telford's second Report was a measure of their alarm at the reports of distress in the Highlands and, perhaps even more worrying for the Government in the midst of the Napoleonic wars, the threat to recruitment for the Services. The valour of the Highlanders had long been used to great advantage by the commanders of the British army. The townships and glens of the Highlands had provided 34 battalions (1,000 men in each

---

16 L.T.C. Rolt, *Thomas Telford*, 67.
17 Thomas Telford, *Survey and Report of the Coasts and Central Highlands of Scotland*, 1803.

battalion) for the Empire wars in America, Germany and India in the last decades of the 18th century and by 1815 it was estimated that 100,000 Highlanders in total had taken the King's shilling. The parish of Gairloch in Wester Ross had been nearly stripped of all its menfolk by 1799. A survey for the Lord Lieutenant of Ross-shire arrived at the conclusion that hardly any males could be found there, and for the most part the population consisted mainly of women, children and old men because of the sheer scale of recruitment.

By the end of 18th century manpower resources in the region had become virtually exhausted, not only because of over-recruitment. The Parish of Reay in Sutherland had furnished the greater part of two companies of Fencibles for the American war; recruiting parties in Thurso were frequently picking up young men for the army, and South Uist reported 400 recruits to army and navy in the previous 18 years. In 1835 the incumbent of the Parish of Kilmallie pronounced, 'This parish was a nursery for the army'.[18] This claim was repeated by several ministers in Highland parishes. The Revd Martin Macpherson of Sleat on the Isle of Skye viewed both emigration and 'repeated drains to the army'[19] as depredations on the population.

However, despite Telford's assessment of the times regarding Highland emigration and the vital need for improvements to be made across the north and west, the Highlands and Islands experienced an inexorable rise in the birth rate from the 1750s onwards. Across the Western Isles between 1801 and 1841, the population increase was of the order of 53 per cent. Between 1755 and 1821 growth was in the order of 80 per cent. Without the mass dislocation of population caused by the Clearances, and indeed without a prolonged outbreak of typhus in the years 1818 and 1819, increases of this order would have posed an even greater challenge to a society which had always existed close to the very margins of sustainability. In the decades of the 1820s and 1830s, the peoples of the north-west Highlands and Islands had been caught in a contracting vice particular to the region: an unrelenting increase in population on the one hand, and the collapse of economic activities which had sustained them for a time before 1815 on the other. The impact of this demographic change had severe consequences on a people whose lives were precariously balanced on the margins of viability.

---

18 *The Statistical Accounts of Scotland: Kilmallie, County of Inverness 1845*, vol. XIV, 120.

19 *The Statistical Accounts of Scotland: Sleat, County of Inverness 1795*, vol. XVI, 537.

Lairds, Land and Highland Farming

The Lairds have transferred their affection from the people to flocks of sheep – and the people have lost their veneration for the Lairds.

Thomas Telford, *Letter to Andrew Little*, 1803

West Highland landlords in the 18th century had remained convinced of the value of maintaining a large population as an economic resource. Indeed, Robert Ainslie, factor to the Duke of Douglas in the 1760s and 1770s, reported that although the removal of many small tenants was a necessary preliminary to the advance of 'improvement' and in time higher rentals for the landlord, he judged that equally vital to success was the need to avoid large-scale displacement of the existing tenantry. Mass clearance, in his opinion, 'was a dangerous and destructive experiment'.[20] He condemned in the strongest possible terms the policies of wholesale clearances which he understood were being introduced on some Highland estates at that time. He favoured gradual dispossession (the non-renewal of tenancies) rather than mass evictions, a practice adopted by many Lowland estates. Perversely, it was a lingering sense of patriarchal obligation by some Highland landlords to former clansmen who had served their families loyally for generations which had merely accelerated the economic demise of many Highland estates.

In his submission to the Statistical Accounts at the end of the 18th century, North Uist minister Revd Allan Macqueen stated his concerns over the social dislocation taking place throughout his parish; both emigration and clearance. He was of the opinion that putting a stop to

> the present rage for emigration requires very nice management in the proprietors. The old attachment between them and their people must in some measure be renewed; long leases must be granted to secure the tenants the possession of their lands for a period of years, to remove their apprehensions of frequent calls upon them for augmentation of rent.[21]

25 years previously, Dr Johnson on his Highland tour was well aware of high levels of emigration and forcibly stated:

---

20 *Report of Robert Ainslie for Sir Alexander F. Douglas-Home*, 7th September 1769.
21 *The Statistical Accounts of Scotland 1794: North Uist, County of Inverness*, vol. XIII, 318.

> Some method to stop this epidemick desire of wandering, which spreads its contagion from valley to valley, deserves to be sought with great diligence. In more fruitful countries, the removal of one only makes room for the succession of another: but in the Hebrides, the loss of an inhabitant leaves a lasting vacuity; for nobody born in any other parts of the world will choose this country for his residence, and an Island once depopulated will remain a desert, as long as the present facility of travel gives every one, who is discontented and unsettled, the choice of his abode.[22]

Mr Macqueen harked back to the times when that 'old attachment' between clan chief and clansman could be recreated, but there was no going back. The old order was gone forever and landowners were profiting from a new experience of wealth which wool and mutton provided. He summed up the contrast between the old order and the new:

> The chieftain prided himself upon the number of his gentlemen farmers so much that he looked upon himself as their common father. In their distress he relieved their wants, and when one of them died he became the guardian of his children and the executor of his will. When the chieftain was threatened with danger from invasion or encroachment of his neighbours, his gentlemen flocked to offer their services. They followed him to the battlefield and shared his fate . . .[23]

As Dr Johnson put it,

> The Laird was the father of the Clan, and his tenants commonly bore his name', adding 'not many years have passed since the clans knew no law but the Laird's will. He told them to whom they should be friends or enemies, what King they should obey, and what religion they should profess.[24]

The rebellion in 1745 had weakened that attachment. Mr Macqueen concluded, 'Since that period the chieftains have withdrawn themselves from their estates, have become unacquainted with their people; they visit but seldom and are become less scrupulous in removing them

---

22 Samuel Johnson, *A Journey to the Western Isles of Scotland*, 222.
23 *The Statistical Accounts of Scotland 1794: North Uist, County of Inverness*, vol. XIII, 309.
24 Samuel Johnson, *A Journey to the Western Isles of Scotland*, 196.

from their farms if a higher offer is made than the possessors can afford to pay.'

Both government and the landed class of the north-west and the islands were implacably opposed to emigration in the later 18th century and early 19th. For the former, it meant the loss of a valuable military resource. For the latter, again, emigration removed precious manpower from the estates which was needed for kelp burning, fishing and army recruitment. Landowners were compensated by an enlistment payment for every man recruited. Now military entrepreneurs rather than patriarchal chieftains, these landowners harvested the population of their estates for the army in order to make money, in the same way as they established sheep walks, cattle ranches and kelp shores.

In fact, recruitment to the army provided many benefits for the Highland elites. The rewards could be substantial. Sir James Grant, whose Speyside estate was heavily encumbered with debt, bagged a cushy appointment worth £3,000 a year (£330,000 in today's terms) and his 'connections' secured him the Lord Lieutenancy of Inverness in 1794. Mackenzie of Seaforth, who like most Highland landowners suffered from acute and perennial financial difficulties, did even better. In quick succession he became Lord Lieutenant of Ross in 1794, 'Lord' Seaforth in the English peerage in the same year and in 1800, Governor of Barbados. There is evidence that several proprietors showed a clear preference for securing these 'martial' tenants for their estates. There would be regular income from soldier-tenants, because of pay and pensions, obviating fluctuations in market conditions suffered by small civilian tenantry.

To maintain a healthy stock of manpower on these Highland estates and beyond, emigration was banned altogether in 1775. To arrest depopulation and provide more employment Parliament was forced into action by allocating funds specifically for the benefit of the Highlands and Islands. From 1803 to 1821 Parliament provided more than £500,000 (£40m in today's terms) to finance Telford's ambitions for transport projects in the Highlands, including the construction of the Caledonian Canal. The investment produced 920 miles of new roads, 280 miles of remade military roads, numerous harbour works and over 1000 new bridges were built over small but treacherous streams and spanning the major rivers of the Spey and Tay, Beauly and Dee.

As Telford was writing his 1803 report, the extraordinary rise in the prices of sheep and wool had already brought considerable wealth to the proprietors who had 'improved' their estates in this way. Telford did not dwell on the effects on the displaced local residents but reserved his criticism for what he saw as a short-sighted and misinformed policy. He expressed his strong opinion that sheep-farming on a large-scale was not suited in the long run to the Highlands. He understood the attraction of the high prices, and he knew that many proprietors were gaining unaccustomed wealth from their estates which swamped the rents they had received from tenants. However, he believed that replacing black cattle entirely with sheep would be profitable only until the country would be fully stocked with sheep, and then he would expect that the supply would outstrip the demand and prices would inevitably fall. He strongly recommended mixed farming, with sheep on the upper parts of hills and black cattle and arable land in the lower ground. This would maintain a large population, one with the skills to manage different types of farming and would recognise the variety of terrain in most of the Highland counties.

As it transpired, Telford was quite prescient in his forecast that a concentration in sheep-farming would not be best practice. It was found that sheep defoliated the herbage by consuming only the shortest, sweetest and most luxuriant grasses. Cattle, on the other hand, consumed a mix of rough and fine herbage and, by so doing, improved the sward. Swamped with sheep, over decades the quality of hill-pasture deteriorated. With hill pastures overrun by moss, heather and bracken, this directly impacted the quality of meat. Later in the century the Scottish trade was further hit by better and cheaper mutton and wool from Australia and New Zealand.

Telford's assessment was confirmed. In the returns for the Statistical Accounts presented, in 1797, the minister of Halkirk in the County of Caithness, in describing his parish, recognised the suitability of the land to maintain a stock of cattle in the traditional way:[25] 'Most of our hills or rising ground, and also our moors, are well adapted for what we call Highland pasturage and capable of maintaining a very great number of black cattle.' And he added, 'By appearance there are sheep-pastures in this parish – but they do not thrive to any satisfaction'. In

---

25 *The Statistical Accounts of Scotland 1797: Halkirk, County of Caithness*, vol. XIX, 8.

1795 in Sleat on the Isle of Skye,[26] 'At a moderate calculation, there may be 2600 head of black cattle in the parish. It is impossible to say exactly what number is annually sold, as the sales depend on a number of contingent circumstances. As to sheep, the number in the parish is so few that it is hardly worth the calculating. Such as can afford to eat mutton are obliged to purchase from the neighbouring sheep walks.' By the close of the 18th century traditional methods of animal husbandry still obtained over large swathes of the Highlands and Islands. But the promise of high economic returns invited landlords to consider changes in land management.

The traditional values of clanship had been eroding for well over a century as the chiefs became increasingly assimilated to the British establishment in Edinburgh and London; even before 1745, heads of the clans had adopted the practices of landed gentry. Mr Macqueen, the North Uist minister, regretted the changes in how the land was managed and the minister of Kincardine summed up its effects within the Highland community:[27] 'The people still retain a sacred regard for the clan and family they are sprung from, but this is in decline. The tale, the song and the dance do not, as in the days of their fathers, gild the horrors of the winter night'. Clan chiefs had glimpsed the financial benefits that could accrue to them as landowners; some had developed financial interests in Caribbean plantations and the Edinburgh money markets, and the 'improvement' of their estates promised to provide the revenue to support a much higher standard of living for themselves than before. The land and the population were subordinated to the revenue needs of the landowners. The land and the population never were to benefit from the accumulating wealth of this new breed of land speculator.

In the space of 25 years, the economic argument for large sheep ranches had been made and the wholesale clearance of lands across the entire north and west was well underway. In 1845 the report for Sleat states that 'lands formerly possessed by labouring tenants are now converted to sheep farms. This has reduced the people's means of support. There are no manufactures and an extent of poverty prevails among them now to which formerly they were strangers.'[28]

---

26 *The Statistical Accounts of Scotland 1795: Sleat, County of Inverness*, vol. XVI, 537.

27 *The Statistical Accounts of Scotland 1845: Kincardine County of Ross and Cromarty*, vol. III, 516.

28 *The Statistical Accounts of Scotland 1845: Sleat County of Inverness*, vol. XIV, 322.

People and Profits: Disaster Seen as Judgment

By such genuine improvements the land might have been able to support its population and avoid recurring famine and destitution. The only answer the proprietors had to these calamities was one most profitable to themselves, the removal of the people, and in that light they could sometimes think of Clearance as the solemn duty of humane landlordism.

John Prebble's *Scotland*

Quite different from the urban poor of the south, Highland rural peasantry was wholly dependent upon the continued 'benevolence' of capricious landowners and was entirely at the mercy of economics. Tied as they were to the land, the rural poor survived or fell on the fluctuating fortunes of these large estates. The prospect of good profits, however, might raise rents on a whim. These tenants became powerless victims and collateral damage as the economic changes and the compulsion to monetise Highland estates took effect. More often than not, this drive to increase landlord wealth resulted in the peoples' expulsion from the land.

Further, there was particular unease among Evangelical ministers that some more liberal Moderate-inclined ministers appeared to turn a blind eye and be silent when it came to the matter and manner of the Clearances. In these instances, autocratic landowners and heritors, not accustomed to being crossed, thwarted or opposed, were in a particularly strong position using to their advantage the residual feudalism which had carried over from the days of the clans. Like the chiefs of old, the word of the landlord was law and, generally in this, he exercised authority with impunity having complete powers to oversee the business of his estate – including ecclesiastical matters. Also, while the Moderate Party may have acknowledged the uneasy relationship it had with landowners over matters at the interface of civil and ecclesiastical responsibilities, like Thomas Telford and the Tory Governments of the day, Moderates too wholly embraced *laisser-faire* economics which supported the landowning classes. They subscribed to the theory of a free market to drive forward prosperity and increase wealth. Consequently Evangelical ministers, especially those recruited from the Highlands and Islands, were suspicious of Moderate commitment to consolidating and expanding the use of Gaelic, knowing that the *lingua franca* of the wealth-generating south was English. Moderates gave their full-throated support for the capitalist model which was successfully employed in other parts of the nation. Therefore the viability, success and prosperity or otherwise of the Highlands came down to a simple matter of economics now in the hands of free marketeers, speculators and ruthless profiteers. But the application of such economic theory had severe consequences with concomitant social implications. Their effects ravaged the Highland population and destroyed communities over the course of a century. The Clearances changed the face of the land for ever. Above all, Moderates were also advocates for, and strong upholders of the rule of law and were generally supportive of landowners and their agents whose notices to quit were quite lawful. However in many cases Moderates also recognised that 'the law' was immoral, prejudiced, unreasonable and blatantly unfair, but it was the Evangelical ministers who appeared to be more vocal in speaking out against the injustices. They too, though, were as unsuccessful in reversing decisions as their Moderate colleagues.

In the decades up to 1815, established landlord elites in Lowland estates had invested significant sums in enclosure, farm steadings and roads, all aimed at exploiting and maximising returns within the new market economy. Better communications also gave easier access to English livestock markets. This process benefited both landlord and tenant. Investment led to improved productivity which, in turn, raised wages. However, this was not so replicated in the Highlands. As James Loch, chief agent of the Sutherland estates warned in 1813,[29] 'It must, however, be very distinctly stated, that nothing is so dangerous as to conclude that, because a system answers well in one part of the kingdom, it must do well in every other'. The irony here cannot be overlooked as Loch was instrumental in managing the Sutherland estate's attempts to replicate the successes of their landholdings in Staffordshire. The Earl of Breadalbane, among other English-based landlords who rarely, if ever, visited their Scottish estates, penned some thoughts from London on how his estates should be improved which elicited a response from his chamberlain that 'whether what he projects in a coffee house in London can be executed in Luing or Lismore I cannot say.'

There were some attempts by entrepreneurs to improve the Highland economy. Attempts to expand fisheries along the coastlines from Ardnamurchan in the west, to Ross-shire in the east were, in the main,

---

29 James Loch, *Letter to Francis Suther, 23rd November 1813.*

unsuccessful as were attempts to establish manufactories. Further, the general programme of letting unproductive crofts to those who laboured on the kelp shores or in unreclaimed moorland required little investment. The income derived from these activities was unearned and the process was more to the advantage of the landowner than to the tenant. The clearance of the cottars, converted from traditional feudal-serfs, was a remarkable change in the entire structure of rural society. In little over 100 years the old landholding population of cottars had systematically been stripped of their ancestral bond to the land and had completely vanished. An entire social class which had numbered between a quarter and third of the population in many rural parishes in old Scotland was no more. Those who now worked on the 'improved' landscape were landless wage-earning servants and labourers.

Dr Roger Dodgshon writes of the impact of sheep-farming on the higher ground of Ross-shire:[30] 'One farmer suggested that farms, when left of sufficient extent for a sheep-walk, bring three, four or five times more rent than formerly'. He acknowledged that some would see this as against the interests of the country because of the removal of 'many of the aborigines of the soil' but went on to say that others argue, with greater justice, that whatever system brings the highest rent must eventually promote the real good of the community. The economic argument may have been made but the effect upon the native population, now dispossessed of their lands and pushed to the unpromising margins, was catastrophic. It is difficult to make a case that the Clearances 'promoted the real good' of the community. Besides prospering a handful of landowners, economic improvement did not come to those who had been cleared.

By the 1820s the entire economic edifice on which the crofting system had been built was crumbling rapidly. Earnings from military employment fell away after 1815 and peace was followed by a considerable return-migration of demobbed servicemen, which added further to the demographic pressures becoming more evident in several districts. However, there was still no mass movement to desert the land during the economic crisis which followed the end of the wars. According to the New Statistical Accounts there were 85,342 more people living in the west Highlands in 1841 than the total recorded in the 1750s. Despite significant numbers of emigrés, in parts of Skye and

---

30 Roger Dodgshon, *From Chiefs to Landlords: Social and Economic Change in the Western Highlands*, 241.

Wester Ross for example, population numbers continued to rise until the 1840s. Actual decline in numbers occurred at district rather than regional levels, where intense programmes of clearance were carried out with no replacement schemes of resettlement in place.

While the population of Lochaber generally rose into the 1850s, hot-spots of clearance from the 1830s occurred in districts such as Morvern, Sunart, Ardgour and Ardnamurchan, areas where there was a predominately Catholic population. When the potato crop failed in 1836 and then again in 1837, this catastrophe pushed the population to the very edge of mass starvation. The Government was sufficiently aroused to send an agent to report on the extent and causes of the disaster. Robert Graham was appointed and provided his authoritative guide to West Highland society in the later 1830s. The New Statistical Accounts compiled by ministers with returns from the mid-1830s and published in instalments confirmed all of Graham's findings. Ministers, both Evangelical and Moderate, reported high levels of destitution, poverty and near-starvation in parishes generally throughout the north and west but specifically in several localities.

These reports, compiled during the turbulent years of conflict between the two opposing factions in the Kirk, give lie to Evangelical claims that Moderate ministers were generally deaf and blind to the plight of their parishioners. Robert Graham reckoned that the population in the distressed districts was 105,000, with the worst affected localities in Skye and the Outer Hebrides. He confirmed that population numbers had outstripped the land's capacity to provide for their needs.

The introduction of potatoes resulted in new communities growing along the narrow coastal strips and hitherto unpromising moorland but the Sutherland agent James Loch's comment appears pertinent:

> The introduction of the potato was, in the first instance, proved no blessing to Sutherland. This delicate vegetable was, of course, exposed to the inclemency of a climate for which it was not suited. The failure of such a crop brought accumulated evils upon the poor people in a year of scarcity.[31]

There had been widespread famine in the years 1812-1813 and again in 1816-1817. While his comment specified the Sutherland estates, Loch thought it true across the rest of the north and west. The potato failures

---
31 James Loch, *An Account of the Improvements of the Estates of the Marquis of Stafford in the Counties of Salop and Stafford and on the Estate of Sutherland*, 1820.

were but mere precursors for what was to come in 1836 and 1837 and again 10 years later. Latent racism resurfaced from the previous century confirming for many the superiority of the Anglo-Saxon over the Celt. While Ireland and Scotland starved, England was enjoying bountiful harvests and now the Celts had to be taught a crucial moral lesson in order that they might transform their values and rise to be self-sufficient, without the security of public charity or Government assistance. Again for many, it was the Highlander's innate laziness, easy acceptance of charity and the failure of the economy as a whole which was absolute confirmation of racial inferiority. Further, the Highlander was now under the very judgement of God whose wrath had descended upon the ungrateful, unambitious and unmotivated Highlander. Evangelicals strongly believed that this skewed vision resonated well with certain Moderate ministers.

The views of certain sections of the English establishment regarding the perceived inadequacy and inferiority of the Highlander penetrated deeply into the thinking of Governments of the day. Scotland, as a whole, had been regarded as a poor neighbour since the Union of the Parliaments in 1707. Like Ireland in many senses, Scotland constituted a restless and unhappy participant in the new order as a reluctant member of a 'United Kingdom of Great Britain'. Many in the south were unconvinced of Scotland's wholehearted commitment to the idea of the predominant English view of 'nationhood'. Scotland was essentially two lands, consisting of Highlanders and Lowlanders and a country hosting two languages. By the end of the 18th century the Scottish heartlands were a commercial and industrial powerhouse contributing significantly to the British economy. The north, however, was a different matter: the need to tackle the 'Highland Problem' frustrated the best intentions of Governments, industrialists, investors, merchants and the 'great and the good'. There was a collective sense that the Highlander alone could not solve the 'Highland Problem'.

Essay Three

The Clearances and The Consequences

The art of agriculture is no exception: in it, as in all others, the accumulation of capital and the advance of knowledge and of skill dispense with half-employed and unproductive labour . . . a population numerous, but accustomed to and contented with a low standard of living for themselves, and yielding no surplus for the support of others, gives place to a population smaller in amount, but enjoying a higher civilisation, and contributing in a corresponding degree to the general progress of the world.

John Campbell, 5th Duke of Argyll (1723 – 1806)

Across the Highlands changes in animal husbandry began at the onset of the 19th century. Introduced by herdsmen from the Lowlands and the northern counties of England, the traditional herds of black cattle of local tenants were replaced with Blackface and Cheviot breeds of sheep. Although the rental return from sheep was considerably greater than that of the local cattle, sheep now competed for the remaining pasture and also posed a threat to the arable strips which supported traditional townships. Sheep farming consequently undermined the basis of the old economy by means other than direct clearance.

Much more cataclysmic however, was the direct removal of peasants and communities to make way for big pastoral farms. Having been given notice to quit, on occasions as long as 12 months, entire parishes were cleared from ancestral lands destroying not only the fabric of the local community sustained over centuries but also that vital connection with the Church which had nurtured and sustained the faith of the people. Many ministers and families were themselves victims of clearance as were their congregations. Some parishes went quietly while others put up as much resistance as could be mustered. However, with the full force of the law behind them, eviction notices were served and enacted by agents of the landowners and on occasion by sheriff-officers, often brutally and inhumanely. As one newspaper contributor observed, 'But law is one thing and humanity may be another'.[1]

---

1 *Morning Chronicle,* 2nd March 1820.

Essay 3: The Clearances and the Consequences

In the summer of 1819, during what infamously became known as the 'year of the burnings', news that 1,300 men, women and children had been driven from their Strathnaver homes and their houses burnt to the ground had reached the press. The *Scotsman* (usually no friend of the Highlander) and the *Times* reported thus:

> A posse of men are parading the county of Sutherland and ejecting the poor Highlanders from the homes of their fathers. A valuation is put upon their property; a proportion of the expense is retained, the balance is paid over to the occupier; and his humble dwelling – in which he has gone through the various stages in life and which is endeared to him by a thousand ties and circumstances – is set fire to, and consumed to ashes, before the eyes of himself, his wife and helpless family ... [Sutherland] is beginning to wear a depopulated and ruinous aspect.[2]

The Marchioness of Stafford was always alert to adverse press coverage of Sutherland Estate affairs and found comment of this kind upsetting. 'We have lately been much attacked in the newspapers', she lamented in a letter to a friend, 'what is stated is most perfectly unjust.'[3] The Revd David Mackenzie, minister of the Parish of Farr at the head of Strathnaver and a favourite of the Marchioness commented, under the heading 'Miscellaneous Observations', in his submission to the New Statistical Account,

> All the lands, both hill and dale, which [the crofters] possessed, are held in lease by a few sheep-farmers, all non-resident gentlemen — some of them living in Caithness, some on the south coast of this county, and some in England; and the straths, in which hundreds of families lived comfortably, are now tenanted by about twenty-four families of herds.[4]

Mackenzie was non-committal in his judgement over the Clearances in his parish, merely noting the changes. However, as a recipient of the Marchioness's largesse (new church, new manse), the minister was an advocate of the new economic order. Farr had not experienced quite the same dramatic fall in population numbers as Kildonan on the west side of the Sutherland estate, but the figures tell their own story nonetheless. In 1790, Farr's population was recorded as 2,500 but by

---

2 The *Scotsman*, Saturday 19th June 1819.
3 Lady Stafford, *Letter to Charles Kirkpatrick Sharpe*, 25th July 1819.
4 *The Statistical Accounts of Scotland 1845: Farr, County of Sutherland*, vol. XV, 79.

1831 had decreased by 400, with the interior of the parish completely cleared.

Clearances had begun in the 1740s in a limited way on the estates of the 4th Duke of Argyll, who rationalised several small-holdings into larger farming units. By the 1810s, however, 'clearance' had become 'The Clearances', a change in nomenclature which would seep into the souls and bodies of Highlanders everywhere. The Clearances had accelerated to a large-scale enterprise. On the island of Rhum the entire population of 400 people was evicted to make way for one sheep-farmer and 8,000 sheep. This was followed soon by evictions on the island of Muck again under the guise of 'improvement'. By 1831 two-thirds of the population of the Uists and Benbecula were destitute, having been thrown off their lands and who were now living on shell-fish and a broth made of seaweed and nettles. In Skye, 1,000 were evicted or threatened with eviction every year from 1800 to 1840. Elsewhere in the Highlands the record was substantially similar. The author Iain Fraser Grigor stated that 'this was but a hint of things to come'.[5]

Landlords had simply done their sums and stood to gain from more secure returns. Regular and rising incomes were guaranteed from affluent graziers utilising economies of scale, as opposed to many tenants crofting smaller pitches whose rent payments fluctuated with weather and volatility in the markets for cattle. As a consequence, the sheep frontier advanced as did clearance. In Sutherland, an estimated 15,000 people were removed during the 'year of the burnings' alone from internal parishes to tiny crofts at the unproductive and inhospitable eastern coastal margins. In the century following Culloden, three factors of change had operated in the Highlands: the cultural conversion of the old elite; the disintegration of the old social framework of the common people; and the introduction of 'improving economics'. Grigor maintains that to these three must be added a fourth: 'the infrequency and ineffectiveness of popular resistance to these great changes, right through to the end of the 1840s.[6]

One such act of resistance, however, was the rebellion of 1813 in the parish of Kildonan, one of the three principal glens in the County of Sutherland. The parish minister was Revd Alexander Sage. The Strath of Kildonan was a relatively prosperous and self-sufficient area. In the lean years it was sufficiently well-stocked that it could sustain

---

5 Iain Fraser Grigor, *Mightier Than a Lord*, 14.
6 Iain Fraser Grigor, *Mightier Than a Lord*, 14.

neighbouring communities struggling to support their own. According to the 1811 census, 1,574 people lived in the parish of Kildonan. The Stafford's management agents had identified two large expanses of hill country, well in excess of 100,000 acres, for the establishment of a farm and the introduction of sheep and measures were subsequently put into action to evict those living in the strath. A deputation consisting of the minister, the local catechist and several other local worthies met with the Staffords' agents with a view to persuading them to overturn the decision but their entreaties were rebuffed, having been reminded that not only would resistance be seen as an act of defiance in the face of their landlords, but also as a flagrant breach of the law. The decision was irrevocable and the area would be cleared after the legal notices to quit had been served.

However, a few days later and with no other option available, around 100 local Kildonan men then threatened violence against the handful of shepherds who had accompanied the land-agents to survey the ground. They were run out of the area and the agents on horseback fled to report the findings to their superiors. This was only a stay of execution however. Kildonan was cleared in its entirety in 1816, including the church, manse and glebe.

Many of the more notorious Clearances took place in the years immediately following the return of demobbed servicemen from the Napoleonic Wars. While these men were fighting for King and Country, it was left to wives, women and girls to keep things going at home. The crofting duties of animal husbandry and planting and harvesting still had to be done, in the absence of the menfolk. The Clearances were met with many acts of resistance, and on occasions it was the women who faced up to the factors and sheriff-officers arriving with eviction notices. This led many women too into resisting the law, if not into breaching it.[7] Having invested their energies into ensuring there was a croft for the returning war-hero menfolk, women were determined not to be ejected from their family homesteads.

It is not entirely clear what level of support Alexander Sage gave to the rebels as they fomented civil disobedience. Conscious of his high standing and reputation within the community he nonetheless enjoyed a cordial relationship with the Staffords having been entertained by them several times over the course of his incumbency. It is improbable

---

7 Sally Magnusson refers movingly to the resistance of the women of Glencalvie in Strathcarron, in her recent novel *Music in the Dark* (John Murray/Hachette 2023).

that Sage shared his anti-eviction opinions with the Marchioness, expressed in private in correspondence with his son Donald. One renowned authority on the Clearances states, 'It is equally improbable that he denounced either clearances or their perpetrators from his Kildonan pulpit'.[8] Like most Presbyterian ministers of the time, Sage adhered to the conviction that placed stress on it being the duty of Christians to obey and to submit to all secular authority. One had to know one's place. James Hunter concludes: 'While Sage may or may not have counseled his parishioners to submit quietly to eviction orders issued in connection with the establishment of the farm ... it is certain that Sage was in no way minded to accept the loss of land he farmed himself.'[9]

Sage had a substantial glebe of 50 acres which supported a number of tenant farmers together with Kildonan's miller who leased property from the minister. He also had fishing rights on the Helmsdale river and employed several fishermen. Sage successfully petitioned the Presbytery of Dornoch to support his claim that certain grounds had been made available for Kildonan's ministers to use since 'time immemorial'. The Staffords' agents relented, cobbling together a compromise but perhaps wishing as much as Sage himself to tread lightly in this contentious matter. Sage was a leader among men and as such was in a position to make much trouble and create much adverse publicity which would have undoubtedly, in certain sections of the press, reflected badly upon the Staffords. The agents possibly considered that losing a few acres out of the 100,000 surveyed would be a small price to pay for a peaceable outcome.

However this temporary solution did not deter subsequent efforts by the Staffords' agents to clear entire townships in the years following. In 1814 the agent Patrick Sellar oversaw a series of evictions which resulted him being arrested on a charge of culpable homicide. It became a show trial with one purpose: to make very public the unchecked sweeping powers and aristocratic authority which the Staffords (and all other landowners for that matter) wielded with impunity. Not only was Sellar acquitted but the presiding sheriff-substitute Robert McKid was obliged to make a public apology to the accused.

This verdict emboldened Sellar and his agents to clear the townships and crofts with indiscriminate recklessness. However, that said, the

---

8 James Hunter, *Set Adrift Upon the World – The Sutherland Clearances*, 265.
9 James Hunter, *Set Adrift Upon the World – The Sutherland Clearances*, 266.

serving of eviction notices upon individuals rarely went without incident. The years 1819 and 1820 saw the wholesale clearance of many parts but it became necessary that most evictions were carried out in the presence of sheriff-officers, constables and on occasions the militia. Often writs were seized and burned and the landlords' agent assaulted and run off the land. But deadlines were strictly adhered to and families were unceremoniously thrown off their property, the remaining goods and chattels destroyed and the houses unroofed and fired.

In the main the Clearances were swift, brutal, unrestrained and inhumane. Any objection in the way notices of eviction were served or the manner in which evictions were carried out were usually summarily dismissed and those who brought objections branded as troublemakers, making any future employment problematic. In these matters, estate owners and their agents were acting in an irregular quasi-judicial fashion as judge, jury and executioner. These powerful families simply *were* the law. They had the power to decide what constituted 'the law' and how it was to be enforced. Their decisions were final. Appeals, from any quarter including the clergy, were not entertained and resistance in the end was futile.

The Land-owning Elite

The response of the landlords [to Highland famine] was less than benevolent: they complained bitterly at being required (as rate-payers) to spend some of their money to preserve a population which they now considered to be quite redundant. Where they were obliged to provide such support, they made sure that it was earned, by enforced labour at starvation wages.

Iain Fraser Grigor, *Mightier than a Lord*

By the 1830s not only were many Highlanders the victims of the Clearances, but the threat of mass starvation now loomed on the horizon as disease began to wipe out the potato crop, further impoverishing a population already dispossessed, oppressed and vulnerable. Yet Highlanders were not the only ones feeling the pinch.

Tom Devine (*The Scottish Clearances – A History of the Dispossessed*) and other commentators state that by the 1830s most hereditary estates in the western Highlands were burdened by heavy debts and insolvency, and a process of considerable transfer of ownership from the old proprietors to the new was underway. All the Outer Hebrides, from Barra to Lewis, and extensive districts in the islands of Skye and Mull, together with Morvern, Moidart, Knoydart, Glengarry, Glenshiel, Arisaig and Kintail on the western mainland, had been acquired by a new wealthy elite, few of whom had any traditional or family connections with the Highlands. By the mid 1850s this transfer of landholdings was complete with over two-thirds of the estates under new ownership. This new breed of Highland landlord had no use or desire for a native population encumbering their properties. The old clanship loyalty between chief and soldier/crofter, existing for centuries had all but disappeared and these newly-acquired estates were geared only for profit, either through the economic advantages of large-scale sheep farms or by income through the promotion of hill-sport activities, such as stalking, made possible by improvements in shotgun and ammunition technologies. As the writer Alistair Moffat observes, 'the Highlands began to fit the romance of its imagined past as the emigrations emptied the glens and straths and a working landscape slowly decayed into scenery, a vacant stage set for epic tales.'[10]

Strategies on several estates now started to move away from containment of the crisis to systematic dispersal of the people through mass eviction and forced emigration. The conversion of lands to profitable sheep farming was the surest and quickest method of maximising income. The possibility of a rise in poor rates, a financial burden on landowners, was an even clearer incentive to hasten the process. The conversion from people to sheep had worked well in Lowland estates and generally throughout England, where people lived closer to towns and alternative sources of employment. Profit and order, promoted under the guise of 'improvement' and the ideals of this *nouveau* establishment, were now the standards by which good and bad were to be judged in the Highlands.

For the heirs of the old clan chiefs the choice was stark: oblivion or enter into the service of the new order. A combination of those clan chiefs who had survived and adapted to the new ways, new venture capitalists and the aristocracy with their 'old' money controlled all the estates in the north and west. Further, Highland and Island representation in Parliament had been maintained by an influential elite of landowners returned as MPs. The influence of that landowning political elite undoubtedly helped to grease the wheels of commerce: Cameron of Lochiel owned 130,000 acres; for Caithness, Sir John Sinclair of Ulbster held 80,000 acres; for Ross-shire, Alexander

---

10 Alistair Moffat, *Scotland's Last Frontier – A Journey Along the Highland Line*, 211.

Matheson owned just shy of 250,000 acres; for Sutherland, the Marquis of Stafford, heir to the Duke, held over 1m acres (almost the entire county); and in Argyll, the Duke's estates ran to more than 170,000 acres.

The restricted franchise meant that it was titled barons, aristocrats and some *nouveau* industrialists and financiers who represented the remaining numbers of crofters and tenants on the land and the growing mass of dispossessed now pushed to the margins. These MPs in the Commons complemented their brethren who sat in the House of Lords, most of whom were still in control of ancestral lands. In the 1830s, the small select coterie of landowning aristocracy had been joined by free market speculators and a new wealthy elite seeking to maintain a grip on the management of landholding, all to their benefit and mostly to the cost of those whose very survival was controlled by capricious market forces and who were at the whim of their lords and masters. Some landowners whose main concern was the commercial exploitation of their assets now regarded the world of politics as a legitimate vehicle for securing their aims and ambitions and to reinforce the interests of their own estates.

As a case study in point, the Clearances which took place on the watch of the Marquis and Marchioness of Stafford are well documented. The 1785 marriage between Elizabeth Gordon and George Granville Leveson-Gower created an aristocratic powerhouse whose management of family lands in Staffordshire and Sutherland offered an insight, at its simplest, into the pursuit of profit at the expense of people.

Relocation

No doubt there were improvements of various kinds ... but the people who were shovelled down to the sea coast were not improved; and it was not for their improvement in any shape that the new roads were made or the new bridges constructed ... It was not the happiness of the great mass of the people, but the hasty enrichment of the few, that was the alpha and omega of their economic gospel in the Highlands.

Professor John Stuart Blackie, Scottish scholar and patriot

The main objective of Elizabeth Gordon was to substantially increase income from the vast estate through the creation of enormous sheep farms across the interior using 'imported' specialist herdsmen from the borders and northern England. As both 'Countess of Sutherland'

and 'Marchioness of Stafford' she had been given extraordinary authority over the county by her husband. The aim was not dispersal or expulsion but relocation of the population. The Sutherland experiment of the relocation of tenants and families into planned villages where fishing was meant to supplement their meagre incomes from the land failed miserably on two crucial counts: first, the Countess and her estate managers, who had little understanding of traditional values and culture of the people and their attachment to time-honoured ways of life, demanded instant transformation from farmers to fishermen. Essentially, sons and daughters of the soil now suddenly needed to become harvesters of the seas; and secondly, Sutherland's north coast, to where many had been forced, lacked harbours so there could be no local fishery. Further, these former crofters lacked the capital required to get into fishing on their own account.

Gradual and relentless displacement ran alongside episodes of mass eviction. The numbers involved were considerable and suggest a systematic process of enforced movement on an industrial scale. Removals on Mull and especially on Lewis, contemporaneous to the Sutherland Clearances, attracted much adverse publicity and were more extensive than many other 'resettlements'.

The real effect of the Clearances before 1840 was not to depopulate the Highlands in the short run, but to increase the terrible poverty and congestion of those townships which were spared but forced to accept more and more of the evicted by the process known as 'crowding in'. Colonies of impoverished cottars were to be found scattered across the western Highlands. Many of the settlements, optimistically planned to support a thriving fishery for the crofters in the 18th century like Tobermory, Bunessan, Lochcarron, Plockton, Lochaline, Tobermory, Dornie, Sheildaig and others, now became slum villages, packed with the dispossessed and destitute poor in the wake of the extensive clearances which became common after *c.*1820. The people, on the edge of starvation, lived in overcrowded and unsanitary conditions.

This in turn intensified the splitting of holdings into even smaller units in order to accommodate the displaced. As a result, the north and west became even more at risk to the impact of crop failure and the volatility of markets for fish, cattle and kelp. Increases in the population placed further pressures on local church accommodation and upon the work of already overstretched ministers.

Emigration

From 1841 to 1861 many west Highland parishes experienced an unprecedented fall in population, primarily caused by large-scale emigration. Over 10,000 emigrants were 'assisted' to move to Canada, mainly from the four great landed estates, those of the Dukes of Argyll and Sutherland, John Gordon of Cluny and Sir James Matheson covering Lewis, North and South Uist, Barra, Tiree, Mull and Skye. Between 1851 and 1855, the people were offered a bleak choice: be cleared from the land into destitution, or be 'assisted' in supported passage to Canada. From Matheson's Lewis estate alone nearly 2,500 souls were compulsorily transported. Summonses of removal were targeted at specific parishes and areas, with Barvas and West Lewis coming off worst. The poorest, who invariably had the smallest voice, were always targeted first. Estate managers came across as rigorous guardians of Victorian morality rather than as impartial administrators. Those who chose to remain were herded onto the fringes of the land, where opportunities to develop an economy barely beyond subsistence were few and far between.

At the census of 1861 the four Highland counties, even after famine and clearance, had a population of nearly 300,000, an increase of more than 36,000 from 1801. Of course, there had been substantial haemorrhage of people through migration, emigration and disease in the intervening years without which the population totals would have been much higher. By the later 19th century, several of the smaller Hebridean islands like Eigg, Muck, Ulva, Lismore and Rum had been swept clear of their inhabitants. But elsewhere, particularly in the Outer Hebrides of Barra, Harris, Lewis and South Uist, the population recovered after the destitution, widespread removals and compulsory emigration of the famine years.

In a sermon preached in London by Dr Ewing, Episcopal Bishop of Argyll and the Isles on 13th July 1852,[11] the text was from Genesis, 'Now when Jacob saw that there was corn in Egypt he said to his sons 'Get you down thither.'" The sermon rehearsed the tragic history of the Highlands from the beginning of the 19th century: the steady increase in population; the destruction of the kelp manufacture; the suppression of illicit distillation; the decline of the herring trade; the decreased value of black cattle; the failure of the potato crop. The only remedy was emigration, specifically to Australia. Nowhere in the sermon does the

---

11 As reported in the *Inverness Courier,* July 29, 1852.

subject of the Clearances arise, neither the callous and indiscriminate nature of evictions, nor is there a word about landlord indifference to the plight of the natives. The Bishop is effusive in his description of the people however, their 'hardy, uncomplaining character, their bravery during the late wars, and their religious reverential character at home'. Compliant and 'knowing one's place', these Highland character traits appear to have justified and legitimised the actions of landowners over decades.

The sermon was published and proceeds of the sale were to be appropriated in aid of 'the fund', which appears in the text unspecified. Dr Ewing appears to have found favour as mouthpiece for the Highland landlords, giving their actions a veneer of religious respectability. Evangelicals had railed against Moderate ministers for the same thing thirty years previously. Whatever 'the fund' was, it benefited by £5129 5s 7p and included, amongst others, sizeable donations from the Dukes of Buccleugh, Argyll and Sutherland, the Marquis and Marchioness of Stafford and Sir James Matheson, all who substantially gained, first by clearance and then by forced emigration.

Land Economics

And while the people were impoverished – in the name of the prosperity of the Highlands – the great tide of sheep flooded north ever more strongly. In 1811 there were perhaps a quarter of a million in the Highlands; by the 1840s they numbered close on a million, and that number continued to grow relentlessly.

Iain Fraser Grigor, *Mightier than a Lord*

The traditional belief existed, inherited from the old martial society, that crofters had an inalienable right to the land they tended and farmed and, even after the death of clanship, that the elites had an obligation to protect the people on the lands in return for rental and service. Forced eviction was seen to be the grossest violation of that ancestral bond. When these bonds were broken and families cleared as landowners went bankrupt in the bad times after 1820, or saw the economic benefits of sheep-ranching accruing to the landed classes, the sense of betrayal was complete. Bitterness and a profound sense of injustice simmered eventually passing down the generations in the oral culture and traditions of the people. Each new generation was infused by these tales of dispossession, deceit and duplicity. The history of the Clearances tells us that these people simply became an expendable commodity

Essay 3: The Clearances and the Consequences

and the following extract reveals that government documents of the time played up the economic advantages and, ignoring the human cost, lauded the consequences of naked capitalism:

> In the Island of Skye alone no less than a sum of £100,000 has been expended by the late Lord Macdonald in the erection of buildings and other improvements. I may here also mention a fact, from which the general state of the Highlands, before the parliamentary works were undertaken, may be inferred: namely that at the period of his Lordship's accession in 1795, to his estates in that island, comprising nearly five parishes, there were throughout their whole extent no churches, only one manse, two or three small slated houses and only one slated inn.
>
> The price of property in Inverness and its vicinity has risen ten fold in the space of twenty-five years: the lands of Merkinch saw rent income increase from £70 -£80 to £600; Redcastle Estate was sold in 1792 for £25,000 and sold again in 1824 for £135,000 [£12,250,000 in today's values]. These increases are to be found generally throughout the north and west: capitalists from Edinburgh and Northumberland have caused increases in rents on the Stafford Estates and this has had a roll-over effect on the more inaccessible parts of the Reay Estates. On the Chisholm estate rents have risen from £700 in 1785 to £5000 in 1824. On the Glengarry estate annual income did not exceed £800 before 1783. In 1824, the land generates an income of between £6000 and £7000 per annum.[12] [£600,000 in today's values]

The author of the report is clear in his conclusion: 'The increase in wealth in the Inverness area is down to the benefits of better communications and the establishment of the sheep and wool market [1817] at this central point in the Highlands to which traders from all parts of the country including England come to do business'.

Rising prices certainly advantaged the landowner, in some cases an absentee aristocrat, especially in areas where historically the value of land, in many parts of the north and west, had been so low as to be almost worthless. Over the course of a few short years owning substantial holdings of land would prove a financially prudent enterprise, but it must be noted that in the space of a further fifty years over half the Highland estates were burdened by massive self-indulgent debt or had either entered into administration or were completely

---

12 Commissioners for Highland Roads and Bridges, *Fourteenth Report*, 1828.

bankrupt. Overblown ambition, over-extended credit and the failure of the kelp industry seem to have been the cause of estate failures in most instances.

Many factors conspired against the promise of prosperity and improvement expected by investors and speculators from the south, all of whom awaited investment returns commensurate with those made elsewhere. First, there was an over-optimistic anticipation of financial return and an under-appreciation of population increases which outstripped the land's capacity to provide enough food to meet the people's needs. Many estates simply could not feed their tenants. Second, little account was taken either of the limitations of natural endowment in the Highlands or the limitations on employment prospects. There were limited opportunities to exploit any potential Highland businesses because the Highlands were judged to be too far from southern markets. Highland enterprises simply could not compete with Lowland industry and commerce, driven as they were by ambition and mercantile enterprise. Third, human assets were perceived to be lacking in the north and west and finally, increasing numbers of absentee landlords who left the day-to-day running of estates to agents often found themselves too far removed to pursue best business practices.

Justice and Poverty

Can Law be Law when based on wrong?
Can Law be Law when for the strong?
Can Law be Law when landlords stand
Rack-renting mankind off the land? . . .
By 'Law' evictions dreadful crimes
Are possible in Christian times

Extract from *St Michael and the Preacher*
by Revd Donald MacSillar

Those Highland families who did escape to the conurbations of the south for work and prospects traded one type of poverty for another – from the vast empty expanses of northern glens to the over-crowded unsanitary vennels and lanes of the cities. Those who remained were forced either to the coasts as wholesale clearance emptied the land of people or to consider emigration to the American colonies as the only viable survival route.

To whom did the victims of Highland poverty eventually turn in the face of blatant injustice? Certainly not the landowners whose eyes would be firmly fixed upon extracting maximum profit by a revolution in farming practices for minimum expenditure. However, an early subsistence crisis which lasted over 1782 and 1783 revealed that many of the Highland estates were not producing enough food to feed their tenants – a first indication of systemic failure. The Highlands and Islands were facing a catastrophe. This crisis ought to have been both an early warning for things to come and an opportunity for change. Neither was heeded. Instead, out of the crisis came the founding of the Highland Society of Scotland in 1784. The product of Enlightenment thinking, the society was a worthy enterprise with the express aim to enquire into 'the present state of the Highlands and Islands of Scotland, and the condition of their inhabitants' and into 'the means of improvement of the Highlands'. Its President was the Duke of Argyll, an enthusiastic improver, and other office-bearers of the society included titled barons with large landholdings, Edinburgh lawyers and several 'noblemen and gentlemen'.

In the matter of addressing Highland depopulation particularly, the Society began to press the Government for action. It was recognised that improvements in communications were urgently needed; principally the building of new roads and small harbours which brought Thomas Telford to prominence. By the first two decades of the 19th century 'land management' and the means of its 'improvement' were the headline issues. Concern for the 'condition of their inhabitants', although stated clearly enough in the society's founding mission-statement, in truth seemed a secondary concern. To many of the directors and officers of the Highland Society of Scotland, 'land-management' clearly meant 'clearance', which in their eyes paved the way for 'improvement'. That its representatives were granted a special audience with King George IV on his Edinburgh visit in 1822 demonstrated that the Highland Society of Scotland was held in high regard and was seen to be an engine and agent for good governance and change. Notwithstanding the jaundiced view of many Highlanders, many of whom regarded themselves as 'victims' and suspicious of any endeavour that smacked of paternalism, the society had noble aims at its heart. There was a growing recognition by the society and others of the desperate need for a general improvement in the conditions of living in the north and west.

Tartanry

Demonstrating the disconnect, however, between the carefully-choreographed Celtified pageantry of the King's visit and the brutal reality of life in the Highlands as experienced by the majority of its inhabitants, in the eyes of some at least, there was now a serious attempt to domesticate the Highlander and rehabilitate His Majesty. This further skewed perceptions of both native and monarch. That the arrangements for the monarch's visit were put in the hands, mainly, of the Celtic Society, founded in 1820 by a group of high-profile Highland gentlemen, cemented the belief that there was a strong case to be made for the promotion of a distinctive Scottish culture and heritage, too often ignored or dismissed by a disinterested English establishment.

Soon after his succession in 1820, it was thought that the monarch should pay a state visit to Scotland. He had visited Ireland, rebellious and uneasy, and the intention was to strike a balance and journey north. Coincidently, there had been arranged a summit meeting for Government officials of all the European states to discuss important matters of state and British civil servants decided they did not want King George anywhere near it. The proposed visit to Scotland could not have come at a more opportunistic moment so the Monarch was hurriedly packed off north. Sir Walter Scott was the Celtic Society's first Vice-President and took charge of arrangements.

One critic commentating on the visit stated that 'Sir Walter had ridiculously made us appear as a nation of Highlanders, and the bagpipe and tartan was the order of the day'.[13] The Whig, James Stuart of Dunearn, quoted above, wasn't the only sceptic. Scott's own son-in-law John Lockhart reported,

> With all respect for the generous qualities with which the Highland clans have often exhibited, it was difficult to forget that they had always constituted a small, and almost always unimportant part of the Scottish population . . . it was a cruel mockery in giving so much prominence to their pretentions.[14]

Lockhart gave no credence to the contributions made by Highland regiments in the three great wars of Empire. It was evident that whatever happened in the north and west hardly registered or impacted upon the lives of those living in relative ease and comfort in the fine dwellings of Edinburgh and London. Some saw through the tartanry and trappings

---

13 James Stuart of Dunearn writing to Robert Ferguson of Raith, 17th August 1822.
14 John Gibson Lockhart *Memoirs of the Life of Sir Walter Scott Bt*, 481.

for what they were. However, many others were convinced, along with the King, that the pure, national characteristic of the Scotsman was a Highlander.

Some Highland landowners were complicit in this deception. Only five clans attended 'The Gathering' organised for the King's pleasure: the Sutherland Men, the Breadalbane Campbells, the McGregors, Glengarry's Men and the Drummonds. Many more prominent clans were conspicuous by their absence: there were no Camerons, Macdonalds, MacLeods, MacPhersons, Rosses, Munros, Gordons, Macleans. Indeed, one writer stated, 'When the clans gathered to honour His Majesty, the Sutherland turn-out was contemptible. Some two or three dozen of squalid-looking, ill dressed and ill-appointed men, were all that Sutherland produced.'[15] Clearly an embarrassment to the parade organisers these men were quickly shepherded out of public view. The Marquis of Stafford and his chief administrator James Loch who were in attendance were said to have 'reaped little honour' by the men's appearance. Represented by a dishevelled bunch on parade was not a great advert for promoting the benefits of rule under titled barons such as the Marquis, Lord Francis Leveson Gower. The Sutherland turn-out may also have been a foolish but brave act of defiance or sabotage on the part of the men intent on showing what life was really like under the yoke of the Staffords. Indeed, while accusations of 'improvement', eviction and forced emigration were all gaining currency, sending a contingent of men to the festivities was the Marchioness of Stafford's retort to those who claimed she had depopulated her estates.

There was a further incongruity, however. Given a free hand, these very clan chiefs and landed proprietors of great Highland estates, now infected by profit-driven economics, would have happily expunged all traces of Highland traditions of dress, custom and language, seen as mighty hindrances on the drivers of wealth and prosperity. Integration with English ways, means and measures was the real intent. Alastair Moffat states:

> It was more than a bitter irony that, at exactly the moment when Edinburgh was filled with tartan-clad lowlanders and a German king all pretending to be Highlanders, the real originators of this bowdlerised version of their culture were being ruthlessly cleared off the land as aristocrats forgot the bonds and obligations of the past and focused on future profit.[16]

---

15 Alexander MacKenzie, *History of the Highland Clearances*, 38.
16 Alistair Moffat, *Scotland's Last Frontier – A Journey Along the Highland Line*, 224.

As a commercial exercise in promoting a picturesque, romantic portrait, it was a triumph. The reality was somewhat different. Yet the King's visit and Scott's stage-management of it inspired a whole new tourist industry and forever changed the general perceptions of those who did not live in the Highlands and Islands but who, nevertheless, were presented with a confused and conflated image of 'Scotsman' and 'Highlander'. And in a wider context, served only to blur further definitions of what it was to be both 'British' and 'Scottish'.

As the monarch stepped over the border (the first to have done so since 1641), this was a crucial time for the Kirk, embroiled as it was in patronage disputes. While still keen to display its 'Establishment' credentials and loyalty to the Crown, it was all the more forcibly engaged in affirming the primacy of ecclesiastical law over the civil courts and affirming the Church's *right* to determine its own affairs. For all its pageantry and procession of the King's visit, neither the debate about what it was to be 'Scottish', nor the arcane nature of Church-State relations touched the Highlander working his meagre strip of unpromising land. His focus was simply on *survival*.

Lies, Damn Lies and Statistics

Across Scotland, Kirk ministers were instrumental in providing exhaustive information which set out the situation at the time, offering an 'on-the-ground' record parish by parish. Whether this information from Highland parishes when compiled into the 'New Statistical Account' reflected the full picture is highly debatable. In his contribution to the Statistical Account of 1834 Revd David MacKenzie of Farr, Inverness-shire and much favoured by the Sutherlands, practically ignores the effect of the Clearances upon the people of his parish, merely remarking that decline in population was 'owing to introduction of sheep-farming system. By its adoption, the farmers and tenants who occupied the straths and glens were, in 1818 and 1819, all removed from these possessions'.[17] The minister of Kildonan, Revd James Campbell, reporting in 1840, had even less to say stating, 'Almost the whole of the parish is occupied as sheep-farms. The Cheviot sheep are estimated at 18,000 head. These are divided among 6 tenant farmers'.[18] Elsewhere on the Sutherland estate, ministers of Lairg and

---

17 *The Statistical Accounts of Scotland 1845: Farr, County of Inverness*, vol. XV, 73.

18 *The Statistical Accounts of Scotland 1840: Kildonan, County of Sutherland*, vol. XV, 147.

Essay 3: The Clearances and the Consequences

of Clyne echoed Telford's assessment that the economic benefits were accruing. Yet these ministers were wholly silent on injustices and cruelty wrought by the Stafford family and were in full praise of the Duchess.

Those in Government whose business was to read the Statistical Accounts were immediately handicapped by reports from across the Highlands and Islands which did not present the whole picture; they contained erroneous information; the information which was offered was often sanitized for the benefit of interested parties; and some reports were clearly and blatantly misleading. There were some undoubtedly important and influential people in Government, with the welfare of their citizens in their hands, who simply did not know what was going on in the north and west, or turned a blind eye to the realities of the situation.

By the 1830s the Staffords were in control of 700,000 acres in the County of Sutherland but this was to rise to over 1 million acres by the end of the Clearances and the evictions and displacement of 15,000 individuals. The Presbytery of Tongue, not unaware of the continuing misery which evictions caused, was almost blasphemous in its adulation of the Duchess when she arrived for her annual visit in 1857 – while evictions were still being carried out. In 1841 the minister of Durness threatened the people opposing eviction with punishment here, and eternal damnation in the afterlife. Evils inflicted upon them were believed to be ordained by God and any opposition was Devil-inspired.

Moderate-dominated clergy were by far the majority of incumbents in Highland pulpits at the end of the 18th century and beginning of the 19th and many of them were generally believed to be unsympathetic towards the plight of those threatened with eviction. Not only were the rural poor without many friends to prosecute their grievances, these same prisoners of geography at the mercy of natural elements beyond their control clearly found themselves impotent in the face of arcane abstractions of market capitalism. Further, they were evidently expendable first casualties when, in the pursuit of profit and gain, they were cleared from the land of their forebears with the suspicion that in many occasions, too many of the clergy were simply unable or unwilling to take up their cause. But generally, all ministers knew that pleading for minds to be changed and calling for eviction-notices to be withdrawn were hopeless tasks.

Clergy Caught in a Cleft-stick

Amid scenes of starvation and pitiful suffering, the Countess of Sutherland wrote to a friend in England, 'Scotch people are of a happier constitution and do not fatten like the larger breed of animals'. It was all done in the spirit of progress – to make the land more productive – and the Countess remarked of her husband, that 'he is seized as much as I am with the rage of improvements, and we both turn our attention with the greatest of energy to turnips'.

Alistair Moffat, *Scotland's Last Frontier*

Since too many Moderate ministers preferred to ignore the plight of the Highlander, some even accused of cosying up too readily to the landowning classes, it was to the Evangelical ministers the rural dispossessed eventually turned. They filled the vacuum created by Moderate and landowning interests unable or unwilling to understand the impact which the new Highland order introduced. These changes had the profoundest effect upon a population disadvantaged by the drive for economic advancement. In a PhD thesis, its author J.R. Stephen states, 'Once established in the hearts and minds of the lower classes of Highland society, the spirit of evangelicalism produced a new breed of leadership that embraced the political and economic concerns of Highland life.'[19] Stephen also argues that the Highland minister was a different breed to his Lowland brethren, 'reflecting the peripatetic nature of Gaelic society similar to the traditional bardic circuits'.

In effect, Evangelicalism by recapturing something of a lost Calvinism offered the dispossessed and rural poor a different type of religion. Those ministers who did protest against social and ecclesiastical injustice, especially in the matter and manner of clearance, were most likely to be Evangelicals. In general terms however, and barring one or two brave and outspoken individuals such as Alexander Sage, ministers were reluctant to upset long-standing practices of traditional Highland society by speaking out about injustice; especially when it challenged the legal position of landowners. Some Moderate ministers would be too conscious of not wishing to jeopardise stipend or social position. In truth, ministers usually advised restraint, arguing that to engage in civil unrest or communal insurrection would be certainly harshly dealt with by the courts, habitually superintended by landowners

---

19 J.R. Stephen, PhD thesis, *The Impact of Geography on Ecclesiastical Endeavour in the Highlands*, 2004.

and other upper-class Justices of the Peace and magistrates. Indeed, a London Times correspondent went further by suggesting that it was only 'religion' which had prevented the 'open and turbulent resistance of law'.[20] He maintained that the clergy had prevented wholesale civil disobedience. Both Moderate and Evangelical views would seem to support this view: Moderate strict adherence to the enforcement of the law and Evangelical acceptance of witnessing God's hand at work despite clear injustice. Arguably, it was the combination of effective preaching on 'passive obedience' by clergy, the natural demeanour of the Gael to 'know his place' and the 'uncomplaining character of the people' as Dr Ewing had it in his London sermon, which facilitated the aristocracy, on the whole, to clear the land with little opposition.

The judgement and verdict of many was clear: Moderate clergy's social sympathies which embraced both *laisser-faire* economics and the inviolable rights of inheritance and property ownership, and their natural leanings towards law and order, actually aided and abetted the landowning classes, casting them in the role of apologists for the oppressing landlords.

As late as 1821 two Scots in three were still tied to the land, on farms or tending crofts and living in small towns and villages. Clearly, the fortunes or otherwise of the vast majority of the Scottish people were still wholly dependent for their living upon the actions of mainly absentee landowners and their local agents. In the matter of the Clearances, there were accusations of total duplicity on the part of some ministers.

During the most active years of the Sutherland clearances of 1816 – 1820, the Duke had discouraged his wife from travelling north from their estate in Staffordshire. In 1820, however, the Duke thought the lands in a fit state to merit a 'royal visit' from the Marchioness. Accompanied by her son Earl Gower all was made ready. There is a hint in the reporting that some of the crofts in the newly-developed areas around Brora may have been especially well chosen as the Duchess and the inspection party were greatly satisfied by what they witnessed. 'We went into every house,' the Duchess reported, 'and talked to all the people and gave great satisfaction.'[21] Prizes were awarded to the builders of the best cottages and to those who had made the best efforts at cultivating the strips of wasteland given to them. In her letter to

---

20 Article covered by several newspapers including *The Atlas, Liverpool Standard, John o' Groat Journal*, May 1845.
21 Letter from Lady Stafford to Lord Stafford, 5th October 1820.

Lord Stafford she wrote that her trip was a 'great encouragement' to her and she was more than satisfied that the people were 'quite happy in thinking they are attended to'. However, there is another side to the visit, since the Duchess of Sutherland relied upon her factor and the local minister for translations, as she herself being from the south had no Gaelic whatsoever. She was assured on visiting many cottages, despite blatant evidence to the contrary, that her people were 'quite comfortable' while the minister himself was fully aware of the horrors of the situation. Those newly-established upon the ribbons of dirt they were encouraged to cultivate understood perfectly that to speak out against their miserable conditions was to risk further sanction. Perhaps the minister, being aware of this, sanitised in translation some of the more critical comments.

Some of those who suffered most by way of eviction, however, did speak out forcibly. Some unafflicted by the prevalent and somewhat pathological Highland fatalism paint bleak pictures which do not reflect well upon either master or minister. From his collected memoir, Donald J. Macleod tells the story of a particular eviction from the township of Timsgarry in 1824, demonstrating beyond doubt the complicity of the minister:

> I knew a man at Aird, Uig, Donald Macleod (Doimhnall Ban). I think it was his grandfather who was evicted from Timsgarry and trekked to Aird where he built a hovel on a hill opposite the village. His heinous crime???? A woman visiting his house as his family was eating said, 'Your table is as good as that of the Balnacille minister.' He replied, 'Am I not just as worthy of such a table as him?'
>
> Someone told the minister who said that anyone who spoke to Macleod was banned from communion. The minister, made out to be a great preacher, Rev Alexander MacLeod, then had Donald Macleod evicted. MacLeod was from Sutherland and in the pay of Seaforth. The Highland Clearances lasted for over a hundred years and Presbyterian ministers were in collusion with the landlords and Anglicised clan chiefs who were evicting the people. In 1826, Timsgarry, Uig, was cleared by MacKenzie of Seaforth to make a glebe for the sheep of Rev Alexander MacLeod, Balnacille Church. However the evicted tenants and their children toiling and starving in the scrub and mosquito-infested backwoods of Canada, were not enamoured by the Christian creed of this cleric, which was hellfire in the

pulpit, sheep on the glebe, and Seaforth's lucre in his back pocket. Since the Act of Union the Kirk had been in the yoke of patronage, harmoniously fitting into a corrupt scabbard along with associates in the political establishment at Westminster.[22]

This incident appears to have been an extreme example of personal vindictiveness lacking in any Christian charity, although many Moderate ministers were accused of complicity in facilitating local clearances. Donald MacLeod was cleared off his ancestral land to the benefit of the Uig minister Alexander MacLeod, a perpetrator and a fervent Evangelical who enjoyed full-throated support from the landowning Seaforths.

Another recorder of events comments on the Strathnaver clearances of 1814. James of Glencarr notes the willingness of the clergy to turn a blind eye and make a profit from the misery of their flocks. He writes how 'the Landlord built new manses for the men of the cloth, with carriage roads to their doors and granted them a few acres of sheep pasturage, in order that they might turn a tidy profit. In return for this, the churchmen gave God's authority to so-called "improvement" and threatened those tenants who resisted eviction with eternal damnation.'[23]

Many folks, compliant and obedient, accepted the changes imposed as in accordance with the will of God. As if to emphasise the point, Donald Sage, son of Revd Alexander Sage, recalls hearing a sermon expounding 'The truly pious acknowledged the mighty hand of God in the matter, humbling themselves and receiving their chastisement at His hand', a blatant misreading and sorrowful interpretation of 1st Peter chapter 5 and no doubt preached by a minister sympathetic to the expansion policies of land-management, to his own advantage and to the detriment of his congregation.

The Duke of Sutherland handsomely rewarded the Moderate-minister David MacKenzie with the parish of Farr, an impressive manse, a fine church and glebe consisting of the best land in the area. This, in exchange for telling his flock that it was God's will that they leave the land of their ancestors and obey those whom God had placed above them. In his coruscating memoir, James of Glencarr rails against the 'evil shepherds who preyed on their own flocks' and the writer

---

22 Donald J. Macleod, *The Highland Clearances on the Isles of Lewis and Harris*, ed. Alastair McIntosh, 2005, 14.
23 James of Glencarr, *The Praying Men of God*, clanjames.com.

quotes from a sermon heard at the time of the Clearances based on the text, 'that the Lord had a controversy with the land for the people's wickedness, and even in his mercy, he had sent this scourge to bring them to repentance', again a grievous conflation of a number of Old Testament prophesies from Jeremiah and Hosea. He recalls the 'silence' of clergy who refused to speak out against social injustice in order to secure their own wealth and comfort. Generally across the county of Sutherland, it was reported that 17 clergy, with the one exception of Alexander Sage, acted at the behest of the Staffords. Alexander MacKenzie wrote, 'The clergy also, whose duty it is to denounce the oppressors, and aid the oppressed, have all found their account in abetting the wrong-doers, exhorting the people to quiet submission, helping to stifle their cries, telling them that all their sufferings came from the hand of God and was a just punishment for their sins.'[24]

These accounts and reminiscences were recorded from a post-Disruption perspective when the faithful churchgoers of Sutherland, Ross, Caithness and Inverness-shire had given their verdict on the Kirk and its clergy. Both Kirk and clergy were found wanting. It was the Free Church which took its stand to oppose patronage and to be finally independent of the power of the landowner. However, it is clear that neither Evangelical nor Moderate minister was, to any degree, successful in overturning land-management decisions irrespective of how vocal or silent they may have been. It appears that any protestation from ministers was ignored, despite the moral righteousness of many of the cases.

It is agreed that clergy generally were in a difficult position, on the one hand, patently lawful estate plans could deprive him of his congregation, if not his church and manse (as in the case of Alexander Sage of Kildonan, and many others), and on the other hand if he voiced concerns there was in reality very little further scope for resistance. It is also worth noting the relative silence of successive General Assemblies on the matter. Concerning the competing national claims of Church and State, and the local claims of minister and landowner, the uncompromising stance of the two more powerful civil forces within the compact easily trumped the ecclesiastical pleadings, such as they were, of the weaker two. The working relationship between these parties was rarely to the advantage of the Kirk's courts. This inbuilt bias in favour of the civil claimants lay at the basis of the problem which took generations to work out.

---

24 Alexander MacKenzie, *History of the Highland Clearances*, 7.

Essay Four

Facing the Difficulties

One of the many inconveniences...
The Statistical Accounts of Scotland 1791: Lismore and Appin, County of Argyll, vol. I, 495

Ministers in Highland Parishes

The Revd John Nicolson was parish minister of Portree on the Isle of Skye including the islands of Raasay and Ronay. When the Statistical Accounts of Scotland survey was delivered to his door in 1795, Mr Nicolson was ill, and it fell to the local schoolmaster to complete the survey and return it to Edinburgh. The schoolmaster Alexander Campbell, later to succeed Mr Nicolson as minister in 1799, spared no effort, and the information he provided on the land, the sea, the hills, the valleys and plains, the caves and the rivers, the fishing and the farming, the virtues of the people and their poverty were set out precisely and sensitively. Under one of the final headings – 'Church, Poor, School, etc.' – he provided a carefully-drawn picture of Mr Nicolson as a Highland minister of the finest kind. The minister had a deep care for the souls of the parish and had established a Poor Fund of £140 (£15,000 in today's value) which, despite many calls upon it, through interest and good governance was still largely intact 50 years later as the 1843 Statistical Accounts were to show.

By Campbell's account Mr Nicolson was an extraordinary man of dedication and drive, absent just four times during 39 years of ministry. He was then 88 and the schoolmaster reported that he got a fall that dislocated his shoulder, and confined him to the house during the rest of the season – however:

> Till that unfortunate accident he never was troubled with any sort of indisposition, and what is rather singular, never travelled on horseback for one mile in all his life. As may be supposed, he is now extremely weak and can scarcely walk to the next place of worship; an assistant, therefore, or missionary, between Raasay and the farther end of the parish is much required, and greatly wished for by the people.[1]

---

1 *The Statistical Accounts of Scotland 1795: Portree, County of Inverness*, vol. XVI, 155.

This urgent request for assistance was noted in the returns for the Commissioners of Religious Instruction, Scotland, published in 1838. However, Presbytery minutes reveal that the formal request for assistance was still 'on the table' in a proposal on 4th December 1833, and only by early 1842 was a missionary minister appointed to support a catechist who had arrived nine years previously.

Mr Nicolson never received from Presbytery the support so patently needed, dying just months after the Statistical Accounts had been submitted. Further, Portree Parish had supplied no manse. Mr Nicolson had been effectively homeless his entire ministry and could only rent various properties round the parish. Whether local heritors whose legal obligation included ensuring stipends were appropriately paid made an additional allowance 'in lieu of manse' to Mr Nicolson is unclear. In 1798 the population was 1,980, the stipend not quite 1000 merks Scots (about £70), and the glebe was worth no more than £6 a year, about £600 in today's value. There were four places of worship, all expected to be served by Mr Nicolson, but only one of these was a church, built around 1730, described by Mr Campbell as 'slated, but rather small, and indifferently finished within'.

Mr Nicolson seems to have been an exceptional man, but many ministers in the Highlands and Islands encountered 'many inconveniences', with similar experiences of far-flung parishes, difficulties of terrain and weather, inadequate resources, and insufficient support. The Old Statistical Accounts, compiled in the closing years of the 18th century, reveal the extreme difficulties under which the majority of ministers laboured as they endeavoured to serve their parishes.

The most persistent and disheartening problem with church buildings in the Highlands and Islands was that the population living in remote and inaccessible areas, which were peppered with ancient ruins of pre-Reformation churches, were effectually unserved by the Church of Scotland, or served sacrificially by ministers like the Revd John Nicolson; and there were many others like him.

An example of an individual stretched to the physical limit of his endurance was identified by the compiler of the Statistical Account as the minister of North Uist. Five places of worship in the parish were listed (see Map): Kilmuir, in very good repair, where he preached on two successive Sundays, and Clachan, 13 miles (20 km) away, where services were held every third Sunday. There was no church in Clachan, and the house used previously was then in ruin. The minister preached once in a quarter in Sollas, seven miles from Kilmuir, and once a year on the islands of Borreray and Heisker. The compiler gave his opinion that it was 'impossible that one clergyman, however assiduous he may be, can be equal to the task of instructing in the principles of religion such a multitude of people dispersed over a great tract of country, many of them in situations so discontinuous to the place of worship that they hardly have the opportunity of hearing the word of God preached in a twelvemonth.'[2]

Clerical isolation, lack of assistance and unwieldy parishes continued to be specific sources of complaint among ministers in the north and west. By the time of the New Statistical Accounts of 1841 matters had improved little.

Nearly 150 years earlier, in 1699 and to alleviate these same historical concerns, the General Assembly, convening for only the third time since the Presbyterian re-establishment of 1690, sent 20 probationer ministers to the north as a matter of urgency to vacant or under-staffed parishes: three to the Presbytery of Perth, Auchterarder, and Dunkeld; six to Angus and Mearns, four to Aberdeen; three to Moray; two to Ross, Sutherland, and Caithness; and two to Orkney.[3] They were to remain for 12 months, and their expenses would be met from the King's gift to the church ('the King's Bounty'). That same General Assembly in 1699 appointed a committee to visit the Highland parishes of Ross, Sutherland, and Caithness. Forming that committee were two or three lairds and six Highland ministers, from the parishes of Thurso, Golspie, Fearn, Farr, Kiltearn and Reay. The committee was instructed to 'visit the kirks, manses, glebes, and, if need be, perambulate the parishes, and consider how they may be more commodiously divided or annexed; or where there is need of new erections, and how the same may be most conveniently accomplished'. The fourth Assembly convened and the following February empowered the Commission of the General Assembly 'to give advice and assistance to the Presbyteries of Caithness, Orkney and Shetland . . . particularly, to be assisting in purging and planting kirks, and in application to the civil magistrate for repairing and building kirks and manses'.[4]

Clearly, the General Assembly was attempting to get to grips with the Highland Problem. Year after year the General Assembly Acts and

---

2 *Statistical Accounts of Scotland 1794: North Uist, County of Inverness,* vol. XIII, 323.

3 'Acts: 1699', in *Acts of the General Assembly of the Church of Scotland 1638-1842,* 277-289.

4 'Acts: 1700', in *Acts of the General Assembly of the Church of Scotland,* 1638-1842.

Proceedings recorded evidence from various official Church sources for the necessity for more buildings and more help for Highland parishes. The sending of 20 probationers north was one such response in dealing with one difficult situation. At least, the General Assembly was correct in identifying the need for a rolling programme of surveys across the entire north and west, for in later years this became more focused on the western Highlands, particularly on Ross, Caithness and Sutherland, northern Argyll, parts of Inverness, and the Hebrides. It is worth noting that as early as 1699, the General Assembly was considering applying to the civil authorities to assist in the matter of financing churches and manses, if only as a recourse in law to ensure local heritors met their full financial obligations. One parish minister however traced the problem of ensuring a properly-financed church even further back.

Ministry and Mission, Popery and Politics

The General Assembly's commitment to the spread of the Gospel particularly in the Highlands and Islands was motivated by both a spiritual concern to bring the Gospel of Christ to all people, and a political imperative to encourage loyalty to crown and constitution and to reassure the monarch of the loyalty of the Presbyterian Church; their aim to work towards eradicating popery could be seen as both spiritual and political. In 1690, at the first meeting of the General Assembly for 40 years and at the end of the period when the Episcopal Church had ruled in Scotland, the Assembly's [5]Reply to His Majesty's Gracious Letter spoke of the unity and order restored to this Church and added that 'God hath been pleased to bless our endeavours . . . in providing for the propagation of religion and the knowledge of God in the most barbarous places of the Highlands, which may be the surest way of reducing these people also unto your Majesty's obedience'. In 1714 the Assembly wrote 'a humble Address' to Queen Anne,

> Your Majesty's known zeal for the true reformed Protestant religion, and the renewed gracious assurances we have from your Majesty, to maintain and protect the Presbyterian government of this Church, do encourage us to lay before your Majesty these things that so nearly concern the interest of religion and of this Church.[6]

---

5 General Assembly Sess. 26, November 13, 1690.
6 General Assembly Sess. ult., May 17, 1714.

> The Assembly expressed its 'extreme sorrow' at
>> the bold and insolent Carriage of Popish Bishops, Priests, Jesuits, and other Trafficking Papists in several Parts of this Nation, and that not only by secret Practices, but by avowed keeping of Mass Meetings, and Chappels, to which People do openly resort, by whose Artifices, several Hundreds have of late been perverted in a few Parishes, and that their Bishops do presume, at stated Times, to confirm great Multitudes, as in a Popish Country.

One year later another attempt to place a Stuart king on the throne and re-establish Catholicism was very nearly successful. The threat from home-bred Catholics but more, from overseas supporters of the Old Pretender was very real. The impression was of an aggressive, perpetually expanding Catholic population, but the situation in reality was very different. Even under James VII the Catholic mission had struggled to expand significantly beyond its north-eastern heartlands, and the number of converts remained small, despite the assertion in the Assembly's letter to the monarch that 'great Multitudes' had been confirmed into the Catholic church. There were some conversions after 1690, but problems of personnel and money meant that Scotland's Catholic revival was precarious.

Was the anxiety about Catholic expansion genuine but focused less on the Highlands and more in the industrial heartland of Scotland? Was it more revealing of the insecurity felt by the Presbyterian church? Did the Church of Scotland position itself front and centre as stout 'defenders of the faith' to convince central government of the necessity of Presbyterian expansion to defend the peace of the kingdom? The same humble address of 1714 discouraged the Queen from turning back to the Episcopal Church for 'defending the peace of the kingdom' and who still posed a threat to the Presbyterian Church. It also stressed the constitutional position of the Kirk which was safeguarded under the terms of the Act of Union. However, a cautionary note was expressed privately in that political sympathy in England for the Episcopalian cause, which aligned itself with the Anglican Church, meant that such accusations had to be deployed carefully.

Despite certain Episcopal sympathies continually voiced from England, the Crown was sensitive to the ever-present possibility of a Catholic resurgence. It looked to the Kirk for assistance as gate-keepers of the Reformation north of the border. In 1725 King George II contributed £1000 a year for work in the Highlands and Islands –

the 'King's Bounty', later the 'Royal Bounty' which funded itinerant preachers and catechists to go to the Highlands and Islands. Here they would promote the knowledge and practice of the Protestant religion.

One year later, the General Assembly passed a ruling which effectively kept ministers in their parishes 'where Popery abounds'.[7] Communities where vacancies existed were perceived to be under the threat of slipping back into pre-Reformation ways. With no Kirk presence or oversight such communities were regarded as vulnerable to Catholic influences. The preachers and catechists so appointed were to be pious and of undoubted loyalty to his Majesty, as well as competently skilled in principles of divinity and in 'Popish controversies', that is, able to argue the case.

It is notable that there was no overt attempt to make a working knowledge of the Gaelic language a pre-requisite despite the efforts over the previous fifty years to ensure that the Highlands and Islands were served by 'persons capable of preaching to them in that language which they are acquainted with'. In 1728 the Royal Bounty Committee suggested that 'colonies of protestants be planted in the popish parts, with long leases'. In the main, these measures successfully kept the threat of Catholic incursion, real or imagined, at bay.

Gradually, Presbyterian ministers gained the ascendancy and secured appointments to Highland parishes consolidating the Kirk's presence across most of the north and west. The unsuccessful Stuart uprisings in 1715 and 1745 softened the assertive mood of Jacobite Episcopalian heritors. Episcopalian chaplains had supported the clans on the battlefield. Post Culloden, the Highland estates of Catholic chieftains were forfeited. However, those estates held by Episcopalians sympathetic to the Stuart cause were retained, but thereafter these heritors were much more amenable in offering fewer obstacles to the settlement of Presbyterian ministers.

In 1782 the General Assembly identified specific islands where Catholicism still maintained a grip: South Uist, Small Isles and Harris.[8] Distance from the mainland, weather and a lack of Kirk presence in these parts made superintendence particularly problematic. However, vast areas of the west-coast mainland were also vulnerable to Catholic incursion. The Assembly named 'Moidart, Glengarry, and Lochaber, and other parishes of the Synods of Glenelg and Argyle' as areas of

---

7 General Assembly Sess. 13, May 17, 1726.
8 General Assembly Sess. 9, June 1, 1782.

concern. The continuing threat of Catholicism and the possibility of a resurgence in Episcopal sympathies prompted the King's Bounty, introduced in 1728, to be doubled. It was also acknowledged that the small salaries payable by the Bounty Fund did not provide much personal comfort for the missionaries and catechists. Salaries would not be doubled. The fund would merely allow more personnel to be employed.

At a practical level, the minister of Lochgoilhead and Kilmorich, the Revd Dugal Macdougal, compared the conditions in the Highlands in 1792 unfavourably with the days before the Reformation. He wrote:

> Under the Church of Rome, the people everywhere had easy access to the places where they were to perform their devotions, and to receive religious instruction. But after the Reformation, owing to the scarcity of Protestant preachers, and to the avarice of the Reformers (particularly the laymen who conducted the revolution), so few places of worship were permitted, and these consequently so distant from one another, and so divided by mountains, rivers and arms of the sea, as to render it difficult and sometimes impossible for the ministers to perform the duties of their office, or for the people to attend on their instructions.[9]

In their haste to rid the country of its popish ways, Protestant heritors dismantled many of the Catholic places of worship which effectively rendered complete swathes of the Highlands and Islands without buildings where congregations could gather. Also, the reference to avarice suggests that the location of parishes created after the Reformation was determined not so much by where the population was most gathered but where the heritors would provide the means, the costs, of establishing a church and parish and minister. These would more often than not be for the convenience of the heritor and sometimes very much to the inconvenience of the minister and congregation. Since heritors held the purse-strings, the price paid for that approach was the sometimes-eccentric drawing of parish boundaries and location of church buildings. The ministers of Inveraray Parish in 1843 also harked back to 'the days of Popery records [which] indicate that this parish had 5 churches, so that no inhabitant lived more than 2 miles from a church. Now there are two churches, one for Gaelic and one for English congregations, between 6 and 8 miles

---

9 *The Statistical Accounts of Scotland 1792: Lochgoilhead and Kilmorich, County of Argyll*, vol. III, 161.

from the extremities of the parish'.[10] The conclusion was that in pre-Reformation times attending church and securing the services of the local Catholic priest was much easier.

In the parishes of Lochgoilhead and Kilmorich and in Inveraray at least, it appeared that the Reformation of 1560 had replaced the theological objections to Catholicism with the practical difficulties of Protestantism. Limited access to the parish church was due to the terrain in many of these places: small pockets of population separated by a mountain that could be crossed only in the summer; by rivers that became dangerous barriers in some seasons; or communities living on small islands storm-bound in winter. It was not unknown for the parish minister to make his quarterly visit and be unable to leave the island for a week or more.

Also, on the west coast especially, large sea-lochs inhibited travel and made church-attendance hazardous or impossible. In Applecross the parish was divided into three districts, each separated from the other by a ridge of mountains, inaccessible in stormy weather. In Kincardine parish there were two preaching stations besides the church, one 10 and the other 14 miles distant from the manse. The distance of many members from the parish church made the journey tedious, fatiguing and at times dangerous. The Revd Dugal Campbell of Kilfinichen and Kilviceuen on the Isle of Mull reported that there were four places of worship in the parish but only one church which had been condemned by Presbytery because of its ruinous state.[11] He was awaiting the replacement of one, and another to be built in Kilfinichen. The two buildings were finally completed in 1804. Up until that time, services had been held on the hillside. The good people of the parish had waited over 200 years for appropriate church accommodation.

The bounds of the parish of Kilmallie were vast. One part of the parish lay in Argyll but the greater part lay in the County of Inverness. The Old Statistical Account reported that the parish was 'intersected in three different places, by as many arms of the sea, [and] is of an irregular form: the length from NW to SE is about 60 miles in a straight line and the greatest breadth from NE to SW is 30 miles in a straight line. It comprehends about 589 square miles, or nearly 376,960 English acres, measuring in straight lines. Adding the surface of the hills and valleys

---

10 *The Statistical Accounts of Scotland 1843: Inveraray, County of Argyll*, vol. VII, 36.
11 *The Statistical Accounts of Scotland 1795: Kilfinichen and Kilviceuen, County of Argyll*, vol. XIV, 207.

it must be at least one-third more'.[12] The Reformation principle of 'one minister serving one parish' seems ludicrous in these circumstances with an expectation that a single individual could adequately perform his duties with any measure of effectiveness. However, the minister of Kilmallie, Revd Alexander Fraser, thought that his account of such an extensive parish may, to the natives of the low country, appear 'romantic'.

To the minister of Moy and Dalarossie, mainly within the County of Inverness-shire, there was nothing 'romantic' about his situation: 'Divine worship is held alternately in the two churches. They are 9 miles distant from each other; the road is always rough, and in the stormy season, frequently impassable'.[13] When the General Assembly in 1699 instructed those six Highland ministers to visit and review the ministry and building resources in the parishes of Ross, Caithness and Sutherland, and if necessary 'perambulate the parishes', it must have had a parish in central Edinburgh in mind; the very notion of perambulating the fifty and more parishes of Caithness, Ross and Sutherland exposed the Assembly's utter failure even to imagine these extensive and remote places. Those outsiders remained largely ignorant of the magnitude of the task facing individual ministers in the north and west.

The reply sent to the Statistical Account of 1845 from Moy and Dalarossie opens with the words, 'There is perhaps not a parish in Scotland which has undergone less change than this since the former Account.'[14] Nor does it appear to have been much changed since the proposed 1699 'perambulation commission'. But it did report that after the 1829 flood had carried off all but two bridges, one fine new stone bridge was built, at the cost of £2600 sterling and the other was replaced temporarily in wood. These two new constructions would surely have assisted the minister in getting about the parish.

Infrastructure improvements also came to the Parish of Glassary in the period between the first and second Accounts. By the 1830s steam ships arrived and brought wealth and prosperity for some. Furthermore, 21 miles of good road had been made and maintained by

---

12 *The Statistical Accounts of Scotland 1793: Kilmallie, County of Inverness*, vol. VIII, 408.

13 *The Statistical Accounts of Scotland 1793: Moy and Dalarossie, County of Inverness*, vol. VIII, 508.

14 *The Statistical Accounts of Scotland 1845: Moy and Dalarossie, County of Inverness*, vol. XIV, 97.

local rates levied within the county, including eight miles along Loch Awe at the cost of £1500. Better roads would certainly have improved the minister's ability to access the remoter parts of his parish.

In 1841 the Revd Coll Macdonald of Portree stated that the church in the village 'was built 16 years ago and is in excellent repair. The manse was built about 30 years ago, and any repair is immediately supplied by the liberal heritors'[15] – a far cry from the resources available to Mr Macdonald's predecessor, the Revd John Nicolson. In 1840 the Revd John Mackinnon was minister in Strath in Skye, and he also wrote of very changed circumstances in Strath from those recorded in the first Statistical Account, with a 'handsome and commodious church for 600' being built there, and in the district of Strathaird where a comfortable church had been fitted up a year earlier.[16] The previous incumbent of Strath Parish had conducted worship at Strathaird in a crevice of rock for 52 years: he was John Mackinnon's father.

Notwithstanding a few episodes of positive heritor-obligation in maintaining fabric or replacing ruinous buildings, the old and constant challenges for the Highland Kirk remained: to augment the numbers of ministers whose mission-work was hampered by the physical obstacles of river and mountain; to appoint missionaries, schoolmasters and catechists to every parish; to establish additional places of worship throughout the north and west to better serve scattered and remote communities; and finally and importantly, to encourage every heritor and landowner to abide by their legal obligations in providing accommodation, by way of manse and glebe, suitable for a minister and family, and to pay an appropriate stipend.

Yet certainly at the time of the Old Statistical Accounts of 1791, penury was the lot of nearly every Highland and Island minister, despite a general reluctance to complain. Reports suggested that by the time of the New Account compiled in the years 1836-1845 not much had changed.

Shortage of Gaelic-Speaking Clergy

Educating youth having ye Irish language at colledges for ye work of ye ministrie

National Records of Scotland, *Synod of Argyll Minutes*, CH2/557/3, 1690

---

15 *The Statistical Accounts of Scotland 1845: Portree, County of Inverness*, vol. XIV, 232.
16 *The Statistical Accounts of Scotland 1845: Strath, County of Inverness*, vol. XIV, 312.

The Revd Dugald Campbell of Glassary believed the essential problem for the Highlands and Islands was not so much the shortage of church buildings but the scarcity of ministers. There were simply too few of them and the erection of more churches would not solve the core problem. In his submission to the New Statistical Account of 1844 he states: 'During the early period of the Reformation, no good result would be considered to arise from the multiplication of church buildings, due to the paucity of ministers. There were only a few ministers scattered over the extensive bounds of what now form the Synod of Argyle and Glenelg.'[17] The Synod of Argyll and Glenelg covered a vast area consisting of the mainlands and islands on the western seaboard of Scotland, from Kintyre in the south to the lands in the most northerly west coast, the Isle of Skye and the inner and outer Hebrides to include St Kilda.

The lack of ministers had been a continuing problem for the Kirk and those ministers in the more remote parishes, where lack of assistance was most severely felt, were among the first to raise the issue. The Revd Archibald Clerk of Ardnamurchan remarked that more than a century after the Reformation, the mission of the Kirk had been hampered by a considerable shortage of Gaelic-speaking ministers resulting in long vacancies. This had long been recognised since the Presbyterian settlement of 1688. Also, many Gaelic-speaking ministers were opting for lowland parishes. Gaelic-speaking Highlanders and Islanders were travelling south to find work in towns and cities, hoping for Gaelic-speaking ministers there too. Argyll Synod had successfully petitioned Parliament in 1690 to secure its vacant ministerial stipends to be used 'for educating and maintaining youth having ye Irish [Gaelic] language at schools and Colledges for ye work of ye ministrie within this province'. There was now a real incentive to address the situation.

In 1703 the General Assembly set up a commission to find and direct Gaelic speakers into ministry in the Highlands and Islands and to encourage ministers 'with Irish' to spend summers in the north, and that 'the Commission be empowered, when they get notice of students having Irish, fit to be entered on trials for the ministry, to recommend such students to Presbyteries, in order to pass; and when they pass, to send them to the Highlands, and this may prevent their being settled in Lowland congregations'.[18] In 1710 the General Assembly

---

17 *The Statistical Accounts of Scotland 1844: Glassary, County of Argyll*, vol. VII, 693.
18 General Assembly Act IX, Sess. 9, March 22, 1703.

enacted and appointed, 'that the one-half of the whole bursaries of all the Presbyteries within Scotland be applied for the education of such youths as have the Irish language, in philosophy and divinity at the Colleges of Glasgow, Edinburgh, St Andrews, and Aberdeen'.[19]

By devoting such a considerable budget resource in this important way, the Church showed some foresight in recognising and taking steps to resolve the specific problem of the shortage of Gaelic-speaking ministers. By 1716, the General Assembly had firmed up its policy regarding Gaelic, forbidding Gaelic-speaking preachers, [20]'especially such as have been educated upon the Highland bursaries', from being appointed to Lowland congregations. A few years later the General Assembly ended these bursaries, apparently satisfied that the many vacancies in the Highlands and Islands had been filled, but found it necessary in 1756 to restore the practice of giving 'augmented bursaries to Gaelic-speaking divinity students'.[21] This policy of the Kirk to expand a Gaelic language-led mission across the north and west to reach those areas which only knew Gaelic, or where English was not generally understood, ran counter to Government suppression of all things culturally related to the Highlander, including language. It had only been 10 years since the bloodbath of Culloden. Wounds were still raw, on both sides, and the dismantling of the clan system and much of Highland culture changed life forever. In the aftermath of that final Stuart uprising, Roman Catholicism had been chased underground or to the very margins in the west but the Gaelic language, like Catholicism, refused to die and remained the common currency among the greater number of Highlanders.

The words at the top of this essay, 'one of the many inconveniences', come from the Revd Donald McNicol, minister of the United Parishes of Lismore and Appin. He was not referring primarily to the shortage of buildings or the difficulties of travel, but to the need for two languages. But it was also 'inconvenient', to say the least, that in the face of Government aggravation, the Kirk was rolling out a policy of facilitating the very language which was under restriction; potentially awkward for the Government and dangerous for the Kirk. Aiming at its very heart, Mr McNicol nevertheless reported in the Statistical Account that

---

19 General Assembly Act X, Sess. 12, May 9, 1710.
20 General Assembly Act VIII, Sess. 10, May 14, 1716.
21 General Assembly Act VII, Sess. ult., May 31, 1756.

the common language of the parish is Gaelic. The minister preaches, in the long day, both in Gaelic and English, particularly in Appin where there are some who understand English only. It is believed that few preachers, in any part of the world, except those in the Highlands, preach in two languages.[22]

In his Preface to the first volume of the Old Statistical Accounts of Scotland, Sir John Sinclair provided a 'line of enquiry', with a view to creating from the responses a highly detailed and wide-ranging survey of life in Scotland in the last decade of the 18th century. The list of 56 topics in the line of enquiry (see Appendix one) seems comprehensive, but, surprisingly, it does not enquire about the use of the Gaelic language. Perhaps 50 years after Culloden the steam had been taken out of the language problem and certain assimilations and accommodations had been made by both sides. By this time in the Highlands and Islands Gaelic was now widely in use within the schools' system, being taught alongside English. Gaelic, by the time of Sir John's Preface, no longer posed the threat it once was perceived to be, although in the eyes of some, Gaelic was seen as a brake on progress towards cementing a unified Great Britain.

In 1836 Parliament ordered Commissioners to undertake a survey of religious instruction in Scotland: a much narrower and more defined view of the provision of places of worship, the size of parishes, the number of poor, attendance at church services, the range of denominations, the price of seat-rents, etc. In all some 46 questions were asked focusing on these aspects and not one of them about the use of Gaelic in worship. Despite this obvious omission, some responders to both the Statistical Accounts and the Commission to report on Religious Instruction did refer to Gaelic, simply because the language was part of their daily lives and their church lives.

The matter of language-led worship was becoming clearer however. Dedicated Gaelic chapels were appearing from the end of the 18th century onwards across the Highlands and Islands, leaving parish churches, very much depending on the ministers' preferences, to offer services in English, Gaelic or both. While the Revd Donald McNicol was the only individual calling the task of preaching in two languages an 'inconvenience', most other submissions offered no opinions one way or another. There are many responses similar to that of Tarbat in

---

22 *The Statistical Accounts of Scotland 1791: Lismore and Appin, County of Argyll*, vol. I, 495.

the Presbytery of Tain which stated that 'The Gaelic being the common language of the people, the greater part of the religious service on Sundays is performed in that language,'[23] the inference being that some part of the service was conducted in English. The Revd John McLeish of Kilchoman on Islay affirmed that in addition to preaching in the parish church he attends worship out of doors on the 'skirts of the parish' for more than one half of the year, conducting in both languages. He voiced a common complaint: 'A fourth minister is much to be wished for in the island, as upon some occasions three clergymen have to dispense communion to 1200 communicants'.[24] And Trumisgarry on North Uist: 'Service in Gaelic, only occasionally in English. Evening service, short sermon in Gaelic for twicers'.[25]

The tone of the report from Kilcalmonell and Kilberry in Argyll changed from the first Statistical Account: 'There are two places of worship, 5 miles apart. The minister preaches in both Gaelic and English',[26] to the response made to the New Statistical Account in 1843, 'The Gaelic is the vernacular language of the parishioners, but the English is displacing it, and the sooner it overmasters it the better'.[27]

A different approach was taken in Cromarty, where Gaelic services were provided not so much for the natives of Cromarty but for the incomers:

> There are two ministers in the parish – the parish minister and the minister of the Gaelic chapel. There was no Gaelic preached in this place until the building of the Gaelic chapel for the accommodation of Mr Ross's numerous labourers who came from neighbouring parishes to the manufacture of hemp. The place of worship was built solely at the expense of Mr George Ross in 1783, and he obtained a grant of £50 from the Exchequer.[28]

---

23 *The Statistical Accounts of Scotland 1793: Tarbat, County of Ross and Cromarty*, vol. VI, 430.

24 *The Statistical Accounts of Scotland 1794: Kilchoman, County of Argyll*, vol. XI, 283.

25 Appendix to the Fourth Report by the Commissioners of Religious Instruction 1835.

26 *The Statistical Accounts of Scotland 1794: Kilcalmonell and Kilberry, County of Argyll*, vol. X, 57.

27 *The Statistical Accounts of Scotland 1843: Kilcalmonell and Kilberry, County of Argyll*, vol. VII, 410.

28 *The Statistical Accounts of Scotland 1845: Cromarty, County of Ross and Cromarty*, vol. XII, 257.

There appears to be a mixed bag of arrangements across the north and west from the end of the 18th century regarding language-led worship. The increasing appearance of Gaelic chapels certainly accommodated those natives whose only language was Gaelic. As the schools' system flourished pupils became bi-lingual as English was taught as the dominant language. In their submissions to the Statistical Accounts published in the years 1801, 1821 and 1841, many Highland ministers noted that English was overtaking Gaelic as the language of preference. Trade was conducted in English and there appeared to be an increasing appetite among the young, ambitious to get on, that English would open up a world of opportunity when Gaelic did not. Some ministers could not wait for the demise of the Gaelic language, and the comment from the minister of Kilberry was not untypical: 'the sooner the English language overmasters [Gaelic] the better'.

Perhaps more ministers than only Donald McNicol thought Gaelic an 'inconvenience' but did not wish to put their opinions down on paper. There were of course Gaelic 'strong-holds', especially in the Western Isles and in the more remote straths and glens of the Highlands where English had had limited impact. It was to these places that mainly Gaelic-speaking evangelical ministers went.

Among themselves they found not only common cause in matters of faith, they were bound together by their culture, heritage... and language.

The Standard of Property

> *Our churches are, in general, exceedingly cold and dirty and there is little hope of this evil being soon remedied.* [29]
>
> Revd Lewis Gordon of Drainie

The Revd Dr Joseph McIntyre of Glenorchay and Inishail, mentioning that the church of Glenorchay was neither 'uncomfortable nor incommodious', if far from elegant, regretted that places appropriated to the public worship of God were not of a standard suitable to such a sacred and important act. He observed that the Church of Rome, the Church of England and other churches had places consecrated to the service of God made decent and comfortable; 'whilst, with us of the Church of Scotland, many of our country kirks are such dark, damp and dirty hovels as chill and repress every sentiment of devotion.'[30]

---

[29] *The Statistical Accounts of Scotland 1792: Drainie, County of Elgin*, vol. IV, 81.
[30] *The Statistical Return of Scotland 1793: Glenorchy and Inishail, County of Argyll*, vol. VIII, 352.

The kirks in the Western Highlands were, generally, in a miserable condition and the Statistical Accounts are peppered with reports of buildings in a ruinous state: Applecross, Fearn, Ardersier are examples of buildings barely able to accommodate congregations in safety, while the minister of Wick maintains his church is the 'worst in Caithness'.[31] While quick to compare the Kirk unfavourably with the Church of England and The Catholic Church, Dr McIntyre of Glenorchy would not be unaware of the funding arrangements pertaining to all three. First, the fabulously-wealthy English church could look to the State to fund its buildings, maintain its fabric and pay its clergy. It was almost in receipt of a blank cheque. Second, the Catholic Church, again wealthy beyond imagining, was known for its magnificent cathedrals, abbeys and monasteries across Europe and beyond. No shortage of cash there either. And what of the Kirk? How was the Kirk to be funded, its buildings, its schoolmasters and its ministers?

Perhaps Dr McIntyre's comment was the most acerbic he dared to write, given that his stipend, his churches and the upkeep of his glebe were in the hands of (probably) one local individual or (possibly) two or three. These men, 'heritors' and usually from the local landowning or mercantile classes, had nothing like the vast resources of the English or Catholic churches to call upon. They were paupers by comparison. The financing of local ministry came out of local pockets, especially in places like the Highlands and Islands where congregations were too poor to pay for stipends and the upkeep of both manses and churches. It was down to these local heritors to ensure that ministers were paid, had appropriate accommodation and that local congregations should worship in buildings that were kept, at the very least, safe, wind and watertight. The Good Lord, it seemed, could not even ensure His people could keep His own House in decent order.

In some places, ministers waited in vain for new buildings to be constructed, making do in the parlous situations which often extended to manses, variously described as dank, damp, and draughty. Given the lack of support, the vast distances to be covered, the inhospitable terrain, the inclement weather and often the advancing years of ministers themselves, the physical task of providing services of ministry was hard enough without there being any creature comforts at home.

The situation was made more difficult when the heritors were not resident in the parish. Absentee landlords and heritors, a more common occurrence from the 1820s onwards, often left the affairs of

---

31 *The Statistical Return of Scotland 1794: Wick, County of Caithness*, vol. X, 19.

estates to factors and land-agents, under strict financial obligation to undertake no unnecessary expenditures. Maximising profitability was the goal, especially for the new breed of landowner; often speculators from the south with money to burn and moving into land ownership for the first time. When it came to dealing with expenditure on church buildings, or even in cases of the payment of stipends, factors and agents turned delay, obfuscation, broken promises and making themselves 'unavailable' into an art form.

Money for ecclesiastical purposes was rarely handed over willingly or without a grudge. Ironically, it was Revd Thomas Jolly of Dunnet Parish Church in Caithness whose submission to the Statistical Account included a reminder to the local heritor of his legal obligations pertaining to church and manse upkeep, neither of which were in decent condition. That local heritor was none other than Sir John Sinclair of Ulbster, the very compiler of the Statistical Account. Mr Jolly may have hoped this little reminder would encourage Sir John to improve the situation in Dunnet. It did not work. Sir John had to die before the minister's little reminder for repair was answered – in 1837, some 43 years after the fact. Mr Jolly, however, ministered in the repaired Dunnet Church for a further eight years, dying at the age of 91 after serving the parish for 60 years.

In remote Highland settings churches and manses were only as good as the competence and skill of the local builder would admit. Often it was the district undertaker who doubled as the builder and as a man hardly considered to be a craftsman, would have had at best only a rudimentary knowledge of construction techniques. He would have employed local unskilled labourers. Shoddy workmanship, even in new builds, was a common complaint. The Revd Walter Chalmers of Deskford Parish in Banffshire was similarly aggrieved about the work on his manse and offices:

> Had the undertaker done his duty, it would perhaps have been a model of abundant and genteel accommodation; but the work, in every department, is insufficiently executed. Such instances are too common, and they are exceedingly distressing, both to heritors and ministers. The heritors justly complain of the hardship of incurring further expense; and ministers must daily feel the grievance of inhabiting houses that will not defend wind or rain. Necessitated to apply for repairs, they are considered as troublesome, and sometimes loaded with much unjust and illiberal abuse.[32]

---

32 *The Statistical Return of Scotland 1792: Deskford, County of Banff*, vol. IV, 362.

The want of decent domestic arrangements pitched ministers against heritors, and *vice versa*. This often caused unnecessary strain in relationships, themselves seldom repaired in the long run. Several clergymen expressed regrets that no easily-accessible law existed to force unwilling heritors to provide and maintain decent and appropriate church buildings. Recourse to the Presbytery rarely helped. This Court of the Church appeared to have had no more leverage in these matters than individual ministers.

Manses were an obligation, responsibility and financial burden that rested upon the heritors and had done so since the Provincial Council of the Scottish Clergy in the 13th century: 'We ordain that every church shall have a manse near the church in which the bishop or archdeacon [or minister] can be comfortably accommodated; and we decree that such [manse] must be made within the year.[33] In 1649 a further Act made it plain that heritors were financially responsible for the maintenance and repair of manses, and not the minister. When a minister could not occupy his manse on account of necessary repairs or additions, he was entitled to receive from the heritors manse rent, or manse 'maill'.

Such arrangements varied from parish to parish, an inconsistency which caused further annoyance. There are reports in the Statistical Accounts of ministers receiving differing amounts of manse 'maill', reimbursements for out-of-pocket expenses and money in lieu of manse. The 1649 Act was not applied uniformly, mainly for want of some governing body, either national or local to oversee compliance. A level playing-field in this matter would have aided relationships between heritor and ministers considerably. The Act was clear enough but the lack of consistency in its application more often than not allowed the heritor to take advantage of the situation. The absence of governance meant that heritors in reality did as little as they could get away with.

A few heritors took their responsibilities seriously enough to ensure that matters between them and the manse and minister ran without rancour. By no stretch were all ministers living in sub-standard conditions and several very fine manses graced a number of parishes across the Highlands and islands, adding to the contentment of both parties. While appreciative of the liberal help received from some heritors in this matter, any grievances ministers may have had were aimed mainly at shoddy workmanship and the scarcity of trained and experienced builders in the Highlands. This created problems between heritor and minister – another of the 'many inconveniences' experienced.

---

33 *Statutes of the Scottish Church 1225-1559*, Scottish History Society, vol. LIV.

Glebes, Teinds and Stipends

In 1905 the Revd Dr Thomas Burns delivered a course of three lectures to candidates for the ministry in all four divinity colleges in Scotland. The second lecture covered the topics of teinds, manses and glebes. His purpose was to guide young parish ministers on matters of law which concerned their own welfare and that of their congregations. The Very Revd Dr James Macgregor wrote the preface to the published lectures, and remarked, 'Had such a book as this existed many years ago, there are church glebes which would have been broader and stipends which would have been larger than they are today'.[34] As well as receiving appropriate stipends, ministers appointed to parishes were to enjoy 'entitlements', payments in cash or kind which in effect were additional benefits over and above. In a nutshell, ministers were entitled not just to stipend but also to manse and glebe.

The lectures set out the heritors' obligations under law (much more strictly observed in 1905 than in 1805) and what ministers could expect in how these laws were applied. The students attending Dr Burns's lectures would hear that the benefits of 'glebe' had existed for over 1,000 years. As early as the 8th century a portion of ground was attached to each parish church for the use of the minister, long known as 'the glebe'. Enshrined in an Act of 1572[35] it stipulated that the glebe should consist of four acres near to the church. Heritors invariably tried to get away with offering only the roughest and least productive land as 'glebe', keeping the best for themselves.

Matters were tightened up in 1593 by another Act of Parliament[36] which directed that the land for the glebe should be of former pre-Reformation kirk lands, and they were invariably the best quality of land. In this respect, as in the upkeep of manses and churches, the obligations of heritors were not always carried out. A final Act of 1663[37] now required heritors always to give the land nearest to the church for the minister's use, even if was not formerly kirk land, and in addition ensure that 'every minister have a horse and two kyes grasse [sufficient pasture for his horse and two cows], and that, by and attour (over and above) his gleib'. The 1663 Act added that the minister's grass was to be in addition to the four arable acres, and if

---

34 'Church Property', The Benefice Lectures, ix.
35 Scottish Parliament Act, 8 July 1587, Edinburgh.
36 Scottish Parliament Act, 3 April 1593, Edinburgh.
37 Scottish Parliament Act, 9 September 1663, Edinburgh.

the minister did not possess 'grass' he should receive a payment of £1, 13s. 4d. (£290 in today's value). Four arable acres would allow for the cultivation of a considerable amount of produce, either for the consumption of the manse family, or more probably to supplement the diets of parishioners in seasons of need. Many glebes effectively operated as parish 'food banks'. In theory, the glebe and its potential bounty was a welcome and necessary asset which enriched the minister's situation but, as in other instances, the law governing the entitlement to glebe was observed as much in the breach as in the observance and a surprising variety and flexibility of arrangements were made.

Again the Statistical Accounts, both Old and New, record many instances of complaints levelled at heritors for ignoring their legal responsibilities. When the incumbent of South Knapdale in Argyll came to the parish in 1771 he found neither church nor manse nor glebe in the whole bounds. Was the minister lured there under false pretences? More likely, the 'promise' of a new kirk and manse was simply not carried through. Heritors always seemed to have other things to do with their money. In 1772 out of necessity however the minister sued the heritors at law to build a kirk, the manse family having rented accommodation nearby.[38] The successful court action, however, did not produce instant results. The new church was completed six years after the judges had ruled and in the meantime the minister had continued to preach in local fields.

The regular 'augmentation of stipend' also appears to have caused upset, perhaps the most important legal obligation of local heritors. In the Parish of Kintail in Ross-shire, there had been no increase in stipend during the entire 18th century and, indeed, the missionary employed at £15 per annum had his wage reduced to £5. Stated elsewhere in the 1801 Statistical Account was the comment that prices and servants' wages are now twice or thrice as much as in 1742; this is 'not sufficient to support a family suitably for the rank of a clergyman'.[39] Prices were on the increase, throughout the 18th century running at about 1% per annum, while income remained static. Inflationary pressures are not a modern phenomenon.

---

38 *The Statistical Accounts of Scotland 1797: South Knapdale County of Argyll*, vol. XIX, 321.

39 *The Statistical Accounts of Scotland 1793: Cross, Burness North Ronaldshay and Ladykirk County of Orkney*, vol. VII, 482.

Essay 4: Facing the Difficulties

The power of the influential landed gentry also put some ministers at a disadvantage. Lord Reay, chief of the clan Mackay, owned a large swathe of the County of Sutherland, and maintained the stipend of the minister of Eddrachylis at below the legal minimum. The minister complained it was one of the smallest in the entire Kirk.[40] Further, Lord Reay had, himself, written into the contract with the Church exempting his estate from having to pay any future augmentation of stipend, irrespective of whatever arrangements had been made elsewhere. It seemed that there was little that Presbytery could do about this, such was the almost brazen authority of the landed classes and their easy facility to make up rules just as it suited them.

As far as the 'augmentation of stipends' went, ministers could rightly believe that Acts of the General Assembly were inviolate and that security of payment was assured. An Act of 1750 had made matters clear enough:

> The General Assembly, considering the distressed circumstances of many ministers of this Church, arising from the smallness of their stipends, the expense of processes for augmentations, and the dilatory payment of stipends, do resolve on an humble application to be made to the King and Parliament on a number of issues: 'That ministers' stipends, if not paid within the year, shall bear interest from the first half year after they become due.'[41]

Difficulties were further complicated most especially when heritors did not reside in the parish. Despite the carefully-crafted legislation designed to protect ministers from the vagaries and inconsistencies relating to the payment of stipend, Parliament did not agree to the proposals. Perhaps the interests of the land lobby outgunned any firepower the Kirk may have thought it had – another instance when the judgements of the civil law trumped any law which General Assemblies had crafted.

In his lectures, Dr Burns held to the view that the origin of 'teinds', from which stipends were paid, could be traced back as far as the reign of David I in the 13th century, although other scholars maintain an earlier record: Professor John W. Sawkins dates teinds from the reign of King Edgar (1097 – 1107) which related to the parish of Ednam near

---

40 *The Statistical Accounts of Scotland 1793, Creich County of Sutherland*, vol. VIII, 370.
41 General Assembly Sess. 7, May 17, 1750.

Kelso.[42] Whichever dates are recognised, the matter of 'teinds' has been woven into the fabric of Scottish church life for 1,000 years.

In Scotland the teinds (a tithe or tenth part) were originally a separate legal 'estate' attaching to land, rather than a burden on the land itself. They were expressed in terms of quantities of various grains grown in a locality with parish ministers legally entitled to draw an agreed fixed stipend payment in 'victual', that is in *kind*, directly from the fields. Land may change ownership often over the years but could not lose the obligation of payment of stipend to the parish minister, and this applied irrespective of a landowner's Church connection. Put simply, the heritors, in acquiring their lands, also inherited the obligation of teind attached to the land exclusively for the purposes of maintaining the ministry. In 1808 to tidy up a cumbersome practice Parliament enacted that the victual should be paid in money. Across all parishes the minister's stipend was the primary charge against the teinds but often, by themselves, were insufficient to supply an adequate annual income to individual parish ministers. Consequently in 1810 and 1824 parliament voted financial aid to the Church for the purpose of making up to £150 *per annum* stipends in parishes where the value of teinds had been insufficient to pay the full amount.

In matters where a minister felt short-changed by the heritor in relation to teinds, he could apply to the Court of Teinds for an adjudication. This Court was presided over by a judge from Scotland's Court of Session. The Revd Walter Ross of Clyne with a stipend that had not been increased from 1722 till 1797 (20 years after he was inducted to the charge) took the heritor to court – to the Court of Teinds – for an augmentation, and won his case.[43]

Dr Burns warned the young ministers that they should be well advised before taking legal steps to enforce an augmentation of stipend. He suggested they approach the heritors privately and, if possible, reach a friendly arrangement before contacting the Teinds Court. 'An amicable adjustment contained in a mutual minute between minister and heritors, and presented to the Teinds Court for its sanction, is sometimes the wisest expedient, preventing, as it does, the interruption, so hurtful to spiritual interests, of good feeling in a parish.'[44]

---

[42] Professor John W. Sawkins, 'The Financing of Ministerial Stipends in the Established Church of Scotland: the Rural Parishes'.

[43] *The Statistical Accounts of Scotland 1793: Eddrachylis County of Sutherland*, vol. VI, 281.

[44] 'Church Property', The Benefice Lectures, 70.

Revd Walter Ross of Clyne's case is a curious one. Clearly a favourite of the Countess of Sutherland as reports about the minister's support for wholesale clearance of the Countess's estates confirm, Mr Ross nonetheless felt compelled to seek reparation in the matter of 'augmentation of stipend' through the Court of Teind. The Countess was the major local heritor and it was she who had responsibility over ensuring Mr Ross's stipend, a legal obligation she clearly failed to carry out. In her defence, the Countess would surely not have involved herself in the minutia of bill-paying or maintaining oversight of household budgets. She would have been ignorant of such matters. These would be left for lawyers, agents and factors to deal with. However, perhaps the close relationship with the Countess was not quite as cosy as Mr Ross assumed. Whatever was the case, the Countess was quick to identify this minister as one whose influence over parishioners would be to the Countess's advantage and one who would do her bidding in the matter of 'encouraging' people to clear the land in favour of sheep. Mr Ross had been appointed to the charge over the head of an applicant much more favoured by the community; an example of the power of the heritors at that time. The minister died in 1825 and in his will left £985 sterling - around £100,000 in today's terms – which implies that a highly successful augmentation was achieved.

While Lord Reay was maintaining the Eddrachylis minister's stipend below the legal limit, he was also depriving the man over his rights to glebe. The minister believed he had a right to the sea-weed on the shore of the glebe but found himself opposed by Reay's family and was obliged to defend himself on a process for damages before the Court of Session who thought fit to decide against him.[45] At a stroke the minister was deprived of the benefit of the sea-weed growing on his glebe as manure to the land and pasture to his cattle in the winter. Despite Lord Reay deciding his own arcane rules to suit himself over his personal responsibilities towards minister's stipend and glebe, the ruling in his favour by the civil court gave him *carte blanche* to impose any conditions upon ministers' settlements he fancied. As individual ministers brought their grievances to the civil courts they often found themselves facing, on the bench, friends or colleagues from within the close circles in which the accused moved. It was often felt that the scales of justice were weighted very much in favour towards the upper classes.

---

45 *The Statistical Accounts of Scotland 1793: Eddrachylis County of Sutherland*, vol. VI, 281.

The Revd Alexander Campbell of Kilcalmonell and Kilberry was succinct in his judgement and spoke in his report of 'the inability of Scotch clergy to cope with superior power'.[46] It appeared that the clergy might have God on their side but the 'superior powers' had the law and in the vast majority of cases it was 'the law' which trumped any claims the earthly agents of the Deity might prosecute. Therein lay the great conundrum for the Kirk, how to acknowledge the claims of the civil authorities while upholding the *right of the Kirk* to determine its own affairs.

State Assistance

When the King's Bounty was at the previous level of £1000, it was sorely stretched. In 1794 the Revd John Macleod of Harris longed for a missionary to be appointed there but, 'the funds of Royal Bounty being already appropriated, there is no hope from that quarter.'[47] The minister of Stornoway believed that 'no parish stands in greater want of a missionary with upward of 1000 souls who have worship only every 5th Sunday.'[48] A Royal Bounty missionary worked every third Sunday in the high grounds of Creich parish, paid £25 by the Royal Bounty, and £7 by the parishioners, but then the Royal Bounty was withdrawn. 'People pled loudly for continuance and Lady Rose Baillie appointed a permanent missionary on a better salary, and large accommodation.'[49]

Submissions to the Statistical Accounts routinely stated the need for ministerial support throughout the Highlands and Islands, conscious that the students coming through the Divinity schools were small in number. But other solutions were presenting themselves with the assistance of the new level of support from the King's Bounty. An additional £1,000 went a long way and further initiatives were employed. Instead of being allocated to work with one minister in one parish, often the missionaries were shared between two or three parishes or more: the missionary established in Lismore and Appin worked between Glencoe and the neighbouring glens which lay in the parish of Ardchattan, and the missionary at Strontian preached four

---

46 *The Statistical Accounts of Scotland 1794: Kilcalmonell and County Kilberry of Argyll*, vol. X, 57.

47 *The Statistical Accounts of Scotland 1794: Harris, County of Inverness*, vol. X, 381.

48 *The Statistical Accounts of Scotland 1797: Stornoway, County of Ross and Cromarty*, vol. XIX, 251.

49 *The Statistical Accounts of Scotland 1793: Creich, County of Sutherland*, vol. VIII, 370.

times a year at Kingairloch. North and South Uist shared a missionary between Benbecula and Carinish. On the Western Isles with seven worship places to serve on Harris, the Royal Bounty missionary officiated in three, and the minister in four. The Royal Bounty missionary appointed to Torosay on Mull worked at the boundaries of Torosay Parish and Kilninian, and in addition on every third Sunday travelled over the mountains to Kilfinichan – three parishes in all.

The Revd Archibald McArthur, minister of Kilninian, had two churches, one at Kilninian and one at Kilmore.[50] Again, both minister and missionary worked at their physical limits. To fulfil his duties Mr McArthur had to traverse '6 measured miles, one hill and 2 torrents of water between [the two churches]'. The minister preached alternately in the two churches, but also went once a quarter to the Island of Ulva, to preach in the open air, for want of a church. He also preached at Aros twice in the quarter, eight miles from his residence until the Committee of the Royal Bounty established a mission in Mull, by which Aros and the outskirts of the other two parishes were supplied. The missionary was only paid £25, without any accommodation whatsoever. The old matter of adequate remuneration was raised in the Mull submissions to the Statistical Account: the minister considered that the stipends drawn by the three ministers were barely an adequate living for two, adding that schoolmasters were equally affected by this 'improvident frugality'.

The minister of Lismore and Appin voiced the old conundrum: how should additional funds be allocated; church buildings or personnel? He stated in his submission that 'the funds for missionaries and catechists should all have been allotted long ago, for building new churches in these extensive parishes. It would unquestionably turn out to much greater advantage to the public'.[51] The argument that buildings were needed ahead of men while successive General Assemblies prioritised the need for more personnel reveals that the Church struggled to allocate limited resources. There were those who argued, 'If we build it, people will come'. The counter argument preferred an emphasis on increasing ministry resources. Accommodation for a church could always be found. Additional buildings, however, with its attendant increase in the number of church services expected

---

50 *The Statistical Accounts of Scotland 1795: Kilninian and Kilmore, County of Argyll*, vol. XIV, 150.

51 *The Statistical Accounts of Scotland 1791, Lismore and Appin, County of Argyll*, vol. 1, 491.

would have stretched the resources of ministers and missionaries even further. The Church at national and local levels appeared to have worked conscientiously in trying to offer solutions given the financial constraints under which it laboured.

Missionary Colleagues and Parochial Assistance

In 1834 the Revd John Munro, now minister of Halkirk and a former missionary himself, was assisted by one missionary who was still partly supported by the Royal Bounty and partly by the inhabitants of the mission district of the parish. The missionary had three preaching stations one of which included a part of the neighbouring Latheron parish. Mr Munro drew a desperate picture of an unworkable job: 'Is it to be supposed that a minister can administer religious instruction to a population of at least 2500, scattered over the remote parts of three parishes, and the greater number of the distant glens and valleys in the high and mountainous districts of Caithness?'[52] He describes a parish between 40 and 50 miles across, home to several scattered communities whose endeavours to attend worship were solely dependant on there being decent weather, with attendance usually impossible in winter and spring. The people's inability to reach church resulted in an 'indifference to the means of grace. This was not to be attributed to the missionary', Mr Munro continued, 'nor, humanly speaking, to the people, but to the system on which the mission is established and the utter impossibility of any one man being able, however gifted, to perform these duties with either success or efficiency,' a comment which echoes, almost *verbatim*, that of the compiler of the Kilmallie submission to the old Statistical Account some 35 years earlier.

Missionaries showed themselves as selfless and devoted individuals, having a great care for the souls of their parishioners. They were as vital to the mission of the church as ministers but were often regarded as second class, not having the status of 'minister'. However, such was the arcane nature of the Reformation principle of 'one minister, one parish', it was impossible to place additional ministers 'ordained to word and sacrament' to serve the outlying districts of a parish, hence those who were appointed had the status of 'missionary'. Some were ordained and thereafter referred to as 'missionary minister', able to fulfil all clerical functions but working under the direction of the parish minister.

---

52 *The Statistical Accounts of Scotland 1845: Halkirk, County of Caithness*, vol. XV, 80.

Again, the categories of 'missionary' or 'missionary minister' were funded from a variety of sources. Local collections from among members of congregations were sometimes gathered to supplement the set annual stipend of £50 from the Royal Bounty. The stipends of some missionaries were paid in full from the Royal Bounty, some partly by heritors and many had their stipends subsidised by the generosity of locals, who themselves would probably have been from the poorest orders. There was a reliance upon local funding which in turn became a worthy obligation which congregations appeared happy to pay, such was the high regard in which these men were held by congregations. People were willing to give sacrificially in order to retain their services.

The number of missionaries grew rapidly in the years between 1800 and 1840 and reports confirm they were well received. Missionaries were appointed across the length and breadth of the north and west and especially where it was felt they were needed most. In Argyll two worked Lismore and Appin, where there was a strong Catholic presence; one was appointed to Tarbert while a third worked between two churches in Glassary. There were appointments at Fort Augustus while another worked in 'the Catholic north' of Kilmorack and in Kiltarlity. Yet another worked in Reay with the funding shared by the Royal Bounty and local subscribers. Missionaries worked Tarbart in Harris and two appointed to Portree and Bracadale on Skye, all serving the Church in especially inhospitable locations. In the Northern Isles there was a missionary for Weisdale and Whiteness on Shetland and one each appointed to Stronsay and Eday, two relatively remote islands in the Orkney archipelago. On Eday, further assistance was given to finance the building of a manse for the missionary's use, by both public subscription and a donation from the parish minister. In all, 36 missionaries and missionary ministers were appointed across the four Highland counties, mainly to serve the Church in the remotest and most physically challenging areas. It could be worthily said that without their tireless efforts and complete devotion to their congregations the work of the parish ministers would have been, not made more difficult, but simply made impossible.

The role of the catechist was vital to the Church as it prepared people for the annual catechising which took place prior to the seasonal communions and examined churchgoers in matters of faith. Catechists also prepared parents for the sacrament of infant baptism. With no academic training, catechists were paid a small sum of around

£7 per annum from the Royal Bounty. It was said of catechists that their 'homely faith and power in prayer' won them love and respect. In the late 18th century and into the 19th some missionaries and catechists were settled into specific areas but many were itinerant, supplementing the labours of parish ministers and moving to where they were most required.

In order to serve congregations and parishes, the Church of Scotland deployed a variety of classifications of men. The Reformation principle of 'one individual serving one parish', was quite unworkable, as many testimonies state. This arrangement stretched resources to breaking point and it became increasingly obvious that more ministerial assistance was required especially in remote and mountainous parishes in the north and west. Without the necessary assistance, it was clear that the ordinances of the Church could not be fully carried out nor the services of the minister fully accessed. Many communities were simply not being served.

Ministers ordained or admitted to the 'Parliamentary Churches' across the Highlands and Islands (see Essays 9 and 10) became yet another category of clergy, an invention of the time to meet the peculiar constitutional arrangements of these 'additional churches'. However, as 'layers' of ministerial assistance were added, the primacy of the parish minister remained incontestable. It was the parish minister who sat on the Courts of the Church; Presbytery, Synod and General Assembly, as well as moderating his own Kirk Session. These other types of minister, because of constitutional niceties, were simply excluded from the decision-making bodies which determined Church policies, politics and discipline. The parish minister's role, among many others, was merely to represent the interests of these other colleagues, should matters arise, and also to be an advocate for the congregations within his bounds, even if he visited only rarely.

It was a refining of the status of Parliamentary churches and its ministers in the first instance, followed by other changes, that paved the way for the eventual overhaul of the parish system in the north and west, and across the rest of the country.

Essay Five

Moderates and Evangelicals: the Battle for the Soul of the Church

After 1750 members of the Moderate party were closely associated with the reorganisation of the universities, the Scottish philosophy and the literary revival, so that the Kirk came to play a big part in the cultural renaissance. While to many this a creditable performance, there were others to whom it savoured of trafficking in worldly concerns.

Rait and Pryde, *Scotland*

The Enlightenment: Joy or Despair

The Kirk had firmly been under the control of the Moderate Party since the middle of the 18th century. Moderates were influenced by the Scotttish Enlightenment, a new age of intellectual foment and excitement, especially in politics and religion. This liberalism of understanding and belief based on rational thought, much of which was avowedly anti-Christian and atheistic, produced startling new theories encompassing economics, sociology, statistics, geology, morality and aesthetics, epistemology, anthropology, linguistics, chemistry, medicine and historiography.

The Enlightenment reflected the sense that humanity was close to approaching the point at which everything could be known and understood and its ambitions realised without the assistance of a deity. In terms of theology its appeal found favour with many of the educated (and therefore middle-) classes who had either remained resistant to, or deeply suspicious of the doctrines principally found at the heart of the prevailing hard Calvinism. The Scottish Reformation was founded largely on Calvin's teaching, but the Scots Confession, while it emphasised the sovereignty of God and the depravity of humankind, spoke not of predestination but of our election in Christ. However, by the 17th and 18th centuries this had hardened into the belief that God appointed the eternal destiny of some to salvation by grace, while leaving the remainder to receive eternal damnation for all their sins, often leading to the lack of assurance which John McLeod Campbell – expelled from the Kirk as a heretic – was to pinpoint in the 19th century.

By contrast, the educated middle-classes had either retained a belief in, or had been won over to, a solid Enlightenment credo in the power of human will and action to take a measure of control in the shaping of human destiny. This reflected a softer religion which left room for a benevolent God giving humankind a fair and equal chance, for better or worse, of self-determination and of embracing ideals of decency, goodness and beneficence.

In matters of theology, all debate, enquiry and criticism were welcomed, mirroring much of the lively conversations to be heard in Edinburgh drawing-rooms and coffee-houses. Moderates aimed to bring a spirit of reason, civility and tolerance to the church. This would be achieved principally by softening Calvinism's strict puritanism, shaking off the excessive rigours of ecclesiastical discipline, modifying Sabbatarian habits and promoting a saner and healthier life not overburdened by shame or guilt.

Moderatism saw itself as a bulwark against any return to the orthodox, joyless and narrow application of Reformation principles established some two hundred years previously. It was unashamedly elitist and intellectual and highly suspicious of Evangelical elements within the Kirk, which, rejecting the new spirit of the age, clung to puritan ways; the Evangelicals were at the centre of revivals taking hold in several locations.

To those who aligned themselves with Evangelical principles, Moderatism offered only a lukewarm orthodoxy with a distinct lack of interest in theology. In sermons, Moderate preachers in the main were accused of avoiding any reference to the great doctrines of the Church: reformation; sin and grace; or the route-map to salvation which was central to Evangelical thought and practice. Moderate-led universities, where the study of theology and doctrine were not prominent on the curriculum, largely produced ministers who likewise gave scant attention to matters of faith and salvation. Evangelical students however, certainly in the minority, railed against much of the curriculum set down to produce ministers of the Kirk and criticised the competence and capabilities of those delivering the courses. Moderate ministers seemed to have little regard for visiting their congregations, evidence of their disregard for souls, and of being too tolerant and having a lax approach towards the Sabbath. They confined themselves to inculcating the moral virtues with illustrations drawn from secular literature even more than from scripture. Their preference for polite society and their easy manners and urbane ways led them to support the system of patronage, a cosy arrangement with landowners and the upper classes, which forced unacceptable ministers on congregations. It was this diet of rational religion which attracted Evangelical scorn as 'cold morality' and 'legalism' without a touch of gospel warmth to stir, challenge or comfort souls.

The controlling Moderate Party concentrated more and more on matters of direct concern in a rapidly-expanding industrialised and urbanised situation; for example, the growing number of seceding churches and the rise of voluntary societies. Both were viewed as direct threats to the establishment principle so cherished by the Kirk. The rise of the Evangelical Party made the Moderates look for the first time both 'inwards' as well as 'outwards'. For Moderates, order and harmony within the Kirk and in relations between Church and State would ensure peace without and unity within, vital for effective control. In this progressive age, no two principles combined more harmoniously than profit and order. In this the Kirk assumed a leading role. Moderates formed the party of 'law and order' and embraced the new economics of *laisser-faire*. They saw themselves as cultured and learned and, supporting the social mores of the day, somewhat patrician and paternalistic.

The universities were firmly under Moderate control. They imposed strict dictatorial powers over entrance qualifications, candidates' suitability and subjects taught, all of which were, in theory, unbending. Moderates were politically conservative who 'deployed religion as a means of hierarchical influence to underpin social order while driving forward economic change'.[1] It was little wonder Governments of the time could look on the Church of Scotland as a robust ally, loyal and supportive. However, this symbiotic relationship between Church and State was to prove troublesome, and eventually disastrous for the Kirk.

The most able ministers of the Moderate Party often combined large city church livings with university chairs, leaving them open to the charge of pluralism, an appointment to two posts. In reality, however, the duties and responsibilities of one were usually carried out to the detriment of the other. It was not unusual for professors in the university towns to devote themselves wholeheartedly to the cultured and rarefied world of academe. With its ceremony and ritual, its relaxed programme of lecturing and easy air of superiority, it is easy to see why many left the day-to-day pastoral oversight of a busy congregation and demanding parish to assistant ministers.

---

1 Donald Smith, *God, the Poet and the Devil*, 3.

The issue of pluralities had agitated some in the church since the early eighteenth century, a time when relations between the Church and the universities were close. All university teachers had to accept the Westminster Confession of Faith which placed them automatically under the discipline of the Church. A growing number of Evangelicals within the Church began speaking out against this practice but numerically never enough in the late 18th and early 19th centuries to successfully move against it on the floor of the General Assembly. An inbuilt Moderate majority in the Assembly saw to that.

A Conflict of Priorities

Matters came to a head with the presentation by the Crown in 1823 of Revd Dr Duncan Macfarlane to the High Church of Glasgow, the foremost of the city churches. At the time Dr Macfarlane already held the prestigious post of Principal of Glasgow University. The appointment was immediately rejected by Glasgow Presbytery, citing that to be minister of the High Church required a full-time commitment. Macfarlane, however, successfully appealed over the head of the Presbytery to the General Assembly in 1824, which upheld this Crown appointment. In many cases in the large towns and cities, presentations of new ministers were made by Town Councils as well as by the Crown with an expectation that local Presbyteries would merely 'rubber stamp' the appointment. Many saw this as a direct attack on the Church's claim that it should be final arbiter not only in cases of introducing candidates to a pastoral charge but in *all* matters ecclesiastical. In Dr Macfarlane's case as in many others the matter of whether patronage was in the best interests of the Church was a hotly debated topic.

The issue of pluralities was finally dealt with when a Royal Commission ruled against them in 1828, a time when Evangelical ministers were now sufficient in number to lead the arguments for abolition. An opinion had formed, not without some justification, that the Moderate-led General Assemblies in the decades up until the 1820s were open to the charge that it seemed unable to prosecute the claims of the Church's *right* to be final arbiter in matters ecclesiastical. As a consequence, the competing arguments and claims of the Crown and local magistrates in the towns and cities took precedence. To the Evangelical wing, it appeared that the Church deferred too easily and on too many occasions to the secular authorities, all the more so in the Highlands and Islands where the rule of the landowners, and their rights over ecclesiastical matters because of patronage, was unquestioned. In some instances the Court of Session, Scotland's highest court, was called to adjudicate; and their pronouncements, in the main, confirmed the superiority of the civil law over the ecclesiastical. This was a weakness in the Church's ability to govern its own matters which the Evangelicals were determined to rectify.

While the Moderate-dominated city-dwelling clergy moved effortlessly among Edinburgh's elite and held court in the many exclusive clubs in the city, their Highland colleagues were experiencing an entirely different ministry, both in terms of risk and reward. The parlous state of religion in the Highlands and Islands where matters were known to be difficult had been an early concern. As far back as 1690 arrangements were made for the distribution of Bibles and Catechisms in the 'Irish' language, to a population still largely illiterate. A few years later Gaelic-speaking ministers who had settled in the lowlands were encouraged to seek charges in the Highlands, yet Gaelic-speaking probationers were forbidden to accept settlements in the south.

Moderates had correctly identified the Highland challenges, while acknowledging the number of well-documented handicaps. Although inhospitable terrain and capricious weather were beyond the powers of the Church to change, some matters could be addressed: large, unwieldy parishes rendering pastoral oversight hard or impossible; lack of assistance to overstretched and overburdened ministers; the offices of the Church executed by some ill-educated men. Most importantly, some in the Church recognised the over-arching issue of trying to accommodate a distinctive Highland culture and language within the scope of being the *national* Church, and this at a time when the number of Gaelic-speaking ministers was pitifully small. What was happening within the Church across the Highlands and Islands hardly impacted the ministries of those working in the south. But at the Kirk's General Assemblies, concerned voices were beginning to be heard.

Many parts of the north and west where Gaelic remained the first and only language had remained untouched by the Reformation. Catholic rituals and celebrations of saints' days continued in the remotest parts well after the 1560. This 'old religion' was carried among Highland people in oral tradition albeit one that had grown dim through lack of organised religious instruction and divine worship. It continued mainly as an underground movement under the protection of powerful Catholic landowners, far from the seat of central Government and relatively free from both State and Kirk intervention. Clan chiefs such as MacDonald of Clanranald and Glengarry and the McNeils of Barra gave cover to priests who conducted public mass in areas where entire communities were Catholic. Gaelic-speaking Catholic priests could remain relatively untroubled and unhindered as they went about their business ministering to their own communities. That was to change, however, in the immediate aftermath of the events of 1746.

The Kirk, through its Highland ministers, began to gain a toehold in most mainland parishes, in some areas more than others. In remote regions, however, the old religion continued. The picture was patchy. The islands remained a stubborn stronghold of Catholic beliefs infused with a heady mixture of folk religion, superstition and vestiges of Celtic Christianity. But some influential voices in the Kirk were calling for extra resources for 'The Highland Problem'. At the Kirk's disposal were the terms of the 1737 Act of Assembly for the 'Reformation of the Highlands and Islands of Scotland, for promoting the knowledge of true religion, suppressing of popery, superstition, and profanity, and for management of the royal bounty given for that end'. This fund, initially £1000 and later increased to £2000, paid some stipends in full and others in part.

Also, in the Society in Scotland for Propagating Christian Knowledge (SSPCK) the Kirk had a worthy ally. Established in 1709 its purpose was to establish schools in the Highlands and Islands and other 'uncivilised' areas of the country. That the Kirk was engaged in establishing a vital presence through the north and west is unquestioned. Yet its aims centred rather more on 'civilizing' the entire country. The historian J.H.S. Burleigh states that 'The contribution of the Moderates was to the intellectual and cultural development of Scotland rather than to its evangelization'.[2] The evidence is clear, however, that the Moderate Party fell far short in its ambition regarding the Highlands and Islands. Further, Burleigh's conclusion that evangelisation was of only secondary concern to Moderates would have rung true for Evangelicals, convinced that lack of missionary commitment was hampering the spread of the Gospel.

There were other, more salient matters than 'mission' to concentrate the Moderate mind. In the Highland's post-Culloden decades, the doctrines of the Moderates were partly focused on the twin perceived necessities of overcoming the scattered remnants of Catholicism and dealing with a resurgent Episcopalianism. In the Highlands especially, the Presbyterian settlement after 1690 had not been greeted with general acceptance. Catholics and Episcopalians had remained a forceful opposition. At its root was the common cause of supporting

---

2 J.H.S. Burleigh, *A Church History of Scotland*, 303.

the Catholic Stuart claims for the Crown and throughout the following 50 years Scotland experienced a series of religious and political confrontations, culminating in the events on Drumossie Moor in 1746. The counties of Perthshire, Ross-shire, Inverness-shire, Caithness and northern Argyll (modern-day Lochaber) were avowedly Episcopalian in outlook while Presbyterians could look for support from the people of Argyll, Sutherland, and Easter Ross.

Gradually, in these years of revolution as the Moderates saw it, the Church had to hold unwaveringly to two central tenets: first, maintaining the establishment principle. This countered any claim that the Episcopal Church was the true national 'Church in Scotland'; and second, to ensure discipline within the Church, with all Courts and Ministers speaking with 'one Presbyterian voice', and preferably and clearly a voice which reflected Moderatism. Over the decades Presbyterian ministers were gradually gaining the ascendancy by securing appointments to Highland parishes in increasing numbers. Essentially, it was asserted, the much sought-after order and harmony both within the Kirk and between Church and State would finally be established and consolidated, especially as the events at Culloden receded in the minds. Moderates forming the party of law and order would ensure that these relationships would run smoothly.

The Advance of the Evangelicals

Revivals in the Highlands began and were carried out in an atmosphere of believing prayer, and faith in the saving presence and power of the Holy Spirit. The preaching of Christ crucified as satisfying the law, atoning for sin, and saving the sinner, was that which was always used to produce penitence and peace.

Revd Alexander Macrae, *Revivals in the Highlands and Islands in the 19th Century*

While the General Assembly was regularly calling for reports into the health, or otherwise, of religion in the Highlands, almost under the radar a new breed of minister with Evangelical leanings was beginning to appear despite their years in divinity halls led by a liberal and intellectual elite. Their numbers were small and these men were influenced by the Scottish revival of 1742 which had followed eighty years of stagnation in the Church. While not setting the whole country ablaze with a renewed sense of religious fervour, several 'burning bushes' took hold among a number of localised Scottish communities, principally Cambuslang, Kilsyth, Gargunnock, Muthil, Crieff and Auchterarder. In the far north of Scotland revivalism took hold of Easter Ross while the Gaelic-speaking Isle of Arran and parts of Kintyre far to the south experienced a similar phenomenon.

The Moderate Party was highly suspicious of these outbreaks of religious passion, regarding them as the hallmarks of fanatics. Attempts were made to discredit Evangelicalism by dismissing such overt and public demonstrations of emotion as mere hysteria, and by citing the stress on dubious visionary experiences, and the incurring of fear and spiritual pride. A thoroughly dispassionate approach to religion and the sober and mindful dedication to the running of the Kirk by cool heads were the Moderates' priorities. In this way Moderates were able, wrongly as it transpired, to disregard these Evangelical outpourings as flights of fancy, unable to see them as the beginnings of a cultural shift.

Large crowds were beginning to gather around a new breed of itinerant evangelists such as the dissident Haldane brothers. At the end of the 18th century they had established the Society for the Propagation of the Gospel at Home, set up a training college to educate evangelists and had a lively publication business printing tracts and leaflets. In some large towns they had built their own places of worship, 'Tabernacles'. The Moderates saw the activities of the Haldanes and other independents operating beyond the reach of the courts of the Kirk as a direct attack on the authority of the Established Church, undermining the Kirk's carefully crafted bureaucracy, and condemning its theology, dogma and practice. The Haldanes' activities sent the 1799 General Assembly into a froth after having received complaints from all over the country. As Burleigh confirmed, 'Great resentments were aroused'.[3]

As a robust response to this, a number of measures were enacted not only by the 1799 General Assembly but by subsequent Assemblies, all designed to crush the movement. Acts were passed to tighten control over who should be permitted to gain access to pulpits and schoolrooms, and further legislation enforced the requirement to pursue courses of study approved by the Kirk. These Acts of Assembly reinforced the powers of universities and courts of the Church in ensuring that only suitably qualified persons should be employed in occupying pulpits and carrying out the ordinances of the Church. Itinerant evangelists, including those ordained by the Church's own presbyteries, were to be banned from all pulpits, other than their own. The establishing of 'Law and Order' within the Kirk was very much in evidence.

---

3 J.H.S. Burleigh *A Church History of Scotland*, 311.

In the words of the 1818 motion passed by the Assembly the presence of these 'itinerants' was deemed to be 'disorderly, calculated to weaken the hands of the minister of the parish, injure the interests of sound religion and so disturb the peace and order of the Church'.[4] In a bold move to remind congregations of the Kirk's insistence on an educated and accredited ministry, and warn people of other various dangers, a pastoral admonition reminiscent of a papal bull was read out from every pulpit in the land. There was a patriotic reference to the misdeeds of revolutionary France, a warning about the circulation of seditious pamphlets promoting atheistic ideas and finally, a move to ban the dissident Haldane brothers altogether. Moderates concentrated on tightening control, delivering better practice and procedure and reminding congregations of their patriotic duty. When it came to passing these Acts on the Assembly floor, and in a rare act of unanimity, Evangelicals wholeheartedly supported these Moderate-crafted motions having been persuaded that the Establishment principle was under attack.

Towards the end of the 18th century, Moderates may have underestimated that the cultural values underpinning Rationalism were on the move, to be replaced by a new set of values grounded in the age of Romanticism, and in politics, an age of management giving way to an age of reform. This new age ushered in the rise of the Evangelical Party, corresponding with the Whig Party's rising to power in the State. 'In both spheres the champions of liberty sought to correct grievances and remedy defects'.[5] The ultimate aim of the Evangelical Party was to make the Church a living force in the life of the nation while questioning the justice of its subordination to the State.

Secession of Members and their Money

The Moderate Party meanwhile had its eyes still firmly focused on the external threats of Catholicism and Episcopalianism. But new dangers were emerging. From within the Protestant fellowship a number of secession churches were proliferating, mainly those unhappy about the intrusion of unwanted ministers upon congregations and others critical of the Kirk's liberal and worldly ways. The rise in the number of secession congregations had severe financial implications for the Kirk for it was generally the middle-classes who departed taking their wealth with them. 'The growth of dissent was rapid'[6] and authors Rait and Pryde

---

4 General Assembly Sess. 9, 30th May 1818.
5 Sir Robert Rait and George S Pryde, *Scotland*, 266.
6 Sir Robert Rait and George S Pryde, *Scotland*, 263.

calculated that by the end of the 18th century the Kirk had lost to dissent something approaching one-third of its membership. The Secession Church claimed 110,000 members at this time and The Relief Church founded in 1752, 100,000 members. This now forced the Moderates to look both ways. But Evangelicals had a different focus: as far back as the 1780s Evangelicals were beginning to concentrate on the internal threat of a dead faith which promised to undermine the Kirk. For Evangelicals, Moderatism did not offer the solution; Moderatism was the problem.

As the fault-lines between the two parties became apparent, the Moderates were unconcerned by Evangelical views and opinions which were now becoming increasingly strident and critical. They relied on the continuation of their dominance in the Courts of the Church. Moderates also overlooked two important aspects of this growing Evangelical revival: first, an intellectual and spiritual awakening; secondly, a practical altruism. Moderates had considered the Evangelical view intellectually inferior to those who had become 'enlightened' by the new '-isms and -ologies' of the age, while any sense of a heightened spirituality could be left to hot-headed fanatics and enthusiasts. Evangelicals would go on to claim that their developing practical altruism arose as a direct result of parish neglect by Moderates, especially as they experienced it in the north and west.

The crowded urban scene in the cities of the south may have blurred the distinction between the two factions but in the Highlands and Islands there was increasing separation as the unique circumstances of the Clearances, the ensuing poverty, and severe social dislocation impacted upon the business of parish life and ministerial effectiveness. Broad as the Church of Scotland may have been, it did not accommodate the beliefs of everyone within the kirk.

Hauled before the 1831 General Assembly, Alexander John Scott was on trial for refusing to sign the Confession of Faith, the church's principal statement of belief. Scott's position, somewhat as an eccentric visionary, did not sit well with either faction. Some years later, after having been banned from Scottish pulpits, Scott criticised the Moderate position for ignoring justice issues and for supporting the political status quo and the inequities of British society. Nor did the Evangelical position avoid his critical tongue asking how did religion ever come to be 'another name for self-interest, or at best for its extension into eternity, in which the devout are more concerned about the salvation of their own souls than the well-being of humanity?'[7]

---

7 Newell, John Philip, *A.J. Scott and his Circle*, 296.

His analysis summed up perfectly the two opposing positions. Further, while he railed against those who used religion to justify the existing political order, he found himself amongst the most celebrated of dissenters of the day: Thomas Erskine, the mystic Laird of Linlathan and John McLeod Campbell, minister of Rhu Parish Church. Scott himself was assistant to Edward Irving, the romantic and apocalyptic minister of the Scots Kirk, Regent Square, London. These three, together with Scott were denounced as heretics.

Despite the criticisms of Scott and others, banished to the sidelines, an emerging Evangelical approach, based on missionary zeal and personal devotion, now appeared more attuned to the needs of its Highland constituency in the wake of the seismic economic changes and social upheavals taking place. Perhaps the Evangelical wing of the Kirk could solve the Highland Problem. This new approach was well received in the communities of the north and west, paralysed by Moderate torpor and riven by the introduction of new land-management techniques and the wholesale clearance of entire townships.

Change and Conversion

General Assemblies were perceived by Evangelicals to be slow and ineffective in response to these changes, despite the appointment of catechists and missionaries to supplement ministerial numbers. Not envisaging any improvement or change under Moderate leadership, by 1799 the independent dissident Haldane brothers had 40 catechists operating in the remotest parts of the Highlands. Missions to the north and west developed quickly in the years following and it was Evangelicalism that offered a faith-based personal religion which met the needs of people struggling to navigate the social and economic changes. Further, Moderates were content to teach the generalities of religion and theology and to emphasise virtue and the qualities pertaining to good citizenship. Evangelicals, by contrast, laid great weight upon the Christian doctrines of sin, grace and redemption and their aim was to awaken in their hearers a deeper personal religious experience. Evangelicalism also promoted the importance of the supernatural and the emotions, both of which were emphasised in prayer and religious revival. Its core belief was rooted in the necessity of conversion and recapturing to an extent the Calvinist view of the complete unworthiness of the individual. The Moderate position emphasised the 'corporate' response of the community of the faithful while Evangelicals concentrated upon a faith with a personal and individual experience at its heart.

This outpouring of Evangelical enthusiasm was seen as a direct consequence of the Established Kirk's long-term lack of impact upon Highland communities and its over-concentration upon extending its urban presence and effectiveness in the south to the detriment of those rural poor scratching a living beyond the Highland line. As a result, an increasingly strident and organised Evangelical Party emerged holding the Moderate Party's authority increasingly to account: first, Evangelicals provided an alternative approach to faith, witness and service firmly rooted in biblical and doctrinal teaching; second, there was an emphasis upon mission both at home and abroad; and third, the promotion of conscientious pastoral care and parish visitation by a committed and energetic ministry. As they saw it, these were the vital elements severely lacking within Moderatism. Such ministers, who had known nothing of the Covenanting struggles and who were now enjoying a certain Hanoverian prosperity, continued to dismiss Evangelicalism as being a religion of the heart and not the head. Oblivious to the new realities experienced especially by those living and working in the north and west, there was not sufficient recognition by Moderates of the need for fundamental change.

In his PhD thesis[8] David Alan Currie advances the theory that Evangelicalism offered an attractive way to counter the institutional paralysis of the Moderate-dominated Kirk during these years of social upheaval. Moderates were not fully aware of the consequences of the move from a rural to an urban economy, from an agricultural to an industrial economy and the shift from Enlightenment values to those of Romanticism. Currie argues that Evangelicalism bridged the cultural gap between the 18th and 19th centuries which made it attractive to those in crisis as they attempted to navigate the gaps between the two states. Moderates further underestimated Evangelicalism's growing appetite for study, reflection and the search for a deeper meaning in matters of personal faith.

This new intellectual approach was facilitated by the growing number of publications and pamphlets which were in circulation from the 1790s onwards. The production of newspapers and periodicals was one crucial element in the dramatic cultural shifts taking place. The printing and quick dissemination of information meant that alternative views could be expressed, entrenched positions challenged and opinions scrutinised by an increasingly-sophisticated readership which included ministers

---

8 David Alan Currie, PhD thesis 1991, *The Growth of Evangelicalism in the Church of Scotland, 1793 – 1843.*

and students. The new way also served to reinforce and challenge partisan, bigoted and hard-line stances already taken. Within the lively religious periodical scene in Scotland especially, a host of publications supported a plethora of conflicting and contentious beliefs. Debate and discussion were freely aired focusing upon the most disputatious areas of public, private and most crucially Church life. How the Church of Scotland was to progress in its faith and mission became hot topics, especially between Moderates and Evangelicals. The use of periodicals reflected societal changes within the country.

Publications

The *Missionary Magazine* established in 1796 covered a general interest in revivalism and missionary awareness and also promoted new religious voluntary societies, anathema to Moderates. Some subscribers were frustrated by the Kirk's lack of commitment to mission activity and its seeming low spiritual vitality and, reflecting this, the magazine became more strident in its criticism, no doubt fuelled by an increasingly disquieted Evangelical readership. However the magazine unsettled many Moderates in the Kirk who were wary of lay preaching and congregational polity, two matters which commanded much support among Evangelicals.

The *Religious Monitor* or *Scots Presbyterian Magazine* sought to tread a middle path: institutional commitment to the Church while supporting spiritual vitality, mission and spiritual revivalism. The publication lasted fifteen years, its main concerns the promotion of personal piety, education and supporting a vigorous parish ministry. It encouraged professional discussion of pastoral care and helped to spread and strengthen Evangelical influence among the clergy, especially in the more remote parts of the Highlands and Islands.

The *Edinburgh Christian Instructor* became the primary platform for the lively exchange of theological and spiritual opinion and the sharing and dissemination of matters which concerned Evangelicals at large. 'It was undoubtedly the most influential and important publication closely related to the Church of Scotland virtually standing alone between the years 1820 and 1830.'[9] This publication, more than any other, gave lie to Moderate criticism that Evangelicals had an inferior grasp of the intellectual nature of religion.

The first significant Gaelic periodical came from an idea of Principal Baird, convener of the Education Committee. *The Teachdaire*

---

9 David Alan Currie, PhD thesis 1991, 52..

Gaelach appeared in 1829. It was somewhat ironic that Principal Baird, an avowed Moderate, promoted the idea of a Gaelic periodical ahead of any English-language based publication. It appears that the Evangelical Highland and Island wing of the Kirk had no thoughts about producing such a magazine. Further, the Moderates showed little interest in developing this vital medium until the 1830s. As complacent members of an elitist social and intellectual movement in control of the universities and the General Assembly, they were less concerned about influencing popular opinion through the wider audience that publications could reach. This lack of commitment demonstrated the patrician nature and paternalism of Moderatism, always ambitious to preserve two essential ideals: law and order and the imposition of social control.

Through its publications Evangelicals were able to achieve two main objectives: they identified and championed agendas firmly rooted in Reformation principles; and they sought to encourage professional discussion on pastoral care and mission work. Evangelicals established religious voluntary societies for the active expression of translating revival into concrete action.

Pastoral care and mission were two specific areas neglected by Moderates. Although missionaries and catechists were provided to the Kirk through the provisions of the Royal Bounty, the Church was uncomfortable working outside the formal structures of the Establishment. These publications helped to encourage a lively and informed fertilisation of thought and ideas and to spread and strengthen Evangelical influence among the clergy, especially in more isolated areas. The small but growing numbers of Evangelical ministers in the far north and west benefited from their circulation and helped these men, despite obvious geographical obstacles and professional isolation, to coalesce around one set of principles and form themselves into a cohesive and well-informed unit. Consequently, they were able to feel increasingly connected to the quickening of this emergent movement and from the 1820s onwards these publications played a decisive role as Evangelicals grew in influence to challenge Moderate dominance in General Assembly.

Evangelicals embarked on a mission to rescue the Highlands and Islands and revitalise the Church. The recovery of that ground lost through decades of Moderate inactivity, as they saw it, was undertaken by the uncompromising Protestant doctrine of salvation and a developed sense of social justice which only Evangelicals offered. In her PhD thesis, Christine Lodge states that 'The emphasis with the Evangelical doctrine on salvation through suffering, together with a millennial vision of justice, held great appeal to the dispossessed Highlander.'[10] This vision provided a new purpose in life and a certain sense of security in an insecure world. In this, distressed Gaels found succour and encouragement. However, Lodge goes on to state: 'The concept of the necessity of suffering as a preparation for salvation was a major factor in the general lack of insurrection in the Highlands at times of clearance.' Further, the concept of spiritual consolation as opposed to worldly comforts was not conducive to radical protest which inevitably led to a 'fatalistic passivity'.

The theme of the Highlander now 'dispossessed' was taken up by Tom Atkinson in his book *The Empty Lands*:

> The 18th and 19th centuries were a period of horror for the Highlanders with a loss of Scottish nationality, the Scottish State, the Jacobite uprisings, the genocide after Culloden, the Clearances, the potato famines. It left a poor remnant of a once-proud people sad and isolated, licking their wounds, seeking relief in a strict religion, looking for acceptance in a political union which had no use for their culture, their language, their heritage, or anything about them except when war-drums thundered. They grew to despise their own language, to see themselves fit only to be gillies [contemptuous term for 'boy'] or servants in the big house. The Highlander had even lost the remembrance of that which had been lost.[11]

It was into this cultural, linguistic, economic and religious vacuum that young Evangelical ministers boldly entered. They were on a mission and it was to these men that the dispossessed turned in numbers. Evangelicalism addressed the core malady at the heart of these dispossessed: a deep-seated spiritual destitution.

Central to Evangelical belief was the eternal fate of the individual soul, not the divine-led harmony of nature through man-centred institutions and the progress of society as espoused by Enlightenment values and Moderate beliefs. Evangelicalism's primary focus concentrated on obedience to the laws of God as revealed through scripture. Preachers were to act as vehicles for God's grace, confronting

---

10 Christine Lodge PhD thesis 1996, *The Clearers and the Cleared; Women, Economy and Land in the Scottish Highlands 1800 – 1900*, 276.

11 Tom Atkinson, *The Empty Lands*, 7.

listeners with the consciousness of sin and the probability of eternal damnation, until they prayed for release from their torment through divine grace. This was true and undiluted Calvinist theology. Despite a measure of comfort derived from 'saving grace' offered through personal conversion, it was unfortunate that melancholia and fatalism were almost inbred in Highlanders, their roots firmly lodged in the immutability of life, which, to a certain extent, was reinforced through their relationship with landowners. But Evangelical belief held out the hope that all the sufferings borne in the present life would ultimately have their reward in the next, while those architects of injustice and perpetrators of wrong-doing would be justly punished in the great reckoning of the heavenly assizes to come.

Evangelicals and Moderates: Two Distinct Perspectives

One important step for Evangelicals was to reject the growing tendency of people to separate life into religious and secular spheres. Young Highland Evangelical ministers were at the forefront of seeking to re-establish the idea of the 'godly commonwealth' while at the same time maintaining and reinforcing the authority of the Established Kirk over society where personal rescue and spiritual recovery were to be effected. Highland economic life, however, was firmly in the grip of the governing classes, supported by most Moderates, and quite separate from the spiritual life directed by the Church – a separation Evangelicals would come to despise. Despite this apparent division, Highland culture evolved according to the directives of both politics/economics and of religion.

That these two spheres had become so intertwined left Moderates open to the charge, by some Evangelicals, that they were no more than 'country gentlemen' fulfilling their duties in a perfunctory manner. Of his Moderate colleagues, Revd Donald Sage had this to say: 'Dr Ross of Lochbroom's love of controversy and litigation destroyed his ministerial usefulness. Dr Downie of Lochalsh was a man of wealth and gentlemanly manners, a princely landlord, an extensive sheep-farmer, a good shot but a wretched preacher.'[12] Others were contemptuously dismissed as 'complete and respectable specimens of Moderatism'. For Sage, these ministers exercised a 'tepid' ministry. Evangelical ministers strove to improve life 'in all its fullness' for all their congregations. There could be no compartmentalising of 'faith', 'work', 'home life', 'church life'; there was but *one* life, and the whole of that life had to

---

12 Donald Sage, *Memorabilia Domestica*, 188.

be underpinned and informed by a robust and committed Evangelical religion.

Further and crucially, as these young Evangelicals saw it, the Moderate Party embraced authoritarian attitudes whose consequence was a fundamental commitment to subordinating the Kirk to the more powerful secular political interests. It was this tension which Evangelicals regarded as behind much of the unrest and insecurity experienced especially by Highlanders caught in the midst of clearance, economic hardship and social dislocation.

There was a firm belief, espoused by Moderates and Evangelicals alike, that the distinctions of social order and class were inherent in human nature and civilised society and therefore immutable. It was also believed that the educated landowner was best suited to choose a minister than his rough, ignorant and unruly tenants. The superior and middle ranks and the lower orders each had their own duty: the former to govern, the latter to obey. In the Highlands especially it was said that this had its own consequences: it was a near-sacred principle that it was the task of the poor man to create wealth and the task of the rich man to spend it – the lot of the crofter to work the land and that of the landowner to enjoy its fruits. While much of this caste system had its roots firmly entrenched in the old clan system, with its codes of fealty and loyalty inbred in Highland DNA, 'knowing one's place' and the inviolability of the social order was reaffirmed almost without exception to the profit of the landed classes and to the misery and disadvantage of the lower orders.

Most Scottish churchmen at the outset of the 19th century not only accepted the existing order, political, social and economic, as having been divinely decreed, but felt bound actively to defend it with every weapon at their command. As for the disadvantaged, they were required to remember that no virtues were more praiseworthy than submission to one's superiors, patient endurance and gratitude for small mercies received. This ideology left little room for radical protest against the aristocratic establishment. For Moderates, much like their position regarding Roman Catholics, keeping the poor 'in their place' was of supreme importance. The aim was to facilitate harmony and peace by ensuring law and order at all costs and perhaps as a happy consequence of all this, to promote the questionable virtues of power and profit.

Charged with the sin of 'inattentiveness', Moderate ministers were also widely regarded as lazy. Neglect of parochial duties and responsibilities was a criticism regularly levelled by Evangelicals, and in the Highlands and Islands especially, some Moderates were seen to be more farmers than ministers. As Dr Johnson confirmed on his Highland tour of 1773, 'the only gentlemen are the Lairds, the Tacksmen and the Ministers who frequently improve their livings by becoming farmers'.[13] Dr Johnson was impressed enough by the ministers with whom he came into contact stating, 'for I saw not one in the Islands whom I had reason to think either deficient in learning, or irregular in life: but found several with whom I could not converse without wishing, as my respect increased, that they had not been Presbyterians'.[14]

At the time of Johnson's travels ministers would have been overwhelmingly Moderate by persuasion. Some individual Moderate ministers were charged with subordinating their parish duties to secular interests. It was known that some Edinburgh Moderates could not stay away from the gambling tables. In the south, as the cities rapidly grew in population partly as a result of Highland emigration and fuelled by increasing industrialisation, new forms of urban ministry and congregational life were seen as predominately middle-class activities where middle-class ministers led middle-class congregations. The Kirk was only beginning to recognise that the great influx of new city dwellers had become a problem. In these industrial centres, the new underclass was the 'urban poor'. There were new challenges to be faced, both by this burgeoning population and by a Church ill-equipped to serve it, and, if truth be told, not at all minded to much mission work. However, the political, economic and social concerns of the Lowlands were far different from those of the Highlands and these had their unique ecclesiastical challenges. In this respect, the contrast between Highland and Lowland ministry could not have been greater.

Evangelicals and Church Life

Moderates continued to concentrate their focus on maintaining good governance of the Church in the early years of the 19th century: defending the Establishment principle against attacks from secession churches; retaining its strong grip on General Assembly matters; and overseeing the business of the Courts of the Church. Meanwhile, Evangelicals continued to focus on two increasingly important aspects of church life as they saw it: first, the necessity of revitalising the church's

---

13 Samuel Johnson, *A Journey to the Western Islands of Scotland* (pub. 1775), 202.
14 Samuel Johnson *A Journey to the Western Islands of Scotland*, 242.

Essay 5: Moderates and Evangelicals

inner spirituality by recapturing some of the tenets of Reformation and Covenanting theological thought and practice; second, to tackle the difficulties encountered when an 'ungodly minister was inflicted upon a godly congregation', felt especially in the Highlands and Islands where the grip on power by a dictatorial patron was unyielding and his decisions on matters both civil and ecclesiastical final.

To facilitate the rediscovery of the Kirk's inner spirituality, Currie states four vital aspects of the Evangelical movement:[15] *corporate prayer* was Evangelicalism's spiritual dynamism, emphasising the need for divine power to effect conversion and sanctification; *education* was the cognitive foundation, formulating and spreading Evangelical ideas among students; *religious voluntary societies* were the movement's active expression of translating religious revival and mission into concrete action; *religious periodicals* acted as the communication network, spreading information about Evangelical ideas widely through the Kirk.

The force of these dynamics was keenly harnessed by the Evangelical clergy of the Highlands and Islands who were exercising ministries along quite different lines than their Moderate brethren. Rather than hold Kirk Sessions and ministers to account over lapses in church procedure and practice, or focus on the Kirk's institutional organisation to meet the specific challenges posed in the north and west, this new breed of ministers focused on the spiritual discipline of their congregations. Moderates used the Courts of the Church to impose societal disciplines and believed the way to improve individual behaviour was to strengthen the powers of Kirk Sessions and Presbyteries. Evangelicals employed a different tactic: strong uncompromising preaching, to change the personal behaviour of individual believers. That was considered to impact more on the morals of the people and have a greater effect on their spirituality than any growth in intellectualism, as promoted by Moderates still clinging to Enlightenment ideals.

As Alexander MacRae reported, the moral improvements among people newly infused with Evangelical fervour were immediate and conspicuous: 'Immorality, drunkenness, profanity, Sabbath-breaking and other forms of sin practically disappeared from the life of these communities.'[16] Those found to be involved in smuggling, dancing and drinking, and general carousing were refused communion. (There

---

15 David Alan Currie, *The Growth of Evangelicalism in the Church of Scotland 1793 – 1843*, 8.

16 Revd Alexander Macrae, *Revivals in the Highlands and Islands in the 19th Century*, 11.

appears, however, to have been no sanctions against distilling, declared illegal by Act of Parliament in 1824 but a practice which continued to be widespread throughout the Highlands and Islands and which underpinned much of the rural economy.) Personal conversion and revival together with a strong social morality were now at the centre of Evangelical Presbyterianism.

Reinforcing that centrality, a life devoted to the discipline of personal prayer became a priority; prayer became a bedrock of personal and corporate discipline. Regular prayer-meetings for the faithful reinforced religion's corporate nature among like-minded individuals in the community and so became an essential facet of living the truly religious life. Evangelical ministers provided leadership, teaching and admonishing congregations on their faith-journey while emphasising the indivisibility of living a full life.

Congregations in return found a new social cohesion and psychological compensation, values more relevant to their situation and a way of coping with change. Congregations met for bible-study and prayer outwith Sunday worship so churches became the focus of community activity in a way in which Moderate congregations meeting only on the Sabbath did not. It was little wonder that churches led by Evangelical ministers were regarded as communities of consolation for people caught in the maelstrom of clearance and poverty. Evangelicalism was becoming an irresistible force as Highland society in itself did not have adequate means and resources to offer alternatives or to resist the planting and growth of these Evangelical congregations who were now seen to be competing with Moderatism for the hearts and minds of the uncommitted.

Also, Highland society lacked any focus of authority, save for individual landowners, or centres of learning from which any alternative community could derive direction and consolidate resistance. The only socially cohesive gatherings were focused upon the local Kirk led by strong Evangelical ministers. Therefore, Evangelical Christianity not only rooted successfully within Highland culture but fruited to such an extent that it choked off any possibility of any Moderate-led renaissance. Among Evangelical ministers there was an assumption of leadership whose authority in defining acceptable behaviour was admitted without question. In this way, the success of the Free Church in 1843 was guaranteed in the Highlands and Islands and the establishing of the Parliamentary Churches whose pulpits were mainly filled by vocal, energetic and robust Evangelical ministers, eager for change.

Evangelicals and Moderates: contrast and compare

Evangelical ministers became known for being strong preachers in their pulpits, uncompromising teachers in matters of faith and doctrine, and authoritative but compassionate shepherds of their flock. And in return, they had the respect of devoted congregations. In his funeral eulogy of the revered Highland Evangelical Dr Angus Mackintosh of Tain, Dr John Macdonald, 'the Apostle of the North', includes this description of Mackintosh's ministry, the very embodiment of Evangelical piety and ministerial excellence:

> He 'kept the faith'. He believed, loved, felt, and fed upon the doctrines of faith which he preached to others. He lived as became these doctrines, as a father, husband, and friend. His conversation was in heaven. He preached the gospel to saints and sinners faithfully and purely, with authority and tenderness. He spoke to the understanding and to the heart at once. He preached doctrinally and experimentally but as the one arising out of the other. Like Paul, he laboured to promote the success of the gospel, by prayer, by a holy life, by boldly opposing error and reproving sin, by his visiting and catechising and by zeal for the spread of the gospel in the world.[17]

It would be extremely unlikely that any Evangelical would hold these qualities and attributes to be true of any Moderate minister who, with the exception of a few, were regarded as unscriptural, worldly, self-seeking and oblivious to the plight of congregations.

The Evangelical ministry saw itself rooted in the lives of the people they were called to serve. As early as 1730 Revd John Balfour of Nigg was railing against social injustice such as exorbitant rents, luxurious living and oppression of the poor. Constant appeals to the privileged rich to do their Christian duty by dispensing charity to the poor went unheeded. Balfour was also a strict disciplinarian in exerting control over his congregation and during his ministry oversaw 10 weekly Fellowship meetings for prayer and discussion in various parts of the parish. His sermons were uncompromisingly Evangelical in nature and his stance on matters of social justice, and by those ministers of a similar predisposition, addressed the needs of the day. This stance was underpinned by a growing intellectual awareness which better related to how people thought and lived and also provided them with a

---

[17] Revd John Kennedy, *The 'Apostle of the North': The life and Labours of the Rev Dr McDonald*, 277.

specific world view. Evangelical ministers moved to make the Christian life and the Church the central focus of how people lived and worked, in whatever circumstances they found themselves. These emphases found especial resonance for people engulfed by the economic and societal changes taking place throughout the Highlands and Islands.

Moderates, stout defenders of the primacy of the ordained ministry, did not have any developed sense of what might be called 'mission' or 'outreach'. Unwilling to cede control of any spiritual activity to an unregulated laity, they only worked within the bounds of their own congregations. They had no sense of working collaboratively with neighbouring ministers. Accused of moral laxity while promoting an ethic of discipline and rectitude, the contrast between Moderates and Evangelicals could not have been more greatly recognised:

> The [Moderate] ministers of Skye were then literally blind leaders of the blind. Mr Roderick McLeod declared that the first presbyterial act he performed after his ordination [as an Evangelical minister] was to assist his co-presbyters to their beds. They were so helplessly intoxicated. This is an indication of their morals.[18]

Parish visitations by Moderates were unheard of. This effectively left all mission activity to the Evangelicals. Further, the Moderates strongly promoted a society and a culture increasingly becoming *anglicized*. In the north and west Moderates demonstrated an ongoing anxiety regarding the Gaelic language, its place within the life of congregations and in society in general. Among Moderates there existed the prevailing view that the Gaelic language was a severe impediment to economic advancement and cultural integration with the rest of the Union. With the Kirk's activities becoming more and more urban-centred, many Moderates regarded the Highland church with increasing exasperation.

At its root lay an unresolved ambivalence and at times naked hostility towards Gaelic culture and language, regardless of the efforts of the SSPCK and the work of catechists and missionaries. Moderates struggled to accommodate the co-existence of two separate and irreconcilable cultures. While Moderates did much to repress Gaelic, seen by some as a 'foreign' language and a liability, Evangelicals acknowledged the place of Gaelic within Highland tradition and heritage as an asset, and something that did not require to be changed.

---

18 Revd Alexander Macrae, *Revivals in the Highlands and Islands in the 19th Century*, 58.

Again, this was eventually to play out to the advantage of those ministers and congregations who would form the Free Church in the years leading to the Disruption.

As a contrast, missionary activity, Gaelic preaching and catechetical teaching were enthusiastically embraced by Evangelical ministers and congregations. The Gaelic Schools' Society proved an effective asset in consolidating and promoting Highland culture. Revd Murdo Macaulay went further in stating its importance which was transformational: 'There is no doubt that the Gaelic schools paved the way for the complete adherence of the people to the Free Church in 1843.'[19] Mission and catechising gave Evangelical leaders a stronger foothold in Highland culture and facilitated the planting and nurturing of congregations.

Over generations, Evangelicals had been attacking Moderates on several fronts: first, Moderates' appearance of siding with landowners; secondly, their lukewarm attitude towards Gaelic culture and language; and finally, their idleness and parish neglect. Yet Evangelicals, recognising not only the signs and symptoms of Moderate failure, were quick to offer a diagnosis and treatment, if not a cure: according to Evangelical belief, it was a missionary mentality coupled with a missionary zeal that Moderates lacked.

By the 19th century it was the Evangelical catechists and ordained missionaries who were pushing back on the twin evils of Catholicism and Moderatism. Not only was Moderatism seen as the problem, Moderatism was now seen as 'the enemy'. Alexander Macrae states that

> with two or three conspicuous exceptions every pulpit, from the Mull of Kintyre to Cape Wrath along the western shores, and every pulpit on the islands, without exception, was without the light of the living gospel of the grace of God at the close of the 18th century. The philosophic unbelief of the age, led by Hume in Scotland, dominated the theological schools and banished the living Christ from the pulpits of the land.[20]

Macrae further maintained that the landowners on the west coast were 'not noted for their piety or protestantism and had ministers presented to the livings who were in all respects like the patrons.'[21]

---

19 Revd Murdo Macaulay, *Aspects of Religious History of Lewis*, 222.

20 Revd Alexander Macrae, *Revivals in the Highlands and Islands in the 19th Century*, 10.

21 Revd Alexander Macrae, *Revivals in the Highlands and Islands in the 19th Century*, 11.

In these circumstances, the traditional network of patrons or family friends from within the closed circle of the influential elite came into play to advantage the sons of landed proprietors, large farmers and professional classes, Those sons, candidates for the ministry, having enjoyed the privileges of a university education could almost be guaranteed a prosperous church living. Indeed, several Arts graduates did not complete their Divinity studies as they had been earmarked for preferment as certain vacancies arose; contrary to the Church's stance on the supervision of ministerial candidates. Some students were ordained and inducted into charges by powerless, or sometimes complicit, Moderate-dominated Courts of the Church. Other ministry candidates were often 'sons of the manse', following grandfathers and fathers into the same pulpit creating thereby something of a 'dynasty'. Yet, 'it was by the influence of one revival of religion after another that moderatism was gently thawed out.'[22]

By contrast with the dominance of a Moderate elite, the rise of Evangelical ministries throughout the Highlands and Islands was no better demonstrated by that of Revd Alexander Gunn, minister of Watten in Caithness on the east coast. Several communities there had already come under the influence of James Haldane's itinerant Evangelical preaching. Licensed by the Presbytery of Caithness in 1803 after completing his studies, Gunn and other like-minded individuals were deemed by some Moderate clergy to be 'dangerous young men', a characterisation which they would have felt fully justified, for 'very dangerous did their powerful exhibition of true scriptural doctrine prove to the corrupt teaching of these [Moderate] men'.[23] These young committed Evangelicals, so uncompromising in their Calvinist preaching which built upon Haldane's evangelizing, were able to elicit the following from the famed Dr MacIntosh of Tain: 'What I believe to be a genuine revival of religion – the work of the spirit of God – has taken place during the past year . . . The preaching of the Word is the grand means that has been employed and blessed'.[24]

In other parts of the north and west, from the late 1700s to the 1830s, similar outbreaks of revival took hold. This did nothing to foster harmonious relations between Evangelicals and Moderates whose

---

22 Revd Alexander Macrae, *Revivals in the Highlands and Islands in the 19th Century*, 11.

23 Revd Alexander Auld, *Ministers and Men in the Far North*, 20.

24 Revd Alexander Macrae, *Revivals in the Highlands and Islands in the 19th Century*, 83.

members abandoned their own churches, for want of a stronger Gospel message. Evangelicals noted a decline in personal behaviour, as they saw it, a direct result of preaching a 'social gospel' under a Moderate regime.

At the core of true Evangelical belief was the question '*What shall I do to be saved?*' The short answer would be a life that met the requirements of the holy law of God, the requirements of a living conscience and the total subjugation to gospel deliverance. By contrast, the thesis at the centre of Moderate-dominated theology was '*What shall I do to be a better Christian?*' to which Moderate ministers answered 'keep the laws, civil and ecclesiastical, and know your place'. Evangelical belief and that of the Moderates started at such widely differing viewpoints that there was no commonality between them. Evangelicals averred that if you ask the wrong question, wrong answers will surely follow.

Evangelicalism had placed 'salvation' at the heart of all religious endeavour, and what both preceded and proceeded from that. As a focus on this central tenet, Gunn and other Evangelicals now harnessed the twin necessities of 'waiting for God' to direct and control, and to work harder for the complete reordering of discipline which had 'fallen below the requirements of scripture'.[25] Revivals impacted not only upon an improvement in the morals of the people but also had a profound effect upon their spirituality.

These 'dangerous young men' of Caithness began the Bible Society which did much to lower the cost of scriptures and widen its circulation. This made the Bible available to a much wider constituency as never before, a further measure that did much to unsettle Moderate sensibilities. These Caithness men also formed an association with the sole purpose of petitioning the General Assembly to abolish patronage, believing that the civil powers regarded the church as an engine to be worked for political purposes, while patrons looked upon the church as a means of securing comfortable livings for their relatives or dependents.

Moderates acknowledged this position but were reluctant to move for change. The temporal advantages gained from supporting patronage became anathema to Evangelicals. Gunn had gained a reputation for speaking out against this abuse and he was persuaded by the Presbytery of Lesmahagow at the General Assembly of 1818 to be the spokesman on the matter and to deliver a motion calling for its abolition.[26] But procedural chicanery by the Moderates saw to it

---

25 Revd Alexander Auld, *Ministers and Men in the Far North*, 36.
26 Revd Alexander Auld, *Ministers and Men in the Far North*, 38.

that Gunn was disqualified from presenting his motion and the point was never debated. This would be the second occasion when Moderate control of Assembly business came under threat from Evangelical attack. Moderate hegemony was dealt a blow the previous year when Evangelicals persuaded the Assembly to vote for restrictions on pluralities. From 1818 onwards, Evangelicals began to find their voice and challenge the old order, in place for almost a century.

Moderates Lose Control of Church Policy

Moderate control had maintained a strong grip on Kirk affairs, almost unchallenged for generations, partly due to the concentration of Moderate clergy in the city charges and in university faculties more easily able to access Edinburgh during General Assembly. Evangelical ministers from the north and west could rarely afford the cost of the trip to attend, nor the time away from their pulpits, sometimes up to a month. Their voices were seldom heard. One Highland Evangelical, Alexander Sage, admitted that in a forty-year ministry he had attended General Assembly once, this in contrast to university professors who combined their post, under rules of plurality, with an appointment to a prestigious city charge entitling them to attend every year. Moderates almost by default therefore found themselves uncontested in matters of devising and regulating Church policy.

In the years following 1818, this loose alliance of ministers of an Evangelical persuasion, formed themselves into the 'Evangelical Party' and grew in terms of influence and prestige. Until then, they simply were unable to harness their potential into a viable opposition. They were determined to save the soul of the Kirk and acknowledged that the only way was to challenge Moderate-controlled General Assembly business on an annual basis. At home, the Evangelical Party's emboldened members consolidated their ministries through their brand of preaching and visitation while supporting local schoolmasters and catechists. Unlike their Moderate colleagues, these men were highly visible in their parishes. Growing numbers of Evangelical ministers now formed themselves into an effective voting bloc, able to resist and counter Moderate claims on Church matters while prosecuting their own agenda.

In 1821 and for the first time, Evangelicals presented and promoted a nomination for Moderator from within their own ranks. This move was born out of the open hostility of the previous year's Assembly which saw Moderates and Evangelicals head-to-head in a display of uncompromising factionalism. These events were to sow the seeds of what was to come in 1843. The dispute centred round the Privy Council's instruction which commanded ministers of the Church to pray for the King (now George IV) and all the royal household. It had been accepted practice, since Queen Anne's reign, that prayers were offered for the monarch and the royal household but ministers had been free to frame these prayers in their own words. Now a royal command to this effect had been issued and this prayer was now prescribed. The leading Evangelical Dr Andrew Thomson argued that the crux of the matter rested on the spiritual independence of the Church of Scotland which would not take instruction from civil authorities. The royal writ was regarded as interference in its worship and had been framed with Scottish Episcopalians in mind, who followed an Anglican liturgy. However, Thomson and the Evangelicals lost this particular argument which became a running sore for next 20 or so years.

By the early 1820s, the fissures and fault-lines between the two, widening for a generation, now effectively split the Kirk down the middle into competing camps. Moderates were unmoveable in their policies: as stout defenders of the Kirk's relationship with the Crown; as favouring a secular, worldly view; and unbending in their opposition to a return to puritanism and piety. By way of contrast, Evangelicals accused Moderates of being more interested in the trappings of position, stipend, manse and glebe, than in promoting a Christ-centred ministry and advantaged by the thorny issue of patronage where the guarantee of a pulpit often tempted students to disregard their studies. Evangelicals were up against the Church's biggest names: Dr John Inglis, minister of Old Greyfriars and head of the Moderate Party; Principal Nicol of St Andrews University, monied, urbane and owner of a large Morayshire estate. He was a man with 'connections'; Dr Duncan Mearns, Professor of Theology at King's College, Aberdeen and, finally, Dr George Cook, then Minister of Laurencekirk but afterwards Professor of Moral Philosophy at St Andrews University.
Taking the argument to the Moderates was Sir Henry Moncrieff Wellwood, Minister at St Cuthbert's Edinburgh, an able leader, unswerving in his adherence to Evangelical principles and thoroughly schooled in the fundamentals of Church governance. 'As presentable a figure socially and intellectually as any Moderate, [he] excelled most of them in his devotion to the proper functions of the ministry.' Undoubtedly emerging as leader of the Evangelical Party, Dr Andrew Thomson, Minister of St George's Edinburgh came to prominence in

the 1820s. Founder of The Christian Instructor, he established schools within his congregation and was the first Evangelical theologian and scholar more than able to hold his own against the combined forces of Moderate academe. More than any other individual, Thomson's intellectualism scotched the idea that Evangelicals were any less academic or scholarly than those in the Moderate Party. His untimely death in 1831 saw Thomas Chalmers assume leadership of the Evangelical Party. Chalmers, academically gifted in the fields of mathematics, economics, moral philosophy and theology, led the party through the ten years of conflict and was one of the principal architects behind the Disruption of 1843.

Throughout the 1820s, the Evangelical voice was being more loudly heard in the courts of the church, and many especially from the north and west now were enthusiastically prepared to attend General Assemblies. In these middle years of the 1820s they sensed a turning of the tide in their favour. Thomson and Chalmers recognised that Moderatism was on the wane and that the Kirk needed a change of direction. Both realised these were years of opportunity for an emboldened Evangelical Party, replete with enthusiastic young ministers leading equally committed congregations.

After years of drift not only was Moderatism's leadership under challenge, Rosalind Mitchison, the Scottish historian, identified several Scottish institutions generally as needing reform and restructuring at this time. Cultural shift was all too obvious. Society was underpinned by a number of establishments, and towards the end of the 18th century all were beginning to display a measure of institutional fatigue. In short, society had maintaining tired, old and worn-out models: the judiciary and court system had failed; schools and universities were outdated and undisciplined; burghs decaying and corrupt with several burghs insolvent.

Within the Kirk Evangelicals now positioned themselves as the party of change. Its ministers were becoming better organised, meeting several times during General Assemblies, In 1824, A document entitled 'Conference of Ministers, Elders and other Members of the Church of Scotland' was circulated among Evangelicals for this very purpose. Its aim was 'to promote the interests of Christ's kingdom by prayer and mutual counsel with a view to co-operation in the General Assembly'. Evangelicals believed themselves to be more in tune with the needs of their parishes especially in the Highlands and Islands, more ably voicing local concerns and more than able to take the arguments to the

Moderates. No longer were Evangelicals dismissed as fanatics or pious zealots. Evangelical ministers in the Highlands and Islands found they had the vigorous backing of faithful and devoted congregations despite the unique geo-political forces working against them in the north and west. By comparison, they held that Moderate torpor exhibited by some ministers was slowly killing the life of the Kirk.

These changes to congregational life in the north and west, exercised by an uncompromising Calvinist message, consolidated not only Presbyterianism in the first instance but secured the future for *Evangelical* Presbyterianism rising in the early 19th century. Ironically, it was the Free Church that profited from the high tide of Evangelical fervour.

As the party of law and order, Moderates saw the battle for the heart and soul of the Kirk to be fought along party lines but the Evangelical movers and shakers firmly believed that the fight was between two competing forces: one to establish a godly commonwealth; the other to maintain the traditional but tired model of Church governance promoted by Moderates. For Evangelicals this had become more of a spiritual matter than a party one. Year on year the bias of the General Assembly began to tilt in favour of the Evangelical Party, testament, as Evangelicals saw it, to a rise in the spiritual life of the nation. New influential voices such as Robert Candlish, David Dickson and David Welsh were beginning to be heard, railing against the corruptions of doctrine and government in the church. Gaining the upper hand in the General Assembly, and thereby setting and controlling Church policy became one of the enduring features of the battle for the heart and soul of the Kirk as it grappled with old and new challenges throughout the first three decades of the 19th century.

The passing of the 1834 Veto Act, engineered by Evangelicals, and which modified patronage by giving the consent and call of the people a distinct place in the choice of ministers was a crucial victory for the Evangelical Party shifting the balance of power and setting in train the following ten years of conflict within the Kirk. It had taken the best part of eighty years to wrest control from the hands of the Moderates. Inevitably and decisively, matters between the two would simmer but eventually boil over. But change would come at a terrible cost.

Essay Six

'Education, Salvation and Damnation'

Nickname for the Central Library, St Mark's Church and His Majesty's Theatre – three neighbouring buildings on Rosemount Viaduct, Aberdeen

As far as the Church of Scotland was concerned, the subject of 'education' had various aspects: education specifically for the ministry where candidates were examined and prepared for ordination; the education of congregations through the preaching of the Word and expositions on the doctrines of faith and by means of the Shorter Catechism; and the education of children in the schoolroom. From the first days of the Reformation there were emphases on both an educated ministry and an educated people. The reformation of universities and schools was therefore vital in achieving these goals.

Without rehearsing the entire history of education in Scotland since 1560, it is vital to note that, for John Knox, education and Reformation were inseparably linked. The Reformed Church, the 'True Church', was to be restored by a return to scriptural purity in doctrine, worship and discipline. This could only be achieved by the sweeping away of the old Church in its entirety and the anti-Catholic sentiment prescribed clearly smacks more of revolution than reform.

An Educated Ministry

Andrew Melville was the scholar who revolutionised academic studies. First, as Principal of Glasgow University (1574-80) and thereafter as Principal of St Mary's College in St Andrews, Melville established a course of study which produced ministers theologically trained and well-versed in associated disciplines such as the study of Hebrew, Latin and Philosophy. First and foremost, ministers were teachers. The medium may well have been through the sermon; by the minister as preacher and catechist. The role of minister as pastor to his congregation was established and developed within the wider social context of the needs of the parish but the primary objective of the university was to teach the teachers. Minister as teaching elder has a long-established tradition.

According to the early Reformers, the journey towards the ordained ministry consisted of election, examination and admission. Election is the presentation of a candidate for ministry by a third party. The candidate is then examined by competent persons, possibly neighbouring ministers, in Scripture exposition and in the topics of 'controversial' theology. There is also a searching enquiry into the character and conduct of the candidate. This is followed by a test of his ability to preach before the congregation to which he is to be minister; sermons dealing with the main articles of faith. Finally, admission will be by those who examined him after a sermon given by the 'chief minister' on the duties of the ministry, and charges given to both minister and people.

The Reformers had also advanced the ideal of a ministry generously provided for. Ministers were not expected to live in poverty. On the contrary, ministers were to have manses, glebes and adequate stipends. Their sons were to have bursaries enabling them to go to school and university if qualified. Their daughters were to have suitable dowries when they came to marriageable age and their widows were to be provided for. In addition, the reformers envisioned a Church capable of financing schools and universities, and also providing funds for the relief of the genuine poor. These ideals did not materialise in their fullest form, however, for there was a profound failure to secure the transfer of funds from the rich pre-Reformation church necessary to create a new national endowment for the whole Kirk enterprise. It was estimated that only one-sixth of that total wealth made its way into the Kirk's coffers. The remainder was redistributed mainly among landowners, town councils and other vested interest groups reluctant to hand over land, property and wealth and who were determined to hang on to as much as they could. This also included the Crown.

The early Reformers envisioned a scheme of national compulsory education, aimed at instilling wisdom, learning and virtue into the youth of the land. The proposal was to attach a school to every kirk where 'religious' education would be taught, either by the minister or by reader or catechist; to teach the rudiments of the faith as well as the clauses of the Shorter Catechism. Every sizeable town was to employ a schoolmaster able to teach Latin and English grammar, and every notable town should have a college in which Latin and Greek should be taught, together with logic and rhetoric. Those suitably qualified should then attend university. Progress through the various stages was by examination. Poverty was no barrier as bursaries would be provided for the poorest of students. At the age of 24 students should be ready to enter the profession of their choice: law, medicine or the ministry, unless they were retained by the university as teachers. This great blueprint for the education of the nation in its optimum configuration also fell victim to the same lack of adequate funds from the outset.

English and Gaelic

> *Of the Earse language . . . it is a rude speech of a barbarous people, who had few thoughts to express, and were content, as they conceived grossly, to be grossly understood.*
>
> Samuel Johnson, A Journey to the Western Isles of Scotland

Dr Johnson's acerbic comment reminds us that Scotland was a country hosting two native languages (and local dialects), yet was hampered by a considerable lack of Gaelic-speaking ministers to serve Highland and Island congregations. This was acknowledged as far back as 1690 but became more visible after the failure of the 1715 rebellion. While the Kirk wrestled with addressing the lack of Gaelic-speaking ministers in the north and west, advances in economics and educational provision had severely diminished Gaelic in the years after Culloden. The old Highland culture had all but been abolished with the dismantling of much of the clan system but further, the English language had penetrated the north and west particularly through commerce and sheep-ranching.

As English-speakers held all the economic power outside the Highlands, the Gaelic language was seen as an economic hindrance and a threat to the unity of the nation. Thus there was little incentive from the industrial and commercial heartlands of the country to support Gaelic-language schools, so it was the prompting of General Assemblies which incentivised ministers to move to northern parishes by offering bursaries, but they also prohibited Gaelic-speaking ministers from leaving Gaelic-speaking regions.

Church services delivered only in the English language to a Gaelic-speaking congregation, and a school curriculum similarly imposed upon children who knew only Gaelic, were major obstacles. In the immediate aftermath of Culloden and as part of the attempts to dismantle Highland culture, prohibition on the speaking of Gaelic in and around schoolhouses was imposed. This, however, was far from universally enforced and by 1754 the rehabilitation of the Gaelic language was underway with efforts to publish a Gaelic New Testament. The ban, seen to be unworkable in many areas, was lifted in 1766 when the teaching of both languages in school was encouraged. However, antipathy towards Gaelic persisted and as Dr Johnson, perambulating the Western Isles in 1773, observed in the Kirk-run parochial schools 'the children are taught to read, but by the rule of their institution, they teach only English, so that the natives read a language which they may never use or understand'.[1]

This is as far Johnson admits to the incongruity of the situation although subsequent history proved him entirely wrong. Moreover, he is firm in his belief that 'English' ways, means and manners will yet rescue the natives from their unenlightened and unlettered ways. Johnson believed that Gaelic language and culture were impediments to the advancement of a civilisation based on Anglicized values. Yet by 1773, as Johnson and Boswell were perambulating their way across the north and west, this Anglicization of the north and west was underway, promoted by the work of the Society in Scotland for Propagating Christian Knowledge (SSPCK), founded in 1709 whose curriculum was firmly based on the English language.

Efforts by Highland Evangelical ministers and those catechist-schoolmasters employed by the SSPCK after proscription was lifted in 1782 to reinvigorate Gaelic culture and facilitate its re-emergence were largely impeded by many obstacles: the Society itself had a distinct but perhaps unconscious Hanoverian bias; the persistence of anti-Gaelic sentiment; efforts to inculcate Lowland values; the prioritisation of the English language; while much was down to the reluctance of English-based landowners to provide adequate funding. Only after the Gaelic Schools Societies were established in the early 19th century was the language, native to the north and west, reinvigorated.

Education for the Ministry: Contrasting Views

The Evangelical view of the Divinity hall was one of loose discipline, over-indulgence in social activities and a lack of religious fervour

J.R. Stephen, PhD thesis, *The Impact of Geography on Ecclesiastical Endeavour in the Highlands*

Beginning in the mid-18th century, the Enlightenment elevated Scottish learning and discourse to new heights and the nation's cultural awakening began to influence university courses. However, this did not suit those of an Evangelical persuasion now offering themselves for the ministry from the north and west of the country. It had become clear that many of the ministers, after completing their years of study and ordained into parishes, were ill-equipped for the peculiar rigours of the task. This new breed of Evangelicals were particularly critical of

---

1 Dr Samuel Johnson, *A Journey to the Western Isles of Scotland*, 146.

the calibre of men emerging from the universities and Divinity halls. The blame was laid at the door of this new age of enlightenment and liberal thinking. It was firmly believed within Evangelical circles that David Hume and his acolytes were replacing religion with philosophy which led to an assault on personal faith and all to the detriment of the Church. The education delivered by Moderate-led universities which these candidates received fell far short of Evangelical expectations and certainly did not reflect, promote or expound the beliefs of a Reformation church seeking to return to scriptural purity in doctrine, worship and discipline. One Highland commentator put it this way: 'At the Divinity hall in Aberdeen, in those days, the example set before young men and the instructions imparted to them, were little fitted to profit them.'[2] As he saw it, many ministers had gladly accepted the softer, more liberal approach of Moderatism and all the worldly benefits that would accrue. However, the historians Sir Robert Rait and George S. Pryde saw things differently: 'Divinity faculties were reinvigorated by being based on compulsory Hebrew'.[3]

Rait identifies one 'Duncan Dewar' as a good example of the archetypal young aspirant, who had recorded his life as a student at St Andrews between 1819 and 1827. Two years each of Latin, Greek and Mathematics, courses in Logic, Moral Philosophy and Natural Philosophy and some additional instruction in Geography, French, Elocution and English, while his Bachelor of Divinity curriculum comprised Theology, Divinity, Biblical Criticism, Ecclesiastical History and Oriental Languages. From a wealthy Perthshire family, Duncan Dewar managed a budget which included funding board and lodgings, for 'hats, gloves, breast-pin, snuff, sweets, whisky, silk handkerchiefs, gifts and entertainment'.[4] The curriculum was formidable and expectations were high. Dewar's was a future destined for the ministry, certainly the expectation of a ministry based upon Moderate values, having been educated at a university thoroughly steeped in Moderate and Enlightenment ways at a period when all Scotland's universities were in the solid grip of the Moderate Party.

By way of contrast, Donald Sage born 1789 and as a son of the manse had his father's and grand-father's ministries as templates for a life of service wholly committed to the Evangelical wing of the church. Born and raised in Kildonan in the Presbytery of Dornoch in the county of

---

2 Revd Alexander Auld, *Ministers and Men in the Far North*, 19.
3 Sir Robert Rait and George S Pryde, *Scotland*, 330.
4 Sir Robert Rait and George S Pryde, *Scotland*, 330.

Sutherland, within a parish stretching 24 by 17 miles north and west up the strath from Helmsdale, the parish consisted of numerous but scattered townships, with the men working crofts of arable land. Born during the Clearances, Sage experienced at first hand the hardships of a manse family kept in penury by the landowner, or more correctly the landowner's factor, who refused to make good promises to make necessary repairs to church and manse. Sage followed his father into ministry and began by taking up studies at Aberdeen University.

His experience could not have been further from that painted by either Rait or Duncan Dewar. It must be stated that aspiring divinity students from the north and west would, in the main, find themselves enrolling at Aberdeen in the first instance, given the distance and cost of studying at St Andrews, Edinburgh or Glasgow. These Aberdeen students would more than likely be Evangelicals. Divinity students such as Duncan Dewar, products of a more affluent middle-class with money to burn on 'whisky and entertainment', would more naturally be drawn to the brighter lights offered elsewhere and would more likely be of Moderate persuasion.

Sage describes his first day attending Marischal College in Aberdeen which he found to be 'in a state of rapid decay, giving one an idea of a hastily-built granary'.[5] He would attend over a four-year course: the first year in Greek; the second in Humanities, General and Natural History and a first Mathematics course; the third in Natural Philosophy and second Mathematics; in year four Moral Philosophy and Logic. At the end of the final year students were accorded the degree of Master of Arts. Sage did not find the courses taught to be intellectually rigorous, nor was he impressed with the quality of the professors and lecturers delivering the curriculum. Some he found tolerably acceptable but in the main the majority were uninspiring Moderates. In his final year he attended the classes of Moral Philosophy delivered by Revd Prof. Glennie:

> This Reverend gentleman was possessed of the least possible measure of talent or imagination. Whatever knowledge he might possess, he was totally destitute of tact in so conveying it to others as either to arrest attention or excite interest. His lectures were the very essence of dullness and were an ill-digested compilations of the sayings and discussions of more eminent men.[6]

---

5 Revd Donald Sage, *Memorabilia Domestica*, 140.
6 Revd Donald Sage, *Memorabilia Domestica*, 155.

According to the student, as a parish minister in Aberdeen's West Church, Glennie was a 'cold and bitter' Moderate. Clearly, his Arts course as a preparatory to Divinity studies was a disappointment. More was to follow however. At the close of the academic year Sage, with his fellow students, received the literary distinction of A.M. 'The graduation, as it was called, was a farce,' he recalled.[7] The students were given a last *viva voce* but had been given the answers beforehand and each in turn was then dubbed 'Master of Arts' by the Principal Dr Brown. Students then were relieved of much money: double fees to the Professor of Moral Philosophy, double fees to the church officer and janitor of the college. The graduation parchment cost half a guinea (approximately £50 in today's money). This matter of extracting fees from students to supplement professorial salaries disadvantaged students who did not reside in the family homes in the cities. Levying fees was a great disincentive to Highland and Island students, far from a seat of learning, who were obliged to pay travel, board and lodgings, an additional cost not borne by city-dwelling students.

Individual Presbyteries, rather than the universities, had oversight of candidates' progress and, in theory, were required to examine students before entry to Divinity halls in literature, science, philosophy, Greek and Latin. This appeared to be seldom done.

Sage then proceeded to Edinburgh's Divinity hall where once again he encountered Dr Brown. Again he would be disappointed by the calibre and content of the courses. The Theology course was a significant let down, evidenced by a perfunctory delivery of the 'tepidly orthodox' without any enthusiasm or commitment. Delivered by the Principal, Sage states 'I never heard from his lips three consecutive sentences illustrative of any of the doctrines of the Bible; and I can conscientiously say that I never heard him pronounce the name of Jesus Christ in his lectures during my four years attendance at the hall'.[8] According to Sage, Principal Brown was more concerned with pronunciation and composition than the substance of the faith. This constituted considerably less than Sage and his fellow Evangelicals had expected. Sage admits that in six years attendance in Aberdeen and Edinburgh, he was only required to be examined twice. An academic policy of examining students, however, had not yet been formalised at any of the Scottish universities at this time. Attendance was also casual.

---

7 Revd Donald Sage, *Memorabilia Domestica*, 156.
8 Revd Donald Sage, *Memorabilia Domestica*, 168.

Sage's opinion of professors and lecturers was mainly damning. So too his opinion of his fellow students. 'The students who constituted the class presented a dreary and melancholy prospect as the rising generations of ministers.'[9] Most would become ministers with Moderate leanings.

The Evangelical Critique

The general Evangelical verdict on Aberdeen's Divinity hall at the time could be summed up by the comment offered by one Evangelical minister: 'If students entered it with grace in their hearts, they would, if that were possible, lose it before they left.'[10] Sage and his fellow Evangelical students would have arrived with Reformation fire burning in their bellies only to find they were greeted with the cold douche of Moderatism eager to extinguish any flames of enthusiasm.

Sage nonetheless fulfilled the requirements of a Moderate-fashioned course, albeit one thin on content and scant on examination. As a fervent Evangelical, Sage and like-minded others may have regarded university attendance as a necessary evil, a mere marking of time and an inconvenience to be overcome on the way to licensing, ordination and the holy work of saving souls. According to Evangelicals, what the Divinity halls and universities were offering during these years of Moderate dominance fell far short of what was required. For them, the Kirk had spent a century drifting away from its Calvinist foundations and puritan principles in thrall to Enlightenment influences with the introduction of courses, for divinity students, covering botany, mineralogy, chemistry, mathematics and other non religious disciplines. As a result, the Kirk was producing candidates for ordination versed in a breadth of study but lacking the depth of understanding required to fulfil a ministry of word and sacrament worthy of the name.

A broader Evangelical view did exist, one which had high hopes that scientific study would improve the devotional lives of believers by eliciting a strong sense of awe and wonder in the creative work of the Almighty. There was no part of the created order, wrought from nothing, which had not been touched by 'God's almighty hand'. Despite that, many Evangelicals would claim that with such a lack of focus, it was little wonder the Kirk had taken its eye off the ball and, distracted, had become worldly, fat and lazy with its theology wholly unscriptural,

---

9 Revd Donald Sage, *Memorabilia Domestica*, 169.
10 Revd Alexander Auld, *Ministers and Men in the far North*, 19, quoting Revd Alexander Gunn of Watten, Caithness.

uninspired and dead. It had become a Kirk which needed to be rescued from itself and, as Evangelicals saw it, only a return to puritan ways could save it.

If he thought that Prof. Glennie of Aberdeen was a 'cold and bitter Moderate', Sage himself may well be open to the criticism that he himself was a 'cold and bitter' Evangelical, having little good or positive to say about any minister not of a similar persuasion. Sage's comments could be bitingly sharp, offered without a hint of charitable Christian warmth. Faithful, dedicated and conscientious ministers of Moderate persuasion, and there were many, were dismissed out of hand. Sage, along with like-minded colleagues, does exhibit an Evangelical myopia towards any whose views were at variance with his own. He was unforgiving and intolerant and represented the hard edge of Evangelicalism. However, his views found much favour among ministerial colleagues in the north and west.

The Moderate Principal of Edinburgh University, Dr George Baird, also came in for biting criticism. Sage had no good opinion of him either. According to Sage, Baird was 'not a man of talent and who had a very ordinary education'[11] who nonetheless held the twin posts as Principal and minister of Greyfriars Kirk. He had been elevated through his marriage (to the eldest daughter of Lord Provost Thomas Elder) with his wife's own lofty connections acquiring a considerable amount of personal influence. Sage continued caustically that 'money had everything to say and was the passkey to open up all the aspirants to civil, religious or literary distinction. Whoever could command the four-wheel vehicle of money, influence, patronage and moderatism, was sure to be wafted onwards from one step of promotion to the next.'

This characterisation of Baird, however, appears wholly unfair and smacks of naked self-righteousness. As Principal of Edinburgh University, Baird used his considerable talents to enhance the university's credentials by creating new professorships in Conveyancing, Music, Forensic Medicine, Clinical Surgery, Military Surgery and Pathology. He also oversaw an ambitious building programme. Perhaps Sage's silence in this is rooted in his distaste for any expansion of Moderate ways and its refusal to abandon the intellectualism fired by enlightenment principles and from which nothing good would ever proceed! Sage overlooks Baird's untiring work in the service of the Kirk. Little credit is given to him as founder and first convener of the Highlands and Islands Committee of the General Assembly which

---

11 Revd Donald Sage, *Memorabilia Domestica*, 176.

focused particularly on expanding educational opportunities among the poor. Baird travelled extensively throughout the north and west at his own expense and in this he was unstinting.

As one of the architects of the Kirk's Education Committee formed in 1811 and working alongside Revd Dr David Dickson, a leading influential Evangelical, to establish a Gaelic Chapel in Edinburgh, Baird finally received a small grudging compliment from his most vociferous critic. Operating as a busy, high-profile Moderate at the administrative heart of the Kirk would simply be enough to engage Sage's ire. His antipathy towards the Moderate wing at whose feet he laid all that was wrong with the Kirk increased in its wrath and finally came to a head in 1843 when he joined the other 473 ministers who departed the Kirk to form the Free Church. However, his son describes Sage as 'warm-hearted and loveable'. He may have been within the family circle and towards like-minded colleagues, but Sage found himself at odds with the theology and governance of the Established Church so much so that his bitter departure, with others, was inevitable.

The Curious Case of Thomas Chalmers

In the case of St Andrews student Thomas Chalmers, however, ruling Moderates who had set themselves up as the 'party of law and order' were somewhat arbitrary when it came to oversight of courses and applying the rules. Attending just two decades before Dewar and nine years older than Sage, Chalmers applied to be licensed by the Church at the age of 19. The minimum age was 21. Admittedly, Chalmers had had a stellar university career, matriculating at the age of 11 but personal ambition and family poverty drove him to seek a church living, where his expectations embraced high levels of self-indulgence. Strings were pulled, ears were bent, and crucially the leader of the Moderate Party Revd Professor George Hill, was persuaded. The young Revd Thomas Chalmers, after two years as a private tutor and attending lectures at Edinburgh University, took up the charge as minister of Kilmany in rural Fife in 1803.

In the early years of his ministry, Chalmers combined his Kilmany pulpit with lecturing at the university. He taught additional Mathematics and Chemistry courses in premises in the town, beyond the reach of the university authorities and in direct competition with the professors. This put him in a head-long collision course with the Senate, who regarded the young Chalmers as something of an upstart and rebel. At the time, it was still legal for a minister to teach in the university so long as he did not neglect his parish. Nonetheless, in a fit of pique, the university authorities unsuccessfully brought a vexatious case before the Presbytery to censure Chalmers. In 1805, Chalmers produced a pamphlet in response to that of John Playfair, Edinburgh Professor of Natural Philosophy who, opposing the candidacy of a clergyman to the Chair of Mathematics in the University of Edinburgh, asserted he would be unable to adequately fulfil his duties both as an academic and as a minister.

Chalmers' retort was one which he was later to regret. He devoted much of the pamphlet to the argument that a clergyman possessed sufficient leisure to pursue anything that took his fancy, including mathematics because a minister's parochial duties required little time or intellectual effort. He stated, 'After the satisfactory discharge of his parish duties, a minister may enjoy five days in the week of uninterrupted leisure, for the prosecution of any science in which his taste may dispose him to engage'.[12] Chalmers further insisted that no great mental effort was required to produce a sermon on the 'simple and homebred lessons of piety'. Chalmers trailed his coat-tails and cassock as a thoroughly modern Moderate.

This relaxed ministry at Kilmany, while pursuing self-indulgence at the university, made him the archetypal Moderate so loathed by Evangelicals everywhere. However, on a personal front things were to change. Essentially a Moderate in his religious views, Chalmers nursed a vehement antipathy towards Calvinism and, in line with many Moderates of the time, was neglectful of his parish duties. However, during the years 1809 to 1811, after a severe illness, Chalmers underwent something of a *volte-face*, a conversion experience after which he emerged as an enthusiastic Evangelical.

When Chalmers went up to St Andrews in the 1790s, the university was in a state of ruin. Thirty years later, after Kilmany and followed by a vigorous ministry in Glasgow, Chalmers returned in 1823 appointed to the Chair of Moral Philosophy. He may well have lectured Duncan Dewar. There, author Stewart J. Brown states that 'the decline was even more apparent. The buildings had fallen into such disrepair that it resembled, as Chalmers remarked in 1827, more an "old cotton-mill" than a college'.[13] Despite administrative oversight being in the hands of Moderates – the party of law and order – matters regarding

---

12 Revd Thomas Chalmers, *Observation on a Passage in Mr Playfair's Letter*, Cupar-Fife 1805.
13 Stewart J. Brown, *Thomas Chalmers and the Godly Commonwealth*, 163.

the suitability of students and the monitoring of their progress were somewhat lax and casual.

At this time Scottish universities had neither entrance requirements nor entrance exams despite promoting a university education as the passkey for preferment in the professions. Most students matriculated directly from parish schools at the age of 14 or 15, many ill-prepared for college study. Academic standards were in decline: the academic term, a brief five months, allowed professors time to pursue whatever took their fancy. Staff appointments were facilitated by a close network of family, friends and influential connections. Chalmers found the university self-serving and run for the benefit of the academic staff. So much for the university's welfare in the hands of the Moderates, the so-called 'law and order' party.

Chalmers' Reforms

For young men bored with Enlightenment rationalism and Moderate theology, Chalmers' Evangelical idealism offered exciting new possibilities.

Stewart J. Brown, *Thomas Chalmers and the Godly Commonwealth*

In 1814 Chalmers had become the Evangelical minister of the Tron Church sited adjacent to the Tolbooth at Glasgow Cross. Following his social experiment of a 'godly commonwealth' in the neighbouring parish of St John's, he left for St Andrews in 1823. There, he ordered a root and branch clearance of much of the Enlightenment thinking which had infused the curriculum. He ran up against the university authorities, mostly populated by academics with little worldly exposure beyond the university walls.

A major function of the university was to prepare candidates for the ministry and Chalmers endeavoured to infuse the Moderate St Andrews University community with Evangelical fervour. A few weeks after his arrival, as well as reorganising his new department and delivering lectures based on Jesus Christ as the exemplar of 'moral behaviour' (something of a novelty at the time), he began a local Sunday School for children in the poorest districts in the town and set up in effect a parish system of visitation and encouragement, along the same lines as St John's. In a short time his students had embraced the 'godly commonwealth' principle and had begun several Sunday Schools, extending the concept to begin Bible classes for adults. He also was the inspiration behind a vibrant student missionary society.

To the disquiet of Chalmers and his ilk, Moderates had carried over the new theories of rationalism from the classroom into the pulpit. Enlightenment values were enthusiastically embraced by Moderate ministers and now underpinned all their labours. For Evangelicals, however, the Enlightenment had caused Moderates to abandon all Reformation principles. Instead of theological sermons, Moderates had introduced practical, ethical and moral content to speak to, as they viewed it, the needs of society. Moderatism would aver that religion could be supported by reason as well as held by faith.

Not so, Evangelicals would proclaim. To correct the errors of Enlightenment thinking, Chalmers set about designing courses which refocused on Reformation principles and theological certainties. His position recaptured the Calvinist approach: religion was not to be used to enforce morality. Religion was to be used to assert and explain dogma to the faithful which concentrated on three vital aspects of Evangelical theology: election, assurance and salvation. There was also strict adherence to the text of scripture. In essence, Evangelicals regarded Moderatism as pagan. It was this recovery of 'old time religion' and an opportunity to reinvigorate the puritan ideals of the first reformers that galvanised new converts, both to the church but more importantly into the ministry. In this, Chalmers had become the recruiting sergeant, *par excellence*.

Under Chalmers' influence and fame, St Andrews began to attract students of different denominations from throughout Britain and Ireland. However, all was not positive. Chalmers attracted the ire of those academics who believed he had betrayed the Enlightenment's intellectual ideals in favour of a more emotional religion and practical ethics. Chalmers rebuffed the notion that he was 'dumbing down' religion to be simply an affair of the heart. He saw the practical applications extending beyond the lecture theatre. While the university itself embraced Enlightenment ideals, Chalmers believed even the administration of its functions needed to be rescued from its arcane practices which had inhibited student potential and welfare – for example any surpluses in income from student fees were disbursed among the staff, a system unique to St Andrews (Chalmers, to his credit, refused these payments).

With Moderates in control, Sabbatarianism, academic discipline and student supervision began to lose its rigour and holidays like Christmas, New Year and the first Monday of every month crept in. Chalmers' mission, one of many, was to embark on a recovery programme to rehabilitate Reformation values, overhaul university procedures, reinvigorate ministerial values and rescue the Kirk. And it would be the idea of the godly commonwealth which Chalmers believed would kick-start the Kirk's rescue.

Moderate Laxity and the Evangelical Response

Mr Roderick's aim was to foster the growth of Moderatism: he protected and patronised young candidates for the ministry whose characters were unsuitable or exceptionable; by shifts, evasions and the most dishonourable modes of procedure, he defended ministers charged with gross delinquencies, and scrupled not to stop, if possible, all bona fide enquiries into the truth of the charges brought against them.

Donald Sage's verdict on Revd Roderick Mackenzie, fellow Presbyter in Chanonry and minister of Knockbain, in *Memorabilia Domestica*

At the time of Donald Sage's university career, Presbyteries and Synods took little notice by way of supervising courses or students. In error, the Presbytery of Dingwall licensed one John Ross, despite him having been expelled from Edinburgh's Divinity hall in 1812. While working for the *Times* newspaper Ross had heard of a plan to transport Highland labourers to Buenos Aires under a Government scheme. A Church of Scotland clergyman was to be appointed as superintendent, so with the unlawful certification provided by the Presbytery, Ross secured the post at a payment of £300, a sum more than double the average annual stipend of a Highland parish minister and commensurate with a large city charge or university appointment.

For Moderates, regulations appeared to be arbitrarily enforced often by personal whim, or were only applied as rigorously as its administration saw fit. George Urquhart from Rogart had been promised his father's pulpit on his death which occurred while he and Donald Sage were still students. On enquiring why Urquhart was no longer attending classes, Sage was informed that the Rogart student had been removed during his first term to be licensed by the Presbytery, the clear inference being that as the pulpit was in the gift of the landowner it was also in the landowner's interest not to keep the charge vacant until Urquhart had completed his course but to have it filled immediately.

It seemed there was little the Presbytery could do about it. Landowners acted with impunity while Presbyteries often found themselves powerless in the face of the over-riding and overarching authority of both universities and Tory landowners when it came to church livings. It may be construed that the combined interests and power of these two institutions, with complicit or unwitting Presbyteries, had a stranglehold on how and when pulpits were filled and by whom. Some Highland pulpits, were known to remain unfilled for years, despite the best efforts of Presbyteries, because of the intransigence and obstructiveness of landowners. Nor was this the first or the last time where sons such as George Urquhart succeeded fathers into pulpits, all in the gift and convenience of the landowner and often in the face of local congregational opposition. Continuity through preferment and nepotism, as far as the landed classes were concerned, kept things running smoothly. It was likely that a son would be cast in the same pliable form as his malleable father. In the case of the church in Rosemarkie, the Woods family were parish ministers for 140 years, one of the longest family successions in the Church. The Presbytery had little say in the matter, merely rubber-stamping the succession of appointments.

Further, the delineation of parishes followed in the main the boundaries of the Highland estates and were organised for the convenience of the proprietor of the 'big house', not the needs of church and congregation. Neighbouring landowners, with an eye on the money, were not averse to linking congregations across parish boundaries thus sharing the savings of eliminating a stipend. The Mackays and Staffords more than once entered just such a cosy and profitable arrangement on their Sutherland lands. The new parish of Knockbain, situated on the Black Isle, was established in 1762, a result of just such a rearrangement of the former parishes of Suttie, Killearnan and Kilmuir Wester. In another case, James Dingwall was inducted to the charge of Farr in Ross-shire. The Moderate-led Presbytery of Tongue blatantly ignored the set of questions specifically pertaining to 'undue influence' in procuring the position.

It appeared to be a stitch-up. Dingwall's family were themselves from the landed classes, very much 'establishment' figures and Moderates through and through. Against the wishes of the congregation Dingwall was placed there under a cosy arrangement among the parties concerned. His ministry lasted 34 years. He was regarded as a secular character. Donald Sage describes him as disliked by his congregation and 'more interested in lifting his stipend than in the faithful discharge of his divine duties.'[14]

---

14 Revd Donald Sage, *Memorabilia Domestica*, 181.

Essay 6: 'Education, Salvation and Damnation'

Many Evangelicals suspected some Moderate ministers had been generously rewarded for siding with landowners during the Clearances. Such men appeared to be living in relative comfort while their parishioners had been harshly dealt with, confirming the view that Moderates had become mere 'stipend lifters', more interested in maintaining an unhealthy but profitable alliance with Tory landowners and making money rather than saving souls.

Kirks, manses and glebes were mostly situated in low ground and the clergy held their pasturage in common with the tenantry. This arrangement was established by law and usage and no factor or proprietor had powers to alter without mutual consent. One notable historian claimed that

> had the ministers maintained those rights, they would have placed in many cases, an effectual bar to the oppressive proceedings of the factors... but anxious to please the 'powers that be' and no less anxious to drive advantageous bargains with them, these reverend gentlemen found means to get their lines laid 'in pleasant places' and to secure good and convenient portions of the pasture lands enclosed for themselves. Many of the small tenants were removed purely to satisfy them in these arrangements.[15]

The Moderate section of the church appeared to tolerate indiscipline among its own clergy, exhibited and promoted theological heresies, and organised its universities and the welfare of its students around its own Moderate agenda. It was a Kirk that had lost all sense of holy purpose. Evangelicals occupying only a few Highland parishes concluded that the Kirk needed fundamental change and a complete rehabilitation of the foundational principles of doctrine, worship and discipline. They laid the blame for this firmly upon a number of factors: the Enlightenment-infused curricula of the universities and especially in the Divinity halls; a collapse of piety within the family hindered by a lack of educational opportunity; and crucially for the Highlands and Islands, an anti-Gaelic bias.

Despite the Moderate grip on education for the ministry, graduates from an Evangelical background mainly from the north and west and Gaelic-speaking, would have completed their course of studies more firmly convinced of the righteousness of their conviction. If a change in theological direction was not possible within the Divinity halls, it would most certainly begin in pulpits and classrooms populated by

---

15 Alexander MacKenzie, *History of the Highland Clearances*, 37.

a fresh breed of enthused and committed Evangelicals determined to recover the lost soul of the Kirk.

Competing Theories on Education and the Ordering of Society

The kirk, or an odd room, barn or stable frequently did duty as a school, and tumbling roofs, walls or entire buildings were not uncommon. Alike for master and pupil everything militated against comfort, health and success and the wonder is that Scotsmen did somehow contrive to be educated.

Rait and Pryde, *Scotland*

As the Church advanced through the middle and late years of the 18th century it was plain that the education of the Scottish nation, as a key Reformation principle, was to become a battle between the two competing philosophies held by either side in the Kirk. The current thinking of the time supported the establishment view that education was the key which led to benevolent government and neutralised any threat of insurgency. The Government held up the French Revolution as an example of the political consequences of an uneducated society. The argument was further advanced that despotism, ignorance, infidelity, and Roman Catholicism were all closely associated. The threat of a resurgent Catholicism fell like a shadow across much of Highland Presbyterianism.

Holding the patronage of one-third of Scottish Kirks gave both Whig and Tory landowners an expectation of political stability and social tranquillity. There was a reliance on both the Scottish nobility and the Church to maintain law and order, to support the Crown and uphold the Union. London was a long way from the Highlands and Islands of Scotland and so the engines of government could reasonably presume that Kirk ministers together with the ruling classes would act in the national interest. They operated as *de facto* government agents for law and order.

As a consequence of the Presbyterian scheme of discipline, Kirk Sessions handled many matters besides religion and often acted as a social court. Supervision of morals was high on Kirk Sessions' agendas. At the end of the 18th and beginning of the 19th centuries, the Church waged a losing war against sex outwith marriage and the majority of cases brought before it for judgement related to sexual matters. Ministers and Sessions were also legally responsible for poor relief and charitable support. In the north and west especially, the rules which Sessions enforced were designed to maintain social and economic order in a patriarchal land-owning society rather than to bring in an ideal Christian order.

A system based on the courts of the Church implied a basic level of administrative work and its organisation equipped them to act as a civil service. This included elders to superintend behaviour, deacons to look after parish funds and beadles to report. In the burghs Kirk Sessions shared the work of appointing teachers and regulating salaries and fees but a less formal arrangement for the appointment of teachers was in place in rural districts. Since the beginning of the 18th century the Kirk was in general charge of the country's education and was positioned to use it as a weapon of social control. Further, since the mid-18th century and the collapse of the clan system, the new landowners had used their autocratic powers as a means of social engineering.

The Clearances were the prime example of this. As a result, across the north and west, among those who might have been thought of as the rebellious and disaffected there were unexpected degrees of compliance and deference; those who had been cleared to make way for industrial-sized sheep-runs; and congregations who had no say in the appointment of ministers selected by heritors. Parliament looked to the Church, together with local Magistrates, to ensure that smooth ordering of society. Social control and social engineering were to become close bed-fellows.

In theory the smooth ordering of society would be achieved in two ways: first, by establishing schools thus increasing educational provision; and secondly, by confirming the rights of civil courts to hand down fines and punishments. Kirk Sessions were empowered to deal with more minor infractions and misdemeanours. Landowners wielded power, prestige and patronage and had the support of the Moderate Party. Operating with impunity, landowners were secure in the knowledge that the laws favoured the upper classes especially in the matter of the Clearances. These laws were blunt instruments but provided mainly Tory landowners with the economic levers to maximise profits and advance the forces of capitalism.

However, by the middle of the 19th century over fifty percent of Highland estates had changed ownership. Many estates, not as viable as once thought, were now in the hands of administrators, showing that the potential for good economic returns would not always be guaranteed. The tempting bright lights of London and Edinburgh proved financially ruinous for not a few estate owners.

As far as the Moderate Party was concerned, embracing law and order, supporting government and knowing one's place almost guaranteed being handed the keys of the kingdom. That was the Moderates' route-map to salvation. Although the Government used the Kirk as a means to an end, Moderates within Scotland had their own agenda, viewing education as an end in itself, practically equating education with salvation because, or so the argument was advanced, virtue and duty were learned responses.

However, Evangelicals had a different perspective viewing education as only a means to an end. It was one of a number of key components to deepen faith and leaven society with God-fearing individuals. Education therefore became an essential method of encouraging sanctification among believers and conversion among unbelievers. Prayer especially in groups nurtured the emotional responses essential to spiritual growth. How best to reach the illiterate, the apathetic and uncommitted became the focus of much of the attention of both wings of the Kirk, although Evangelicals thought that Moderate efforts in this regard were mere window-dressing. Also, the challenge remained of how to reach into the Gaelic-speaking heartlands of the north and west effectively, regions which still harboured pockets of superstitious folk-religion and a latent Catholicism. Again, Evangelicals believed that Moderates were ill-equipped to address the cultural, linguistic and religious challenges across the north and west.

In his PhD thesis, David Alan Currie states that the basic need was to overcome illiteracy so that everyone could read the Bible. 'Evangelicals held that the message of the Bible served as the primary means for conversion and sanctification, insisting upon Bible reading as an essential part of individual, family and congregational piety.'[16] Education was an essential precursor to spiritual awakenings and revivals, as evidenced by those especially in Lewis and Ross-shire and Caithness. Evangelicals held strong anti-Catholic sentiments contributing to their commitment to education. They viewed education and Roman Catholicism as mutually exclusive, arguing that Catholicism's claims would lead inexorably to an intellectual scepticism among the educated. They simply would not countenance its superstitions. Evangelicals viewed Roman Catholicism as inherently intolerant, its spread therefore a direct threat to Protestantism in general and to Evangelicalism in particular.

---

16 David Alan Currie, PhD thesis 1991, *The Growth of Evangelicalism in the Church of Scotland 1793 - 1843*, 287.

Schooling in the Highlands

> *Of what [Highlanders] had before the late conquest of their country, there remains only their language and their poverty. Their language is attacked on every side. Schools are erected, in which only English is taught, and there were lately some who thought it reasonable to refuse them a version of the holy scriptures, that they might have no monument of their mother-tongue.*
>
> Dr Johnson, *A Journey to the Western Isles of Scotland*

By a succession of Parliamentary Acts, culminating in 1696, the provision to supply a school and a salaried schoolmaster fell to landowners. However, across the north and west especially, coverage of schools was by no means uniform and the quality of teaching patchy. This was mainly because heritors often disregarded their legal obligations in this matter and were generally obstructive to or reluctant to carry out their responsibilities.

Aware of the difficulties, in 1707 the General Assembly established a 'Committee for the Propagation of Christian Knowledge' with the proposal that education provision should come under the purview of the Kirk and funds for such would be ingathered through a charitable trust. The Kirk had one eye on evangelising the Highlands and Islands and the other eye on preserving Presbyterianism against any possibility of a Catholic resurgence.

Out of the 1707 committee came the formation two years later of the 'Society in Scotland for Propagating Christian Knowledge' (SSPCK). Its stated policy was to 'To Erect and Maintain Schools, to Teach to Read, especially the Holy Scriptures, and other good and pious books; As also to Teach Writing, Arithmetick, and such like Degrees of Knowledge in the Highlands, Islands and remote Corners of Scotland.'[17] In an academic paper, Jamie Kelly states 'At the heart of this was a fundamental belief in the improvability of Scotland's Gaels provided that they were equipped with the right tools. It was the ordinary Gael's lack of exposure to religious instruction and literary education that had prevented their effective integration into the Scottish kingdom and, subsequently, the British polity.'[18] Further, the absence of a pro-active, corrective Church institution in the lives

---

17 Founding Principles of SSPCK, National Records of Scotland GD95/1/1, 3rd Nov. 1709 – 6th Mar. 1718.

18 Jamie J. Kelly, *The Mission at Home: The Origins and Development of the Society in Scotland for Propagating Christian Knowledge, 1709-1767*, 8.

of Scotland's Gaels rendered the Highlander susceptible to erroneous religious doctrine. 'Improving' the Gael would have two effects: it would lead to the further domestication of the Highlands and it would ensure the docility of the Highlander. Education was therefore key to making these happen.

The establishing of the SSPCK sought to reinforce the claims of the gospel while making law-abiding citizens out of the population. The society achieved this by managing schools albeit with a political bias of supporting the Hanoverian claim as well as a religious imperative of establishing and strengthening the primacy of maintaining a robust Presbyterian presence. So they taught the Bible and the catechism of the Church of Scotland, both in English. With its Evangelical bias, the SSPCK sought to use its influence to ensure that schoolmasters and teachers modelled and promoted a God-fearing piety. Although the schoolmaster had to be competent, good morals and a strong faith were often considered to be of more worth than any educational qualification.

However, linguistic, cultural and geographical barriers limited the SSPCK's effectiveness. For example, many Gaelic-speakers would not or could not learn to read in English, especially the numerous adult illiterates whose age placed them outside the SSPCK's purview. Cultural resistance to 'all things English' was deeply entrenched in the soul of the Gael, while remoteness of many of the glens and townships physically put them beyond the reach of the society.

Awareness of the SSPCK's limited effectiveness prompted Evangelicals to establish The Gaelic Charity School movement, designed to meet the needs of a near-destitute population and the prerequisite of sustaining a pool of divinity students who would form the base for Gaelic-speaking ministers of the future. The Gaelic Schools' Society vehemently opposed the 'English only' policy of the SSPCK, but acknowledging the direction of travel, by 1767 the SSPCK had produced 10,000 printed copies of a New Testament designed with facing pages of Gaelic and English texts for both languages to be read alongside one another. A Gaelic Old Testament was published in four parts between 1783 and 1801 but it was not until 1828 that the entire bible could be purchased at a cost within reach of many Gaelic-speaking households. There was a Gaelic Psalter available, but set to a ballad metre which worked for English and not Gaelic.[19]

---

19 Jock Stein, *Temple and Tartan*, 172-3.

100 years on from the establishment of the SSPCK and, from its founding principles drawn up in 1811 The Edinburgh Gaelic School Society notes that, 'Although the [SSPCK] maintains 290 schools at which nearly 16,000 young people are taught, it is a melancholy fact that many parts of the Highlands and Islands continue in a state of great ignorance.'[20] There were still areas, especially on the islands, where the impact of SSPCK effort was minimal and for those pro-Gaelic lobbyists the great English language experiment in the north and west among native Gaelic speakers was a continuing failure.

At the time it was estimated that there was a population of 400,000 across the north and west, of whom it was reckoned that 300,000 were unable to read in any language, and the greater number of these could only read Gaelic, knowing little or nothing of the English tongue. Through the Edinburgh Gaelic School Society and for the first time, children were taught their own language in schools specifically established for the purpose. The Glasgow Society quickly followed in 1812 and the Inverness Society in 1818. They attempted to avoid absenteeism and maximise numbers attending by timing the school year to the farming year. English, as a foreign language, had yet been an unwelcome imposition for many resistant to change and, some would say, 'progress', and there was strong recognition too of the ethnic and social dissonance between two competing cultures.

The Gaelic Schools deepened the feelings in the Gael that Gaelic was the spiritual medium and the language of worship and salvation. This had been achieved through teaching the scriptures and nothing else in their own language. For many, this was nothing short of the complete rehabilitation and vindication of the two principles underpinning Highland cultural life: language and religion.

The popularity of the Gaelic Schools was one sign of the growing acceptance of Evangelicalism within the Kirk which reached a peak in the 1830s. Its core policy of teaching in Gaelic won many parts of the Highlands over to Evangelical Presbyterianism, a move from which the Moderate wing never recovered. By resisting the cultural imperatives of the language and being unable to counter the strengthening Evangelical grip north and west the Moderates braced themselves to lose much of their remaining influence in the Highlands and Islands.

---

20 Revd Murdo Macaulay, *Aspects of the Religious History of Lewis*, 123.

Threats to Gaelic

Other cultural forces were at work, placing the rescue, recovery and rehabilitation of the Gaelic language under threat. Emigration, both forced and voluntary to the Americas principally, and to the industrial south reduced the size of the pool which required Gaelic as a first language. Opportunities in employment south of the Highland line together with business, trade and commerce required a literate workforce versed in the prevailing language of the day. Learning English was becoming a more attractive and profitable proposition while the Gaelic language was seen as a drag on progress.

By the New Statistical Accounts, some ministers were predicting the obliteration of the Gaelic language entirely. Revd Angus Kennedy, minister of the Parish of Dornoch, reported in 1834:

> The predilection for the Gaelic language is, however, still manifest, from the well known facts, that the common people prefer to use it in their ordinary intercourse, and that larger congregations attend public worship during the Gaelic services than during the English. Nevertheless, the English is making rapid encroachments on our ancient language; and it is not improbable that, in the course of sixty or seventy years, the latter may be extinct.[21]

In the same Statistical Return, Revd Charles Gordon, minister of the Parish of Assynt Presbytery of Dornoch, foresaw the time when the Gaelic School Society will have actually aided and abetted the demise of the Gaelic language:

> The Gaelic language is still universal in Assynt, and the only medium of religious instruction. The English language, however, is making slow but sure progress. The youth of the parish are ambitious of acquiring it, being sensible that the want of it proves a great bar to their advancement in life. It is likely, nevertheless, that Assynt is one of the very last districts in which the Gaelic language shall cease to be the language of the people. It is remarkable that the Gaelic School Society will probably prove the means, at a remote period, of the expulsion of the Gaelic language from the Highlands. The teachers employed by that useful society, to whom we owe much, taught the young to read the Scriptures in their native tongue. This implanted a

---

21 *The Statistical Accounts of Scotland 1845: Dornoch, County of Sutherland*, vol. XV, 7.

desire to acquire knowledge on other subjects, which induced them to have recourse to the English language as the medium of communication.[22]

Reporting in 1840, The Revd George Mackay, minister of the Parish of Clyne Presbytery of Dornoch supported that view thus 'The language usually spoken among the labouring classes is Gaelic; but, owing to the more general intercourse with the south country, and the increase of education, it has certainly lost ground since the date of the former report, and, as most of the young people now attend school and receive at least the rudiments of education, it bids fair to be altogether unknown at no very distant period'.[23]

Others, it appears, cannot wait for its demise entirely. Revd John McArthur, minister of United Parish of Kilcalmonell and Kilberry Presbytery of Kintyre states (as in a previous essay), 'The Gaelic is the vernacular language of the parishioners, but the English is displacing it, and the sooner it overmasters it the better'.[24] There were those, like McArthur, who continued to view Gaelic as a hindrance to the advances of industry, commerce and the good of society in general where, it was argued, prosperity and well-being would be gained solely within the sphere of strengthening relationships both with Scotland's own burgeoning heartland and with its southern English neighbour. The continued use of Gaelic was still seen by Moderates as a divisive and threatening element to the very Union itself. Gaels were increasingly regarded as stubborn, non-compliant and anti-integrationist.

By the time of the compiling of the Old Statistical Account of 1798, there had already completed 40 of the 100 or so years of the Clearances which devastated the Highlands and Islands. A deep sense of betrayal weighed heavily upon the soul of the Gael. Highland regiments had offered 30,000 men to fight in America, Germany and India, all in the cause of supporting the British Empire 'ere the 18th century had run its course'.[25] John MacMillan, minister serving the Ullapool and Garve areas, addressed a public meeting in 1880, at the height of the crofters'

---

22 *The Statistical Accounts of Scotland 1845: Assynt, County of Sutherland*, vol. XV, 112.
23 *The Statistical Accounts of Scotland 1845: Clyne, County of Sutherland*, vol. XV, 156.
24 *The Statistical Accounts of Scotland 1845: Kilcalmonell and Kilberry, County of Argyll*, vol. VII, 410.
25 Iain Fraser Grigor, *Mightier than a Lord*, 38.

war, offering a perceptive analysis of the mechanics of Highland landlordism but focusing on the early decades of the Clearances and stated,

> While abroad over the earth, and always first in assault and last in retreat, their lowly homes in faraway glens were being dragged down, and the wail of women and the cry of children went out . . . to convert the Highland glens into vast wastes untenanted by human beings – such was the work of laws formed in a cruel mockery of names by the Commons of England.[26]

It was little wonder that the Gael was regarded as 'stubborn', 'non-compliant' and 'anti-integrationist' by his English neighbour.

While in the north and west Gaelic culture was coming under a rising threat from the spread of the English language, there were yet a number of Gaelic-speaking Evangelical ministers maintaining a strong grip on congregations and still exerting great influence upon the people of their parishes. Around 1821, a pro-active group of five leading Evangelical ministers wholly resistant to further Anglicised advances and ever more willing to defend Gaelic's primacy formed the 'Association at Inverness for Aiding the Education of Pious Young Men for the Ministry', convinced that Highland parishes would be better served by native Gaelic-speaking ministers, missionaries, catechists and school-teachers.

From the end of the 18th century a number of factors had combined to weaken the Kirk's authority and influence with regard to school education but mainly Presbyteries' continuing failure to oversee and report on schools within their bounds and the very limited powers Presbyteries had to support and encourage a growing educational sector. The Old Statistical Accounts depict an education system not so much deplete in numbers of schools but a system deteriorating as a result of poor salaries and qualifications of schoolmasters. The statistical return for the small parish of Kiltearn (Ross and Cromarty) for example reveals some 1,616 inhabitants boasting a parish school teaching Latin, French, geography, geometry, book-keeping and mathematics to some 60 to 80 children.[27] By contrast, the parish minister of Forbes and Kearn in Aberdeenshire returns the information that 'there has never been any legal school in this district; only some of the ministers

---

26 Iain Fraser Grigor, *Mightier than a Lord*, 38.

27 *The Statistical Accounts of Scotland 1791: Kiltearn, County of Ross and Cromarty*, vol. I, 285.

kept a school themselves, or a boy for educating their own children, and admitted the children in the neighbourhood to partake of the benefit.[28] Education provision was far from uniform or universal.

Mixed reports from the Statistical Accounts revealed widespread inadequate schooling across the Highlands and a confused and confusing picture of educational provision across the country in general. This prompted the General Assembly in 1824 to form its own board now commonly called the Assembly Education Committee, as a somewhat negative reaction by Moderates who felt under increasing threat from the rise in numbers of Evangelicals. Its remit was to plant schools to supplement parochial schools in areas where additional provision was most needed, particularly in the Highlands and Islands. In fulfilment of this aim the committee set itself to address four main issues: the need for more schools; the need to train schoolmasters and improve their conditions of service; the need to promote and develop the regular examination of schools by presbyteries and parish ministers; and the need to safeguard the place of religious instruction, or perhaps more accurately, instruction in Protestant doctrine, in the school curriculum. The formation of the Assembly's Education Board gave some structure and formality, and reinforcement to the 1802 Schoolmasters' Act which had set a minimum salary range of between £16. 13s 4d and £22. 4s 6d and obliged heritors to provide this salary together with reasonable accommodation.

Literacy

> *The heart-breaking handicaps under which the old-time dominie worked have often been described. His statutory salary varied between 100 merks – about £5 11s sterling – and 200 merks – about £11 2s. The stipend was not always forthcoming.*
>
> Rait and Pryde, *Scotland*

The state of religion in the north and west had frequently exercised those ministers and elders attending General Assemblies, who on occasions had turned their attention specifically to the state of education. It fell to Principal Baird of Edinburgh University to deliver an annual report on the subject. His 1818 report deplored the poor levels of education in the north and west where evidence suggested that up to three-quarters of the population were illiterate with little

---

28 *The Statistical Accounts of Scotland 1794: Forbes and Kearn, County of Aberdeenshire*, vol. XI, 196.

or no exposure to the Protestant religion. Despite the best efforts of a century of SSPCK's work and the endeavours of parochial schools, levels of illiteracy remained stubbornly high until around the years 1819 and 1820. Meanwhile, pro-active Evangelicals in the north and west were lobbying landowners and heritors to convince them of the need to hire pious and godly schoolmasters, efficient at supplementing traditional catechetical teaching supplied by the minister. These actions pre-dated Baird's new Assembly Committee by some years as Baird was able to report in 1824 that heritors in the Highlands and Islands appeared more willing than in the past to support the Kirk's efforts in educational provision. Catechising was increasingly integrated into the school curriculum.

Some Moderate traditionalists within the Kirk objected to this development, citing that proper religious instruction should be done within the home with responsibility lying in the first place with the individual head of the house. The Evangelicals countered this by arguing that the decline of family worship, personal piety and pastoral visitation, laid at the very feet of these Moderate objectors, absolutely necessitated catechising within the schools all the more as an important bulwark against widespread religious ignorance. In April 1824, however, some six years after his 1818 report, Principal Baird reported to a meeting of Edinburgh Presbytery on literacy numbers, which would become the basis of his overture to that year's General Assembly bringing about the new Education Committee. Baird stated he had in his possession the results of an extensive survey (a Parliamentary enquiry conducted by Henry Brougham) which indicated 'the parishes of Gairloch, Portree, Lochcarron, the Small Isles, South and North Uist, Barra, Harris etc, etc, in the Synod of Glenelg... contained a population of about 70,000, of whom nearly 50,000 could not read'. He further concluded that what had been said of Glenelg 'might be applied to the Synods of Argyll, Caithness, etc'.

Dr Baird's report called for the establishment of 'ambulatory schools' based on an English model by which 'more good had been done in six months than in a Gaelic school in six years', and the 'sending of catechists among the people'. These were to be 'plain Christian men' but were not to be recruited from the Gaelic societies, those of Glasgow and Paisley 'he would have nothing to do with'. Baird may have had first-hand experience of individuals from these two areas, some of whom he regarded as Gaelic-speaking agitators keen to promote the pre-eminence of their language and willing to overstep fixed remits.

Ardgour

© Richard Webb (cc-by-sa/2.0) and licensed for reuse under this Creative Commons Licence

Berneray

© Stephen Darlington (link: https://commons.wikimedia.org/wiki/Fi

BERRIEDALE

© Sandy Gemmill (cc-by-sa/2.0) and licensed for reuse under this Creative Commons Licence

CROICK

Photo by Karen Ross Rae

[LEFT] CHURCH AT RISABUS OR THE OA, ISLAY
Photo by John Lumsden

Duror

Photos on this page by John L. Millar

Iona Church

Keiss

© Bill Henderson (cc-by-sa/2.0) and licensed for reuse under this Creative Commons Licence

Kinlochspelvie

© Richard Dorrell (cc-by-sa/2.0) and licensed for reuse under this Creative Commons Licence

NEW LANARK SCHOOLHOUSE
© Rob Farrow (cc-by-sa/2.0) and licensed for reuse under this Creative Commons Licence

POOLEWE
© Roger McLachlan (cc-by-sa/2.0) and licensed for reuse under this Creative Commons Licence

PORTNAHAVEN
© Gordon Hatton (cc-by-sa/2.0) and licensed for reuse under this Creative Commons Licence

QUARFF
© Chris Downer (cc-by-sa/2.0) and licensed for reuse under this Creative Commons Licence

STANLEY
© Maigheach-gheal (cc-by-sa/2.0) and licensed for reuse under this Creative Commons Licence

STENSCHOLL
© John Allan (cc-by-sa/2.0) and licensed for reuse under this Creative Commons Licence

STOER

© Anne Burgess (cc-by-sa/2.0) and licensed for reuse under this Creative Commons Licence

STRATHCONON

© Gordon Brown (cc-by-sa/2.0) and licensed for reuse under this Creative Commons Licence

STRONTIAN

© Russell Wills (cc-by-sa/2.0) and licensed for reuse under this Creative Commons Licence

TRUMISGARRY

© Anne Burgess (cc-by-sa/2.0) and licensed for reuse under this Creative Commons Licence

ULLAPOOL

© Mike Pennington (cc-by-sa/2.0) and licensed for reuse under this Creative Commons Licence

ULVA

© Rude Health (cc-by-sa/2.0) and licensed for reuse under this Creative Commons Licence

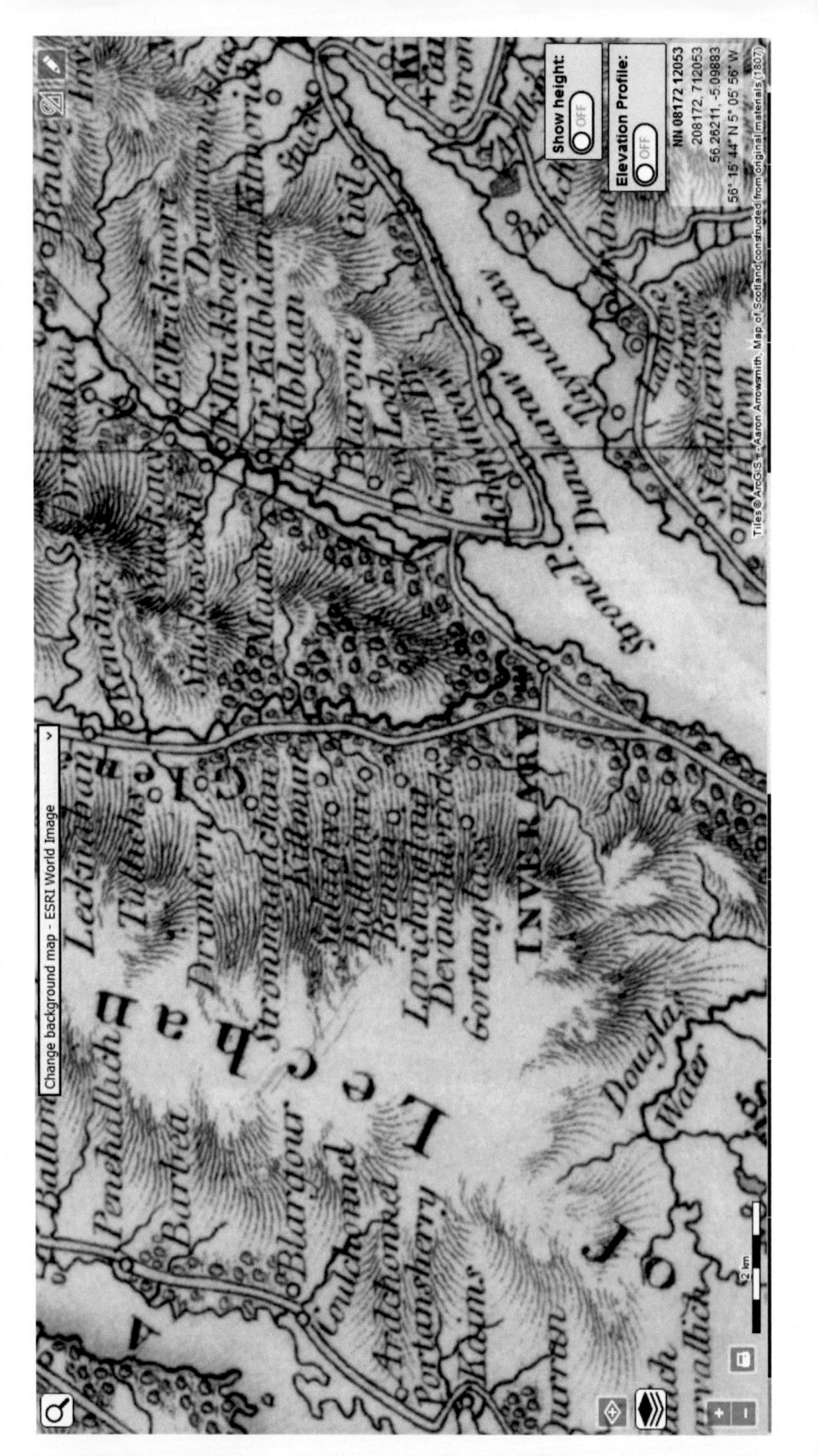

MAP 1　INVERARY, ARGYLE　　Before and after the Clearances, 1807 & 1856

Change background map - ESRI World Image
Show parish details?
Malt Land
Fort
Leacann Mhor
Sgornach Ruadh
Stealltaire Ban Loch
Greag Dhubh
Inveraray Castle
Loch Shira
Strone Point
Pier
INVERARAY
Ferry
Ard
Newtown Bay
An Oitir
Manse
Coille Bhraghad
Loch Righeachan
Buachaille
1060
Town Common
Auchnabreac
Sgeir Bruachaig
Show height:
OFF
Elevation Profile:
OFF
NN 09055 07825
209055, 707825
56.22454, -5.08154
56° 13' 29" N 5° 04' 54" W
Tiles © ArcGIS
500 m

Map 2　Rosskeen, Ross & Cromarty　　Before and after the Clearances, 1807 & 1856

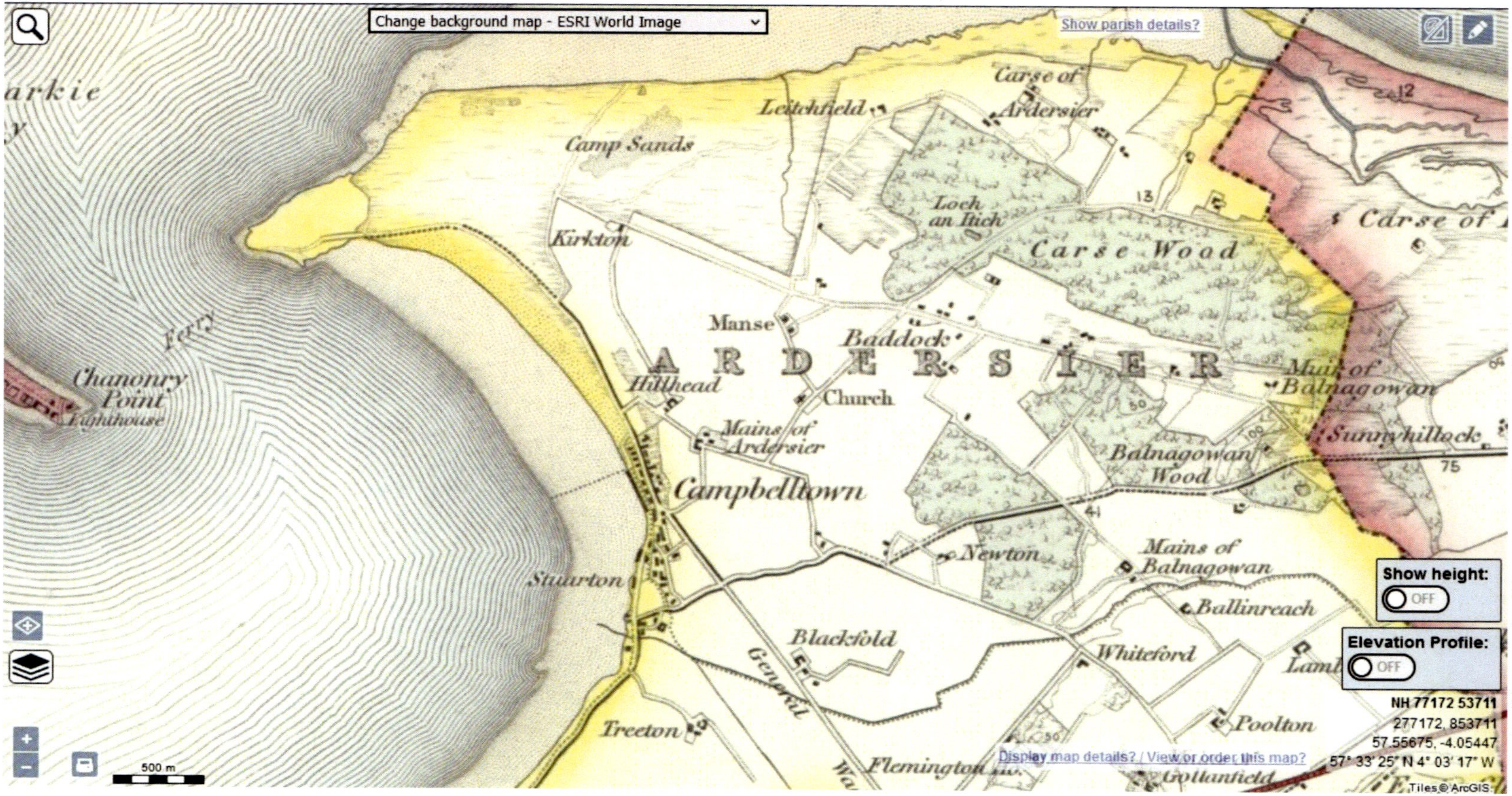

Change background map - ESRI World Image
Show parish details?
Carse of Ardersier
Leitchfield
Camp Sands
Loch an Ilich
Carse Wood
Carse of
Kirkton
Manse
Baddock
ARDERSIER
Muir of Balnagowan
Ferry
Chanonry Point
Lighthouse
Hillhead
Church
Mains of Ardersier
Sunnyhillock
Balnagowan Wood
Campbelltown
Mains of Balnagowan
Newton
Stuarton
Ballinreach
Blackfold
Whiteford
General
Treeton
Poolton
Flemington
Show height:
OFF
Elevation Profile:
OFF
NH 77172 53711
277172, 853711
57.55675, -4.05447
57° 33' 25" N 4° 03' 17" W
Display map details? / View or order this map?
500 m
Tiles © ArcGIS

MAP 3   APPLECROSS, ROSS & CROMARTY   BEFORE AND AFTER THE CLEARANCES, 1807 & 1856

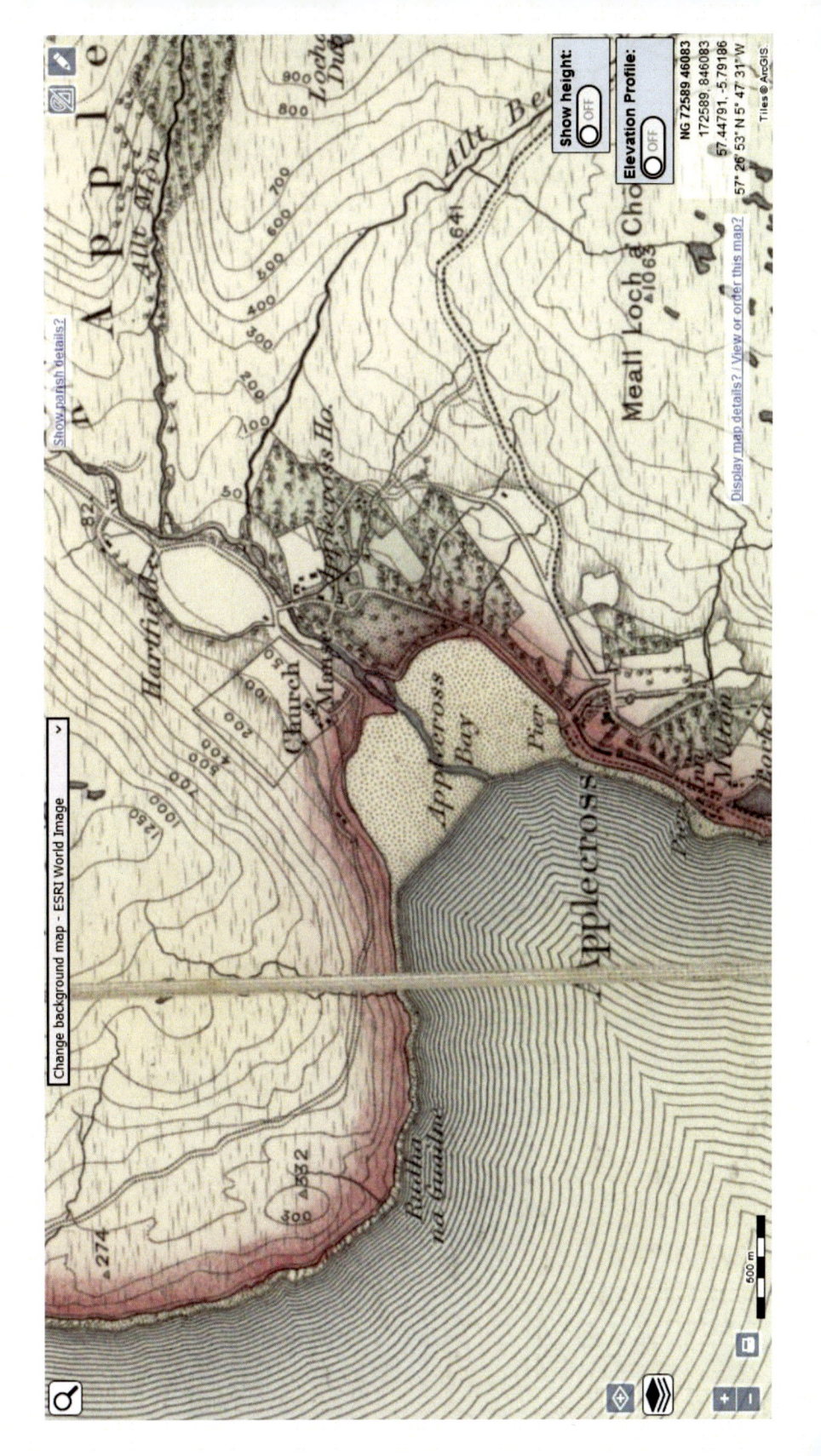

Applecross Bay
Applecross
Church
Hartfield
Pier
Rudha na Guailne
Allt Mòr
Allt Beag
Loch Dubh
Meall Loch a' Chà...

Show height: OFF
Elevation Profile: OFF

NG 72589 46083
172589, 846083
57.44791, -5.79186
57° 26' 53" N 5° 47' 31" W

Change background map - ESRI World Image
Show parish details?
Display map details? | View or order this map?
Tiles © ArcGIS.

500 m

MAP 4 STRATH, SKYE,   BEFORE AND AFTER THE CLEARANCES, 1807 & 1856

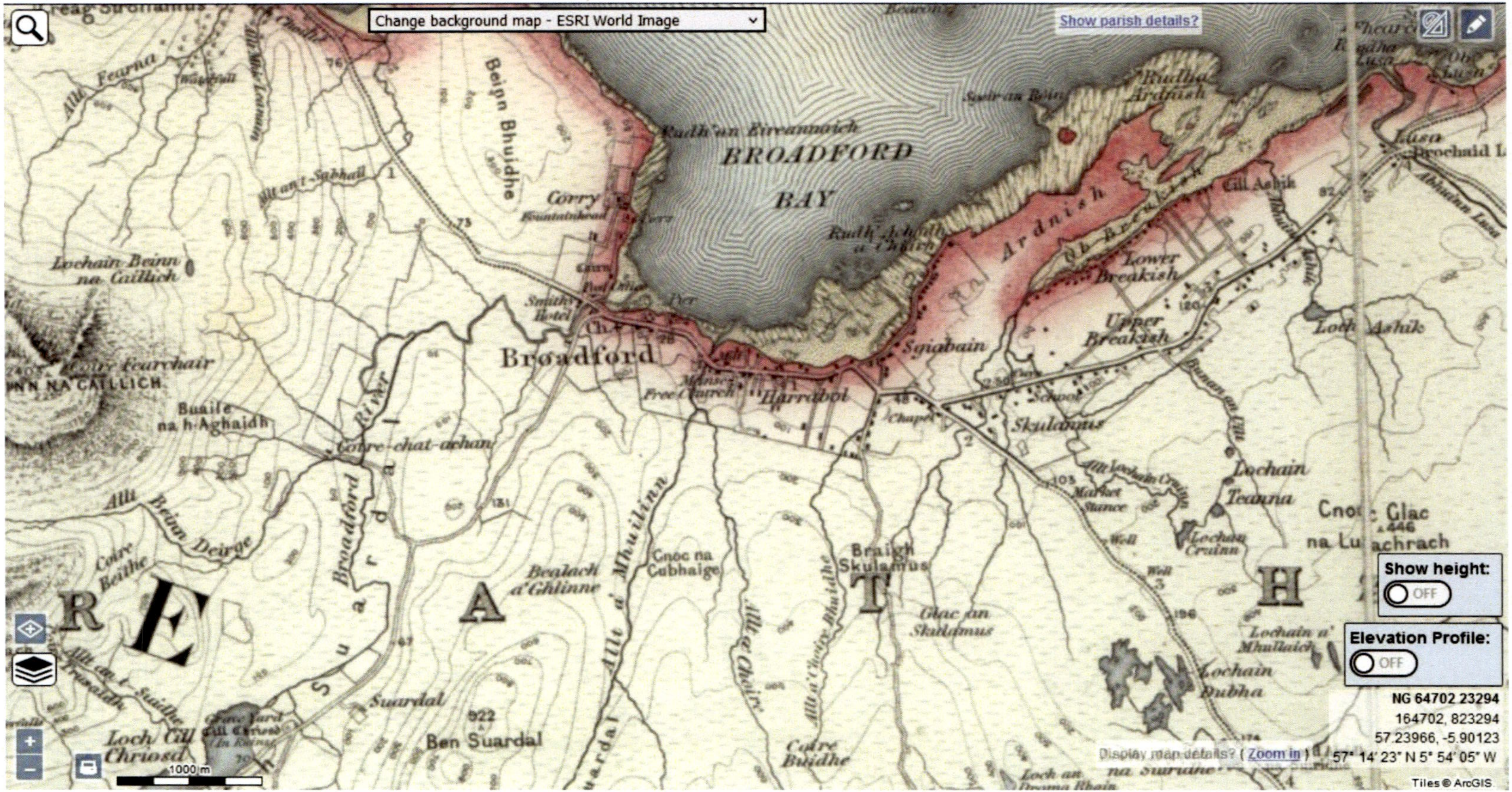
Change background map - ESRI World Image
Show parish details?
BROADFORD BAY
Broadford
Beinn Bhuidhe
Corry
Lower Breakish
Upper Breakish
Skulamus
Harrabol
Free Church
Sgiabain
Ardnish
Loch Ashik
Lochain Beinn na Cailliche
Buaile na h-Aghaidh
Coire-chat-achan
Broadford River
Allt Beinn Deirge
Cnoc na Cubhaige
Bealach a'Ghlinne
Allt a' Mhuilinn
Braigh Skulamus
Glac an Skulamus
Allt a' Choire
Coire Buidhe
Ben Suardal
Suardal
Loch Cill Chriosd
Lochain Teanna
Lochain Dubha
Cnoc Glac na Luachrach
Market Stance
Show height:
OFF
Elevation Profile:
OFF
NG 64702 23294
164702, 823294
57.23966, -5.90123
57° 14' 23" N 5° 54' 05" W
Display map details? (Zoom in)
1000 m
Tiles © ArcGIS

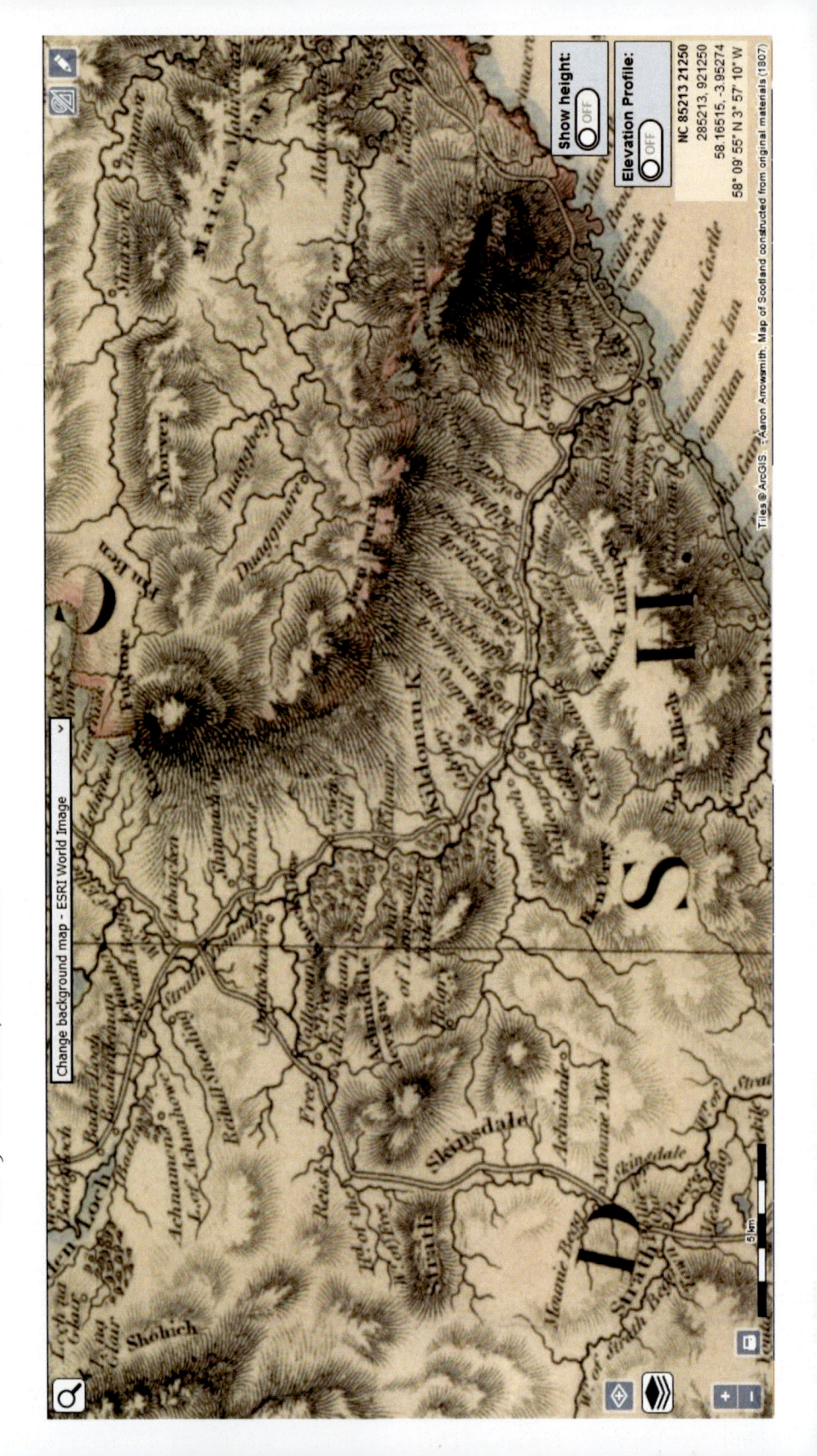

MAP 5 KILDONAN, SUTHERLAND   BEFORE AND AFTER THE CLEARANCES, 1807 & 1856

ALL MAPS: RE-USE © NLS, ARROWSMITH MAPS AND OS.

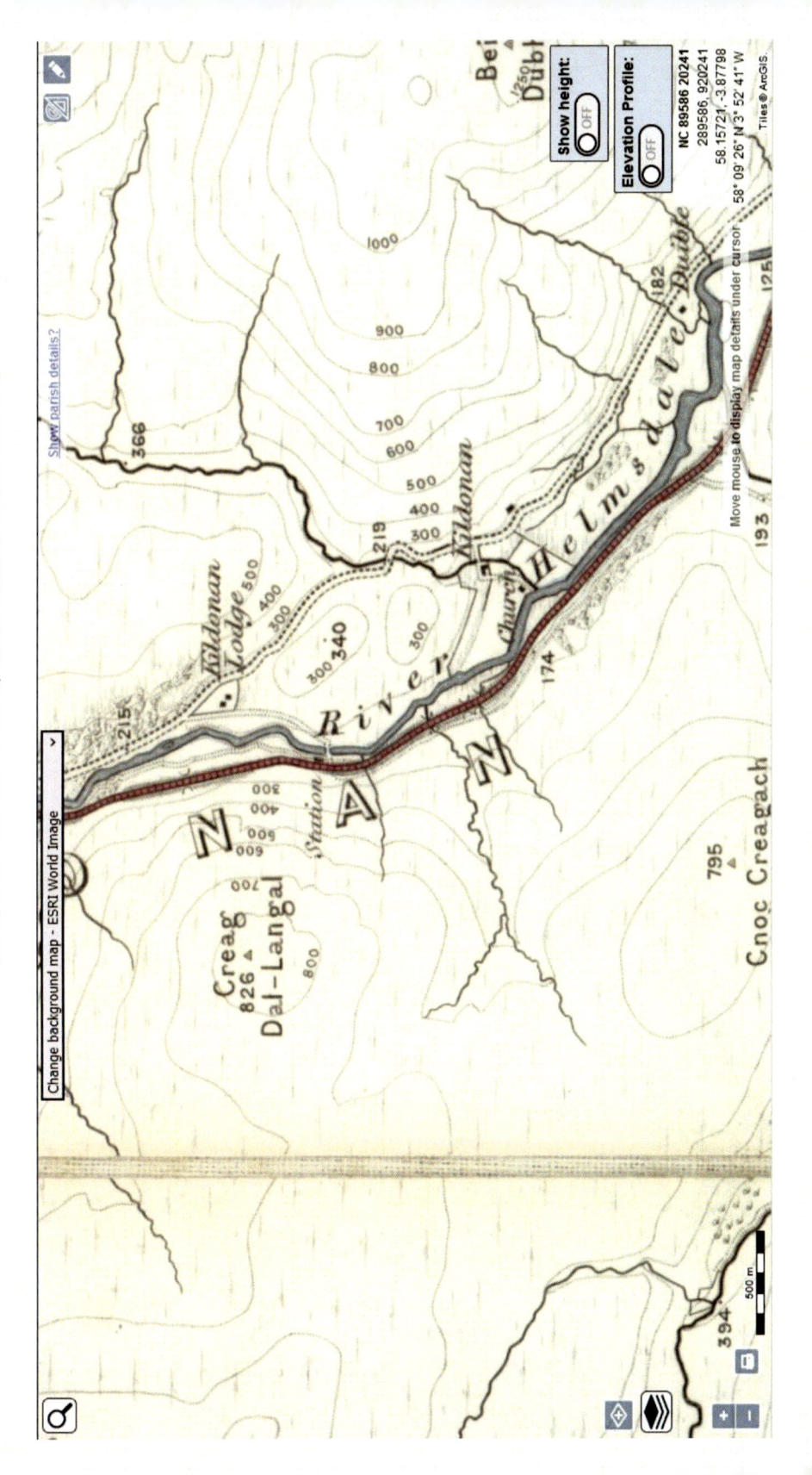

Boreray

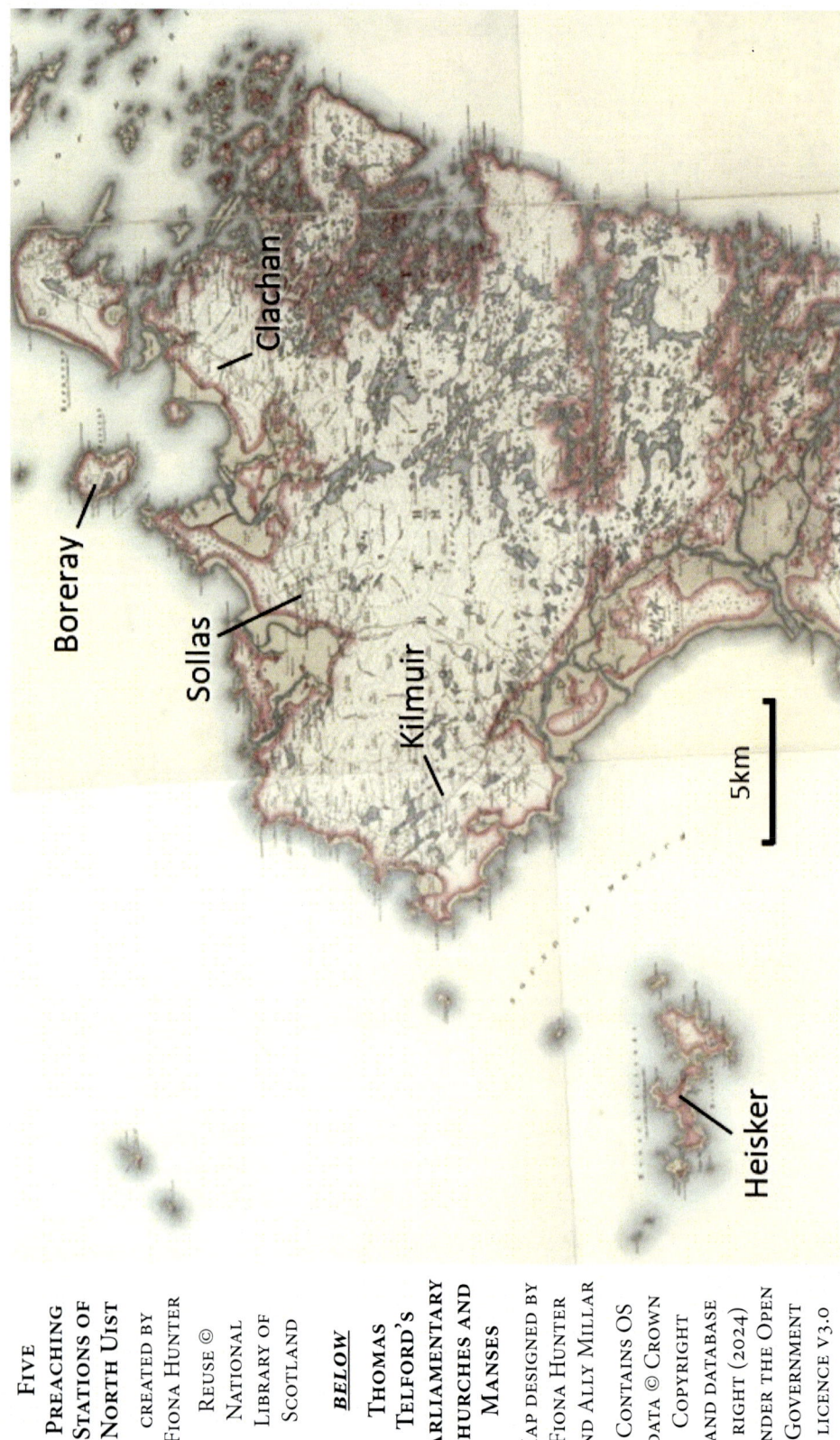

Clachan

Sollas

Kilmuir

5km

Heisker

FIVE PREACHING STATIONS OF NORTH UIST

CREATED BY FIONA HUNTER

REUSE © NATIONAL LIBRARY OF SCOTLAND

BELOW

THOMAS TELFORD'S PARLIAMENTARY CHURCHES AND MANSES

MAP DESIGNED BY FIONA HUNTER AND ALLY MILLAR

CONTAINS OS DATA © CROWN COPYRIGHT AND DATABASE RIGHT (2024) UNDER THE OPEN GOVERNMENT LICENCE V3.0

PARLIAMENTARY CHURCHES – NUMBERED IN RED

MANSES – LETTERED IN BLUE

1 Acharacle
2 Ardgour
3 Berneray
4 Berriedale
5 Carnoch
6 Croick
7 Cross
8 Duror
9 Hallin
10 Iona
11 Keiss
12 Kinlochbervie
13 Kinlochluichart
14 Kinlochspelvie
15 Knock
16 Lochgilphead
17 North Ballachulish
18 Oa
19 Plockton
20 Poolewe
21 Portnahaven
22 Quarff
23 Shieldaig
24 Stenscholl
25 Stoer
26 Strathy
27 Strontian
28 Tobermory
29 Tomintoul
30 Trumisgarry
31 Ullapool
32 Ulva

A Sandwick
B North Ronaldsay
C Deerness
D Rothiemurchus
E Inch
F Rannoch
G Foss
H Innerwick
J Kilmeny
K Muckairn
L Salen

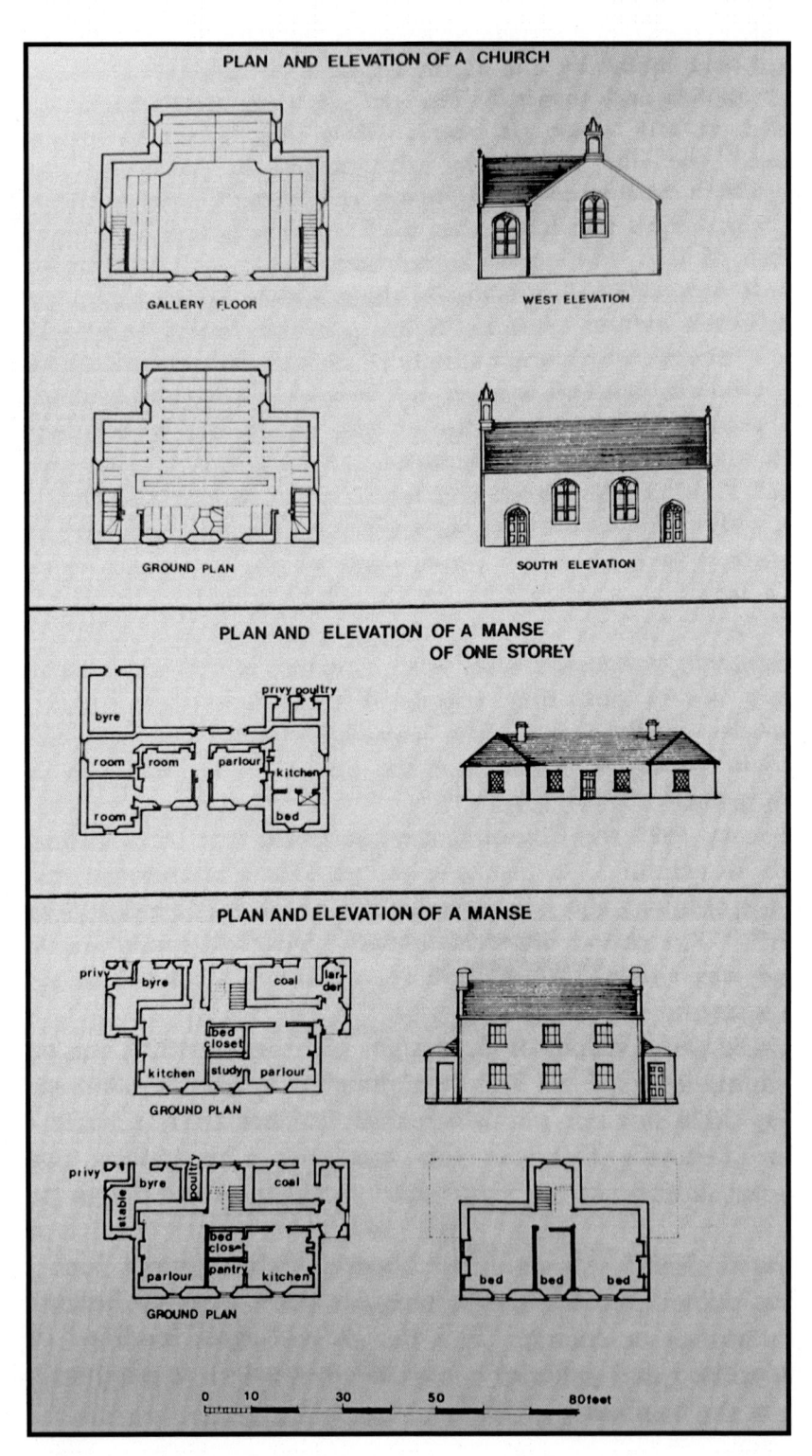

Telford's Designs produced by the Commissioners for the Parliamentary Churches in 1831

Also, Baird's jaundiced view of Gaelic Societies revealed the Moderates' general default position of resisting and opposing any agency not under complete control of the Kirk. Neither were Moderates slow to decry the more Evangelical efforts of others, outwith and within the Kirk.

Partisanship was as entrenched as ever. In response to Dr Baird, Dr Andrew Thomson, quick to defend Evangelical efforts, stated that 'there had been a great deal of work done by SSPCK and the Gaelic Schools' and suggested that the survey had only taken into account the years to 1819, offering statistics that were now well out-of-date and which would have artificially inflated the figures of the illiterates. According to Dr Thomson the statistical basis of the report was highly misleading and there had been significant improvement meantime. It would be inconceivable that as leader of the Evangelical Party Dr Thomson would not be in possession of more accurate figures, gleaned from information freely available in the many publications with Evangelical leanings circulating at the time and distributed widely throughout the Highlands and Islands.

More curious still was a General Assembly report given two years previously in May 1822 on the introduction of a quarto version of the Gaelic bible to the Highlands which included the quote, 'The greater number of Highlanders are at this time able to read the scriptures in their native tongue'. According to Baird's 1824 report, literacy levels among Highlanders had suffered a catastrophic decline! This was not the first time, nor would it be the last when 'statistics' would be disputed.

However, the clamour, *again,* to address the state of education in the Highlands and Islands was overwhelming, finally bringing the Assembly together to endorse Baird's initial proposal in the following terms:

> The Assembly most cordially gave their approbation to the object proposed in the overtures, and unanimously appoint a Committee to enquire and report to the Assembly as to an advisable plan for increasing the means of education and religious instruction throughout Scotland in general where it may be needed, but particularly in the Highlands and Islands, and in large and populous cities and towns, and take what proper and prudent measures may be in their power for the information and direction of next Assembly.[29]

---

29 Principal Baird's resolution passed at the 1824 General Assembly.

It should be noted that in this, as in other instances, General Assembly decisions adopted a 'one size fits all' pattern. While Baird's report initially identified slow progress in the Highlands and Islands, the newly-appointed committee's remit was to consider the entire country including the growing conurbations of the south. Evangelicals in the north and west rightly felt short-changed by this approach. They believed once again that the Kirk's response, too focused as it was on the situation in the urban centres, would simply dilute the efforts of Highland ministers facing unique challenges, and these would be lost in some general future report.

Religious Education in the Highlands

Notwithstanding the above, the General Assembly's verdict was clear and forcibly stated: 'A scheme for giving them catechists, schools and missionaries under the superintendence of this house, was the only plan to ameliorate the state of the Highlands'. It was also a timely response in light of the SSPCK turning down applications for new schools and closing others for want of funds. The verdict of Moderate commissioners on the Gaelic Schools Societies, criticised by Dr Baird and others was that they were ineffective and inefficient. Moderates believed once again that any solution to any problem lay in improving the organisation and administration of the Kirk's affairs.

However, Baird's overture to the Assembly garnered general support from both wings of the church which shared a basic commitment to religious education, especially as disseminated by the Established Church. The survey on education provision commissioned by Baird had revealed an estimated 10,500 children in the six most northerly Synods were without the means of education. In his PhD thesis, author John Stevenson states,

> Few of the poorly paid crofters and fishermen living in the scattered townships in the Highlands and Islands could afford the fees for schoolmasters or the cost of books. Inefficient teachers threatened to dilute educational standards. Absentee landlords (many of whom had associated themselves with the Scottish Episcopal Church) were not interested and in the new towns the old parish system was not appropriate.[30]

---

30 John Stevenson, PhD thesis 2005, *An assessment of the contribution of the Church of Scotland to school education focusing in particular on the work of the General Assembly Committee 1824 – 72*, 59.

Further, Baird's survey revealed that few schoolmasters were sufficiently fluent in both English and Gaelic thus hampering students' progress. This was time for action as it was acknowledged previous attempts at addressing the Highland Problem had fallen far short of what was required. Both Evangelicals and Moderates accepted that education in its broadest sense was the key to society's progress. Being taught to read the Bible in Sabbath Schools or through the auspices of the SSPCK and Gaelic Schools' Societies was the main building-block of religious educational provision. In addition, these schools offered a varied curriculum including English, Gaelic, writing, arithmetic, book-keeping, Latin and Greek and sometimes navigation being taught.

The Statistical Accounts for Stornoway, Isle of Lewis reveal that, in 1833, a number of schools were operating in the parish: one parish, one SPCK, two Gaelic Society schools; one female school where 60 scholars were taught reading, writing and sewing. Several privately-sponsored schools took the total number to 13. Lady Seaforth had endowed three such schools, together with one circulating library. Beyond Stornoway, Lady Seaforth had established a number of spinning schools for girls. A local benefactor, Mary MacKenzie Carn, bequeathed £300 for the establishment of a girls' school in the town.

Despite targeted investment of this type and no doubt harbouring hopes of 'improving' the Highland female, Revd John Cameron who compiled the Account was dismissive: 'The women are miserable slaves; they do the work of brutes, carry the manure in creels on their backs from the byre to the field and use their fingers as a five-pronged grape to fill them.'[31] While the demands of the croft was always the priority for families, 'education' was therefore seen to have only limited use for both boys and girls. The teaching of subjects in English was to extend the ambitions of the young, eager to grasp the opportunities which existed beyond the croft and the need to remain at home.

However, while commitment to rolling out educational provision throughout the land came from across the Kirk, it still faced a further awkward challenge. Many native Gaelic-speaking Evangelicals remained unconvinced of General Assembly's commitment in this and other matters relating to the Highlands. Moderates, on the other hand, had to acknowledge that within their own ranks many were still ambivalent towards Gaelic as a language-medium for both liturgy and learning and to securing and expanding education provision

---

31 *The Statistical Accounts of Scotland 1833: Stornoway, County of Ross and Cromarty*, vol. XIV, 131.

in the Highlands and Islands which included giving both Gaelic and English their place. Perhaps to allay further Evangelical fears, Baird's committee had to decide how much teaching was to be in Gaelic and how much in English. As a working compromise the committee printed sets of schoolbooks in both languages but noted it was expected that the English language would be more or less taught in all schools. Thus the pre-eminence of the English language was assured. Many Moderates in the face of mounting Evangelical challenge more than ever wished to keep Gaels 'in their place' by promoting English as the dominant medium for liturgy and learning. Yet those Moderates faced a competing cultural belief system deeply rooted in Highland history and tradition that affirmed that *Gaelic* was the language of liturgy and learning.

Despite these misgivings, it was the tireless work of Principal Baird and his Education committee which ensured the Assembly Schools found success in the Highlands and Islands. Revd John Smith in his 1912 publication *Broken Links in Scottish Education* applauded the committee's efforts in reaching into the isolated parishes of the Highlands where 'adults from twenty to seventy years of age, crowded everywhere to the newly erected schools'. In some sense, the success of the Assembly schools eclipsed both the efforts of the SSPCK and Gaelic Charity schools. By 1830, 86 Assembly schools had been established.

While the SSPCK had concentrated its work on the coastal fringes of the Gaelic communities, the Gaelic School movement targeted the remoter areas of the Highlands, the Western Isles and the areas north and west of the Great Glen. At its height, the Gaelic Schools Society administered some 83 schools. Baird's 1824 report, resulting in the Assembly's school movement, was delivered at a time when Moderate domination of Church matters was annually under threat by an emboldened Evangelical Party. That said, leading Evangelical Thomas Chalmers thoroughly approved of Baird's overture, stating that Kirk-established schools would do more good than all the missionaries and societies together.

Whatever the merits and effectiveness of the SSPCK, the Gaelic Charity Schools and the Assembly Schools may have been, one thing is clear in that all made vital contributions to the improvements in levels of literacy through teaching scripture and fostering a greater understanding of the bible. Especially between 1819 and 1822 and after fresh impetus by the Gaelic Schools Society, this appetite for learning underpinned and facilitated the rash of revivals which took place in the Highlands and Islands. The schools' systems were now beginning to bear much fruit. During these years, Lewis, Skye, Ross-shire and parts of Caithness were gripped by a succession of 'awakenings'.

In their attempts to regulate and ensure adherence to the discipline of Presbyterianism, ministers were aided by individuals specifically set apart as teachers, known as 'catechists'. Their specific task was to teach both adults and the young to help them commit to memory and to repeat the Shorter Catechism which codified the tenets of Presbyterianism and of which they also gave a short explanation. This was all the more vital in the vast tracks of remotest Highland and Island Scotland where the number of illiterates was almost total.

Entry into a full Christian life and participation at communion was achieved through religious education. First steps to faith began with instruction on the Shorter Catechism. In many respects, the catechism sets out a more rigid Calvinism than perhaps Calvin himself intended. It was completed in 1647 alongside the Westminster Confession of Faith, drawn up specifically to establish clear blue water between the Presbyterian Church and the Anglican Church and its English Prayer Book. The tone and rhythms of the Shorter Catechism penetrated deeply into the Scottish psyche.

Content and Practice of RE, and Revivals

The Shorter Catechism consists of 107 clauses in the form of questions and answers, beginning with 'What is the chief end of man?' *'Man's chief end is to glorify God, and enjoy him forever.'* It concludes with 'What doth the conclusion of the Lord's Prayer teach us?' *'The conclusion . . . teacheth us to take our encouragement in prayer from God only, and in our prayers to praise him, ascribing kingdom, power and glory to him. And in testimony of our desire, and assurance to be heard, we say, AMEN.'*

Clauses 2 to 106 cover the subjects of creation, sin, the elect, Christ as redeemer, the work of the Spirit, justification, sanctification, the ten commandments, punishment and escape from punishment, salvation, baptism, the Lord's Supper and prayer. In all, it is a weighty diet of prescribed knowledge to be learned, memorised, retained, recalled and examined upon and it was the catechist's job to prepare and assess individuals as to the 'fitness' of their right to receive the sacrament. For the catechism to be taught and learned by rote was surely an exhausting task for both tutor and pupil. At any celebration of communion, there was always the stern admonition from the minister about not receiving the sacrament 'unworthily'.

From the first decade of the 19th century onwards Evangelical ministers began more and more to occupy pulpits in the north and west, and an emphasis upon communion seasons took on more importance and meaning than ever before. Ministers were able to impose absolute discipline in the matter of the sacrament, redressing examples of laxity and deregulation permitted under more liberal Moderate regimes. Under Evangelical ministries, out of the congregations of thousands assembled from far and wide, only a few would come forward to receive the bread and wine.

This is surely testament to three truths: first, the result of the failed struggle of the truly pious to learn and be examined on all 107 clauses; second (and in contrast), such a complete understanding of all 107 clauses would have rendered the truly pious as truly undeserving; third, a judgemental fear of failing to embrace 'new obedience'. This was central to the understanding of clause 87, *'whereby a sinner, out of a true sense of his sin, and apprehension of the mercy of God in Christ, doth, with grief and hatred of his sin, turn from it unto God, with full purpose of, and endeavour after, new obedience.'* The ultimate threat of eternal damnation hovered over individuals if their quest for new obedience did not live up to the Almighty's expectations, so that they came forward *'unworthily, [to] eat and drink judgement to themselves'*. All three would engender an overwhelming sense of 'unworthiness'.

That the Catechism, as the ultimate expression of Reformed Presbyterian doctrine, had been written in English put native Gaelic-speakers at an immediate disadvantage. To this extent, evangelising the Highlands was not achieved at a uniform pace. Older Gaelic-speakers showed a reluctance first to learn to read, and secondly to learn to read in English and were mainly resistant to adapting to Anglicised ways. The oral traditions underpinning Gaelic language and culture had served them well enough. Thus, it was the children who became the focus of these new endeavours.

> *It is the case that spiritual and intellectual revival take place together. The Spirit of God quickens the whole of life. Both intellectually and spiritually the Highland people owe more to the endeavours of the Gaelic School Society than it is possible for them ever to appreciate.*
>
> Revd Alexander Macrae, Revivals in the Highlands and Islands in the 19th Century

A 'plentiful harvest' of saved souls was accomplished chiefly by the Gaelic Bible, the Gaelic schools and their schoolmasters. The Island of Lewis had high levels of illiteracy in all age groups with adults particularly resistant to any new initiatives. However, matters took a turn for the better with the arrival of two Evangelicals in particular, Finlay Munro, a travelling evangelist and ex-SSPCK teacher who arrived on Lewis in 1818 and John MacLeod, in 1820, an employee of the Edinburgh Gaelic School Society.

These two individuals, more than any others, sparked considerable appetites for learning among young and old. MacLeod's remit was to teach the people to read the scriptures in Gaelic (from 1801 the complete bible had been available) but he was not permitted to preach or hold religious services. Such work was seen as treading on the clergy's toes. However, being unwilling to desist from 'explaining the scriptures' he was dismissed from the Society. Such was his popularity he was able to continue his work independently among a grateful people whose generosity gave him a living.

Finlay Munro was known as 'the boy with the bible', an English version which Munro translated into Gaelic as he read. Lay-preaching was not looked upon favourably and was opposed by both Evangelicals and Moderates. Presbyteries on a regular basis had to deal with unlicensed, undisciplined and unwelcome itinerants and 'vagrant teachers' disrupting congregational and school-room life throughout the Highlands. Munro the itinerant evangelist was well received, gathering large crowds wherever he went and much to the fury of Revd Alexander MacLeod, Evangelical minister in Uig at the time. However, as Munro was beyond the reach of Kirk discipline there was little MacLeod could do about it. It seems, though, that MacLeod was the ultimate beneficiary of these travelling evangelists' efforts with a significant increase in those attending his own services which required the building of a new and larger church to accommodate the worshippers within a decade of Munro and MacLeod's arrival.

Running concurrently with the Gaelic Schools were the SSPCK schools. A report in 1830 speaks of the Sunday Schools which had been well-established in Stornoway for more than twenty years. Teachers of the SSPCK were actively encouraged to hold Sabbath evening schools for both adults as well as children. Teachers in the General Assembly Schools in Lewis were also obliged to hold Sabbath Evening Schools. In 1833 there were nine such Sabbath Schools in Stornoway, four in Uig and two in Lochs. A total of 15 in Lewis. By this time there were also five SSPCK schools. In little over 10 years there had been considerable improvement in educational provision as the 1819 report on Gaelic

Schools stated that there were only eight such schools across the entire island. In Barvas, there were 100 on the role with a regular attendance of 80, including married couples, again, a considerable improvement upon matters a decade previously when leading Evangelicals had placed the demise of family worship firmly at the feet of Moderates.

Some Moderate ministers, who in the main incurred the wrath and contempt of Evangelicals, did much to promote education on the island encouraging the establishing of the Gaelic Schools. Revd William MacRae of Barvas and Revd Alexander Simson of Lochs were particularly singled out as 'Moderates' being genuinely concerned about the educational progress of the people. Mr Simson reported in a letter to the Gaelic School Society on 13th July 1822 that 'By the acquaintance of their native tongue, the Highlanders obtain possession of a key to other languages, and with the ability to read Gaelic is born the anxiety to learn English'.[32]

Macaulay also singles out for praise seven Evangelical ministers ('honoured instruments of the revival') at the epicentre of the Lewis awakenings: Finlay Cook, John MacRae, John Finlayson, Donald MacRae; Alexander MacLeod; Duncan Matheson and Robert Finlayson.[33] John Cameron, revered minister of Stornoway who would have regarded himself as an Evangelical, but not Evangelical enough for some tastes, is not included in the list. Certainly these 'Lewis Seven' and others displaying more radical tendencies within the Evangelical Party had to be reined in by the likes of Andrew Thomson and Thomas Chalmers when it came to debates on the floor of the General Assembly.

Education and Poverty

Despite a great increase in the number of those who could now read Gaelic, and a Gaelic bible in every household, levels of 'poverty and wretchedness' continued to rise. Crop failure and poor herring landings together with the finishing of road-building across the Highlands meant that most families had been pushed into subsistence living. In parts of Skye and the west coast of the mainland poverty levels rivalled those in Ireland. Education alone, it appeared, was not the passkey to increased prosperity, wealth and prospects that it might have supposed. Increasing levels of poverty and destitution had had a

---

32 Revd Murdo Macaulay, *Aspects of Religious History of Lewis*, 89.
33 Revd Murdo Macaulay, *Aspects of Religious History of Lewis*, 96.

deleterious effect upon the children's schoolwork. Despite the tireless work of the Gaelic School Societies, effort was not always rewarded by good outcomes.

While the benefits brought to the Highlands and Islands by the Gaelic Schools were thought to be considerable, question marks over the effectiveness of the SSPCK's schools remained. From his damning retrospective report in 1865, Alexander Nicolson, assistant commissioner for Scottish Education and an expert in Gaelic culture says of the SSPCK schools, 'Efficiency, on the whole, cannot be considered satisfactory.'[34] A former Inspector said of them, 'The education is of a very low character indeed'. Despite this, there was a considerable amount of educational effort expended on the setting up and running of schools, and in other corners of the land by the three main bodies, SSPCK, Gaelic Schools and General Assembly schools.

A retrospective but pertinent conclusion to the matter of education may be given by Revd Murdo Macaulay, 'There is no doubt that the Gaelic schools paved the way for the complete adherence of the people to the Free Church in 1843'. The Gaelic Schools had consolidated the language for the native speakers of the north and west. The march of Evangelical Presbyterianism and the rise of the Gaelic Schools from the second decade of the 19th century onwards proved to be a potent and irresistible force.

---

34 Revd Murdo Macaulay, *Aspects of Religious History of Lewis*, 118.

Essay Seven

The Distinctive Religious Spirituality of the Highlander

Spirituality is recognised in relationship to a creative or unseen force or forces, forces beyond physical control. It is a relationship which could be defined as a recognising, realising and embracing of the non-material aspects of life. This spirituality was never more apparent than in Highland culture, and from ancient times replete with symbolism, ritual and the numinous. As Christianity took hold, pagan or pre-Christian beliefs were not necessarily abandoned, or indeed extinguished. Despite the best efforts of the Church the new belief system found itself 'accommodating' some of these pre-existing components. Manifesting itself in the practice of sorcery, folk medicine, charms, omens and divination, a firm belief in second-sight together with an unorthodox mixture of Catholic and Celtic rituals, superstition abounded.

Nor did these particular aspects of Highland belief vanish with the coming of Protestantism. Indeed, many of the age-old practices and beliefs, preserved within an oral tradition, lingered on within communities, now under the spiritual leadership of Moderate and Evangelical ministries alike, across the north and west. Many of these practices were still in existence at the turn of the 20th century and beyond.

The New Broom

At first glance, it would appear that the Evangelical wing of the church, with its particular emphases on spiritual or non-material matters would have been more sympathetic towards the old ways. Not a bit of it. Nothing would stand in the way of a return to Reformation principles which abhorred the very idea of superstitious beliefs, or the chanting of charms, or the lingering vestiges of pagan ritual. These age-old practices rooted in especially Gaelic communities were to be swept away – as far as it was possible. One of Evangelicalism's aims was to eradicate any notion which did not have its authority rooted in the Bible. Conversely, it has been argued that 'evangelicalism served to fill some of the gaps between official religion and folk religion.'[1] Prof. McLeod further argues that this gap was created by 'increasingly rational-minded clergy' who had lost touch with the forms of thought of the superstitious masses. Thus an evolving Evangelical spirituality was one of the potent drivers which fuelled the Disruption, assuring the Free Church of its distinctive form of Presbyterianism.

> *Deep impressions of their utter impotence under the power of sin, as well as their utter inexcusableness under its guilt, with a distinct recognition of the necessity of regeneration and of the sovereignty of grace, distinguished the experience of the awakened.*
>
> Revd Dr John Kennedy, *The Days of the Fathers in Ross-shire*

Revitalising the church was not a solely human endeavour, it required the work of the spirit as well as the intellect. 'Divine aid was needed and so prayer became a bedrock of personal and corporate discipline.'[2] Evangelicalism saw its full blooming in the Highlands and Islands of Scotland; those who aligned themselves with Evangelical principles were able to uncover and nurture a distinctive spirituality for the new post-Reformation age, some of which had existed since pre-Christian times.

At the age of just 37, the young minister John Macdonald, later to acquire the moniker 'Apostle of the North', reassessed his personal priorities thus: 'earnest, frequent, importunate prayer; the reading and searching of the scriptures; meditation; assessing the state of his personal godliness; devotion to public ministry; zeal for God; love to the souls of men; preparation for the work; readiness to speak the word.'[3] These would enable him earnestly to devote himself more in three vital areas: the work of the Lord; to consider himself not his own, but belonging to the Lord; to be at the Lord's disposal.

As a life devoted to the discipline of personal prayer became a priority for the likes of Macdonald and others, regular prayer-meetings for the faithful placed personal spirituality at the heart of the religious endeavour, reinforcing the centrality of revival, evangelism and social morality. The Evangelical wing produced hard, uncompromising

---

[1] Prof. Hugh McLeod, *Religion and the Peoples of Western Europe 1789-1970*, 39.

[2] David Alan Currie, PhD thesis, *The Growth of Evangelicalism in the Church of Scotland 1793 – 1843*, 349.

[3] Revd Dr John Kennedy, *The 'Apostle of the North'. The life and labours of Rev Dr McDonald*, 81.

leaders with a firm grip on Reformation principles offering a more rigorous religious experience which was for many a welcome and essential change from the less stringent, less intrusive and more benign religion offered by Moderates. For Evangelicals, there was no hope of salvation in Moderate theology. Evangelicalism offered a highly personal religion with its core belief in the necessity of conversion and the acceptance of the Calvinist view of the unworthiness of the individual.

Evangelicalism was beginning to find a home within and among Highland people already primed with a sense of the numinous, highly-seasoned with mysticism, superstition and a deep sense of the sacred. Evangelicals highlighted the importance of the supernatural and the emotional in religion, both of which they considered to be central to religious revival and essential to prayer. As the age of rationalism gave way to the age of romanticism around the end of the 18th century, Evangelicals were able to harness the new thinking of the day while Moderates, clinging to the old arguments and philosophies based on Enlightenment doctrines, found themselves unable to change and as a consequence lost ground especially in the north and west.

Prayer Meetings and Salvation

Prayer meetings reinforced religion's corporate nature among like-minded individuals in the community and so became an essential facet of living the truly religious life. It was believed that only the Holy Spirit could create within the individual the response of true faith and prayer which was paramount for divine activity. As the nation progressed through the many cultural, industrial and relational changes during the early years of the 19th century, many believed that their only hope was to seek divine assistance through both personal and organised corporate prayer. Family prayer was encouraged as the hallmark of evangelical piety, serving both as a primary outlet for the deeply felt spiritual experience and as a means of reproducing that experience in succeeding generations. Within the community of the faithful the sole question upon the lips of sinners was expressed as this: *What must I do to be saved?* The answer to this core tenet was the fundamental aim in achieving the true religious life through three central aspects: confession; forgiveness; and the hope of redemption. The Evangelical minister confronted sinners with the person of Christ: 'You are a lost sinner; Christ is here; He calls you to come to him now; Nothing can excuse disobedience.' This is Evangelical preaching at its bluntest and it broaches neither qualification nor caveat.

In their purest form, Reformation principles laid bare the human soul's unmistakeable and abject degradation. Salvation is found 'only in the Lord'. It was a pious hope and certainly not an expectation. Salvation through a personal conversion rested on election tempered by grace, but those who remained outwith the community of the faithful and who did not participate in divine services were not necessarily lost forever. Through encouragement by their community, reprobates might be made receptive to grace through the recognition of their sins. Election of the truly repentant could be made by God alone, but assurance of salvation could be found through the sacrament of communion, which was in itself an affirmation of God's covenant with the elect.

The communion seasons were therefore very important in the Highlands. Through prayer and contemplation the godly were able to confirm their faith at these sacramental occasions (though as we have seen, in Highland areas few in practice went forward). These foundational principles certainly confirm the gravity of nurturing an Evangelical faith. An Evangelical approach to religion was not to be taken or accepted lightly.

The Theological Heart of the Matter

The Church of Scotland . . . considers its ministers as men of understanding, of taste, and of sentiment, capable of thinking for themselves, who . . . may be permitted to exercise their talents, with a coming independence upon Divine aid, in the sacred and important office of leading the devotions of Christian worshippers.

Principal George Hill addressing students, 1803

Deep theological disagreement concerned the cleansing or purging from sin, with very clear differences between Evangelicals and Moderates. The issue concerns *justification* when God, in a one-time act, declares a guilty sinner to be righteous, setting the sinner free from sin's penalty. Following on, it concerns *sanctification* when God in a continuous process sets the sinner free from sin's power; allowing the sinner to grow in righteousness.

Fifty years before Evangelicals and Moderates engaged in the fateful battle for the soul of the Kirk which culminated in the Disruption, Revd John Erskine, a leading Evangelical, had reflected upon the nature of a saving faith and the measures sufficient for sanctification. Erskine wondered if the Moderates' position 'simply' of being a communicant member of the Church of Scotland stood up to scrutiny. 'Membership' was the passkey to the sacrament of the Lord's Table where receiving the bread and wine was an affirmation of righteousness. For Evangelicals, placing a name on the congregational register was clearly not sufficient in itself, and sanctification required a personal commitment by way of conversion. In this, Evangelicals saw themselves as more rigorous gate-keepers of both the sacrament of communion and the kingdom of God. For the Evangelical, personal conversion was a first step in the new relationship with God with an affirmation of the true unworthiness and complete degradation of the self which only God in Christ could repair through forgiveness. In turn, this new state of forgiveness gave the *hope of election* of the truly repentant which again could be made by God alone. However, for Evangelicals like John Erskine, *assurance of salvation* could be determined through the sacrament of communion, which was itself a declaration of forgiveness and an affirmation of God's covenant with the elect.

Erskine was leader of the Evangelical Party in the second half of the 18th century and a theologian, scholar and committed churchman. He ably expressed the Evangelical viewpoint which was eagerly taken up by the new breed of ministers emerging at the end of the 18th century and at a time when Moderates thought little of theology and matters of faith. The seeds of dissension and schism were sown in Erskine's time.

For the Evangelical, self-examination of the state of one's soul, which was held to account against Christ's own example, and a deeply held sense of personal 'worth' or 'worthiness' permeated every aspect of life constantly tested by a minister's exhortations and preaching. The believer had to be in a state of constant readiness to be examined on the Shorter Catechism. Faith, a complete change of heart and a sense of renewed Christian experience were crucially and critically put to the test. To be 'worthy' was to be accepted and sanctified and to be in a fit state of grace for receiving the sacrament. This placed conversion at the very heart of personal witness. 'Conversion' was absolutely essential for the true Evangelical.

Salvation through a personal conversion, resting on election tempered by grace, was at the very heart of every revival. 'Rooted in Puritan faith, almost every believer had had a profound conversion experience. They preached it, they sought it, they recounted it in spiritual autobiographies and hagiographies, they checked its authenticity with those already converted and they had disdained those who had not experienced it.'[4]

---

4 Revd Ian Muirhead, *The Revival as Dimension of Scottish Church History,* 185, The Scottish Church History Society, 1980.

Awakenings

> ... the land was held in the deadening grip
> of the black frost of moderatism
>
> Revd Alexander Auld, *Ministers and Men in the Far North*

As early as the 1730s, the first 'awakenings' or evangelical revivals occurred in Nigg, Ross-shire occurring simultaneously with outbreaks in Golspie, Tongue and Strathnaver and coinciding with the revivals in Cambuslang and Kilsyth in the south. A decade later many parishes in the Presbytery of Tain were similarly affected, together with parishes in the Presbyteries of Chanonry, Dingwall and Dornoch. Further east, there was a revival in the Nairn area. During the first two decades of the 19th century a further series of revivals broke out almost at the same time in districts far removed from one another. Although 'awakenings' took place in Kintyre and Argyll it was mainly in the counties of Lewis, Sutherland and Caithness and in the scattered townships of Kilmuir and Snizort in Skye where revival had the biggest impact.

All involved shared the common belief that the Kirk had to recover its inner soul, sacrificed during the years of Moderatism, and the necessity to promote a doctrine of a personal rather than corporate relationship with God in Christ. Revival also put a firm halt to the resurgent claims of both the Catholic and Episcopalian churches while Protestantism was regarded as the only medium for bringing and establishing 'civilisation'. When Jacobite heritors ruled, however, it was said that 'ignorance, profaneness and superstition' abounded and in the north and west, the distinctive characteristics of Evangelical Protestantism and especially in its Presbyterian form were taking root. As these flourished so dogma, belief and faith began to underpin religious life. Events over a relatively short period demonstrate the speed with which revivalism took hold.

On Skye a revival had begun in 1805 led by one minister and an itinerant preacher. This isolated phenomenon gathered pace with prayer meetings increasing numbers of those 'awakened', presumably from the torpor of Moderatism, and by 1817 a substantial meeting-house had been built at Snizort which held 200 souls. The Government Report by Commissioners into educational provision listed seven parishes including Raasay and Scalpa, clergy serving all areas, four missionaries, two Parliamentary Churches, several catechists and Gaelic schoolteachers as well as three small Baptist congregations. Revival of a similar nature reached the Isle of Lewis, especially around Uig.

Presbyteries in the north and west until the late 1820s were still mainly Moderate controlled. However, growing numbers of Evangelical ministers began to occupy pulpits across the north and west from the early years of the 19th century onwards, shifting the balance away from Moderates as revivalism took hold. The building of 32 new 'Parliamentary Churches' across the north and west towards the end of the 1820s (see Essays 9 and 10) gave an immediate boost to numbers as ministers sympathetic to the evangelical cause were appointed, and across the north and west, a pronounced Evangelicalism began to undermine Moderate domination of Presbyteries.

Orthodoxy and Heresy

Revd Alexander Macrae [5]complains of a Moderate stranglehold in the Kirk throughout the north and west at the end of the 18th century, blaming Enlightenment teaching, influenced by the philosophies of David Hume and others. The universities were under the command of the Kirk who had total power over appointments. Although at the epicentre of Enlightenment thought, Hume's departure from theological orthodoxy prevented him from securing the Chair of Moral Philosophy at Edinburgh in 1745 or the Glasgow chair in 1752.

The universities had deep concerns over Hume. An allegation that he considered the soul to be mortal, i.e. to perish at death, had been one of the six 'Remonstrances' mounted by the Kirk, successfully sabotaging any thoughts of a life in academe. It was most certainly the case that the universities, filled with Moderate churchmen, were more alert to heretical thinking than the Evangelicals supposed, but it was true that many evangelically-minded ministers regarded any alternate view to their own as heretical. The universities continued to teach divinity subjects regarded as too liberal for evangelical tastes, and also continued to teach 'non-core' subjects such as botany and chemistry to prospective ministers.

Writing in 1866 Revd Dr John Kennedy in his memoir *The Days of the Fathers in Ross-shire* reflects upon the county 'in its best days', building on its reputation as a hot-bed of Evangelical orthodoxy from the mid 18th century. He sets out an *apologia* defending the distinctive character of the religious spirit in the north as having 'certain peculiarities', which became the subject of southern criticism and misunderstanding. For example, in critics' eyes the Highland Christian

---

5 Revd Alexander Macrae, *Revivals in the Highlands and Islands in the 19th Century*, 10.

was a 'gloomy bigot', as compared with the more cheerful and liberal Christians of the south.[6] The Christian Highlander was too readily accused of being too focused on the state of his own soul to determine whether he is a true servant of Christ or not, when he should be proving that he is so by being 'busy for God'. Excessive self-suspiciousness and an over-concentration on an individual's spiritual health, said the critics, gave rise to the Fellowship meetings, essentially a private prayer group. In defence of the Fellowship meetings, Kennedy affirms they were the product of a lively, questioning spiritual faith, a need arising from within a healthy Christian community but completely unknown in Moderate circles. For Evangelicals this confirmed the Moderates' abject lack of spirituality.

However, Kennedy states:

> Highland Christians did not take for granted that they were "the Lord's", nor could they speak peace to themselves and that, unlike many others, they were dependent upon the Lord for their hope and their joy. They were grave but not gloomy. They had not the light cheerfulness of unbroken hearts.[7]

The Highland Christian certainly was predisposed to introspection to ascertain the state and progress of his soul. Kennedy continues, 'Must he not keep an eye on his spirit while engaged in his work, lest his service be found by the Lord to be a graceless formality?' In contrast to others exhibiting an easy assurance which is but a 'covering for deadness and decay' are those truly pious 'more deeply stirred by a sense of corruption, more aware of their own deceitfulness, more moved by the solemn realities of eternity, and therefore less likely to declare their hope'.[8]

Kennedy, in one sentence, reveals the Highlander's pathological sense of his own unworthiness, deeply rooted in his Calvinist upbringing, a condition which can only be redeemed and redressed by the Lord's unfathomable grace and limitless mercy. Nor should the Highlander take his own Christianity for granted or be easily satisfied with the profession of faith of others. The truly pious constantly tested his own faith against biblical standards and he remained reserved and cautious of those labelling themselves 'Christian'. This habit of maintaining a constant watching brief on the Bible standard

---

6 Revd Dr John Kennedy, *The Days of the Fathers in Ross-shire*, 117.
7 Revd Dr John Kennedy, *The Days of the Fathers in Ross-shire*, 117.
8 Revd Dr John Kennedy, *The Days of the Fathers in Ross-shire*, 117.

of godliness, affirms Kennedy, may lead to accusations of an air of exclusiveness in his bearing towards others.[9] Some Moderates found any evangelical display of spiritual credentials deeply disturbing and offensive.

Dr Kennedy appears impervious to criticism and wears such as a badge of honour. He reflects upon a series of general awakenings of faith which flourished under a number of individuals exercising what Kennedy calls a 'spiritual ministry' from the late 18th century onwards. From this first 1739 revival in Nigg, Kennedy states that 'the influence of the Gospel spread over the community', even reaching parishes where there was no evangelical ministry. 'Personal Christianity was the great object on which their attention and their labour were bestowed. They were not anxious merely to spread a layer of religion thinly over the face of society, but to obtain from the Lord's hand, living specimens of the power of His grace.'[10] Kennedy, writing of the early years of the 19th century dismissed the trend to establish 'social Christianity' defined as a diminution of personal godliness and a 'superficial religious excitement'. According to Kennedy 'ordinary decency' had now replaced 'true religion' and appeared to be the aim of the religious life. For Evangelicals, the pursuit of 'ordinary decency' seemed to be the sum and substance of Moderate preaching.

'The Men'

> *An unfavourable opinion is entertained of them by some, because they know them not. Not a few have been accustomed to speak of 'the men' whom it would not be impossible to persuade that, if they caught a live specimen, they would be found to have both horns and hoofs.*
>
> Revd Dr John Kennedy, speaking of the Fellowship meetings in *The Days of the Fathers in Ross-shire*

Besides offering a theology at whose heart was the imperative of conversion, puritanism laid a practical emphasis on the Fellowship meeting, a peculiarity in the Highlands and emerging only from within the Gaelic Evangelical tradition. These meetings were to play a central role within worshipping communities. With its roots in the early 18th century, the Fellowship meeting was a lay elite known as 'The Men' or *Na Daoine*, whom many believed were the 'most gifted and godly in

---

9 Revd Dr John Kennedy, *The Days of the Fathers in Ross-shire*, 122.
10 Revd Dr John Kennedy, *The Days of the Fathers in Ross-shire*, 123.

congregations and who had enlarged views of Divine truth and deep experience of its power'.[11] Many of them seemed to possess to a high degree the Highland bardic facility for recalling from memory texts and indeed entire passages of scripture they had heard, sometimes only once. They played a pivotal role in converting communities to Evangelical Protestantism.

This spiritual elite, drawing on aspects of older Highland belief systems including Celtic Christianity and which appealed to a people particularly sensitive to the supernatural, came to prominence during the religious revivals, combining the roles of clergymen with that of the traditional Highland seer. On occasions they stood over and against the prevailing views of the incumbent minister and, for this reason, they were sometimes regarded as a disruptive and divisive element within congregations, operating as an alternative leadership. Auld, however, is kindly disposed to them stating that 'pre-eminently they were men of prayer',[12] though he did go on to hint that their special powers extended to disseminating the will of God, and knowing what God was thinking in the here and now, and knowing his future plans.

Potential 'men' were recruited in the first instance by 'godly Highland ministers' discerning that an individual was truly converted, he was then invited 'to speak to the question' at a normal congregational meeting. This was taken to be a test for further possible advancement to be enrolled in the Fellowship meeting, as a 'Friday speaker'. The Friday Fellowship was an exclusive meeting whose membership was confined to those deemed worthy enough to be invited to join and which gave an especially powerful platform to 'The Men'. In Uig on Lewis, for example, the first resolution of the Fellowship meeting established in 1826, and recorded by Revd Alexander MacLeod, was that

> none will be admitted as members of the meeting but such as are in the opinion of the church partakers of real grace. They are to be examined upon their faith, change and experience, and though in the opinion of Christian charity we might receive scores into this meeting ... none will be received but such as give evidences that they are decidedly pious, and thus we exclude all others from this meeting, however promising in their first appearance.[13]

---

11 Revd Alexander Auld, *Ministers and Men in the Far North*, 88.
12 Revd Alexander Auld, *Ministers and Men in the Far North*, 89.
13 Revd Alexander MacLeod, *Diary and Sermons*, 17.

There was the possibility however of future membership for those who were seen to 'grow in grace, knowledge and conversation becoming the gospel of Christ'.[14] This meeting was an exclusively male assembly and from its earliest inception became a powerhouse of decision-making which, at times, ruled over the head of the Kirk Session. Not all Elders were of 'The Men' and not all of the Men were Elders. MacLeod was laying the foundations for building a highly privileged inner coterie with almost dictatorial powers over the lives of the community. This template was replicated in many other communities where the raising of 'The Men' coincided with revivalism.

'The Men' were not above criticism mainly from Moderate-led Kirk authorities. Some were accused of spreading apostasy, of fomenting discord and speaking out in defiance of ministers and Kirk Sessions, as Revd George McCulloch observed in 1793 regarding the Parish of Loth, Presbytery of Dornoch:

> However though there be no open schism to divide them in public worship, they have their lay leaders, some of the boldest and most conceited speakers at fellowship meetings, whom they implicitly believe merely on account of their high pretensions and affected sanctity by which they impose upon the people, and frequently mislead them. Of late they have begun to keep fellowship meetings without the presence of a minister. To these meetings they convene from different parishes, propose questions in divinity, explain scriptures, and give a sanction to any doctrines or opinions of the presiding saint – The evil consequences of these meetings on the heads and hearts of the people are begun to be seen most clearly by clergy; but they have not been able as yet to devise a method for suppressing them.[15]

However, by the time of McCulloch's report there had already been a history of attempts to rein in these groups over the preceding fifty years. Regarding them as a disruptive and unregulated laity, the Synod of Caithness and Sutherland at various times between 1737 and 1758 tried to suppress the Friday Fellowship Meetings and curb the power of 'The Men'. In this, they were singularly unsuccessful. Synods and Presbyteries were Moderate-dominated at this time and any unorthodox or unaccountable power bloc, operating within

---

14 Revd Alexander MacLeod, *Diary and Sermons*, 17.
15 The Statistical Accounts of Scotland 1793: *Loth, County of Sutherland*, vol. VI, 319.

congregations, was viewed with high suspicion but the failure of the party of law and order in this matter allowed 'The Men' to operate with impunity.

Such was the unregulated nature of the Fellowship meetings and the unbridled influence of 'The Men' that neither the threat of discipline nor sanction imposed by the Courts had much bearing on their activities. 'The Men' were regarded by Moderates as mavericks disrupting the smooth administration of the Kirk especially when delaying the filling of vacancies and also as a threat to the well-being and stability of congregational life.

However, it was also the case that some Evangelical ministers had difficulties with them. This highly influential group could act as sole arbiters of those making a 'profession of religion', on occasions stubbornly opposing the minister. In some instances, they also assumed the role of judge and jury, acting as guardians of the Lord's Table to ensure the health and righteousness of the Church. Critics dismissed them as 'enthusiasts', operating at the extreme edges of evangelicalism and there were many ministers, including native Gaelic speakers, keen to keep them 'in their place'. Generally, however, Evangelical ministers were wise enough to harness the talents of 'The Men', conscious of their long-standing history within communities. Ministers acknowledged the relative short-term nature of their own tenure, conscious that 'The Men' would see them come and would see them go.

Lewis in the 1820s: Cross

When Finlay Cook arrived on the Island of Lewis in 1829, having accepted the call to the newly-established Parliamentary charge of Cross, he apparently encountered a population devoid of any spirituality: 'rude in manners, filthy in habits, and lying under the thickest folds of moral and spiritual darkness',[16] this in a letter to his brother-in-law Donald Sage and despite there being a beloved and revered minister occupying the Stornoway pulpit, some 25 miles away. Clearly the Lewis Revival which had begun several years previously and was so dynamic, but localised in the south of the island around Uig, had not reached the northern parishes of Lewis. Finlay Cook had arrived to reports that in the churches in Stornoway and in Barvas, Cook's nearest neighbour 10 miles distant, baptism of children had never been refused and that everyone who attended seasonal communion was admitted to the

---

16 Revd Donald Sage, *Memorabilia Domestica*, 296.

sacrament. Those ministers were, respectively, John Cameron, and William Macrae who ministered at Barvas for 43 years; both great advocates of Gaelic education but whom Cook dismissed as 'models of Moderatism', even if Cameron might have regarded himself as an Evangelical.

However, Cook appears to have been taken in by some mischief-making and rumour. It is clear from the 1836 Report to the Commissioners for Religious Instruction submitted by Macrae that from a population of 1,840 in the Parish of Barvas, 'all belonging to the established kirk' and with an average weekly attendance of about 300, the number of communicants 'does not exceed 12'. While in Stornoway, the same census return gives a parish population of 4,500, again 'all belonging to the established church'. John Cameron states that there were two quite distinct congregations, Gaelic- and English-speaking, both having average attendances of 1,500. At the seasonal communion prior to the census, the number receiving the sacrament amounted to 45.

It appears that some Evangelical ministers themselves, keen to display their undiluted puritan credentials, were not averse to criticising their own colleagues who failed to come up to the mark. As an Evangelical, Cook's first motivation was to bring individuals to a personal knowledge of the saving grace of God through Jesus Christ. To him and others, strict Calvinist doctrines remained unchanged, impervious to the social, cultural and religious upheavals taking place as the pace of 19th century life quickened. As well as remnants of popery, Cook also found there to be widespread practices from Celtic Christianity which he dismissed as 'pagan'. Cook's second objective was to correct the ill-informed teachings of Moderatism which Cook believed had done nothing to challenge or correct these pagan practices.

Donald Sage again quotes the letter received from Cook which states 'the people of the Hebrides were 'utterly unacquainted' with the ordinary means of religious instruction. Their public teachers were idle and inefficient', possibly a jibe at the SSPCK's efforts to teach only English in the classroom. However, this sweeping generalisation of an 'utterly unacquainted' Hebridean people whose teachers were idle and inefficient does not seem to be borne out by the facts, as reports of invigorated teaching and enthusiastic scholars from Uig are well-documented and where the parish school was in the capable hands of one John MacRae from 1825 onwards. MacRae was ordained to the charge of Ness, Lewis in 1833 and became one of the most revered ministers of the time.

Joseph Mitchell, assistant chief engineer to Thomas Telford, penned this reflection on the situation in Lewis as he found it around the year 1832. 'There are 4 parishes in Lewis, 2 of which were recently added [Parliamentary Churches]. The clergy who are educated men have great influence upon their flocks, but they are reported to lay more weight on matters of faith and doctrinal points than on ordinary cleanliness and conduct [a thoroughly Moderate view, surely]. Such is here the power of the church. Although Protestant, the minister appears to rule with popish sway. The minister of Barvas [William Macrae] is a man of intelligence and culture and is a friend and favourite of all the educated people in the island but he is not, it is said, evangelical enough for the taste of the country people, although much beloved for his kindness of heart and attention to their distresses and wants.'[17]

Mitchell evidently witnessed for himself a sense of 'degrees' of evangelicalism among the clergy. Clearly, William Macrae as a much-revered figure conducted an effective Evangelical ministry. However, among Evangelical ministers further differences became evident. It appears that the voice of the more radical elements among the clergy was quick to offer criticism, even of its own. The uber-Calvinist Cook had a deep suspicion of John Cameron, the Stornoway minister. Further, a very public dispute arose between Cameron, as minister in Stornoway and Alexander MacLeod, as minister in Uig, who along with Cook was another vocal and somewhat unforgiving individual. MacLeod believed in the severe purging of his roll while Cameron did not. Those like Cameron who showed the slightest tolerance towards any religious indiscipline or mercy towards the sinner were regarded as no better than the Moderates.

Another contemporary commentator was Lord Teignmouth, an English baronet and first president of the British and Foreign Bible Society. He embarked upon two visits to the Highlands 'to survey the scenery and acquire information respecting the moral and social conditions of regions which he regarded with early and strong predilection'. In his account of the 1828 visit to Lewis he states that the 'upper class' of Stornoway and presumably the better educated did not relish Cameron's preaching, advising that the better-off classes found Evangelical preaching 'an embarrassment' – this despite Cameron being well-loved and respected among his own people. Here was further evidence, not only of a theological divide, but of a class divide too. Evangelical preaching had found its home chiefly among the poor

---

17 Joseph Mitchell, *Reminiscences of my Life in the Highlands*, 1884.

and labouring classes, apparent also in the cities, while the 'better-off classes' (however Teignmouth defines them) still found their way to churches whose ministers had Moderate leanings. On Lewis, as Joseph Mitchell reported, some of the better-off classes had deserted Cameron in Stornoway and found their way to Barvas to hear William Macrae. Finlay Cook himself certainly did not warm to either the Barvas or Stornoway ministers as his own reflection penned some years after departing Cross reveals. Cook names fellow Evangelicals on Lewis as worthy and righteous colleagues. Unsurprisingly, nowhere do the names of either Macrae or Cameron appear.

Lewis in the 1820s: Revival in Uig

The Revd Alexander MacLeod arrived on Lewis after two years in the Gaelic Chapel in Dundee followed by three years in the Gaelic Chapel in Cromarty. He succeeded to the Uig pulpit after a Moderate incumbent who was seen to be ineffectual, lazy and ignorant and uncaring of the needs of his congregation. On his arrival, MacLeod's vigorous ministry coupled with an uncompromising puritan message from the pulpit began to 'awaken' the congregation from their slumbers and fire them with evangelical zeal. Uig's revival was underway and resulted in an expanding congregation and a general upsurge in people's faith and commitment.

Such was the people's 'thirst for gospel knowledge', the minister wrote from the manse on 30th November 1824 to the Seaforth MacKenzies, Lewis's landowners, to ask for a new church to accommodate expanding numbers. MacLeod also requested that the Edinburgh Gaelic School Society supply three new teachers together with 100 copies of the Gaelic Bible, 100 copies of the Gaelic New Testament and 200 copies of scripture extracts in Gaelic. Access to the Gaelic Bible, supported by ministers and catechists, became the essential resource for individuals to embrace fully the hope of salvation confirmed by participation in the sacraments and latterly to underpin revivalism. MacLeod had also applied to the Royal Bounty for the supply of the island's first catechist.

Uig was experiencing a prolonged and deep revival, and the establishing of the Friday Fellowship Meeting was obviously deemed necessary and desirable. The impetus for this would have come from MacLeod himself. He regarded 'The Men' as an important and valuable local resource as revival took hold. Appetites for gospel truths were invigorated and opportunities for personal prayer and devotion extended. The new church was duly completed in 1829 to accommodate upwards of 800 souls and major upgrading to the manse was also completed.[18] MacLeod also favoured a deep purging of his communion roll, small though it was, which denied people the sacrament if MacLeod and the Elders deemed any 'unworthy'. When he arrived in 1823 the church's role stood at 900. MacLeod swiftly reduced this to nine. Also, if the clearing of the township of Timsgarry to provide an enlarged glebe for MacLeod's own sheep in 1826 is to be believed, then the minister and Seaforth were as complicit as many Moderates and Tories in the matter of clearance.

While the situation on Lewis is illustrative of the different relationships found there among ministers and congregations caught up, as they were, in the *realpolitik* of the day, one can safely assume that this situation is also indicative and holds to be true across much of the rest of the Highlands and Islands but especially so in Evangelical hotspots on Skye, Caithness, Sutherland, Ross-shire and Cromarty.

Minister, Congregation, Communion

One year after accepting the call in 1823 to be minister in Uig, Alexander MacLeod reported on the moral and religious state of his people. In Uig there was also much resistance to his ministry among the community but the opinion expressed by Evangelicals was that the entire island had been badly infected by the disease of a lax and careless Moderatism. At the start, his people were 'astonished at the truths delivered and at a loss as to how to comprehend them'.[19] They were 'grossly ignorant of the truths of Christianity, had an idea of the hope of heaven that showed that the polluted remains of Popery was the only notion they had of Christianity', another possible reference to the mass whose crucial clause states, 'Lord, I am not worthy to receive you; but only say the word and my soul shall be healed.'

The easy and casual access to divine grace by the Catholic faithful was anathema to Evangelical discipline and rectitude and again explains the vehement anti-Catholic sentiment that remained among Highland Evangelicals long after it had dissipated in the south. MacLeod and others opined that spineless and ineffective Moderate ministries were either unable to correct these heretical propositions from the 'old religion' with its associated deep-seated superstitions, or were indeed indifferent towards their continued existence. MacLeod

---

18 Basically a much larger version of a Telford church and not built as a 'Parliamentary Church'.
19 Revd Murdo Macaulay, *Aspects of the Religious History of Lewis*, 173.

placed poor standards of personal behaviour – swearing, lies, stealing and drunkenness were common – firmly at the feet of ill-discipline within the Kirk, presided over by ignorant and lax Moderates. He further states, however, that as revival deepened many were converted to faith bringing about an immediate improvement to society.

MacLeod's ministry was centred in the south of the island and on Sundays many travelled from the parishes of Ness, Back and Knock, distances of between 20 and 40 miles, to attend his services. However, as far as the celebration of the Lord's Supper was concerned, such was its history of past, ill-disciplined affairs, with reports of between 800 and 900 flocking to the table and all communicating, only in June 1827, some four years after his arrival, was MacLeod able to conduct his first communion service. Only after a considerable time of preaching and teaching did he deem his people to be in a ready state of grace to receive the sacrament. The cautionary warning against receiving it unworthily was emphasised. He recalled that between 800 and 1,000 from the parish attended that first communion season and it was reported that over 6,000 from other parishes joined the congregation that day. However, out of that vast assembly only six felt called to be served.

On their respective arrivals at Cross and Uig on Lewis, both Finlay Cook and Alexander MacLeod did find the communion seasons (annual celebrations of the sacrament taking place over one weekend beginning on Friday and concluding on Monday) to be undisciplined, casual, formulaic and wholly irreligious affairs, according to their own strict standards. Cook's letter to his brother-in-law Donald Sage stated that 'one poor man had to testify that he never either witnessed or heard of a diet of catechetical instruction and another that five of his children had been baptised but that not one question was ever asked of him by the "reverend" incumbent concerning his own salvation or that of any of his children'.[20] Cook could only be referring to the situation at Barvas or Stornoway, as stated above, where evidence certainly counters Cook's own belief at the time. However, Cook continues by stating that the sacraments were administered, 'but in a stupified manner' and the usual services were curtailed or mutilated. 'Tents for the sale of intoxicating drinks were erected on the communion Mondays and from them proceeded all the riot and drunkenness of a Highland country fair, commencing almost immediately after the benediction was announced at the thanksgiving service in the open air'.[21]

---

20 Revd Donald Sage, *Memorabilia Domestica*, 296.
21 Revd Donald Sage, *Memorabilia Domestica*, 296.

MacLeod at Uig found much the same thing. Similar events took place on Skye. Revd Alexander Macrae states that what passed for 'religion', a potent mix of Druidism, Romanism and Protestantism, was nothing short of a 'grotesque superstition':

> The island was populated by witches, faeries and ghosts: darkness covered the land, and gross darkness the people. Drunken and riotous excesses abounded. The most outrageous orgies were indulged in: bagpipes were played, songs sung, filthy tales and jests recounted. The gatherings on the Lord's Day were fully utilised for business and pleasure. At communion seasons, pedlars, spirit-dealers and others erected their booths round the churchyards, and pushed a lively trade.[22]

The inference was clear: all the above vulgarities were allowed to flourish under the ministries of previous incumbents, the ever-detested Moderates.

The Holy Fair

Riotous and ill-disciplined Communion seasons were not confined to the Highlands and Islands. In Ayrshire, a blacksmith's account of a seasonal communion possibly provided the basis for Robert Burns' poem 'The Holy Fair'. The blacksmith's account describes all the rich and sour elements which Finlay Cook and Alexander Macrae encountered: 'In Scotland they run from kirk to kirk, and flock to see a sacrament, and make the same of it as the papists do of their pilgrimage and processions; that is, indulge themselves in drunkenness, folly and idleness ... in this sacred assembly there is an odd mixture of religion, sleep, drinking, courtship, and a confusion of sexes, ages and characters.'[23]

The blacksmith's account ends with the words 'there is such an absurd mixture of the serious and comic that, were we convened for any other purpose than that of worshipping the God and Governor of Nature, the scene would exceed all power of farce.'

In the poem, Burns mocks both Evangelical and Moderate preachers. Here, Moodie, an Evangelical minister, clambers into the pulpit:

---

22 Revd Alexander Macrae, *Revivals in the Highlands and Islands in the 19th Century*, 57.

23 Quoted from 'A Letter from a blacksmith to the ministers and elders of the Church of Scotland. In what the manner of publick worship in that church is considered; its inconveniences and defects pointed out; and methods for removing them humbly proposed.' 8th May 1758.

> For Moodie speels the holy door,
> wi' tidings o' damnation.
> Hear how he clears the point o' faith
> wi' rattlin and wi' thumpin!
> Now meekly calm, now wild in wrath,
> he's stampin and he's jumpin!
> Smith opens out his cauld harangues,
> on practice and on morals;
> an' aff the godly pour in thrangs,
> to gie the jars an' barrels
> a lift that day.

Smith, the Moderate, soon turns his listeners off who then leave to prepare the bar for the selling of alcohol. Those who had come to hear about matters of faith would be sorely disappointed. Burns continues:

> What signifies his barren shine
> of moral powers an' reason?
> His English style, an' gestures fine'
> are a' clean out o' season.
> Like Socrates or Antonine,
> some auld pagan heathen.
> The moral man he does define,
> but ne'er a word o' faith in
> that's right that day.

Burns wrote 'The Holy Fair' in 1786. Contemporary accounts suggest that the behaviour and demeanour of those attending seasonal communions in the south rapidly improved, no doubt due to the proliferation of buildings erected in the first three decades of the 1800s. Communion, in the urban setting, had moved indoors. For Finlay Cook, arriving in Ness forty-three years after Burns wrote his poem, little had changed in over a century.

By way of contrast, an article entitled 'State of Religion in the Highlands' had appeared in a London magazine and was reproduced in the Inverness Courier, coinciding with Revd Alexander MacLeod's arrival as minister in Uig. The piece contains a description of a celebration of the sacrament as witnessed by the author. Taking place in Lochinver, Sutherland, it was an altogether more sober, seemly and serious affair. The author came across the congregation seated on a grassy mound silently awaiting the arrival of the minister. 'I guessed them at three thousand; but was told I greatly underestimated the number. What a glorious sight! Everyone so neatly attired, so patient, so serious, so solemn!'[24] Many had travelled fifty miles to attend. He went on, 'I never thought about creeds; I thought only of what was before me – devotion! How poor are "gay religions full of pomp and gold" compared to their simple and sincere worship'.

The prayer lasted half an hour, the sermon an hour. Despite his lack of Gaelic, the correspondent listened 'unweariedly' as the minister preached with grace and dignity and 'the smile of good-will never left his countenance'. After the sermon, he addressed the assembly on the subject of Communion, ensuring that only those who 'obtained permission' received the sacrament. He was impressed with the solemnity of the congregation considering the service lasted eight and a half hours. Clearly, a more appropriate and disciplined approach to Communion prevailed in Sutherland in 1823 than on Lewis. The correspondent contrasts this austere event with 'gay religions full of pomp and gold', a jibe at Episcopal and Anglican occasions with their rituals and ceremonies.

The sacrament of communion itself became a battlefield where common ground was difficult, if not impossible, to determine: Evangelicals began to hold more frequent, emotionally-charged communions; Moderates adhered to strict communion seasons, celebrating the sacrament once or twice in the year; the Evangelical approach emphasized the 'exclusive' nature of the sacrament (only those deemed 'worthy' shall receive the sacrament) while Moderates favoured a more 'inclusive' approach ('none shall be turned away').

Theological Concerns over Communion

It was certainly the case that very few came forward to receive the sacrament under the strict leadership of Evangelical ministers. However, although the memorialist Revd Dr John Kennedy answers that criticism from the standpoint of the 'Ross-shire Fathers', the same would hold for the circumstances on Lewis and elsewhere across the north and west. For Dr Kennedy, the righteous Evangelical was being true to scriptural doctrine: baptism is a recognition of the need to be cleansed from sin by Christ as Saviour and its lessons are given as to a class of beginners. There are 'good grounds for maintaining that the way to the table of the Lord be more strictly guarded than

---

24 *Inverness Courier*, 29th May 1823.

the outer door of His house'.[25] The applicant for admission is expressly commanded first to examine himself as to his knowledge, experience and conduct which will, secondly, come under the strictest scrutiny by the Church and whose faith must demonstrate that he has been 'regenerated and justified already'. Having been prepared to the satisfaction of the catechist only those whose profession of faith had been 'accredited' by minister and Elders (and in many cases 'The Men' would have a hand in this too) will be admitted to the 'inner circle', by the sealing ordinance of the Supper.

Dr Kennedy defends the charge of 'exclusiveness' which inevitably was levelled by Moderates who stated that 'a few pious people scare themselves away from the Sacrament by superstitious notions of its sanctity'.[26] Kennedy considers this a mistake and 'it might be an improvement on the state of matters elsewhere if all the communicants had as much respect for this ordinance as many of the non-communicants in the north'. In any respect, he added, 'it is the invariable experience of a Highland minister that all whom he would wish to bring forward do, sooner or later, apply for admission to the table of the Lord'.

Kennedy's statement discloses the tight control ministers had on those presenting themselves for communion. Assisted by Elders and in some locations 'The Men', by controlling numbers, ministers were able to guard the propriety and efficacy of the sacrament. It is true to say, however, that the Evangelical dying and infirm came forward at the very last in numbers perhaps admitting that little time remained for an opportunity for 'sinning'. Having being cleansed by the sacrament they were now fitted for heaven, if the Lord would have them.

The matter of numbers communicating remained a cause for concern, especially in the Moderate-controlled Presbyteries of the north and west. While Evangelical ministers purposely and fiercely guarded the sacrament, lest those who took it unworthily faced eternal damnation, some Presbytery Clerks questioned a practice of maintaining a sacrament exclusively for the hand-picked righteous irrespective of the rigorous preparations by those under instruction seeking a seat at the table. The Moderate Revd James McLauchlan offered this criticism on these Evangelical practices in The United Parishes of Moy and Dalarossie, Presbytery of Inverness: 'Attendance

---

25 Revd Dr John Kennedy, *The Days of the Fathers in Ross-shire*, 138.
26 Revd Dr John Kennedy, *The Days of the Fathers in Ross-shire*, 144.

at worship is good, but the number of communicants is small, owing to the doctrines instilled by demagogues in regard to the sacrament of the supper.'[27] A further criticism by another Moderate Revd Archibald Clerk noted similar practices in the Parish of Duirnish, Presbytery of Skye. Writing in 1841 Clerk stated:

> By the influence of some men (some are lay-preachers) the majority of people have come to regard the sacraments, especially the Lord's Supper, with a degree of horror. There are nearly 200 children unbaptized and the table of the Lord is unfrequented. Piety is expressed by avoiding the sacraments. These unscriptural notions are daily gaining ground in the place. An open and unshrinking profession of religion is more frequent and more honoured than it was not many years ago. And although the wicked are becoming bolder in their wickedness, believers are becoming more courageous in the cause of the Lord.[28]

Despite Dr Kennedy's assurances, the number of those coming forward to receive the sacrament did remain a tiny proportion of the total who attended seasonal communions reportedly to be as many as 20,000 or 30,000. An unrelenting diet of Evangelical sermons emphasising the corrupt nature of the human spirit seemed to consolidate every sense of an individual's 'unworthiness' and at each seasonal communion the congregations gathered from far and wide were constantly warned about receiving the sacrament 'unworthily'. Celebrants often quoted Paul's 1st letter to the Corinthians ch.11 vv.27-29, 'He that eateth and drinketh unworthily, eateth and drinketh judgement to himself.'

The threat of judgement for many Evangelicals was such a powerful deterrent that it actively prevented them from communicating. Also, it was not an uncommon belief that participation in the sacrament was seen as 'popish' and therefore to be avoided. Perversely, keeping away from the communion table was often seen as proof of righteousness. However, Revd Dr MacKintosh MacKay of Harris, venerated Gaelic scholar and Evangelical minister did not agree. He held a positive view regarding the sacraments and thought it dishonoured the Lord's Table if individuals held back. For him, non-participation was no evidence of grace or proof of righteousness. Here was further evidence of fault-lines

---

27 *The Statistical Accounts of Scotland 1845: Moy and Dalarossie, County of Inverness, vol. XIV,* 112.
28 *The Statistical Accounts of Scotland 1841: Duirinish, County of Inverness, vol. XIV,* 355.

within the Evangelical ministry itself as in the case of attitudes towards communicant rolls. Some Evangelical ministers favoured purging, so retaining a small membership list of only the 'truly righteous' while others were less strict in the admission of new members who were therefore able to gain access to the communion table.

As far as numbers relating to baptism and communion were concerned (and which statistics support) statistical returns reveal a deal of over-zealous policing did take place among Evangelical congregations but, conversely, there is certainly little evidence that the sacrament was administered either casually or perfunctorily, an accusation laid on Moderates. Indeed, the rigorous examination of people seeking admission to communion continued to cause trouble throughout the Highlands.

Among Evangelicals themselves there was not one consistent view regarding an individual's fitness to attend the Lord's Table. While the Synod of Ross attempted to make one rule for all its ministers to adhere to, individuals continued in other parts of the north and west to order matters according to their own likes. All Evangelicals however had common cause in opposing Moderate-held views on communion. The stinging charge levelled at them was that admission to the Lord's Table was made too easy, a criticism similar to the Catholic mass. Evangelicals believed that those anticipating a seat at the Lord's Table had not been sufficiently or rigorously examined upon their faith by catechists and ministers. Only in isolated and extreme cases was laxity and ill-discipline among clergy recorded, with both sacraments administered in the same casual manner. Communion was regarded as a 'second step' because the baptised were deemed 'qualified'. Some communion seasons under the authority of a small number of Moderates were known to be unseemly, undisciplined and riotous affairs. As a result, Evangelicals all too easily characterised Moderates as self-regarding, ignorant, indolent and uncaring of their congregations and, above all, perfunctorily indifferent towards the sacraments. The accusation of demonstrating a casual and unscriptural attitude towards the great themes of faith condemned Moderate ministers out of hand.

Evangelical and Moderate Approach to Preaching

Alexander MacLeod in Uig, Finlay Cook in Cross and every other Evangelical minister across the north and west would aver that the 'preaching of the word' was central to the education of their respective congregations. However, Moderates were accused of ignoring the great themes of faith and the contrast between Moderate and Evangelical sermons could not be more marked. The latter never deviated from the central tenets of Reformation theology, emphasising confession, the need for forgiveness and the possibility of salvation depending on the grace of God. The cause of the fractured relationship between the Almighty and humankind was 'sin'; and this fractured relationship required repairing which was undertaken solely by the grace of God. This was a religion for and of the elect with a distinct emphasis on *spirituality*.

On the other hand, with a clear emphasis on *morality*, Moderate sermons favoured a more liberal approach with instructions on how to live a better life. Matters of faith intruded little into day-to-day living, there being clear demarcation between the 'religious' life and the 'social' life, as typified by Prime Minister Lord Melbourne's overheard remark after hearing a sermon on sin: 'Things have come to a pretty pass when religion is allowed to invade the sphere of private life.' Becoming a 'better Christian' by improving behaviour was central to Moderate theology. Moderates were unmoveable in their policies favouring a more secular, theologically liberal world view and rejected any possible return to puritanism. At times, it was difficult to believe that Evangelicals and Moderates belonged to the same Church.

Evangelicals were too ready to condemn wholeheartedly the entire Moderate wing while certainly disregarding worthy individuals who held the care of souls and the plight of congregations as a priority and the concern to match. Statistical returns such as the Report of the Commissioners of Religious Instruction, Scotland 1836, reveal in parish by parish throughout the Highlands and Islands deep concerns for the spiritual well-being of congregations. These returns, reported by Moderate and Evangelical ministers alike, point to the remoteness of many communities, lack of buildings (there is strong support for the Parliamentary Church model) and lack of ministerial support. These reports echo the situation in 1793 when ministers were preparing the Statistical Accounts. Nothing had changed. These reports, however, suggest that Moderates were as well-attuned to the needs of their congregations as Evangelicals and similarly moved to suggest remedies.

The Balance Tips

However much the statistics reported the situation on the ground Evangelical ministers believed themselves to be more in tune with the needs of their parishes than Moderates, especially across the

Highlands and Islands. By the 1820s Evangelicals had begun to take control of more pulpits across the north and west which allowed two vital situations to develop: it enabled and facilitated the flowering of local revivals under strong Evangelical leadership; and it promoted and reinforced with increasing vigour the Reformation principles at the very heart of the religious life.

These increases in numbers also began to alter, slowly but surely, the theological balance of Presbyteries and Synods. Evangelicals held that Moderates were exhibiting institutional fatigue. As they saw it, the Moderate-controlled Assemblies oversaw the continuing failure to address adequately the problems of a rapidly expanding urban population outstripping the Kirk's response. Specifically, in the north and west and despite the investment of many resources in terms of manpower and money, Moderates were continually failing to address the challenges posed by the Highlands. Further, the theological failure at the heart of Moderatism gave rise to a diminished and dead spirituality, eager to focus too readily on worldly matters.

For the Evangelical, the persuasive Enlightenment voices promoting liberalism and moralism had all but drowned out the message at the core of Reformed theology: how to embrace the saving grace of Jesus Christ. For strong Evangelical leaders such as Andrew Thomson and Thomas Chalmers, deft, masterful theologians and Church politicians, the Kirk had become directionless but worse, it had lost focus to challenge, inspire and win over hearts and minds.

The ramifications for the north and west were clear: Moderate theology and the Moderate critique had failed and as the Highlander now saw himself a victim of clearance, poverty and patronage, his very culture seemed at odds with the rest of the country. The Highlander was in the main unserved by the Kirk. Evangelicals were determined to rescue the Highlands and Islands out of Moderate stupor but by doing so introduced a narrower, more rigorous and more proscriptive religion in its place.

Ancient and Modern: a Clash of Temperament

> *The Celtic spiritual tradition is one that has long emphasised an awareness of the sacred essence of all things. This tradition is in fact part of our Western Christian inheritance, although it has been largely forgotten and at times suppressed.*
>
> John Philip Newell, *Sacred Earth Sacred Soul*

The documented religious, moral and social transformations occurring in the Highlands and Islands of Scotland, and which took place over time, are well documented. The complete and unbidden reordering of Highland life for most people came painfully. The people of the north and west, from the earliest years of the 19th century, were becoming more and more subject to the influence of strong Evangelical leadership. From the perspective of many of the social and religious practices whose origins were formed in the mists of time, life now seemed less vibrant, less tolerant and more restrictive and restrained.

In his volume *Carmina Gadelica* (The Songs of the Gael), a collection of Gaelic poems, songs, prayers and benedictions, Lismore-born author Alexander Carmichael assembled a vast treasury of material collected throughout his working life as an excise-man in the latter half of the 19th century, working extensively across the north and west. The collection was published in 1900. Contained in the narratives, the collection is a powerful expression of the wisdom of the human soul over the centuries. John Philip Newell states, 'In times of loss and adversity it is the song of the soul that has safeguarded a memory of life's sacredness and a belief in love's grace.'[29]

This deep spirituality, acknowledging the divine within the created order, certainly pre-dates the arrival of Ninian and Columba. In Carmichael's collection of prayers and blessings, earth, air, fire and water are seen as sacred, and life-giving energies of the divine are viewed as both encompassing and interpenetrating the human. These prayers and blessings carry pre-Christian wisdom which finds its way into Christian expressions of faith. Nurtured within the oral Gaelic tradition these words also point to the rites and rituals, superstitions and ceremonies which the Gael had performed since the coming of Columba. A distinctive Celtic Christianity was born here. Much of this had similarities to Druidism. Many deemed them to be 'pagan', as when Carmichael once heard a young man rebuking his grandfather for his 'lying Gaelic stories'[30] and it was the threat to Reformation orthodoxy which ultimately moved the Kirk to begin to excise these distinctive expressions of faith. In theory, within Reformation orthodoxy, especially as Evangelicals viewed it, there was no possible accommodation with any aspects of pre-Christian or Celtic spirituality.

As Evangelical influences began to extend across the Highlands and Islands, communities were forced into a more rigid expression of

---
29 John Philip Newell, *Sacred Earth Sacred Soul*, 97.
30 Alexander Carmichael, *Carmina Gadelica*, 24.

faith in an attempt to extinguish these ancient practices from times past but now regarded as 'corrupt'. Aspects of Celtic Christianity and lingering Catholic superstitions were both incompatible with puritan ideals. One anonymous commentator opined that 'corrupt, guilt-ridden Catholicism had been replaced by joyless, guilt-ridden Presbyterianism'. Prudish legalism began to replace this particular form of the vibrant and life-affirming spirituality of the Highlands and Islands. 'Even the rooster was locked away on the Sabbath, lest it think of doing anything 'natural' with the hens.'[31] Newell offers this quote from 19th century Lewis as a ludicrous example of rigid and proscriptive behaviour.

Further, it must be recognised that age-old practices and superstitions did not vanish overnight with the coming of the reformation, or with the re-establishing of a Presbyterian form of church government, or with the arrival of Evangelical ministers. The 'lapse of Halmadary', from the county of Sutherland's past, is a salutary tale and demonstrates the tension experienced by faithful Presbyterians yet reluctant to relinquish old habits and customs from deep within their Highland cultural, spiritual and religious DNA, or even from more ancient pagan times.

In this case from 1740 the incident focused on the frenzied exhortations of a lay leader in an unauthorised prayer meeting, although there was a suggestion that a minister was in attendance. The lay leader who had a fanciful fixation on the story of Abraham's sacrifice of Isaac led the assembled company to prepare a fire whereupon the young son of an unpopular tacksman was to be sacrificed. Fortunately, a travelling merchant chanced upon the situation and his timely intervention broke the spell. The incident was minuted by the Presbytery in 1749 as 'the melancholy scene that happened years ago in one of these unauthorised meetings in Halmadary', an incident which demonstrated that such attitudes could linger at the deepest level of the soul and might rest unacknowledged or unrecognised until triggered by events which allowed them to surface.

Revd Kenneth Morison was appointed the Stornoway minister before the Presbyterian settlement of 1689.[32] He was described as a highly-gifted man, 'well-suited to repress the turmoils in Lewis at the time, between Papists and Protestants. For protection he carried a

---

31 John Philip Newell, *Sacred Earth Sacred Soul*, 109.
32 Revd Murdo Macaulay, *Aspects of Religious History of Lewis*, 44.

sword and stationed two guards with weapons drawn at the door of the church during services. On one occasion after he had administered the sacrament of baptism to a child, a woman dipped her hand into the remaining water in the vessel, and threw as much as she could lift in her hand on the face of a female servant to prevent her from seeing visions. The report concludes it had the desired effect.

Superstitions surrounding baptismal water as a curative may have been widespread across much of the north and west. Further, a curious incident from the life of Finlay Cook, first minister of Cross on Lewis, reveals that even strict Evangelicals like him were not immune from employing old and ancient superstitious practices which had no place within the liturgy and learning of the Kirk. On a visit to Uig, Cook fell into conversation with Alexander MacKenzie the catechist, regarding how sinful the latter's life had been in each of his three appointments, Assynt, Lochbroom and Lewis.[33] Cook came to him and laying a hand on his shoulder stated he was going to give him 'three dips in Loch Roag', the first for his Assynt sins, the second for his Lochbroom sins and the third for his sins while on Lewis. This was certainly not any kind of 'baptism' as the Kirk would recognise it but might be regarded as a cleansing ritual which had decidedly baptismal overtones.

These two irregular incidents perhaps smack of a Celtic echo from long past, one in the use of charms and the second from within Cook's own Gaelic heritage. The consolidation of Evangelical Presbyterianism across the north and west from the early 19th century onwards by strict ministerial practitioners and an unyielding church discipline combined to combat these practices from more ancient and superstitious times. But it took the best part of the next hundred years for both the Evangelical wing of the Kirk and the Free Church to finally eradicate and expunge all doctrinal 'impurities' across the Highlands and Islands.

A Growing Austerity

The colourful and joyful expression and celebration of life's gifts were replaced by an altogether more austere and sterner behaviour, under the proscriptive eye of Evangelical ministers as this tale from the Isle of Lewis demonstrates. For his collection of Gaelic tales, Alexander Carmichael asked a local woman if there was still music, dancing and singing at wedding feasts:

---

33 Revd Murdo Macaulay, *Aspects of Religious History of Lewis*, 76.

Oh, indeed, no, our weddings are now quiet and becoming, not the foolish things they were in my young days . . . In my young days [we can hazard a date around the 1830s and perhaps coinciding with the arrival of Rev Finlay Cook] there was hardly a house in Ness in which there was not one or two who could play the pipe or the fiddle . . . A blessed change came over the place and the people, and the good men and the good ministers who arose did away with the songs and the stories, the music and the dancing, the sports and the games, that were perverting the minds and ruining the souls of the people, leading them to folly and stumbling . . . They made the people break and burn their pipes and fiddles. If there was a foolish man here or there who demurred, the good ministers and the good elders themselves broke and burnt their instruments, saying, 'Better is the small fire that warms on the little day of peace, than the big fire that burns on the great day of wrath'. The people have forsaken their follies and their Sabbath-breaking, and there is no pipe, no fiddle here now.'[34]

The same woman went on to explain to Carmichael that men and women were now kept apart at the wedding feasts, the women on the one side, the men on the other. Unmarried girls were not even allowed to be seen at the feast for 'fear of their life', lest they be reported to the minister and denounced the following Sunday from the pulpit. But when Carmichael proceeded to ask if they were still allowed alcohol at the wedding feasts, the woman replied, 'Oh, yes, the minister is not so hard as that upon them all'.

In other words, Newell concludes, dance was denied, the natural socialising of men and women on such occasions demonised, but drink was allowed. As Newell observed, 'Increasingly the abuse of alcohol began to dominate the culture of the islands. A people's soul was being numbed.'[35] The Statistical Accounts reveal a population on Lewis of 14,000 and an annual consumption of 4,520 imperial gallons of spirits.[36] Small-scale whisky distilling was a traditional part of Highland life but laws passed in 1822 and 1823 sought to introduce more regulation into the industry which effectively outlawed illegal distilling. However, those who enforced the new regulations saw

---

34 Alexander Carmichael, *Carmina Gadelica*, 26-27.
35 John Philip Newell, *Sacred Earth Sacred Soul*, 111.
36 *The Statistical Accounts of Scotland 1845: Stornoway County of Ross and Cromarty*, vol. XIV, 140.

little wrong in the practice and often turned a blind eye to the continuing illegal industry. In a letter used as evidence for a revenue commissioner's report in 1822, Sir George Mackenzie of Coul said, 'There is not a justice of the peace who can say, that he does not, in his own family, consume illegal whisky.'[37] Justices of the Peace were often local landowners and well aware that income from illegal distilling was frequently the only thing enabling their tenants to pay rent and so normally imposed ridiculously low fines on those caught breaking the law. The unforeseen consequence of stamping out illegal whisky production was a population unable to make ends meet eventually leaving the district, extending the diaspora.

Superstition or Mystic Reality?

We cannot rule out the possibility that in death the relationship we have with the world is not abolished, but is rather, for the first time completed . . . through death the soul becomes not a-cosmic but all-cosmic.

Karl Rahner, *On the Theology of Death*

The particular Highland and Hebridean approach to death and dying was yet another set of traditions under attack from Reformation legalism and Evangelical demands. Having existed for a thousand years, Celtic Spirituality commonly spoke of angels and heavenly messengers, visible to the dying and others supervising the transporting of the dead to paradise. There was also the mystical awareness of a death happening in a faraway place. The author Ian Bradley asserts that this is indicative of second sight, and the 'ambiguity between the orthodox Christian doctrine of the post-mortem state as a long period of sleep before a general resurrection and the popular belief in the immortality of the soul and a more immediate passage to heaven after death.'[38] At funerals, prayers, chants and singing were expected on these occasions together with revelry, much whisky and cake shared. These occasions were important community opportunities to celebrate a life well lived.

The 1560 First Book of Discipline put a stop to all that, expressing a profound Presbyterian unease regarding prayers for the dead, which was regarded as 'popish'. All rites and rituals were thereby proscribed but this was in reality unworkable. A thousand years of tradition,

---

37 Rachel McCormack, *Chasing the Dram*, 211.
38 Ian Bradley, *The Coffin Roads*, 38.

encompassing magic, superstition, the use of charms, a belief in faeries, the use of folk-medicine and the practice of second sight, rooted deeply in the soul and body of the Highlander could not easily be overturned. Entrenched pagan beliefs held their ground with dogged persistence.

The Kirk had neither the ministerial manpower to ensure compliance, nor was the presence of a minister expected at funerals. Such ordinances, as it transpired, were somewhat 'unregulated'. Yet, as Dr Johnson discovered on his Highlands and Islands tour in 1773, 'The various kinds of superstition which prevailed here, as in all other regions of ignorance, are by the diligence of the Ministers almost extirpated' but adding 'They still have among them a great number of charms for the cure of different diseases; they are all invocations, perhaps transmitted to them in the times of popery, which increasing knowledge will bring into disuse.'[39]

The prevalence for superstitious behaviour and practices were decidedly ingrained into the Gael. As far as 'second sight' was concerned Dr Johnson also observed, 'It is the common talk of the Lowland Scots, that the notion of the Second Sight is wearing away with other superstitions; and that its reality is no longer supposed, but by the grossest people.'[40] He concluded his findings by commenting, 'The Islanders of all degrees, whether of rank or understanding, universally admit it, except the Ministers, who universally deny it, and are expected to deny it, in consequence of a system, against conviction.'

Lord Teignmouth visited Bracadale in 1827 as part of his more extensive Highland tour, also looking for evidence of 'second sight', which was not dying out as Dr Johnson had attested but which was thriving and was especially prevalent. He found the population generally 'peculiarly susceptible of religious impressions'. He offered a personal view on the unique and peculiar beliefs and practices of a 'mongrel' religion, current at his time of writing. He adds,

> Unhappily, during many ages, ignorant or instructed only in error, they blended with the pure faith which they had received from missionaries of the gospel, all the absurd poetical fictions derived from the stock from which they sprang, from Scandinavian invaders, from monks, or from the innumerable hoard of imposters, bards, minstrels, seers and dealers in second sight, who preyed upon their incredulity. In spite of education

---

[39] Dr Samuel Johnson, *A Journey to the Western Isles of Scotland*, 151.
[40] Dr Samuel Johnson, *A Journey to the Western Isles of Scotland*, 154.

and intercourse with strangers, they cling to the superstitious delusions and practices of their forebears.[41]

Lord Teignmouth again noted the absence of religious ceremony at a funeral he attended on Jura, reflecting the fact that most funerals were organised and conducted by family members without the professional services of either minister or undertaker. The funeral was conducted with all due solemnity which gave way to much revelry after the short prayer of thanksgiving had been offered. Teignmouth further records other occasions where excessive and disorderly scenes followed certain funerals.

The significance of the graveyard is also a distinctive Highland belief, as a place to maintain contact with those who have died and in which to grieve and remember them. Bagpipes were regularly played at Highland and Hebridean funerals, although as early as 1836 Teignmouth received reports from Highlanders that dancing and the playing of the pipes at funerals had ceased. The clergy disapproved of these practices which they thought encouraged drinking and carousing. The practice across the north and west appears to have disappeared entirely by the middle of the 19th century, no doubt under pressure from Evangelical ministers, especially those associated with the Free Church. However, these prohibitions could not remove the rich seam of paranormal and supernatural lore permeating both Protestant and Roman Catholic communities which later became the subject of psychical research.

> ... *The journey of death was viewed as holy. It was a voyage into the heart of nature, a returning to God ... Waiting on the other side of death's waters are the midwives of eternity, waiting with outstretched arms to receive us. In the Celtic world there is the hope that, just as the newborn child is received with love through the waters of birth, so upon death's crossing we are welcomed back to the place of our beginning.*
>
> John Philip Newell, *Sacred Heart Sacred Soul*

Peculiar to Highland and Hebridean spirituality was the chanting of the 'death-croon' over the dying by one specifically known as the 'soul friend', this having its origins in the days of monasticism in the Celtic church. The position of 'soul friend' evolved over the centuries

---

41 Charles John Shore, Baron Teignmouth, *Sketches of the Coasts and Islands of Scotland, and of the Isle of Man*, 133.

and was held, in turn, by elders in the community, a semi-professional class of 'mourning women' and latterly by midwives. The singing of the death-croon assisted the soul's journey into the next life. Carmichael records in his *Carmina Gadelica* that the figure of the 'soul friend' had developed into a specialised form of lay ministry to the dying which was still very much in existence in the Hebrides in his own time.[42]

There appears to have been a particular custom in certain Island communities regarding the laying out of a body in preparation for its burial. A story known to the writer relates to the death of the old father whose body is persuaded into his Sunday suit and then laid out on the kitchen table. At the end of the day with only the fading glow of the peat fire and two guttering candles for light, one at the head and one at the feet, does the eldest son with great ceremony reach for the family bible from the shelf to place it on the chest of his dead father. There he will rest until morning. At the arranged time, the undertakers duly arrived to coffin the old man. It was then one of the undertakers called the son aside to enquire if there was a specific reason why a copy of Webster's Etymological Dictionary had been placed on his father's chest. In the poorest of light, the two volumes were identical in size and heft.

Ian Bradley states that some of Carmichael's collection of death-croons contained a certain developed theological content, reflecting the influence of Evangelical Christianity's doctrine of 'Christ buying the salvation of the human soul through the shedding of his blood'.[43] Such chants emanated from both the Protestant northern islands of Lewis, Harris, and North Uist and the Catholic southern islands of South Uist, Vatersay, Barra and Eriskay. Bradley continues, 'So too are themes of penitence, repentance and forgiveness of sin. In the chants from the Catholic islands, as one might expect, there is more emphasis on confession and absolution from a priest and anointing with oil in the last right of extreme unction.'

Carmichael's collection, translated as 'The Song of the Gael', has nothing to say regarding any exposition of the Christian doctrine of resurrection from the dead as expressed by the creeds of the church. Carmichael notes that there is almost nothing about hell and only occasional hints regarding God's judgement, nor has the collection anything to say about purgatory, the Roman Catholic belief in the intermediate post-mortem state in which the souls of the departed will be tested and cleansed to make them ready for heaven.

---

42 Alexander Carmichael, *Carmina Gadelica*, 578.
43 Ian Bradley, *The Coffin Roads*, 105.

Celtic Spirituality and the Bible

From this Celtic spirituality might be characterised as a joyous expression of humankind's place within the firmament of God's creation, a union of the temporal and the eternal, the seen and the unseen and to be in tune with the resonances and rhythms of nature. This gives us one angle on Celtic Christianity, which of course did include orthodox features not mentioned by Carmichael.

Christ's birth was celebrated as a manifestation of the light that already existed in the earth, sea and sky, the deep mystery of the intermingling of the divine and the human, the conjoining of spirit and matter. Newell asserts that, crucially, to know the sacred essence of one's being was to know also one's calling to serve the sacredness in each other and in the relationships of self with the world.[44]

This heightened sense of a religious life lived in community was predicated upon acknowledging the interdependence of its society. This ensured the welfare of each individual. Celtic Christianity stressed the significance of Creation and the Incarnation, as well as the Cross and Resurrection, and had a positive view of humankind and life in general, which contrasted with the narrow legalisms of the Evangelical wing of the church at that time.

It is little wonder that the Kirk, gaining evangelical ground in the north and west, expended great energy to suppress and extinguish every aspect of these age-old traditions and superstitions. Further, the great concern of successive General Assemblies was the continuing presence and possible resurgence of the Catholic church. Again, to deal with the beliefs and practices as they existed entailed the suppression of an unregulated laity and the imposition of a severe religious discipline as laid down, controlled and exercised by the tenets of Reformation orthodoxy. Such orthodoxy placed the doctrines of eternal damnation, hell and judgement, not so stressed in Celtic Christianity, now front and centre of the new order. There was a concerted effort by Evangelicals to banish all beliefs and practices which were held to be unorthodox.

At the same time Evangelical Presbyterianism asserted the primacy of the ordained ministry, wresting any control from the laity and bringing discipline, obedience and restraint to bear upon congregations. In these, the Evangelical ministers of the Highlands and Islands had themselves become the party of 'law and order'.

---

44 John Philip Newell, *Sacred Earth Sacred Soul,* 105.

As the oral traditions lost their potency, all teaching, learning, sharing and disseminating was to be achieved eventually through the written word. The wider accessibility of the Bible and the importance of the Catechism, a tool for formalising and regulating the religious life, in addition to the efforts of the SSPCK and Gaelic Schools Societies, effectively replaced the wisdom of the old pre-Christian age.

This particular wisdom had been honed and codified from the time of Columba onwards in hearts and minds but Evangelicalism had rendered much of it redundant and anachronistic – but most of all unorthodox. Having codified a new orthodoxy, the Reformers first attempted to expunge these expressions of Highland and Hebridean spirituality, and Evangelical Christianity in the 18th and 19th centuries finished the job.

Celtic Christianity with its particular brand of spirituality found it had no place in the theology, liturgy or life of the Kirk.

Essay Eight

The Kirk's Growing Pains

Towards the end of the 18th century and for the first decades of the 19th, Scotland's population was in a state of constant flux. Large swathes of the Highlands and Islands were being systematically and cruelly cleared to make way for more profitable sheep-ranching, then deer-stalking. Highlanders were faced with three options: to be forcibly cleared to the coastal margins leaving the interior of the land entirely stripped of people; to be 'emigrated' by rapacious landlords who paid the passages to America or Australia; to migrate to the expanding industrial central belt of Scotland and find work in the iron, chemical and glass industries. There Highland workers were tempted by work, wages and accommodation. The large cities of Glasgow and Edinburgh, and their surrounding satellite towns, all needed fresh recruits to feed the factories and dye-plants, mills and forges as Scotland began to make its significant contribution to the great Victorian age.

The Kirk, as the Established Church in Scotland and in whose care the peoples' education, welfare and the message of the hope of salvation rested, was not always alive to the new challenges posed by a population on the move. The old parish system of 'one church one minister' was essentially a mediaeval model founded upon, and better suited to, more stable, rural, agrarian times. This old model was beginning to creak at the seams as it attempted to address the new age. And there were many within Moderate-controlled General Assemblies who appeared reluctant to make the necessary changes, comfortable as they were fulfilling their duties (perfunctorily, Evangelicals would say) and lifting their stipends.

Thankfully, there were others, Evangelicals and Moderates, who were reading the signs. They recognised that what was needed were more ministers, more churches, better administered poor laws, more schools and more school-masters. The realignment of old parishes, both in the north and south, was also essential but for different reasons: in the south, it was becoming increasingly obvious with the explosion in population numbers that the old parish system was failing; in the north, an increasingly elderly ministry was expected to fulfil the ordinances of religion to a scattered population across vast areas of inhospitable country. The pressing need for an expansion in church provision, and all that came with it, became a priority as the demographic changes accelerated. In the north and west, the challenge for the Kirk was how to meet the needs of a population whose situation in terms of geography, history, language and culture simply did not fit patterns of parish and congregational life more familiar to the majority of the commissioners who annually attended General Assemblies.

Those who recognised that times were changing moved the Kirk to engage in three areas of action: to recognise that the Highlands and Islands required different solutions to the challenges posed by the Lowlands; to roll out a policy of church extension across the country; to enter into discussion with Government for assistance with building costs and to establish a national endowment to help with the payments of stipend. During the 20 years from 1818 to 1838 the issue of 'Church Extension', in its various forms, was one which commanded constant attention.

Since the introduction of the Royal Bounty in 1725, the Church of Scotland had already been receiving financial assistance from a third party, initially given to seriously promote Protestantism in the Highlands and to check any further growth in Catholicism. From as early as this time, there was a recognition that the Kirk could not possibly achieve all it was called to do without financial help coming from an outside source. This was especially so in the north and west where the basic provision of a minister's stipend was beyond a congregation's financial capabilities.

On this basis, the Kirk in 1817 made a formal approach to Government for financial assistance, resulting in the Highland Churches Act of 1824 which provided additional churches across the north and west. The 'Parliamentary Churches', a unique category within the panoply of church provision, will be the subject of the final essays.

Evangelicals on the March

In the south, 'Mission' was reinvigorated by committed, enthusiastic and hard-working Evangelicals who had recognised that the old and tired ways of the Moderates were no longer fit for purpose and did not meet the needs of the people. Moderates were accused of presiding over a Kirk that was falling asleep on the job. But Presbyterian Evangelicalism was on the march. In many parts of the country the

Church of Scotland was revitalised: popular Evangelical preachers were filling churches; increased numbers of Evangelical students preparing for ordination; Highland pulpits beginning to be filled by Evangelical ministers.

Evangelical influence, suffusing every aspect of church life from local congregations and eventually to the Courts of the church, was attracting a new constituency. At the 1824 General Assembly, such was the Evangelicals' compelling argument for developing a 'mission strategy', that it garnered support from many Moderates and so was formed a permanent General Assembly Committee on Foreign Missions. This was a breakthrough. For 25 years Moderate-controlled Assemblies had rejected calls to support overseas mission which had left the field open to voluntary agencies such as the British and Foreign Bible Society to fill the vacuum. Now the Kirk was able to harness its formidable fire-power by becoming involved.

Running concurrently was an effort to strengthen 'Home Mission'. 20 years earlier, such a phrase would have had little meaning.[1] The challenges were now recognised: in the south, how the Church might serve a people crowding into the slums of the industrial heart of Scotland; in the north and west, how the Church might serve a scattered population, often on the move. Thus, a new Evangelical impetus was underway: to build new churches; plant new congregations and strengthen existing ones; and reach out into parishes.

The Kirk's Response

The first concerted effort by the national Church to address the accommodation shortage saw the building of 66 'chapels-of-ease' between 1790 and 1834. In 1789 the Assembly passed the Chapel Act. This Act gave permission to Presbyteries to erect chapels where additional accommodation was needed, enabling them to procure an additional pastor. All were erected by private subscription. Other than a few, most of these churches were unendowed, that is to say that no public or General Assembly funds were available to pay for ministry. Congregations therefore were obliged to pay their ministers out of seat-rents and church-door collections. Local heritors, who commonly contributed to the build-costs but who were legally obliged to pay stipends, had first call on any surpluses and should make good any shortfalls. The historian J.H.S. Burleigh, states, 'Doubtless, sometimes,

---

[1] Stewart J. Brown, *Thomas Chalmers and the Godly Commonwealth*, 212.

the purpose to be served by a chapel-of-ease was to provide an alternative to the local parish church when the minister was unpopular or unacceptable. Moreover church door collections were the main source of funds for the relief of the poor, supplemented if necessary by an assessment on the heritor'.[2] The chapel had no area allocated to it as its parish, and had no kirk session of its own. Its minister had no seat in the courts of the church, and his congregation came under the supervision of the kirk session of the parish church in whose area the chapel was sited. Yet heritors were still able to remain obstructive in filling vacancies.

One Kirk One Minister: One Size Doesn't Fit All

But the [Parliamentary Churches] arrangement originated entirely in the jealousy of the dominant Moderate party, who wished the parochial ministers (although not bishops either in name or de jure) to be regarded as having Episcopal powers in the respective parishes.

Donald Sage, *Memorabilia Domestica*

It was certainly the case that the status of both chapel and minister was 'irregular'. In the urban setting chapels eased accommodation pressures and provided 'over-spill' from the crowded parish churches. The majority of these were erected in the larger cities while a small number were established in the Highlands to solve a different set of challenges namely, to make the services of the Kirk and offices of the minister available to those living and working in the remotest parts of the country.

Procedures to plant new congregations by the division of existing parishes proved well nigh impossible as legal and economic hindrances were formidable. To alter parish boundaries which by tradition were aligned with the civil parish would have brought the Church into potential conflict with landowners. For Moderates, chapels provided an unpopular but necessary solution to the problem: they tended to be filled with Evangelical ministers who operated free from the yoke of patronage as the appointment of such ministers was vested in the male members of the congregations; Moderates, stout upholders of the old parish system and keen advocates of patronage, supported the landowners' right to appoint ministers of their own choosing, having no confidence in any choice made by an uneducated rabble.

---

2 J.H.S. Burleigh, *A Church History of Scotland*, 319.

Moderates appear to have hindered the expansion of the chapel system and certainly ensured through legislation a lower ecclesiastical status for these chapel ministers thus guaranteeing such ministers 'knew their place'. In effect, Moderates guarded the rights and privileges which historically had accrued to the parish minister and it was parish ministers who alone controlled Presbyteries and Synods. All other forms of ministry, those ordained as missionaries, those appointed and ordained to chapels, those ordained and working under the auspices of the Society in Scotland for Propagating Christian Knowledge (SSPCK) were excluded from all decision-making responsibilities in the courts of the Church. Complete control of Kirk affairs was vested in the parochial ministry.

Crucially, those appointed as ministers to the Parliamentary Churches at the end of the 1820s were also in the same category as chapel ministers. While Moderates clung on to the old pattern of parish ministry, it was becoming increasingly obvious that this particular Reformation principle was unsuited to the new situation, both in the vast empty landscapes of the north and west, and in the burgeoning heartlands of the south.

Historically, one-third of the Kirk's ministers were paid by the Crown from the sequestered monies accrued from the considerable wealth of the pre-reformation church. James VI granted funds, known as tiends, to local heritors who were not necessarily landowners but empowered to distribute funds to maintain the ministry, with the proviso that in theory these monies be set apart for the payment of a fully-funded clergy. Therefore in Scotland, some ministers' stipends were paid from a variety of sources: Crown, Exchequer, landowners or more likely by local heritors, as well as church-door collections and seat-rents.

This arrangement put missionary-ministers especially at the mercy and whim of extraneous forces. A mission station at Achness within the Presbytery of Tongue and Dornoch was the victim of the Duchess of Sutherland's policy of clearance. The townships were deserted and the mission dissolved. Influential aristocrats, such as the Staffords who acted as Crown Agents had easy access to those administering the Royal Bounty and records show that the dissolution of the Achness mission was not an isolated case. By contrast, historic parish churches were 'ring-fenced' thereby remaining exempt from any changes in circumstance.

In short, by accident or design the Kirk had adopted a multi-layered approach to planting congregations, building and financing churches and ensuring how ministers were paid.

Stipends, Dissent and Taxation

In Scotland the issue of providing adequate financial support for churches moved some into breaking the law. There was growing resentment among the middle-classes during the 1820s due to the levying of the Annuity Tax, peculiar to Edinburgh, which was essentially a church rate of 6% on all valued rentals of shops and houses in the capital. This was used in part to pay the stipends of the Edinburgh parish clergy. In Glasgow and the other towns ministers were paid from seat-rent income and church-door collections. In the capital it was argued that merchant families often had to pay twice, once for their shop and again for their home. Because of certain iniquities within the system, 650 of the wealthiest households, to include the judiciary and members of the College of Justice, were exempt.

A further argument claimed the Kirk supported too many Edinburgh ministers at too high a cost. City clergy were paid at a rate three times the average of a rural clergyman, £450 against £150. In short, the Annuity tax set mainly middle-class dissenters, forced to pay for the upkeep of a Church they did not believe in, against the privileged professionals in the law and against the Established Church. Those who refused to pay were charged with civil disobedience.

To make the point and to set an example to discourage others, a few were arrested, charged and sentenced to short prison terms. On release from prison, the *refuseniks* were greeted like heroes and shouldered down the High Street to the acclamation of 10,000 voices. This episode did nothing to quell the growing opposition to the tax and dissent rumbled on. In 1833 there were 846 prosecutions for withholding payment. One dissenting minister chose imprisonment rather than pay the fine.

Further, dissenters believed they were themselves the victims of a grave injustice. They felt their children were discouraged from attending parish schools and further, that their poor were being discriminated against by local poor laws whose benefits were traditionally distributed through the parish churches. Teaching posts in the parish schools and universities, under direct command of the Kirk, were also closed to them. Above all, they resented being regarded as inferior in the eyes of the state. The increasingly strident and influential voice of Scottish dissenters who embraced the voluntary principle and opposed the connection between Church and State found its way into the politics of the day and was set to play a bigger part in the argument.

Secession congregations had multiplied church buildings and in most cases, seceders were the educated middle-classes who had taken a positive step to abandon the Kirk taking their wealth with them and leaving the parish churches with little money to support a minister. Dissenters strongly objected to their hard-earned taxes being redistributed to a State-funded organisation they no longer supported. Statistics gathered in the two years 1835/36 reveal that 40% of Glasgow's, and 42% of Edinburgh's populations were members of secession churches.

The Kirk's reliance on denominational loyalty was crumbling. In Edinburgh especially, there was a veritable explosion of new secession congregations being planted, mainly out of disputes and schisms within their own numbers. A prime example of splits and splinters concerned the Cowgate congregation who, in 1818, had applied to Edinburgh Presbytery to erect a chapel-of-ease. This request was refused. The congregation merely shifted its allegiance to the rival Relief Presbytery of Edinburgh. Another split in the congregation in 1825 led to the forming of the Arthur Street congregation. Those who were left abandoned the Cowgate building in 1831 because of its size and erected a new church in Bread Street to accommodate growing numbers. Meanwhile, the old Cowgate building was bought over by another secession congregation forming Infirmary Street Church.

This was a situation which was replicated in all the major towns and cities at the time. The mania for erecting churches caused, basically, because people fell out with each other was to come back and haunt the Kirk a century later as these secession congregations found their way back to 'Mother Church' in large numbers while insisting they still hold on to their own buildings.

More widespread was the increasing influence dissenters were to play in Parliamentary business itself. English non-conformists were becoming a powerful vested interest group which successive Governments ignored at their peril. This group opposed the Church of England and with Scottish dissenters opposing the Established Church in Scotland, these two formed a loose but sufficiently potent alliance to the extent that successive Governments began to take account of the large constituency from which they were drawn. Strong dissenter opposition, combined with some influential Radicals and some Tory Landowners, was finally to scupper Chalmers's last throw in 1838 in his attempts to secure Government funds for further church extension by way of funding a national endowment to pay for stipends.

The Kirk's Further Ambitions

> ... the doors of our churches are hermetically
> closed against the middle and lower orders of society.

Editorial 'Church Accommodation', *Inverness Courier*, 13th July 1825

The passing of the Highland Churches Act in 1824, which brought into being what became known as the 'Parliamentary Churches', did not quieten dissenting and opposition voices. It may very well have emboldened them. Before the first ground had even been broken, an editorial in the Inverness Courier questioned the justification of more new churches. It stated that the building of new churches alone had not improved the 'moral feeling and conduct' of the working classes.[3] The piece compounded the error by stating that the cause of this lay with the assertion that the Established Church, 'endowed beyond any in the world, shut the doors of the House of God against all who cannot pay for admission'. The editorial went on,

> We shall perhaps be told of the free sittings that are to be found in some of these churches, of the holes and corners, and one-shilling galleries, in which a working man and his family may by accident gain accommodation; but these, bad as they are, form but sorry exceptions to the rule; and generally speaking, we assert without fear of contradiction, that in the metropolis and other large places, the doors of our churches are hermetically closed against the middle and lower orders of society. The Dissenters of all denominations feel the force of this; and do not fail to avail themselves of the opportunity which the lukewarmness of the Government upon this subject affords them.

Indeed, in the following dozen years, successive Governments would blow hot and cold over the issue of improving Scottish church accommodation.

The focus on improving church accommodation, vigorously opposed by the dissenters, was aimed primarily at the city and urban situation. Some in the kirk optimistically saw the 1824 Act, focused on the Highlands and Islands only, as the first in a two-step process of addressing the needs of the whole of the country. Indeed, the wording of an 1822 letter from the Government to the General Assembly said as much. Now, by 1824 and with the Highland Churches Act up and running there was a clamour to press home a similar claim for the

---

3 *Inverness Courier*, 13th July 1825.

Lowlands. In the parliamentary session of 1825 a Bill for 'Building additional places of worship in the Lowlands of Scotland' began its progress through the two Houses. The terms of the Bill had been drawn up in London by civil servants and on the face of it was a noble attempt to address inadequate church provision, especially in the cities, in the face of the rapid expansion of industry and the explosion in population which outran the kirk's ability to educate the new working classes.

Paisley Presbytery was first to raise doubts over the terms of the proposed Bill for new churches. At its first gathering of 1826, the Presbytery did acknowledge the worthy and benevolent aims of the Bill but expressed dissatisfaction with its terms and could not look upon the proposals favourably. The primary objection declared there was no provision for erecting new Parish Churches; the new churches were to come under the jurisdiction not of the General Assembly but of Commissioners yet to be appointed; the new charges would also introduce another order of clergy; civil judges were to determine the bounds of the new charges when the kirk's own resources were better placed to make these judgements; and finally, the right of nomination to pulpits was to be held exclusively by the Crown but the Bill made no provision for the Crown to bear any of the costs of paying stipends in perpetuity.

It was further argued that the people would not take the smallest interest in them so long as patronage was vested in the Crown. Attendance at either a chapel-of-ease or a dissenting church would be a far more attractive proposition where male heads-of-families would select a candidate to fill pulpits. Moreover, the Kirk would have no say in the appointment of commissioners who in theory might be drawn from the English upper classes not at all acquainted with the situation in Scotland, nor was there any provision in the Bill for representatives from the Kirk itself to go along with the commissioners in the execution of the act. Finally, the Bill as presented did not make clear that remuneration should be on a par with the then current minimum stipend. To all intents and purposes, the terms of the proposed bill looked like an English political solution to a Scottish ecclesiastical problem.

Glasgow Presbytery, meeting one month later, endorsed the Paisley findings: 'the proposed erections would be *neither* Parish Churches *nor* Chapels but would possess a character wholly different from everything at present known in our ecclesiastical establishment'. The matter advanced no further. Beside these Scottish misgivings, the legislation itself ran into trouble in the House of Lords and the proposal was quietly dropped.

Thomas Chalmers' Mission Project

> *This system is now, I grieve to say, greatly broken up, and one must signalize himself by resisting every established practice, or spend a heartless, hard driving, and distracting, and wearing out life among the bustle of unministerial work, and of no less unministerial company.*

Thomas Chalmers' observation of the parish ministry in Glasgow

Chalmers, one of the leading Evangelicals of his day, while minister of Glasgow's Tron Church had raised funds to plant a new congregation just east of Glasgow Cross, named St John's. The building cost £9,000, financed entirely by subscription. This, in 1819, was to be Chalmers' new solution, albeit an *urban* one, as an experiment and personal first pitch at what became officially known as 'Church Extension'. Aimed exclusively at tackling the vast numbers of the unchurched, the uncommitted and those for whom there had been little exposure to Christian values, it catered also for those Kirk members who had migrated to this part of the city, especially from the north, looking for new opportunities in employment.

In the years prior to this, Chalmers had begun to formulate the concept of a Christian Community in which a shared missionary ideal strengthened both piety and benevolence. Chalmers regarded poverty as a 'moral disease', its cure to be found in the apotheosis of the covenanted community where industry and benevolence would be encouraged by a missionary ideal transcending individual interests. Chalmers' plan was to revive Scotland's communal traditions among all social orders through the establishing of one covenanted commonwealth and the focus for this initiative was aimed directly towards the new urban poor, equally susceptible to economic changes as the Highlander.

There were serious recessions of trade in 1816, 1819 and again in 1826 with factory closures and resultant high unemployment. A typhus outbreak had ripped through the city in 1818-19, due to unsanitary conditions. Glasgow's Radical Wars which prompted troops on the streets in 1820 showed the industrial belt on the brink of revolution. Chalmers' years in Glasgow (to 1823) were tense with strikes, protests, marches, and public executions for treason. St John's parish was at the very epicentre of social unrest and upheaval.

Chalmers' concept of the 'Godly Commonwealth' was his blueprint for instituting his vision of the Kirk. His credo was rooted in the responsibilities of the ideal parish ministry, albeit based still upon a rural model, one which had begun to prove effective towards the end of his Kilmany years: Sabbath preaching; supervising education in the parish, both at school and in the home; purposeful visitation; encouraging family devotional exercises and enforcing moral discipline; together with the kirk session to gather and administer funds for parish poor-relief. The Godly Commonwealth, encouraging the poor out of poverty through education, self-respect and self-sufficiency, was to be assisted by the kindness of neighbours and the charity of the rich. Chalmers was determined to apply his blueprint founded in St John's for social change.

His plan hinged on the Town Council granting St John's freedom to organise its own poor relief instead of being obliged to contribute to the 'General Session', a consolidated fund operated by Glasgow's historic parishes, which would normally distribute monies as it saw fit. Also, Chalmers recognised that the parish system in Glasgow had all but collapsed. He had heard Dr Inglis address the 1818 General Assembly stating that the parishes of St Cuthbert in Edinburgh and The Barony, Glasgow were the only churches serving upwards of 40,000 people each. It had become all too clear that this explosion in the urban population, fuelled by industrialisation, was quickly outstripping the number of parish churches required to meet the needs of the people. Indeed, the number of parish churches had remained almost unaltered since the 16th century.

Chalmers advocated the creation of 30 new parishes within Glasgow, thus decreasing the average parish population from about 10,000 to 3,000. The aim was to restore the urban population to the traditional Christian communal ideal of the rural parish. At the heart of this endeavour was the need to abolish the evil of assessment-supported legal poor relief. Despite increasingly large amounts being ploughed into relief for the poor, there was increasing pauperism, social unrest and political disaffection.

As the Kirk faced up to the twin challenges of serving an increasing population in the urban sprawl and reaching those in the remotest parts of the north and west, its response in the first instance was to continue with an informal policy of adopting irregular solutions to the problem. The provision of supplying additional places of worship began in the closing decade of the 18th century, corresponding with an increase in the numbers of missionaries and minister-missionaries.

Choppy Waters: Westminster and State Support

It had long been accepted that the Kirk could not finance both the building of new churches and sustain the stipends of the new ministers without a measure of State funding, which the State had acknowledged as early as 1818. There were indications from Government, given on several occasions, that it would not be unsympathetic in its consideration to finance one or the other.

Author Stewart J. Brown argues that through the influence of Evangelicalism, the Church had become revitalised during the 1820s.[4] By requesting Parliamentary grants for church-building, and by emphasising its 'Establishment' credentials, the Church demonstrated its intention to employ its state connection to its advantage. This was the only way the early Reformers' blue-print for a fully-funded Church could be implemented. The proposal would be that the Kirk would look after the erection of buildings, whether through its own money-raising capabilities, or in the case of Glasgow and Edinburgh to persuade these Town Councils to foot the construction costs. The big money prize however would come through securing Parliamentary grants to fund a national endowment to pay for ministers' stipends. To this end, in 1828, the General Assembly appointed a Church Accommodation Committee to press Parliament for an additional grant to support church building in the Lowlands, and particularly in the growing cities.

Chalmers was at the heart of this new effort, having seen at first hand how Kirk and Government negotiated the Highland Churches Bill. The same argument of State assistance obtained: only a Parliamentary grant providing an endowment for paying part of the minister's stipend would allow the new *quoad sacra* parishes to set their seat-rents low enough and thus enable the lower social orders to attend regularly as families. Without such an endowment the labouring poor would continue to be excluded from the national Establishment. The fear was that religion in Scotland would become an exclusively middle- and upper-class affair, 'while the poor would be relegated to ignorance and depravity, endangering both their souls and the social stability of the commonwealth'.[5]

Following a number of unsuccessful overtures to and fruitless negotiations with Government, eventually in 1835 the General Assembly beefed up its Accommodation Committee and formed the Church Extension Committee led by Dr Chalmers himself.

---

4   Stewart J. Brown, *Thomas Chalmers and the Godly Commonwealth*, 222.
5   Stewart J. Brown, *Thomas Chalmers and the Godly Commonwealth*, 242.

While convening the new Church Extension Committee, Chalmers was already working on a second front. There was a concentrated effort to increase church accommodation in Glasgow. Spearheaded by the publisher William Collins, an elder in St John's, in 1834 a five-year plan was set up to build and endow through private subscriptions 20 new church buildings with seating for 1,000 in each, thus doubling existing accommodation in the city. Each new church would be built at a cost of £2,000, with a similar amount as an endowment attracting interest payments which would go towards the payment of stipend. Seat-rents, therefore, would be set low enough to attract even the poorest member. Collins embraced Chalmers' ideal of the Godly Commonwealth where educational opportunities and poor relief would be well funded. This local initiative was followed by a similar one in Aberdeen and was a new departure for the Church.

Chalmers was to become the most influential figure in the Kirk. After the death of Andrew Thomson in 1831, Chalmers assumed the role of 'leader' of the Evangelical wing of the Church. In terms of status, he was a towering figure in the Kirk, feared and lauded in equal measure but coming with an impressive pedigree: a Doctor of the Church, Edinburgh University's Professor of Divinity and architect of the new and dynamic 'Church Extension' impetus.

He was not universally popular. He was regarded by many as having an unstable character who courted controversy, a shrewd and uncompromising political opportunist who lobbied whichever Parliamentary party suited his purposes. He was still loathed in Glasgow because of the St John's experiment and for disrupting long-established poor-relief procedures a decade earlier, a favourable change for Chalmers at the time which was only secured by some influential Tory magistrates. His reputation did not fare much better in St Andrews who long-remembered him impugning the integrity of its professors, and especially in the north and west of the country with its focus still on the dangers of Catholic practices, he was regarded with high suspicion over his support for Catholic emancipation.

However, in the matter of promoting 'Church Extension' by lobbying to secure a national endowment towards the payment of stipends where efforts had come to nought in 1828, Chalmers now gave the Committee fresh impetus and renewed vigour and immediately engaged with Viscount Melbourne's Whig Government to reopen talks regarding a national endowment for Lowland Churches.

Chalmers' committee soon found itself ambushed by strong and persuasive dissenting voices within the Government, wholly opposed to any State intervention in church matters. The debate initially became focused on whether there was the need to provide more church accommodation. This was a replay of the Government's argument in 1821, persuaded by the Prime Minister Lord Liverpool who did not think there was any compelling case for additional churches. Now, in these middle years of the 1830s, the Government once again questioned the soundness of an argument based on numbers.

Both Kirk-supporting proponents, and opponents in the shape of that loose alliance of dissenters began to employ a blizzard of statistics to support their respective positions to present to Government. Heads were counted, seats were numbered, additions and subtractions used to deliver so-called 'accurate' figures with each side, Kirk and dissenter, accusing the other of manipulating and massaging the statistics to shore up their own arguments, accusations that went as far as each side accusing the other of deliberately misrepresenting the true picture and knowingly submitting false numbers. The 'numbers game' had successfully been deployed as a stalling tactic for almost the entire time the Government had been in discussions with the Kirk regarding Highland churches between 1818 and 1824. Gathering statistics was time-consuming, labour-intensive, exhausting for those involved in number-crunching and an easy way to kick matters into the long grass.

As the arguments in Parliament raged on, in 1835 William Downe Gillon, Scottish Whig MP for Falkirk Burghs was at the forefront of championing the dissenters' cause and forcibly stated, 'that we were indebted [to the dissenters] for keeping alive the flame of pure religion in the country, during a long period in which members of the Church had been sunk in a species of lethargy'.[6] Gillon went on to accuse the General Assembly's use of statistics as a blatant attempt to obtain money under false pretences. The level of contempt for the Kirk was plain to see. 'The fact was,' continued Gillon, 'that most of the ministers of the Established Church were of the Tory party, and the present Government, knowing how unpopular they themselves were, backed the clergymen in their demands, in order to obtain in Scotland a partial support'. Seven weeks later, Gillon presented Petitions from 35 different bodies in Scotland 'against any grant of money out of public funds for the purpose of extending the endowments of the Church of Scotland'.[7]

---

6 *Hansard* 3rd April 1835, Church of Scotland debate vol 27 column 783.

7 *Hansard* 20th May 1835, Church of Scotland debate vol 27 column 1255.

These petitions had all emanated from public meetings and had been subscribed by 13,500 individuals. The nub of the dissenters' argument stressed that Scotland was not short of church accommodation and that by nefarious means statistics to include the number of sittings provided by dissenting congregations had been omitted from the General Assembly's Committee charged with the task of ascertaining an accurate picture. Gillon complained that the dissenters' voice was being wilfully suppressed.

Opposing Gillon's view, Sir William Rae, Tory MP and serving as Lord Advocate stressed that church accommodation especially in Glasgow and Edinburgh was totally inadequate and that dissenting churches, in levying high seat-rents to pay for clergy, had excluded 'the poor' from attending worship. 'Let those who oppose this grant,' Rae concluded 'look at the increase in crime in Scotland. It was lamentable to make the observation, but depravity was fearfully on the advance there, and the consequences must become truly alarming if adequate means of religious instruction were not provided in due time for the people.'[8]

Tories, as the party of law and order were not slow in linking the lack of church accommodation with increasing levels of lawlessness. Support for Rae came in the person of Major Charles Cumming-Bruce, Tory MP for Inverness Burghs who stated that Parliament had no difficulty in voting large sums of money for education in Ireland or approving a grant of £17,000 (£1.5m in today's terms) for the British Museum. The endowment requested by the Church of Scotland was paltry by comparison and Cumming-Bruce concluded by echoing arguments which had first been aired decades previously, 'It was the duty of the State, and one of its most important duties, to see that the means of spiritual instruction were afforded to the poor.'[9] He claimed on this ground the support of all 'who were favourable to an Establishment'.

In 1837 and following a conspicuous two-year silence from Viscount Melbourne's Whig Government, Sir William Rae finally brought forward a motion relating to the 'Endowments of Churches in Scotland' in similar terms to those he made in 1835. That he had to do so further highlighted the opposition's stalling tactics employed to hinder any progress as a promised commission set up two years

---

8 *Hansard* 20th May 1835, Church of Scotland debate, vol. 27, column 1261.
9 *Hansard* 20th May 1835, Church of Scotland debate, vol. 27, column 1263.

previously to investigate further only brought forward a short report on church accommodation in Edinburgh. In any case, those findings were completely disregarded by the Government. Noticing the direction of travel the Parliamentary debate was taking, the contribution from the Scottish Tory Major Cumming Bruce was succinct and brutal. 'The Church of Scotland asked for bread and the noble lord gave it a stone. They asked for a grant and the noble lord gave them what? - a commission.'[10]

It was clear that for the good Major the noble people of Scotland had as much expectation of Government assistance in this matter as it had ten years previously. The nation would have to fight for every penny. For the people of Scotland, stated Sir William, this was a question 'more exciting from one end of the country to the other than any other question that affected their interests'.[11] The Commons itself was divided over the issue: Whig opposition, siding with the dissenters, did not support the Church's claim to additional endowments from the state, instead, preferring to direct any grants to the delivery of better religious instruction for the poor. The nub of the matter was clear enough: was social and cultural improvement better secured through education or increased church provision? Sir William found himself deploying the same argument from twenty years previously, under Lord Liverpool's Tory Government, when the Highlands Churches Bill was being argued: it was the church itself which was in the best position to deliver that religious instruction, stating again that it was the 'duty of the state to provide for the support of the established religion of the country'[12] and the petitioners were arguing that an endowed church would provide all necessary spiritual instruction. The church certainly had not come 'cap in hand'.

The Scottish Contribution

> *The inhabitants of Scotland were ready to come forward, and at their own expense to provide all the churches that might be necessary. They were willing to leave the patronage of those churches to the disposal of the Government, and all they asked for, was that the Government should give a small endowment, in order that cheap seats be furnished to the poor.*
>
> Stewart J. Brown, *Thomas Chalmers and the Godly Commonwealth*

---

10 *Hansard* 5th May 1837, Church of Scotland debate, vol. 38, column 645.
11 *Hansard* 5th May 1837, Church of Scotland debate, vol. 38, column 604.
12 *Hansard* 5th May 1837, Church of Scotland debate, vol. 38, column 605.

Despite the numerous and exhausting trips to London by coach and four, Chalmers had not been idle at home, keeping a tight rein on matters in Edinburgh. His Church Extension committee, by 1835, had raised the sum of £66,000 by private donations to aid the object of the petition, and had secured the building of 64 churches. As part of the negotiations Chalmers was willing to make over to the Government this entire property portfolio in exchange for guaranteeing stipends.

Sir William Rae and his supporters certainly regarded this as a good deal, for both sides. Indeed, the self-same argument Sir William had put forward in 1835. He was now able to update parliament with current figures as at 1837: 90 churches had been completed and a further £32,000 had been subscribed to meet building costs.[13] Sir William stated that the subscribers would be offering upwards of 100 churches at a build cost of £150,000 to government in the hope and expectation that a fully-funded clergy from state coffers would be the *quid pro quo*. He sincerely hoped that the argument over the Government's duty to maintain and aid the Established Church had finally been settled and was no longer in question. That commitment, however many times it had been challenged, was embodied in the Highland Churches Act of 1824.

For Sir William, the dispute lay in statistics. He was sure that if the grant now sought was to be given, 'decency of dress and general morality of conduct would soon appear in the class for whose benefit it would be made'.[14] The liberally-minded Moderate aim of the 'improvability' of the people was still being advanced. Sir William continued that a grant would also enable the pew-rents to be reduced from the current rate to lessen the burden on the poorer classes. Dr Chalmers, on behalf of the Church, stated that two things were necessary for the religious instruction of the poor: to remove the barrier of fixed seat rents, and to bring Christian charity and fellowship home to the poor.

Chalmers had still not given up the hope of establishing his 'Godly Commonwealth'. Chalmers considered that evil and criminality thrived from within the unchurched classes, a view very much supported by Tory MPs such as Sir William Rae. An endowment of between £10,000 and £12,000 was a small price to pay compared to the advantage of reclaiming so many from their evil ways and degraded condition. The endowment proposed would allow for 64 ministers to be paid between £156 and £187 per annum. As well as saving a stipend, the

---

13 *Hansard* 5th May 1837, Church of Scotland debate, vol. 38, column 605.
14 *Hansard* 5th May 1837, Church of Scotland debate, vol. 38, column 610.

advantage to the Kirk would also be found in its ability to reduce seat-rents which in turn would encourage an increased attendance. Money would be freed up for the vital work of mission to the unchurched and the poor. Chiming with Tory opinion, according to Chalmers crime had increased as a direct consequence of the lack of church accommodation. Chalmers countered William Gillon's stout defence of the dissenters' claims by again declaring that, as a consequence of the build costs and supporting stipends of dissenting churches being financed by the members themselves, seat-rents were still exorbitantly high. Thus only the wealthier classes could afford to attend. Where then would the poor go?

Lord John Russell, aristocrat and leader of the Whigs in the Commons, reminded the House that Rae himself had said levels of crime had been growing rapidly during the previous 30 years. But as Lord Advocate in a number of successive Tory Governments, Rae had been 'all talk and no action', yet had no qualms in approving 'lavish' expenditure of £140m in one year[15] (£10 billion in today's terms) in financing 'unnecessary and expensive' wars with France but never occurring to him to see fit to turn his mind to the plight of the Church of Scotland which he now so readily championed. Russell suspected that Rae was motivated more by guarding the rights and privileges of landed proprietors of Scotland against any financial call made on them to contribute to the upkeep of local churches more than was strictly necessary. Any Government endowment towards stipend would greatly reduce landowners' financial obligations to provide church livings.

Despite Rae and others now championing the Kirk's cause, resistance to the endowment proposal was building and the view was the Government, facing other parliamentary difficulties, was ready to stall progress with the debate yet again. Not only was there the tricky business of assembling statistics to support the cause, made by both sides, the debate was now fully focused on the problematic correlation between non-church attendance and levels of crime and degeneracy and the resultant endangerment to the peace of society.

Other MPs agitated by the breakdown of law and order now acquired a foothold in the debate. Joseph Hume, radical Scottish Whig MP for Middlesex, asserted that the decline in morals could be laid firmly at the feet of the clergy. Ministers were to blame for failing to attend to

---

15 *Hansard* 5th May 1837, Church of Scotland debate, vol. 38, column 616.

their duties and as a consequence education in their neighbourhoods had declined. A more democratic solution was necessary: money was needed towards bolstering education for all.

In a July sitting of Parliament the debate continued where it had left off two months previously. The Earl of Haddington rode to the clergy's defence, regretting the 'ungracious attack' on these men, but accusing some ministers of interfering with the political processes.[16] Lord Aberdeen accepted that the deficiency in spiritual instruction had led directly to a great increase in crime, quoting the cost of pursuing criminal prosecutions had risen in the years 1813 to 1828 from £5,000 to £30,000. The Earl of Camperdown did not think that building new churches would reduce the crime rate while regretting that some clergy were now openly critical of Government.

In March the following year hostilities resumed.[17] The Earl of Aberdeen lamented the lack of Government progress under the leadership of Prime Minister Melbourne on the matter. Scotland had been palmed off with the promise of surveys and reports and the Earl concluded that the 'people and Church of Scotland were naturally tranquillised by that hope'.[18] Melbourne warned the house that if the Church of Scotland had come cap-in-hand, the Church in Ireland would come looking for funding too. The cost of the commission to date had risen to £20,000 (and would rise to £30,000 by the end of 1838). Dr Chalmers's had estimated grant assistance at between £10,000 and £12,000. This figure now appeared cheap at the price.

The Conclusion of the Debate

> *The people of Scotland did not ask to have churches built on speculation. Those that had been built and financed from within its own membership were built out of necessity.*
>
> Sir George Clerk MP[19]

The turning point of the debate came with Whig Prime Minister Viscount Melbourne displaying a certain cooling towards the proposal. Lord Liverpool himself as Tory Prime Minister displayed a similar 'cooling' towards the Highland Churches grant almost 20 years

---

16 *Hansard* 3rd July 1837, Church of Scotland debate, vol. 38, column 1747.

17 *Hansard* 30th March 1838, Church of Scotland debate, vol. 42, columns 112-152.

18 *Hansard* 30th March, Church of Scotland, vol. 42, column 115.

19 *Hansard*, 5th May 1837, debate on 'Church of Scotland Endowments'.

previously. In 1834, Melbourne had declared that the extending of church accommodation in Scotland was one which the Government 'ought to take speedy and serious consideration'. This was the same worthy intention voiced by Liverpool's Government in 1818, an intention which took six years to come to fruition. All the signs indicated that Melbourne was supportive of the Kirk's claim. Now however, by 1837 Melbourne's stance had changed by stating that not only were levels of destitution far greater in London than in either Glasgow or Edinburgh, thereby diluting somewhat the Kirk's claim, but also that if an increase in church accommodation was possible then that it ought to be done from the resources of the Church of Scotland itself:

> Everybody would agree the religious wants of Scotland should be provided for by Scotland itself. It was better, much more wise, much more prudent that this should be, than that they should rashly and imprudently plunge themselves into a course by which a great change and burden would be imposed on the country for providing church accommodation, which would, no doubt, begin small at first but which would necessarily increase and become a most onerous impost on the general resources of the country.[20]

Melbourne had not only put the brakes on the whole question of endowments, but had completely reversed a Government policy signalling that the national Church of Scotland was not in the financial position to do all that was expected of it, and that a modicum of State assistance was absolutely necessary. Coming to the Kirk's rescue, the Archbishop of Canterbury declared his wholehearted support for the Scottish claim stating that these wants 'appear to be small in comparison with the wants of the Church of England'.[21] He praised the Scottish clergy. Scotland had been well-served for the 'good order and economy that had been observed through the influence of the parish ministers'.[22] The Archbishop concluded, 'What Scotland needed was not more churches but endowments for ministers,' and that the Government should listen to the General Assembly who were the proper authority on the matter.[23]

The debate continued with both sides offering numbers and statistics to shore up the arguments for and against. The Earl of Haddington

---
20 *Hansard,* 30th March, Church of Scotland, vol. 42 column 129.
21 *Hansard,* 30th March, Church of Scotland, vol. 42, column 131.
22 *Hansard,* 30th March, Church of Scotland, vol. 42, column 131.
23 *Hansard,* 30th March, Church of Scotland, vol. 42, column 132.

had read the mood of the house and concluded that anti-establishment forces within Government ranks and among the various dissenting groups lobbying MPs were enough to scupper the Church's hopes. The Bishop of London tried another tack. If parliament approved the grant, the Bishop argued, then the Government would 'reap an ample harvest in the increased respect, affection and adherence of the people [of Scotland]'.[24]

Lord Aberdeen accused the Prime Minister of 'breaking faith' with the Church of Scotland. Melbourne had never objected to grants made to the Church of England: £1.5m for building churches plus an endowment of £100,000 per year for eleven years, making a total of £2.6m. And further, the people of Scotland never objected to these grants. Under this attack, Melbourne denied he had broken faith with the Kirk, and stated he had given no previous undertaking to support a grant on the terms now proposed although he admitted he had shifted his position once he had been satisfied as to the situation regarding church accommodation, the statistics regarding the number of vacant sittings and the amount of destitution of spiritual instruction which prevailed. However, it appeared to all that political expediency had won the day.

Chalmers had listened intently to the ebb and flow of the debates and which had taken up his flagging energies for almost a decade, but by the end of the summer of 1838 it was clear that the claim for Government assistance to provide for stipend endowment had run into the sand. It was suspected by Chalmers, and many others, that this had been a political decision manoeuvred by an ailing Whig Government reliant on dissenter votes in Parliament to stay in power. Dissenters naturally would oppose any public funds being so directed towards the Kirk.

The game was up and Chalmers knew it. He and his deputation left London for the final time with only the promise of the Royal Commission to investigate the extent of 'religious destitution' within Scotland which would turn out to be another laborious exercise in fact-finding and compiling statistics. The names of commissioners did not fill Chalmers with hope either, as nearly all had dissenting or radical tendencies not at all sympathetic to the Established Church's cause.

From 1834 to 1838 Chalmers and his deputation were almost fixtures in London and he prosecuted the Kirk's case with his usual

---

24 *Hansard*, 30th March, Church of Scotland, vol. 42, column 146.

eloquence of language and persuasion of argument. But to no avail. It was galling for Chalmers to hear Melbourne's comment about mounting 'rash' and 'imprudent' arguments to support the Kirk's claims. The arguments had been mustered coolly and rationally since 1825! Instead, Melbourne put forward three proposals: unclaimed Crown tiends would be used to build more churches in the Highlands; unclaimed tiends in the possession of private landlords would be sequestered to build additional rural churches where needed; nothing would be done for the towns and cities.

Chalmers believed wholeheartedly that he had been the victim of Government chicanery, too focused on keeping radicals and dissenters on side. He returned north and immediately went on a charm offensive attempting to win over public support on a national level which would provide him with a stronger mandate with which to engage Melbourne's Government yet again. However, he failed to mobilise sufficient numbers to the cause. There would be no further negotiations in London. That door was now firmly closed. Chalmers himself was exhausted and beaten and at home people lost interest and the great Church Extension programme dwindled to a trickle, eventually becoming a side-show while more important matters took up the energies of General Assembly Commissioners. A full-scale schism in the Church was becoming a reality.

The Situation in the Highlands and Islands

However, it is testimony to Chalmers' powers of oratory and persuasion that he steered the Church Extension Committee in its time to oversee the erection of 222 buildings and the amassing of a considerable war-chest to fund the planting of new congregations. Melbourne's much-vaunted Royal Commission served no real purpose other than to state the obvious. It did however provide a 'mid-term' report before the Statistical Accounts of 1841 and which gave much information about the state, not only of religion in the Highlands, but of the social, industrial and educational provision throughout the north and west. It provided useful information regarding the Parliamentary Churches, scattered throughout the Highlands and Islands, all built between 1826 and 1830. The statistical return, compiled by ministers, achieved almost 100% compliance. Almost to a man, the same deficiencies and difficulties in parishes, especially in the north and west, were identified, echoing reports from the Old Statistical Accounts at the end of the 18th century: churches left isolated and deserted by local congregations due to the Clearances; lack of adequate roads and bridges linking communities despite Telford's comprehensive road-building programme; the desperate need for additional buildings; rising levels of rural poverty; lack of ministerial assistance; continuing poor levels of stipends. It appeared that nothing had changed.

Before the 1750s, the Highland population had remained for the most part geographically settled. These folks were not itinerants. Generations of families, tied to the land by clan fealty and ancestral loyalties, were raised in the same townships and crofts as those who had gone before them. The bare necessities of life were pretty much to hand. The Clearances changed all that. The latter half of the eighteenth century saw the beginning of massive population dislocation with the forced march of entire districts to the coastal margins or to seek new opportunities in the Americas.

The geographical reordering of large swathes of the Highland population which continued for a hundred years, meant that the provision of new infrastructure required to meet the peoples' needs: roads, employment, housing, schools, churches, was always behind the curve. John Knox, travelling in the Highlands in 1786 on behalf of the British Fisheries Society found no roads in Sutherland, Caithness or Ross-shire. He advocated the construction of new roads for civilian use and called attention to the magnitude of the task, not only of making but of maintaining them. For nearly 20 years the situation in the Highlands was ignored until Thomas Telford's appointment as Commissioner of Roads in 1803.

Chapels-of-ease (as mentioned above) followed by Parliamentary Churches went some way to meet local ecclesiastical needs. These years of the early 19th century also saw an expansion in the provision of specifically Gaelic Chapels together with the appointments of missionaries, especially when entire townships and areas had been cleared to the coasts. The provision of schoolmasters and missionaries was undertaken first, by SSPCK and then subsequently assisted by the Church of Scotland who administered the Royal Bounty. *The Moorland Mission Churches of Caithness* by George Watson states that local residents provided mission-houses for preachers, initially the parish minister, but later a resident missionary. Parish ministers still regarded the congregations of mission-houses as part of their flock, but could only manage to make infrequent visits to these outlying communities.

Chalmers himself was an advocate of missionaries and, later, ordained missionary-ministers stating that the first point of building a congregation lay with a missionary, able to cultivate the district. Although ministers were ordained to mission stations they remained under the complete jurisdiction of the parish minister within whose bounds the mission station was sited. Mission-houses were rudimentary but still substantial buildings. The building erected at Bruan in 1798, for example, provided accommodation for 585 sitters from an immediate population of 1,800. At Dirlot, the building sat 403 from a population of 2,500.

It would appear that these buildings were constructed to a standard design. According to their circumstances, it might be that a missionary was only able to preach in one of his stations every three weeks, but that was a considerable improvement in what the parish minister could provide. Watson concludes that 'given the independent nature of the communities who established and supported these mission stations it is quite understandable that the majority were drawn to the Free Church in 1843'.[25]

Mission stations were erected in the more remote parts of Caithness and Sutherland and along the coast where many of the dispossessed/cleared had created new communities. For example, a new mission church was built at Eribol in 1804 to serve three scattered upland districts together with the missionary maintaining a presence in Kinlochbervie. With the coming of two Parliamentary Churches, at Strathy and Kinlochbervie, in the late 1820s, missionary activity was restricted and provision remained poor in some districts. To meet local needs congregations took it upon themselves to build rudimentary churches, as in Strath Halladale where a thatched church was built in 1830 with assistance from the Sutherland family.

However, for landowners in general, it was 'business as usual'. Despite new locations and some congregations able to choose their own minister, the local patron still wielded considerable control in the matter of ministry, manse and church. He was able to use them as levers wherever he could, to retain as much control as possible in terms of influencing the choosing of ministers, appropriating glebes, closing churches or moving parochial boundaries when it suited. In cases such as these, no minister, or Presbytery, or Synod, or General Assembly appeared to have much fire-power in countering these abuses. These landowners had the whip hand and using the threat of legal action landowners were further emboldened, especially after the law on

---

[25] George Watson, *The Moorland Mission Churches of Caithness* (first published in the Caithness Field Club Bulletin 2011).

occasions had been tested in the Court of Session where decisions seemed to favour more often the claims and rights of landowner and heritor over the Church whenever disputed cases had come before it. Donald Sage and many of his fellow Evangelical colleagues found, in general, dealings with heritors were fraught with difficulty. Many landowners delayed repair-work to churches and manses, deferred stipend payments and defaulted on promises made, despite being under orders from Presbyteries. Even the threat of legal proceedings against the heritors failed to bring swift results. Donald Sage, reflecting upon his life in his later years, stated that 'For the twenty years consecutively in which I was minister in the Established Church (Sage left the Kirk at the Disruption) I did not receive a farthing of my stipend without a *grudge*, or even without the *curse* of my heritors along with it'.[26]

> *In the 18th century there is a clear pattern of building up and strengthening the inherited pattern from pre-Reformation days of many parishes, each with a church, to which were added small chapels in other places, relics of a previous non-parochial system. With the Reformation, and its aftermath, there were new dimensions to the story, first due to the scarcity of qualified Reformed clergy, and then with the changes from Episcopalianism to Presbyterianism, the need once again to win over the affections of the people.*
>
> Allan MacLean, *Telford's Highland Churches*

The raising of Gaelic chapels went some way to address the 'Highland Problem' and only was possible when a ready supply of native Gaelic speakers felt the call to the ministry and presented themselves for ordination. Local landowners were encouraged to provide the build costs while applications were made to the Crown to pay stipends from the Royal Bounty. Of the necessity for improved accommodation, one Lewis writer stated 'The parish church is situated in Kirkhill, and the manse in Tong is now four miles by the new road. Between the manse and Tolsta, there is a population of 12,000 without a seat in a church, and destitute of any place of worship. The present church was built in 1794 and holds 800. On Lewis there were no chapels-of-ease. There is one Government church built in the district of Ui [Eye], four miles from the parish church'.[27] The 1841 Census figure for the

---

26 Revd Donald Sage, *Memorabilia Domestica*, 326.
27 Revd Angus Macaulay, *Aspects of Religious History of Lewis*, 65.

whole of the island recorded 23,082 souls, the heaviest concentration of people did indeed live on Skye's eastern seaboard, very likely to have lived within the bounds so described by Macaulay. The planting of new congregations and the building of additional church accommodation, first chapels-of-ease followed by Parliamentary Churches, provided an expedient solution to the Highland Problem but reveals the unfocused way in which the Kirk, local and national, attempted to manage the situation.

Inverness: a Case in Point

In this Highland town a local dispute demonstrated the mismanagement of just such a situation: weak superintendence by Presbytery, compounded by every exertion by certain individuals to 'get their own way'. Local jealousies, rivalries, and enmity between Gaelic- and English-speaking congregations and within Gaelic congregations themselves formed the basis of the dispute and led eventually to splits and dissension. This marred inter-church relations for generations and set congregation against congregation and native Gaelic-speakers against English speakers.

Between the Statistical Accounts of 1791 and 1831 Inverness's population had doubled to nearly 10,000 souls possibly due to redundant canal workers remaining in the town and incoming displaced peasantry from the Clearances. The 1791 Account states that several religious preferences were catered for as well as the English-speaking congregation in the Old High Church: a small congregation of anti-burghers; Episcopalians; a Methodist meeting house (John Wesley had preached there in 1764) and a Roman Catholic congregation.

The first minister of the town's Gaelic Church was Revd Ronald Bayne. Known as Inverness's 'East Church', Bayne remained there until 1808. During the incumbencies of three successive Evangelicals, attendances rose considerably and debt upon the building cleared. Finlay Cook came to the East Church in 1833 after having been inducted as first minister of the Parliamentary Church at Cross on Lewis in 1829.

The dispute arose when after two years in Inverness he accepted a call to the Parish of Reay in Caithness, leaving the East church facing a vacancy. Part of the East's membership unsuccessfully petitioned to call Finlay's brother Archibald, missionary-minister in Bruan and Berridale in the Parish of Latheron Caithness to succeed his brother, and the subsequent fall-out led to the creation of the town's

North Church. Revd David Campbell was Archie Cook's rival for the position and was himself first minister of the Parliamentary Church in Glenlyon, Perthshire but there was delay in inducting him to the Inverness charge because of doubts over the voting eligibility of certain male members. This hiatus lasted months resulting in a petition from the Cook camp, brought before Inverness Presbytery, to build a new church. They would have their man come what may and so the new North Church was duly opened in 1837 to accommodate between 1100 and 1200 with Archie Cook as minister. His supporters identified him as a 'Christian of great experience' hinting a preference over a more learned and educated minister.

Clearly for some, a minister's education was less important than his piety, a veritable premium on ability in 'marks of grace' theology, highly venerated by Evangelicals in general. On the other side, the questionable purity of Archie's fluency in Gaelic seems to have been an issue. While David Campbell was noted for the exactitude and eloquence of his Gaelic, Archie Cook may have failed to modify his 'Southern Gaelic accent', not acceptable for many people. Although his brother Finlay's Gaelic does not seem to have been a barrier, Archie's 'cosmopolitan' accent occasioned the response, 'Oh, it is a hotch-potch gathered from Arran, Lewis, Inverness and Caithness'.[28]

The issue more probably was simpler: Archie Cook was a poor preacher compounded by an unsophisticated approach to language. Donald Sage, Finlay Cook's brother-in-law whom he respected and spoke of in warm terms, does not hold a similar opinion of the brother. For Sage, despite being a 'devout and pious man' Archie Cook nonetheless possessed a 'limited range of intellectual ability' and combined it with a considerably inflated sense of spiritual pride which 'greatly interfered with his usefulness'.[29] Further, Sage picks up on Archie's language skills. 'His literary attainments are not high; his Gaelic is bad, his English worse.' It seems Archie managed all too successfully to mangle both Gaelic and English languages in the pulpit and on the street. Having forgiven Archie for all his human shortcomings, Sage's final words are, however, complimentary: 'I question if there be any of the age in which we live who . . . more nearly approximates to the divinely-trained disciples of Galilee than does Archibald Cook'.[30] Archie was obviously a plain speaker, in every

---

[28] Revd Alexander Auld, *Ministers and Men in the Far North*, 68.
[29] Revd Donald Sage, *Memorabilia Domestica*, 298.
[30] Revd Donald Sage, *Memorabilia Domestica*, 299.

sense of the word, less afraid than others to take on authority and his humanity outscored any obvious lack of erudition or scholastic accomplishment. Part of Archie's appeal to the ordinary Highlander may have lain in his very vocal opposition to the Clearances.

The Inverness situation was not the only controversy to embroil Cook. The Parliamentary Charge of Kinlochbervie fell vacant in 1834 and Revd Robert Clark of Duke Street Gaelic Chapel, Glasgow was called as minister but 137 heads of families objected petitioning that Archie be called. This the landlord rejected. Some petitioners held out against Clark's appointment while others reluctantly accepted the landlord's decision. However, these 137 families left the Kirk in 1843 and joined the Free Church, as did David Campbell, and both Cook brothers.

In Inverness and despite the internecine spat over choice of minister producing an additional church building, statistics suggested that there was still a severe lack of church accommodation in the town. To this end, the town's missionary-minded Evangelical ministers directly petitioned the General Assembly to build a new church in the west side, while ignoring the usual first step in securing Synod's approval. A further row ensued with accusations by Evangelicals on one side, of Moderates deliberately stalling further expansion, and by Moderates on the other side critical that Evangelicals did not follow proper procedures. Finally in 1835 permission was granted and work commenced, having secured a suitable nearby site on a feu owned by Macintosh of Raigmore.

The disputatious events in Inverness demonstrated the growing strength and influence of the Evangelical wing of the Kirk. Evangelicals were gaining the upper hand. Against Moderate opposition in Presbytery and Synod, Evangelicals on this occasion were able to drive through their plans based on local conditions to the point of splitting established congregations and forming new ones. Highland Evangelicals were well aware that the Kirk's Church Extension plan, when it came into being as approved by the General Assembly and under the bullish leadership of Dr Thomas Chalmers, was firmly urban based but necessarily so to confront the challenges of a burgeoning industrial situation.

However, the local situation in the Highlands and Islands was dislocated from Chalmers's efforts in London and untouched by the arcane machinations of party and Governmental politics. It is doubtful that any living and working in the north and west would give the least thought to what was happening in Westminster. The Highlands and Islands remained a world apart. The Church in the north and west was not slow in conjuring new solutions to local problems and challenges when the need arose. In the Inverness case in point, Evangelicals experienced no difficulty raising the funds necessary from local sources to further their own ecclesiastical ambitions. They were already on the road to self-sufficiency independent from hand-outs from others, Government included. There was also a growing realisation that these congregations were thriving despite their 'detachment' from the Kirk's centralised bureaucracy.

The Problem of Funding – Who Pays the Piper . . .

As the Church continued to address the challenge of religious provision throughout the Highlands in the 1820s, others too had begun to take matters into their own hands: Principal Macfarlane reported to the 1828 General Assembly that the Buchanan family, owners of the Stanley Mills near Perth had built and endowed from their own pocket, 'accommodation and religious instruction' for the workforce.[31] It was an imposing example of Georgian Gothic architecture (see photo on the eighth page of the colour section). 'How desirable', continued the Principal, 'would it be were other manufacturing establishments to follow the example of the Stanley Company; for if that was done, there would then be far less occasion to complain of the want of church accommodation'.

In response, Dr Chalmers concurred in the sentiments of the report. He then furnished his own details of the circumstances: 'The public spirited proprietors, on their own responsibility, at their own risk, and at an expense of £1000, erected that chapel to accommodate no fewer than 1200 people and had endowed it with an annual allowance of £150 for a clergyman. This they had done purely for the character and moral good of the people', all this at a time of fevered discussion with the Government as to the provision of additional places of worship, and the question of how these were to be financed. Chalmers and others recognised a strong correlation between improved church accommodation and improving morals.

While welcoming such examples as the Stanley Mill chapel-of-ease, it was clear that there were those in the General Assembly content to cede responsibilities in this matter to any philanthropic third party, untroubled by what was in effect the establishing of a private chapel,

---

31 As reported in the *Scotsman* newspaper, 30th May 1828.

or in the Inverness scenario to let local congregations fight it out among themselves and find local solutions, despite some acrimony, dissension and disruption. One wonders if Principal Macfarlane, in lauding the proprietors of Stanley Mills, had glossed over the unhappy and unsatisfactory situation which had occurred some years before, on this occasion, not a private chapel but a private school but, as will be shown, the Kirk's authority in matters of oversight would run up against independent wealthy mavericks unmoved by the arcane manoeuvres of Presbyterial oversight.

Robert Owen had taken over the running of New Lanark Mills from his father-in-law David Dale, a devout Christian. Notwithstanding this, the mills were known to be a hotbed of vice and desperate poverty with little Christian charity on offer. Owen and his co-owners set about establishing a new community based on socialist principles. Work, discipline and religious education were the new watchwords. As most of the families were 'Calvinists', Owen thought it appropriate that scriptures should be read and the shorter catechism be taught in his Sunday Schools, open to both mill children and their parents.

Owen, it must be stated, had no particular denominational allegiance. Further to this, Finlay Cook (he of the Inverness controversy and brother of Archie but here launching his ministry) was appointed catechist by the Presbytery of Lanark in 1816, during his summer vacation from university to 'lecture to the Highlanders' at the mill. However, Cook did not offer himself on further occasions but, keen to make a start on his career, took up the minister-missionary post at Dirlot in Caithness.

Perhaps he had seen the writing on the wall as Owen became less and less enamoured of the curriculum content. Owen was now at loggerheads with his partners over the direction of travel Christian teaching should take. Something of a free-thinking radical and now proclaiming that the Bible was 'evil', Owen espoused extreme liberal views in both religion and education eventually in 1823 forbidding any reading of the scriptures, suspending all catechetical teaching and introducing his own curriculum. Never one to embrace any kind of organised religion, Owen's actions came to the attention of Lanark Presbytery, whose oversight in the matter of education provision was suddenly undermined. Owen's actions fell foul of his business partners and the Assembly's Committee on the Examinations of Schools whose report to the General Assembly that year outlined the whole regrettable situation. Although the Assembly instructed the

Church Procurator to become involved, it seemed there was little the Kirk could do.

The New Lanark situation became a *cause celebre* and generated many column inches in the pamphlets and periodicals of the day. Owen himself penned a detailed defence of his actions in an extensive letter to the editor of the Glasgow Chronicle on 11th September 1823, in response to his nemesis Revd William Menzies, minister of Old Lanark. Menzies had submitted his own letter to the Morning Herald (London) giving his side of the exchange. Owen's main argument was that the Presbytery had no jurisdiction over what was an educational experiment within the confines of his own private school where he felt at liberty to teach any curriculum he so wished. Owen simply disregarded the Kirk's authority in matters of educational oversight. The *Christian Instructor* went as far as describing Owen's revised curriculum as 'a mixture of arrogance, irreligion and absurdity'. Owen went on to found his own religious movement in America, known as Owenism. By 1828 and with the departure of Owen, the Mill School came back under the jurisdiction of Lanark Presbytery and order and oversight were restored.

Schools which were established and financed by private patrons placed them effectively beyond the Kirk's control, despite local Presbyteries having a superintending role. They were an anomaly. Teachers and catechists properly appointed by Presbyteries and Mission Societies but funded from other sources exposed the very nature of these schools somewhat to the whim of the patron. In many respects, control of education was merely one aspect in the Kirk's struggle to assert its own authority in matters it considered its own preserve, such as the appointment of ministers but whose church living depended on the continued beneficence of a local patron. However, as different agencies providing resources sought to push their own agenda, the Kirk's position on occasions was compromised when competing with the likes of SSPCK, mission societies and some independently-funded free-lancers.

The Chapels Act of 1834: the Kirk Runs up Against the Court of Session

In one attempt to regularize the Kirk's organisation and improve oversight, The Chapels Act of 1834 overhauled the constitution recognising existing chapels-of-ease and those to be built as parish churches *quoad sacra*. This change in status meant that parochial bounds were to be assigned to them, Kirk Sessions constituted, and their ministers were to have full status and were to be enrolled as such in the church courts. Importantly, these ministers would be brought into line with their parish colleagues and subject to the more rigorous clerical discipline as exercised by Presbyteries and Synods. This new status accorded to these ministers had the effect of reining in the more maverick elements among the evangelicals, now subject to a more disciplined oversight. This monumental alteration to its constitution was met with general approval within the courts of the Kirk for it cleared up a blatant anomaly by finally bringing chapels-of-ease and their ministers into line with the parish model which had underpinned the Kirk since the Reformation. Those who believed this fundamental and hugely important change would improve matters in terms of establishing more parishes were to be sadly disappointed.

One year after Chalmers had effectively wound up his endeavours, events in 1839 caused uproar in the church and threatened the entire church extension movement by questioning the legal principles upon which the parish system had been established. Eleven congregations of the Old Light (Auld Licht) Burghers were received back into the Church of Scotland. They had seceded from the Kirk because of certain quibbles regarding the Confession of Faith.

However, their position gradually softened over the years and they found themselves gravitating back towards 'Mother Church'. In terms of the Chapels' Act of 1834 their ministers were now to be enrolled as members of the appropriate Presbyteries which were instructed to allocate to them territorial areas as their parishes *quoad sacra*. The parish of Stewarton within the Presbytery of Irvine was redrawn to accommodate one of the eleven new congregations. However the patron and the heritors protested, the decision effectively reducing both power and income, and their case was heard by a Commission of Assembly which ordered the Presbytery to proceed but, as the historian Burleigh explained 'in express words to reserve the rights of heritors and their tenants to all their privileges in the original parish church'.[32]

This Assembly ruling appeared less than clear but certainly did not go far enough for the heritors and they sought civil redress in the ever-obliging Court of Session obtaining 'suspension and interdict'. Upholding the heritors' claim, the Court declared the Chapels' Act was illegal, but more, the ruling declaring that Presbyteries in which

---

32 J.H.S. Burleigh, *A Church History of Scotland*, 347.

chapel ministers had been enrolled was illegally constituted and their decisions therefore invalid. Thus the Church's discipline since 1834 was called into question and once again the old uncertainties in the relationship between Church and State reared their heads. By this time there was open warfare between Moderates and Evangelicals showing little common ground between them in terms of settling the matter of patronage and the rights of the Church to determine its own ecclesiastical laws free from interference by the civil courts. This led the way to the Church adopting a lengthy resolution which became known as the Claim of Right, as a way to break the impasse. However, the Stewarton case had finally been settled, confirming that any Court of Session decisions would be the last word. There was now no way back, secession and schism were inevitable.

Gaels in Glasgow and the Recurring Highland Problem

It cannot be said that in the vital concerns of health, housing and cleanliness the Scottish nation was any better off in 1850 than in 1800; rather, as a result of the inrush of Scottish peasants and low Irish to towns unprepared and unfit to receive them, social evils had been intensified.

Rait and Pryde, *Scotland*

Throughout the decades of the Clearances there had been a steady stream, and in growing numbers, of Highlanders forced to quit their townships and crofts in search of better prospects in the south, this as an alternative to emigration or the forced march to the coastal margins of the north and west. However, incoming Gaels to the south now faced a new type of poverty and poor prospects and as the Rait and Pryde attribution above opines, the blame for increasing social depravation lay squarely at the feet of 'Scottish peasants and low Irish'. These very people brought with them their religion and their faith, and not a few grievances. The Gaelic Missionary Societies especially rose to the challenge in providing ministry and mission to these new communities and the building of Gaelic chapels followed.

The Gaels who had ventured south and who were now caught up in the fevered atmosphere of city living were not slow in reinforcing their Highland credentials by voicing their demands for appropriate church accommodation. In March 1823, Glasgow Presbytery ruled on a petition with over 2,000 signatures for a fourth Gaelic Chapel to be established in the city. The crux of the argument centred around the number of sittings available to accommodate the city's 40,000 Highland souls. Those who opposed the petition maintained there was plenty of spare capacity in the three existing chapels, Gorbals, Duke Street and Ingram Street. By increasing the supply, a fourth would only spread the congregations ever more thinly and reduce the income, especially at a time when there was debt outstanding on all three buildings.

To counter this, other statistics were offered which seemed to bear out a severe lack of accommodation among the three existing chapels supporting a great need for a fourth. A site had already been chosen in Union Street. Those who objected advancing the argument that it would reduce income were roundly condemned while those proponents splitting hairs over 'West Highland' and 'Northern' dialects were similarly ridiculed. It will be remembered that the purity, or otherwise, of Archie Cook's Gaelic was an issue. In Glasgow at least, two distinct Gaelic communities had established themselves. The vote was narrow, with the petition to build a fourth chapel granted.

From north to south and from east to west there was a steady increase in the number of new or replacement places of worship, heralding the great Victorian age of church building, but now with no prospect of Government funding. In Aberdeen, Edinburgh and Glasgow a concentration of wealth and mercantile expertise facilitated the planting of many new congregations and the erection of fine buildings, often carved out of existing parishes.

The Kirk employed a mixed bag of financial resources from which to draw appropriate funding to facilitate this acceleration in activity. At its heart was Chalmers's core belief, as the convener of the Assembly's Church Extension Committee, that in order to provide sufficient overall national coverage in terms of deploying ministerial resources it was fundamental that the Kirk enter into a political pact with Governments of the time to provide all necessary funding, even on a supplementary basis. The precedent had already been established. The Royal Bounty provision set up in 1725 was the clearest indication of third-party funding and Governments in the early decades of the 19th century had given every indication that they were willing partners in this pact. However, for the decade following The Highland Churches Act of 1824 Governments both Tory and Whig began to show a reluctance to continue with the arrangement, despite positive noises to the contrary.

The Parliamentary Church model appeared to be working well and the General Assembly more than once contemplated extending the scheme further. But it was not to be. Instead, Chalmers took up the cause and his 'Church Extension' programme was testimony to the way in which he galvanised the people of the Kirk into providing funds together with encouraging town councils, heritors and landowners to meet much of the financial requirements to expand and extend the Kirk's presence throughout the land.

The ever-present challenge for the Kirk in the north and west was how best to serve the mainly Gaelic-speaking population, many of whom remained resistant to or sceptical about initiatives they suspected exposed them to a Church which still retained cosy ties to landlords and heritors. Marginalised at the time of the Clearances, these same Gaels found solace through their religion within the surviving worshipping communities of the north and west. This was replicated in the urban areas of the south. It is true that mainly Evangelical ministers filled the pulpits of the Parliamentary Churches and chapels-of-ease reinforcing the claims of a specific Gaelic culture, language and religion. That these claims continued to prove troublesome merely enabled the disaffected and dislocated clergy and congregations to come out in 1843 and form the Free Church when the historic opportunity arose.

Essay Nine

Planting New Congregations: the Kirk's Highland Ambitions

The Evangelicals got control of the Church during the 'thirties and started at once to revivify religion. They raised funds in order to provide more parish schools, they pushed forward with the work of building 'quoad sacra' parishes in the newer communities [and] made strenuous efforts to supplement the unsatisfactory results of the poor law.

Sir Robert Rait and George S. Pryde, *Scotland*

The years from the 1750s onwards until the 1820s experienced the greatest expansion of mission work in the north and west. This was driven by enthused Gaelic-speaking Evangelical ministers occupying Highland pulpits who gradually displaced Moderate ministers. As a consequence, the building of churches and the planting of congregations as revivalism took hold in certain localities became a feature across the Highlands and Islands. Successive General Assemblies, although Tory-biased and Moderate in persuasion, were in no doubt of the positive advantages, religious, cultural and political, of building upon an expanding church presence: first, to encourage Gaels to be loyal to the Presbyterian Church; secondly, to promote loyalty towards the government and the Hanoverian succession; and finally, to wean them away from the ever-present dangers of Catholicism, Jacobitism and superstition-infused beliefs.

The Evangelical agenda, however, was focused in other directions and motivated by three urgent points of concern: first, to recover the puritan soul at the heart of the Kirk; second, to redefine the relationship between Church and State; and third, to make 'mission' and the strengthening of congregational life the Kirk's priority. This new Evangelicalism was characterised by three aspects which appeared at odds with the 'Establishment's' ambitions: first, there was less reference to Hanoverian loyalty and its concomitant political agenda; second, it addressed the increasing influence of Anglicisation at the expense of Gaelic language and culture; and last, it was less concerned with extending the benefits of civilisation. The Evangelical imperative was founded upon recovering a personal relationship with the Almighty; on acknowledging sinfulness; the need for repentance and God's forgiveness; and, by his grace, the hope of salvation.

From time to time, General Assemblies fretted about the state of religion in the Highlands and Islands and their responses, late in the day for some, were prompted mainly by this new breed of Evangelical ministers. Many Highland and Island congregations could be termed 'unstable', as depopulation, the Clearances and voluntary emigration took their toll. As the 18th century drew to a close it was firmly felt that the plight of the Gael required specific solutions.

First . . . a Little Bit of History

From the Reformation onwards the procedure for building a new church was vested in the parliamentary Commission for Plantation of Kirks, but the responsibility for the associated costs – church buildings, manses and salaries – lay with the heritors. Few willingly met their obligations. Throughout the 17th and 18th centuries the General Assembly urged Presbyteries on many occasions to bring before Parliament and the Commission the need for improvements to the kirks within their bounds and required Synods to exhort Presbyteries to meet their responsibilities. In time this increasingly focused on the planting of churches in the Highlands and Islands, supplying them with Ministers and Probationers, and promoting Religion and the 'Knowledge of God in these places'.

In 1725 the Royal Bounty of £1000 was placed in the hands of the General Assembly's newly formed 'Commission to some Ministers and Ruling Elders for Reformation of the Highlands and Islands of Scotland, and for Management of the King's Bounty for that end'. The fund was used to appoint itinerant preachers and catechists to go where they were most needed and to work under the authority of the local Presbytery. The Commission reported regularly to the General Assembly, and for nearly 40 years the same purposes were approved. In 1759 the focus was narrowed further: there was now a concentration on the parishes of South Uist, Small Isles, Glencoe, Harris, the countries of Moidart, Glengarry, and Lochaber, and other parishes of the Synods of Glenelg and Argyle. These specific areas were known to accommodate a sizeable Catholic population. After the rout at Culloden, Catholics sought refuge on the very western fringes of the country. The Kirk had been ever vigilant over the possibility of further Catholic insurgency supported by sympathisers from overseas.

It was therefore vital to convert the practitioners of the 'old religion' to Protestantism and establish all means to do so in these areas.

The first Statistical Accounts of Scotland, from 1791-1799, as reported in previous essays, provided plentiful evidence of large swathes of the Highlands and Islands being inadequately served by the church: too few ministers, too few churches, too few well-maintained church buildings, large remote areas with no access to a parish church for months of the year, and insufficient stipend for ministers, and hence many vacancies. But an opportunity to address the 'Highland Problem' would arise from an unexpected source.

The 1819 Act for Building Additional New Churches in England

During a House of Commons debate on 16th March 1818, concern had been expressed in Parliament in part about the inadequate provision of churches for the greatly increased population in towns and cities in England, and in part about the changes in England in religious affiliation and the considerable increase in non-conformist congregations. Nicholas Vansittart, the Chancellor of the Exchequer, stated that even during the nearly eight years of war with Napoleon, 'parliament had made liberal grants to promote the comforts of the clergy, and to confer on the public the benefit of a respectable and moderately endowed ministry. But these grants, however important in their object, could not supply the want of places of public worship, of which there existed so melancholy a deficiency.'[1]

He reported that church services ran from morning till night – in one instance quoted, the work of one curate entailed conducting three Sunday morning services, one full service in the afternoon after which 17 children were baptised and five funerals held. Another report spoke of one vicar conducting 40 to 50 baptisms every Sunday afternoon. Concern was expressed that the dignity and solemnity of worship was not possible to maintain. The ordinances were carried out in haste, with constant repetition and usually in the midst of crowded, noisy sanctuaries. The Chancellor proposed 'a grant, to the extent of one million pounds sterling, to be raised by an issue of exchequer bills, and applied . . . under the direction of commissioners appointed by the Crown.'[2]

---

1 *Hansard*, 16th March 1818, Building of New Churches, vol. 37, column 1118.
2 *Hansard*, 16th March 1818, Building of New Churches, vol. 37, column 1127.

Essay 9: Planting New Churches

The Bill gained wholehearted but not unanimous support (dissenters were quick to voice opposing views) and was virtually 'nodded through'. This proposal became the 1819 Act for Building New Churches, sometimes known as the Million Pound Act, the equivalent value today being around £105 million. The buildings that resulted were often known as the Waterloo churches – 'built', said George Tierney, Leader of the Opposition, 'to commemorate our victories by sea and land'.[3] More than a dozen Church Building Acts followed this one over the next 30 to 40 years; the 1824 Act produced a further £500,000.

During the same debate, Mr William Smith, MP for Norwich, wished to know whether it was intended to extend the operation of this measure to Scotland, where, to his knowledge, 'the parishes were so extensive, that the people were prevented from attending at their parish churches. There were some parishes in Scotland not less than forty miles long'.[4] In reply, the Chancellor conceded that 'Scotland had, in proportion to its wants, equal claims to national support',[5] and he believed parliament would feel equal readiness to come to its assistance: 'but the forms of church government in Scotland are so different from those of England that to attempt to embody in the same act of parliament the provisions applicable to each, could only lead to embarrassment and confusion'. He assured Parliament that Scotland had not been overlooked, and that he 'felt no disposition to object to a separate proposition for that part of the united kingdom'.

However, one year prior to this, the General Assembly had already set up a committee with a view to collate all relevant and necessary information about the serious deficiency in church provision across the entire country and present the findings to Parliament.

The Kirk Launches its Appeal to Government

The focus of what became known as the 'Highlands Churches Act' of 1824 was firmly aimed at tackling problems specific to the north and west: first, how the Kirk might better serve a population very often living on the margins of economic viability in townships scattered across vast parishes where no possibility existed for a local congregation to pay for ministry; further, how to meet the challenge of indigenous

---

3 *Hansard*, 16th March 1818, Building of New Churches, vol. 37, column 1116.

4 *Hansard*, 16th March 1818, Building of New Churches, vol. 37, column 1130.

5 *Hansard*, 16th March 1818, Building of New Churches, vol. 37, column 1126.

Gaelic culture and language; also, to push back on the residual and irrepressible Catholic traditions still prevalent in some specific pockets in the north and west and finally; to assert Presbyterian primacy over the stubborn and resistant presence of Episcopacy. In Parliament, the initial consideration was a plan to cover the whole of Scotland, north and south but, as the negotiations developed, the more pressing need began to focus on the far north and west. To the vast majority of English and Scottish MPs the Highlands and Islands remained a wholly 'different' country.

Through the advocacy of Revd Dr John Inglis, minister of Old Greyfriars' Church in Edinburgh, Dean of the Chapel Royal, leader of the Moderate Party and convener of the General Assembly's Committee, the Church optimistically entered into a formal dialogue with the Government. This initial outline report was sent to Prime Minister Lord Liverpool and Chancellor Vansittart and was followed by a more detailed report one year later. By the time the March 1818 debate was underway, both Houses were well aware of the dire situation north of the border.

At the General Assembly some weeks later, the commissioners were encouraged to hear the terms of the Prince Regent's letter, which stated the intention of 'extending at no distant day, pecuniary succour to those Parishes, which either from their redundant population, or from their expanded dimensions, were at present incapable of supplying adequate Places of Worship for their Religiously-disposed inhabitants'. The Kirk's General Assembly had drawn up a strong case to tackle destitution in many parts of the country and the request for a similar grant for Scotland, now with Royal approval, seemed to be on track.

The case for a stronger Kirk presence was the subject of one newspaper editorial. It was reported that in Highland Perthshire, Catholics were 'gaining ground and missionaries sent out by the Church of Scotland were far inferior to Established clergymen and who were often offering 'superstitions and fanatical creeds'.[6] It was not beyond newspaper proprietors, mainly landowning Tories, to stir their readership into a froth. On this occasion, the editorial identified three possible evils before the Kirk: the covert threat of further Catholic insurgency; the Kirk's inability to muster much of a defence against the forces of popery; and lastly the number of ill-educated missionaries stationed in the rural areas. Whether or not the above was true it certainly played into the hands of those fearful for the pre-eminence of the Established Church.

---

6 *Aberdeen Press and Journal,* 15th April 1818.

English MPs generally exhibited a distinct ignorance and prejudice when it came to dealing with Scottish matters: the skewed perception of 'Northern Britain' populated by an ungrateful, lazy and handout-dependent population persisted. This perception circulated among Scottish landowners keen to monetise their estates mainly through the Clearances which, by 1818, had been ongoing for several decades. Further, the Government was already spending considerable amounts on infrastructure improvements in the north and west. By 1821 the Government's investment would amount to £500,000, quite enough for many irritated English MPs. The upper classes viewed the Highlander through the prism of a particular work-ethic combined with the desire and drive for self-improvement. Enthusiastic improver the Duke of Argyll's comment was typical of his class and of the times, 'Highlanders have not yet come to appreciate the true dignity of ordinary labour.'

Despite this it was believed that Government ambition would win the day and Highland communities would eventually be won over to the post-revolution political and religious establishment and would become integrated, ambitious and loyal subjects of Crown, State and Empire. Bringing the Highlander 'into line' with the rest of the country i.e. the south of the country, would solve several problems at a stroke.

However, Highland communities remained obstinately resistant in adopting Southern attitudes or replicating the new commercial practices of the industrialised central belt. The 'Political Establishment' put this failure down to two main reasons: first, that there was little prospect of integration either with the new emerging Scottish cultures of the south or with British polity. The *laisser-faire* approach to economics which Tories and Moderates embraced had not played out well for the lower orders in the Highlands and Islands. Further, the economic theories which drove capitalism could not be similarly applied to the north and west. The Highlands and Islands were simply too 'different' in terms of culture, language and landscape; and second, there was an abiding and persistent religious ignorance which appeared impervious to education or correction in the errors of Catholicism, superstition and Jacobitism.

Additionally, there was a lack of a strong church institution which might have provided leadership in aligning the Scottish nation with Southern ambitions to drive Scotland forward as an integral and valued member of the 'united' kingdom. Despite Moderatism and Tory ambition hand-in-hand it was clear that the lack of effective cohesive leadership by the clergy had failed to help win over a reluctant and suspicious population, already traumatised by the Clearances, to the cultural and economic advantages of the Union. Moderate ministers generally but with some exceptions seemed incapable of prosecuting the Presbyterian case effectively enough in the face of those whose religious allegiances were rooted elsewhere.

The Kirk's Difficulties Begin . . .

The General Assembly's Committee, with Dr Inglis at the head, might have recognised that the levers and gears of government 'grind exceeding slow'. The Bill for new churches in England had gained Royal assent with minimum fuss but if the Committee expected a similarly quick and positive response it was to be sorely disappointed.

To assist the Chancellor's calculations in determining the size of grant, by March 1819 the Committee had drawn up a statistical analyses of populations and the number of parishes, on a strict basis of comparison with corresponding English numbers, together with an explanation of the peculiar difficulties in the Highland and Island areas. Dr Inglis calculated on a *pro rata* basis the Scottish grant should be £200,000. This sum was summarily dismissed. The Chancellor brought forward a Government Bill for erecting Churches in Scotland, with a budget of £100,000. It passed the House of Commons but certain procedural delays meant it could not be read in the Lords during that current session of Parliament. However, the Bill generated much unease about its provisions, since most of the grant would be swallowed up by building new churches in the Lowland towns and cities with little left as a capital reserve to fund new churches and manses in the Highlands and Islands, or to pay stipends for clergy.

Nothing was done for two years. At the 1821 General Assembly, Dr Inglis provided a blow-by-blow account of correspondence between the Assembly Committee and the Lord Advocate, Sir William Rae, which revealed disagreement within the government. In Sir William Rae's letters, it emerged that although the Chancellor of the Exchequer was in favour of the grant in principle, some Scottish members were opposed to the Bill and the Prime Minister was opposed to the application for monies as he thought that 'there does not exist the indispensable necessity for the building of additional churches in Scotland which can justify the application of such a sum at the present moment.' There were many MPs who shared the Prime Minister's concerns and who were eager to curb any enthusiasm for new Scottish churches from the outset.

Essay 9: Planting New Churches 233

By 1821 the effort to raise public funds to finance the building of Scotland's National Monument on Calton Hill had failed miserably. This was to be a memorial to the contribution of Scottish soldiers in the Napoleonic Wars. There arose a motion in Parliament to pay for it by taking £10,000 directly from the proposed (and at the time, *unspecified*) budget to finance Parliamentary Churches in the Highlands whose Bill was making its tortuous way through both chambers.

This proposal had garnered much support from English MPs and it took a timely intervention from the Inverness MP Charles Grant to refocus the argument by stating that £10,000 for the 'erection of splendid buildings in Edinburgh was a gross misapplication of public funds.'[7] When he heard such a sum mooted he 'could not help looking to various parishes in the Highlands, some of which were forty miles in extent, and without a parish church'. The MP went on to say that he thought the question ought to have been submitted to the General Assembly, as had been done before. 'When in England grants had been made for the building of churches, they were handed over to Commissioners, who employed them on their own responsibility.' Why then, Mr Grant concluded, could the same arrangement not be made for Scotland? Mr Grant recognised that expertise on Highland churches rested with the General Assembly and not with any Parliamentary committee sitting 500 miles away.

Sir William's letters to Dr Inglis revealed that Lord Liverpool proposed postponing the matter until another Parliamentary session, and that a different, more economical and more effectual solution be found for Scotland. The Government was obviously seeking a less costly option. The Prime Minister believed the 'Highland Problem' would perhaps be solved by appointing more missionaries. Sir William explained to Dr Inglis that the Government were not very much disposed to vote a sum of £100,000 as there were difficulties as to how the churches would be maintained and endowed (no such fears had been expressed when considering the situation in England) but he was confident that the Bill would be considered again in the next parliamentary session. Sir William's confidence was in direct contrast to the general air of despondency felt by commissioners as Dr Inglis expressed the disappointment of the General Assembly.

On the day he received that letter from Sir William, Dr Inglis replied that he had found in Hansard that the grant had indeed been voted on

---

7 As reported in the *Scotsman*, July 25th 1822.

two years previously in 1819; Hansard did not record the sum voted, but Dr Inglis quoted from the Edinburgh Advertiser: 'A resolution that a sum not exceeding £100,000 be granted to His Majesty for erecting Churches in Scotland was agreed to.' With more than a touch of irony, Dr Inglis assured Sir William that 'We heartily rejoice in the advantages which the Church of England already derives from the liberal Grant which Parliament was pleased to make, but we hope to be forgiven for having, at the same time, a strong desire to participate in this bounty.'

The writer of this essay cannot find the report of a vote in 1819 or in 1818, but notes here a reference in Hansard to the sum of £100,000 in the midst of a Parliamentary debate: Scotland's Lord Advocate, Alexander Hamilton (10th Duke) reminded the House that

> The Chancellor of the Exchequer had last year obtained from parliament the grant of £100,000 for building churches in Scotland, on the ground that the people were in want of such churches, but there was a paragraph in this petition stating that the people could not go to church from want of clothing. Would it not, then, be but considerate in the right hon. gentleman and his colleagues, to consider of the means of supplying the people with that clothing, without which these new churches would be of no utility?[8]

The Chancellor appeared to be advancing an argument which stated that without a suitable 'clothing fund' made available, existing and new churches would remain unfilled.

Another Parliamentary session elapsed and in the following year a meeting was held in Melville Castle, the home of Lord Viscount Melville, the First Lord of the Admiralty, who was a popular figure in Scotland and viewed for a short time as a 'manager' for Scottish affairs in Parliament. (There was no Secretary of State for Scotland between 1746 and 1885. The 'manager' post changed hands from time to time which did not aid communication between the General Assembly and Parliament.) At the meeting which Dr Inglis and committee members attended, Lord Melville made the case for a grant of £100,000 to create 30 new *quoad sacra* parish churches with manses and offices in the Highlands at the cost of £1500 for each parish. He furnished the meeting with the details: 30 new schemes at a total cost of £45,000 would be needed, and a further sum of £15,000 would allow the investment of

---

8 *Hansard*, 21st December 1819, *State of the Labouring Poor in Scotland*, vol. 41, Column 1400.

£500 per parish, the interest from which would prove sufficient for repairing and maintaining the churches and manses, absolving both the government and landowners from that expense, although requiring landowners to grant the land on which to build the church and manse, and a glebe. It was also stipulated that applications should come from two or more heritors per parish. The unused £40,000 would be used for additional churches in the Lowlands. The talks at Melville Castle also proposed an annual grant of £4500 for ministers' stipends – £150 per charge – with the possibility of the cost being reduced with Royal Bounty money.

Despite Dr Inglis' and the committee's expectations, Lord Melville, possibly under pressure from the Government, later rowed back on the details of the scheme. Dr Inglis and the committee had considered the scheme to have been finalised. Not so. His Majesty's Advocate sent a letter outlining what the Government's new proposals were to be and which, timeously, the terms of which were read to the General Assembly. The focus of the Melville Castle meeting had certainly been upon the pressing matter of church provision for the Highlands and Islands, but the Advocate's letter had revived an initial overture from the General Assembly of 1819 that Government would provide grants for additional places of worship *throughout* Scotland. While this, in principle, was to be welcomed, two consequences were plainly obvious: the focus of attention was clearly moving away from the Highlands and Islands; and second, the General Assembly was left in no doubt that a much watered-down scheme was being proposed.

The recast proposal intended to apply £20,000 to the building of churches in the Lowlands, and £57,000 in the Highlands, but 'all that could be given this year would be only £30,000; one half to be applied to the Highlands and the other in the Lowlands'. The phrase 'all that could be given' simply highlights the obstructionism and chicanery of Liverpool's Government, determined to make matters as difficult as possible for the Kirk.

This letter reveals the wholly unsympathetic nature of Government's response to the Assembly's petition and by this time it was fairly assumed by many in the Kirk and those commissioners who sat listening to the proposal in the General Assembly that, there was little indication that the Government would prosecute the Scottish case with much conviction. Four years had now elapsed with precious little Parliamentary time spent on debating the issue. By contrast, thanks to the awarding of the £1m grant in 1818 the erection of additional places of worship in England was well underway. Little did Dr Nicol or other commissioners to the 1822 Assembly know of the Government's intention to award the Church of England a further £500,000 (the equivalent of £52.5 millions in today's terms) towards new church accommodation. Whatever came the Kirk's way was surely going to be crumbs by comparison.

Possibly stung by the parsimonious and niggardly proposal advanced by the Government, the *Scotsman* newspaper ran an editorial on the matter of financing Scotland's Established Churches, the proper remuneration of its clergy and the cost to the nation.[9] By comparison, it reported that the most recent audited figures for the Church of England revealed an income of £9m. The editorial supposed there were 5000 places of worship ('probably an overestimate', it stated). Dividing the one into the other resulted in an average income per place of worship at £1520, a sum that would be 'ample sufficient for the support of *five* Scottish churches'. Quoting Paul's second letter to the church in Thessalonica, the piece continues, 'It has been said, and by very high authority, that those who do not work ought not to eat. But it unfortunately happens, that notwithstanding the unparalleled wealth of the Church of England, the incomes of the working clergy, or curates, are miserably and disgracefully deficient'. It was estimated that, according to these 1817 figures (the latest available in 1822) approximately one-third received incomes of between £40 and £60 per year, with the average being £115.

At the same time, Kirk ministers were paid in an income range of between £120 and £600, the latter which included a university appointment. From these figures it would appear that, as in the case of the Kirk, payment of stipend especially at the lower end was woefully inadequate. However, in Scotland, the Church was *unable* to pay all its ministers at a level envisaged by the early Reformers' blueprint for a well-funded, well-endowed clergy. It was the case in the Church of England that parsimony dictated that it was *unwilling* to pay its clergy a living wage. The clergy, north and south of the border, were indeed held hostage by the old maxim, 'God will keep you humble and the Church will keep you poor'.

After the meeting at Melville Castle, Lord Melville had asked Dr Inglis to write to him, outlining in full (again) the case to be made for the funding of additional churches in Scotland, that he might bring

---

9 The *Scotsman* 27th July 1822.

ESSAY 9: PLANTING NEW CHURCHES

to the attention of parliament. The case for Parliamentary approval for the building of additional churches, first put forward in 1819, had obviously not been made forcibly enough, given the wholly inadequate settlement which came before the 1822 Assembly.

Dr Inglis and the committee must have thought they were back at square one. And so in November that year, Dr Inglis wrote the letter with extended information and further statistics to support the argument: a comparison between the number of churches per head of population in England and Scotland. In England and Wales, there were a few hundred short of 12,000 churches of the Establishment for 12 million people; in Scotland only 956 churches for 2 million, and those spread over an extensive and mountainous country. He considered that it was impossible to doubt that the wants of Scotland in respect of Church accommodation were more urgent than those in England, which Parliament had remedied with some speed. He also pointed out that, unlike the Church of England, the Established Church in Scotland represented more than four-fifths of the population. And with a hint of grievance, he added, 'In these circumstances it cannot be supposed that the people of Scotland, while they pay an adequate proportion of the Grant of Money for the Erection of Churches in England, should not feel it a hardship if the Boon were not to be proportionally extended to themselves'.

Dr Inglis summarized the proposals agreed in the meeting held at Melville Castle earlier in the year. He also reminded Parliament of the promises of the Prince Regent and the King in Letters to the General Assembly encouraging 'the supply of adequate places of worship for the Highlands of Scotland' and the grateful reply sent in 1818 and reported in the London press that year: 'We receive with all thankfulness the royal donation of £2000 for the promulgation of Christian knowledge and the principles of the Reformed religion in the Highlands and Islands of Scotland',[10] and the hopeful reply in 1819, again reported in the same journal: '[With] the assurance that your Royal Highness has not abandoned your wise and benevolent intention of affording aid ... we confirm our reliance on the interest your Royal Highness takes in our church, and from the fulfilment of that intention (which we trust will not be long delayed) we anticipate the happiest consequences.'[11]

---

10 *London Gazette,* 23rd May 1819.
11 *London Gazette,* 29th May 1819.

In the Hands of the Government . . .

As the new year of 1823 began, Lord Melville took Dr Inglis' letter to the Government for consideration. However, further Parliamentary entanglement ensued. The awarding of a further £500,000 to the Church of England clearly had garnered considerable opposition among mainly dissenting English MPs and this certainly did not help the Scottish cause. Some MPs asked why another Government grant was needed to assist the already wealthy Anglican Church and during the same debate other MPs wrongly assumed the Church of Scotland had similar considerable funds at its own disposal. Also, many MPs doubted the strength of the English case on the need for accommodation, asking for statistics to support it, one way or the other. £500,000 would eventually enable a further 50 churches to be built. One church alone cost £77,000.

Demonstrating that the cost of such a scheme for Scotland still exercised many MPs as well as its readership, the *Scotsman* reported that in the House of Lords 'The Marquis of Bute wished to know from any of the noble Lords who are members of government, whether any measures had been taken for the appropriation of £200,000 voted by the House of Commons for building churches in Scotland.'[12] In smoke-filled clubs and in Parliamentary corridors various sums had been aired as to the level of Government funding; the arguments were further confused and conflated as the additional grant of £500,000 for English churches began making its way through committee stages. The Marquis of Bute expected a grant of £200,000 for Scottish churches while Dr Joseph Hume the MP for Montrose during an exchange quoted a figure of £100,000. A figure of £150,000 was also commonly banded about. The lack of Parliamentary debating time simply fuelled the rumours.

The 1824 Bill for Additional Places of Worship in the Highlands and Islands of Scotland

By May of 1823, the clauses of the proposed Highland Churches Bill were clearer, with Government once again having changed its mind over how the Bill was to be financed and what expenses were to be covered. Dr Inglis now was informed of the 'nuts and bolts' of the proposal and duly reported to the General Assembly on 31st May that he had 'very lately been informed by the Lord Advocate' that the Chancellor of the Exchequer would propose to Parliament to make

---

12 The *Scotsman*, 30th April 1823.

a grant of £50,000 (at the rate of £10,000 per annum) to be applied to the building of Churches in the Highlands, leaving no balance for buildings in the Lowlands, the need being greater for churches in the north and west. Each church would have a manse and offices, and each minister would be provided with a stipend. Commissioners would be appointed to carry out the purposes of the Act, and they would invite landowners in the Highlands and Islands to make an application to the Commissioners for the erection of new buildings in their parishes. The Commissioners would enquire into the arguments put forward with each case and would have the power to decide if an additional church would be provided, its situation, its size and design. The Commissioners would report regularly to the Lords of the Treasury.

Dr Inglis concluded by saying that the preparation of the Bill was under way, the terms of which fell considerably short, both of Dr Inglis' initial *pro rata* assessment (£200,000), and the Chancellor's own proposal (£100,000) at which the Prime Minister baulked. This new Bill became an Act in 1823 but was amended a year later to make provision for the appointment of commissioners to execute the Act, with a secretary and clerk, surveyors and other necessary individuals.

The Government was well aware that there was no body in Scotland equivalent to the Church Commissioners in England who were overseeing the spending of the £1 million grant. It appeared that the General Assembly would be disqualified from holding the purse-strings. This oversight could well have been foreseen and a remedy easily incorporated into the terms of the Bill. However, a more necessary amendment concerned applications for a new church which had to be supported by two heritors. Many of the neediest parishes were immediately disqualified because there was only a single heritor responsible for the parish.

Finally, 'A Bill entituled An Act for building additional Places of Worship in the Highlands and Islands of Scotland' went live on 9th April 1824 and was thereafter known as the 'Highland Churches Act'. The *Scotsman* was therefore able to report that

> During the debate on the Building of Churches Act, the Chancellor of the Exchequer declared it was his 'gratifying duty to propose a grant of £50,000 for the building of churches in the Highlands and the endowment of Ministers in the Established Church of Scotland'; that proposition met with the unanimous approbation of the house.'[13]

---

13 The *Scotsman*, 14th April 1824.

The process had taken six years of debate, argument, delay, obstruction, obfuscation, Government silences, mischief-making and chicanery. Its largesse in this matter was to grant the Kirk a sum which equated to three percent of the grant given to the Anglican Church. Many, mainly dissenters, had opposed the Bill from the very beginning and they were to have the final *hurrah*. There existed a standing fund 'For the augmentation of the maintenance of the poor Clergy of the Established Church of Scotland.' By Parliamentary Act, three grants had been made amounting to £30,000 during the reign of George IV. Some English MPs mischievously suggested that this fund ought to be raided to finance part of the Bill, a suggestion that was met with universal disapproval within the Kirk. However much general support there was for the building of additional churches, the General Assembly's response was firm that it must not be achieved by appropriating funds expressly designed to improve the lot of impoverished ministers. Now, at the time of enacting the Highland Churches Bill, MPs voted to repeal the above Act. There would be no more Government contributions to assist the poor clergy of Scotland.

There certainly remained pockets of dogged resistance, not only from English sources but from within sections of the Scottish population itself, to expending any monies, especially tax-payers' monies, on improving the lot of buildings and clergy. There remained those who had resisted the Bill, right up to the last minute – and beyond. While the machinery for this 'great and new experiment' (Revd Prof. George Cook, Moderator of the General Assembly 1825) was being assembled within the corridors of power in London, even yet siren voices at home were withholding support from the combined efforts of the Kirk and Government, and declaring 'far enough but no more!'

The Highland Churches Act was now in force, but subsequent and related legislation was about to come before Parliament. The *Scotsman* reported

> The Michaelmas [1824] meeting of the Landholders and Justices of the Peace within the County of Aberdeenshire resolved to oppose the forthcoming Parliamentary Bill to regulate the building and repairing of Manses, offices and other matters relative to the residence and accommodation of the Clergy of the Church of Scotland. It rejected the measure on the grounds it was unnecessary and inexpedient.[14]

---

14 The *Scotsman*, 18th Oct. 1824.

In Aberdeenshire, much of the land was held by families with Episcopalian sympathies. As local patrons willingly supporting their own, it also fell to these same local landowning families in their role as heritors to provide financial assistance for the upkeep of the local kirk and ensure ministers' stipends. It was therefore not surprising that the influential members of the above organisation baulked at any move, Parliamentary or otherwise, to increase the burden of their personal financial responsibilities solely in favour of the rival claims of Presbyterianism.

Similarly, the Michaelmas meeting of local landowners and Justices of the Peace in Dumfriesshire wholeheartedly supported their Aberdeenshire brethren in agreeing to oppose the Parliamentary Bill. At the same gathering the members also heard a petition regarding improving the lot of schoolmasters who, in terms of the petition, were 'praying for a small augmentation of salary'. This petition was 'very favourably received and it was admitted on all hands, that the Parochial schoolmasters are a class of men so highly meritorious, that their claims are entitled to the utmost consideration'. However, a note of caution in agreeing to this was expressed when it was pointed out that a wages agreement was already in place which would take effect from 1828, raising salaries from between £16 and £23 to an improved £25 to £28 four years hence. Members were therefore advised not to 'interfere' with the arrangement. It would appear therefore that these 'highly meritorious' schoolmasters in straitened circumstances had to endure a further four years of penury before they could enjoy a wage rise.

Despite all the above, the 'Parliamentary Churches' enterprise, as it was now to be known, was finally underway and a new chapter in Scottish church history was about to be written.

The Terms of the Highland Churches Act

The first clause of the amended Act stipulated that the Treasury would issue £50,000 out of the Consolidated Fund of the United Kingdom, to be issued to the Commissioners who were to be appointed.[15] The sum would be invested in Exchequer Bills until needed,[16] and the Commissioners would be required to render accounts of expenditure to the Barons of the Exchequer in Scotland.[17] It had already been

---

15 Essentially, the Government's bank account which was set up in 1787.

16 A type of paper-money that the Government used to borrow from people and repaid with interest.

17 The Court of Exchequer had responsibility for administration of Government

realised that £50,000 was insufficient for building 40 churches and manses, but sufficient for completing 30 churches with manses, and 10 more manses where churches already existed.

The 1823 Act had required 'two or more heritors possessed of land valued at £100' to make an application; this was changed in the 1824 Act to allow one heritor to apply to the Commissioners to have parish buildings built where they desired them to be erected. The minister's stipend was raised in the 1824 Act to £120 per annum, but the salaries of £5 for a precentor and £3 for a beadle, stated in the 1823 Act, were omitted. A significant amendment to the former Bill was to consign funds raised from seat-rents to the heritors and to the future minister, imposing upon them the burden of maintaining the church and the manse respectively, with any surplus deposited in reserve for future expenditure on fabric.

This clause was designed to ensure that the buildings would not be allowed to fall into decay. Details would be required in the application of the type of ground offered for the buildings, whether there would be sufficient space for a churchyard with access, and ground for a garden for the minister of not less than half a Scotch acre. (A Scotch acre was roughly 25% larger than an English acre which became the British standard in 1824). The Commissioners, on receipt of any such application, would send direct notice to the minister or ministers of the parish(es) from which the application came, with the instruction to read out the notice after morning service on the first Sunday after it was delivered, and to attach a copy to the church doors.

The Commissioners would consider each application, gathering information to determine whether an additional church should be provided in such a parish and to ascertain that the land could accommodate the size of the buildings and space for a churchyard etc. If the Commissioners decided to proceed, they would be empowered to require the heritors to reach an agreement with the Presbytery, that a district within the parish should be defined and set apart for an additional place of worship where a minister would be appointed to officiate.

The Act also allowed the Commissioners, before any parish or district was chosen, to consider the type of situation and access, and the size and design of the churches and manses and appurtenances that would be appropriate to a place of religious worship in full communion with the Church of Scotland. 'And be it further enacted that it shall and

---

revenue.

may be lawful for the said Commissioners to accept from any Heritors, in any Parish in which such an additional Place of Worship shall be erected or provided, a Portion of Ground in Name of Glebe, and also to accept any Grant or Privilege of grassing in the Summer.' There is no other reference in the terms of the Act to the size of arable ground or the quality of the ground or its proximity to the manse, nor to the Teinds, and no mention of 'a horse and two kyes grasse'.

Step Forward Thomas Telford

Although the Chancellor of the Exchequer had proposed that the arrangements should be undertaken by the Barons of the Exchequer, 'it must have been obvious that there was already one agency that was eminently suited to act as Commissioners. These were the Commissioners for building Highland roads and bridges.'[18] Thomas Telford, in his role as Chief Surveyor or Consulting Engineer to the Commission, now assumed control of the new Commission for Building Churches in the Highlands and Islands of Scotland. He brought with him a wealth of experience first as Engineer to the British Fisheries Society and then as Engineer to the [Caledonian] Canal Commissioners.

These Commissioners had been working together since 1803 and had formed a redoubtable and respected group of men who had played a vital part in the Government negotiations: Sir William Rae, Scotland's Lord Advocate and Lord Melville – three individuals who 'had history' with getting the Highland Churches Act over the line: Nicholas Vansittart who had been Chancellor of the Exchequer until March 1823, William Smith MP for Norwich who, by asking the question of the Chancellor in the debate of 1818, elicited the reply that Scotland would have 'equal claims for national support' and Sir Charles Grant who poured cold water on the proposal to finance Edinburgh's National Monument from monies set aside for building Highland churches.

John Rickman, Clerk Assistant to the House of Commons, was the Commission's secretary in London and James Hope was appointed Law Agent. John Mitchell had worked for 14 years as Telford's resident deputy on the roads and bridges, covering 10,000 miles every year on horseback and on foot. Telford appointed him to the new Commission for Churches, but Mitchell died suddenly in 1824, and Telford immediately appointed his son Joseph Mitchell, aged 21, as

---

18 Allan MacLean, *Telford's Highland Churches*, published in 1989 by the Society of West Highland and Island Historical Research, 7.

resident deputy, and he proved just as capable and skilled as his father. Two further appointments were made, crucial to the outcome: James Smith, an architect from Inverness and William Thomson, surveyor of the Crinan Canal. These two, together with Joseph Mitchell and Telford himself worked on the plans for both church and manse.

Few books about the work of Thomas Telford have much to say about churches and manses in the Highlands and Islands. They focused on his achievements in road and canals, harbours and bridge-building. L.T.C. Rolt, in his biography, considered that the Government was providing the churches by way of atoning for past crimes against the Highlands. Rolt was unadmiring of the architectural merit of the churches Telford built ('austere enough to satisfy the dourest minister of the Wee Free') but impressed with the financial achievement of building 32 churches and 40 manses at a cost of a little over £54,000.

The Commissioners had met during 1824 and by the following February 78 applications had been made. Some were immediately 'dismissed as outside the remit of the Act, like Fortrose and Perth; at others, the population was too small, like St Kilda and Rhum; or the number of Protestants was too small, like Canna'.[19] Before this meeting Telford had asked Smith, Mitchell and Thomson each to draw up designs for both church and manse which could be built within the £1,500 budget. In the end, with some fettling from Telford himself, it was agreed to proceed with Thomson's design for the churches, and Mitchell's designs for the manses, some single storey and the rest two-storey, erected as to local exposure to weather.

The Commissioners' Reports, Starting in February 1825

In the First Report, the Commissioners gave a brief explanation for the amendments to the 1823 Act and an exposition of the new clauses in the Act of 1824. At its first meeting and the following June, the Commissioners had drawn up a list of 31 churches, to be served by 30 ministers, and the offer of manses and ministers in 10 other cases. The first Table (opposite) shows the places where manses had been offered on condition of the existing church being repaired. The second Table (at the end of this chapter) sets out a list of applications for church and manse that had been received, a few of which were provisionally approved. For Argyll alone, 11 new churches were proposed, for Ross & Cromarty 7, and 6 for Inverness.

---

19 Allan MacLean, *Telford's Highland Churches*, published in 1989 by the Society of West Highland and Island Historical Research, 10.

Essay 9: Planting New Churches 245

Table 1 (manses only)

County	Parish or Island	Place	Population	Remarks
Aberdeen	Crathie & Braemar	Braemar	900	
Argyll	Mull, Torosay	Salen	800	
	Bowmore & Kilmeny	Kilmeny	1,600	
Elgin	Kingussie	Inch	800	
Orkney	St Andrews Deerness	Deerness	700	
	Cross & Burness	North Ronaldsay	467	
Perth	Fortingal	Rannoch	1.269	
Ross & Cromarty	Loch Broom	Ullapool	800	
Shetland	Dunrossness	Sandwick	649	
	Esting	Whalsay (Island)	655	

The decision was taken to employ builders who had established a good reputation in their contracts with the Road and Bridge Commissioners and offers of contract were made. This Report annexed sketches of the church and manse buildings and final versions of the plans and elevation of the standard church and the two styles of manse appeared in the Seventh Report. The Commissioners announced that they were confident that six churches would be completed by May 1826: Portnahaven on Islay, Tomintoul in Banffshire, Brae, Kinloch Luichart, Plockton, and Shieldaig in Ross-shire.

In the Second Report it was clear that the tentative approval of some applications had to be reviewed when visits were actually made to the parishes. The surveyor was eventually despatched to Shetland 'at a large expense, which has produced little more than negative results': neither the proposed new church and manse at Quarff nor the offer of manses for existing churches seemed viable. He visited Orkney on the same trip and confirmed the manses for Deerness and North Ronaldsay, insisting that the churches be properly repaired 'and fit for Divine Service'.

The Commissioners decided that the list of manses needed review, which would allow offers to be made to other places. It was anticipated that three of the applications for church and manse in Ross & Cromarty would be reduced to one 'when the best situation for it shall have been ascertained'. A correction was made to the list in the First Report, amending Brae to Croick. No significant alteration had been made to the drawings, but discussion was continuing on specs and estimates. The Commissioners found that the estimated dates for completion had been over-optimistic, but they expected that four churches and manses would be completed by the end of 1826 – Tomintoul and Kinloch Luichart by July, Croick and Plockton by September or October.

The Building Work

No building work is free of delays and complaints, and both occurred during this exercise, the main grievance being that £1500 was not adequate for the job in hand. However, the Commissioners made it clear to contractors and heritors that that was a strict limit, set by the 1824 Act. The delays were often a matter of getting signatures on documents, but if contractors had waited for the actual signature on every contract, hardly a single church or manse would have been built. The Secretary presented accounts for one year ending July 1826; fees for the secretary, law agent, clerk, for the surveyor resident in Inverness and the two other surveyors, and fees for Mr Telford. Travelling and other expenses amounted to £1,320 17s. 6. 'a larger Sum in all probability than will be required in any future Year.'

The Commissioners opened with a confident statement, that, according to the latest information they had received, 'upwards of twenty churches and manses would be completed before the end of the present year, 1827', this in addition to the four already certified as complete: the churches and manses at Tomintoul in Banffshire, at Shieldaig at Kinloch-Luichart, and at Plockton in Ross-shire and Croick, although in the latter there was a small legal obstacle shortly to be removed.

The buildings expected to be completed before the end of the year were churches and manses at Duror in Appin, at Tobermory, at Kinloch-Spelvie, and at Salen on Mull; a church and manse on the adjacent Isle of Ulva; at Keiss in Caithness; on Berneray Isle in the Parish of Harris; at Stensholl, and at Hallin, in the Isle of Skye; and at Trumisgarry on North Uist'. The churches and manses at Lochgilphead in Argyll; at Portnahaven and at Oa (or Oth) in Islay; at Berriedale in Caithness; at Strathy and at Rhuistore in the South-west part of Sutherland; and a manse at Kilmeny on Islay; most or all of these would be finished before the end of the season. They also reported that a manse at Inch in Kingussie Parish was nearly finished: this was a new addition to the list of manses requested.

Contracts were in preparation for building churches and manses at North Ballachulish in Inverness-shire with a church in Ardgour

Essay 9: Planting New Churches

to be served by the same minister; and for two churches and manses at Back and Cross in the Isle of Lewis. Contracts were also being prepared for a church at Muckairn in Argyll which would be built at the expense of General Campbell of Lochnell, and for a church at 'Interwick' [Innerwick] in Glenlyon (parish of Fortingall), to be built at the expense of the heritors; the Commissioners agreed to assign a manse and a minister to these two churches.

The speed of this whole project was remarkable; most of the areas had been selected precisely because they were remote, and that brought special difficulties over the availability of building materials and the transport of them. By July 1827, the date of the Third Report, the current situation stood at 25 churches with 24 manses, and four manses on their own, already completed or under contract to be built. The Commissioners expected seven more churches and manses, and six separate manses would yet be built. Shetland would have one church and manse, and two other manses; and Orkney would receive two manses. A decision had been reached by the Commissioners to place a church and manse in Poolewe to serve a large area of Ross & Cromarty, having considered in the Second Report three different locations in that extensive area.

The Commissioners reported that heritors and others, accustomed to the usual (inferior is implied) standard of building in the Highlands and Islands, considered the specifications in the contracts to be unreasonably expensive, but the Commissioners 'do not depart from their opinion' being concerned that the churches and manses were constructed with materials and with workmanship of a solid construction to avoid dilapidation, to withstand the effects of a stormy climate, and, just as much, to encourage heritors and ministers to maintain the buildings and not allow them to decay.

The Reports of the Commissioners were condensed, giving very little detail of the experience of building in the remotest areas. A more illuminating insight into human factors in such work is provided in letters in 1835 and 1836 between Bishop Andrew Scott, the Roman Catholic Vicar Apostolic of the Western District of Scotland, based in Greenock, to the local priest, Mr Coll MacColl who assisted the elderly priest Maighstir Raonall MacDomhnaill in 'the Rough Bounds' – the area bounded by Loch Hourn, Loch Shiel, and Loch Moidart. (Coll MacColl, it may be noted, was the son of Church of Scotland minister Revd Archibald Maccoll of Tiree). Some local Catholic landowners were willing to contribute to the Bishop's plan 'to build chapels in six different Missions in the Highlands, viz. Glencoe, Badenoch, Glengarry, Knoydart, Morar and the Island of Eigg'.

The Bishop had imagined that the local inhabitants would do the building, but it emerged that, although willing, they had neither tools nor the skills required. One letter from Mr MacColl commented on the high cost of bringing lead for roofing by cart from Glenfinnan to Arisaig. Timber was brought from Loch Nevis side, but most material was landed at the Rhu pier in Arisaig and transferred to local boats for the coastal stage to the Morar estuary. After being manhandled past the Falls on Britain's shortest river it was taken to Bracara by boat. Mr MacColl wrote to the Bishop, 'Volunteers went from Bracara on a stormy Saturday to unload the Cargo of lime for the Chapel . . . but the vessel did not get that day to the landing place. [They] returned on the Monday following . . . I remember your Lordship was pleased at the exertions they made, it being a heavy and dangerous work they had of it & by which some of them suffered very much in their skins in carrying the Lime'.

The work was done over the winter of 1835-36. Heavy and dangerous and expensive work – the priest commented, 'What could be looked for but heavy expenditure in so difficult a place as Loch Morar?' In late March Bishop Scott told his deputy in the Outer Hebrides: 'We have got a very neat chapel and dwelling house nearly finished in North Morar, the place most difficult of all others to get materials to.'

The Fourth Report July 1828

An Appendix of the Report showed a map of Scotland with the marks placed where church buildings had been erected or were proposed. A final map showing all the properties built was published in the Seventh Report – however, for the sake of clarity, Telford's map showing the location of churches and manses has been replaced by the chart which the reader will see near the end of the colour section.

The Report provided a review of progress on the work; the Commissioners believed that their expectations would be more than realised. They listed 41 additional places of worship, most of them built from the grant provided by Government and a few funded locally. The report revealed successful completion and certification on approximately 50% of buildings, mainly those in the more easily accessible areas. The majority of the others were either in various stages of completion, or in the case of certain sites on Lewis and in Contin, Ross, Sutherland and Orkney and Shetland, work had yet to commence as the requisite funds were not in place.

Essay 9: Planting New Churches

The original plan for a Highland Church was single-story in design, with seating capacity for 312 sitters. This could be augmented by adding a gallery to seat another 200 souls and the cost of adding galleries would be met by the heritors, or other inhabitants. It may be remembered from a previous essay that the Seaforth MacKenzies funded a new church at Uig, Lewis to seat 800 souls. This was built to an adaption of Telford's design (see the last page of the colour section).

The cost of each manse was £718; either single storey for exposed and stormy areas, or double storey manses offering similar accommodation. The Commissioners ensured that the manses were within a reasonable distance of the church, and had received, from the good will of the heritors, more land than the Act had stipulated, with fuel and pasturage available. The final version of the plans and drawings for church and manse appeared in the Seventh Report.

The nomination of ministers to the churches which had been certified as complete was conceded to the heritor or heritors who had applied for the church and granted the site of the manse and its garden, undertaking at the same time to uphold the church to the extent required by the Act; and several missionaries had already been settled as ministers in the newly built churches and manses. The Commissioners received a representation (dated 30th June 1828) from Dr George Baird, Past Moderator of the General Assembly, Principal of the University of Edinburgh, on the matter of the appointment of Royal Bounty missionaries and, crucially, much less critical of Evangelicalism than most of his Moderate colleagues.

Dr Baird was a member of the Acting Committee set up by the General Assembly to appoint the missionaries on the Royal Bounty, fix their salaries, and superintend their conduct. The Royal Bounty had provided modest, very modest, funds for missionaries and catechists for nearly a century, and some of these men had served faithfully in remote districts for many years and become part of the communities they served. Dr Baird's representation strongly recommended that where new churches had been built in areas already served by Royal Bounty missionaries, the Commissioners take steps to forward the claims of these missionaries to be nominated as ministers under the Act.

Dr Baird supported this request on several grounds – a recognition of excellent work done by the missionaries in the areas where they served, and if the missionary were not appointed, an implication that the General Assembly or the missionaries themselves had failed in their duty; a concern also for their hardship if not appointed which would have the effect of annulling their Royal Bounty position, alongside a rather belated recognition that the frugal existence of the missionaries would have ensured they had no savings to fall back on and they and their families would face destitution, and a risk that hardship might drive them to irregular exercise of their ministry, with the danger of irregular baptisms and marriages.

He was also concerned about the loss to the congregations who had received the spiritual care of the missionary, his kind attention to them and their knowledge of him and his family, especially if the change were 'not only without necessity, but contrary to equity and expediency'. While respecting the position of the heritors, Dr Baird trusted that the Commissioners would not accept apparently unfounded personal dislike of the missionary on the part of the heritor; and that they would require satisfactory evidence laid before them of special grounds for displacing a missionary. He concluded by declaring that, of course, no missionary should be presented to a new Church without favourable testimonial and certification of his personal character and professional duties.

The Fourth Report closed with the Account of Charges and Expenses for the year ending July 1828 – a total of £1,252 14s. 4d.

The Fifth Report June 1829

The Commissioners reported that they had distributed the £50,000 granted by the Act around 43 new buildings. 24 ministers (one of them officiating at two churches) would be established in the Highlands and 18 in various islands from Shetland to Islay. They were also pleased that the heritors had supplied larger glebes than the Act required in addition to the right of digging peat, and pasture for the cattle. With a surplus, they were able to fulfil a commitment to build a church and manse in Strath Conan. It was an area (the parishes of Contin, Urray, and Fodderty) where 1100 to 1200 people were living between 12 and 18 miles from any church. The final list of churches and manses, [and manses only] was presented – see Table 3 at the end.

The Commissioners expressed their confidence that the few uncompleted buildings would be certified within a few months. The final Account of Expenditure on churches and manses, including the extra expense incurred at Strath Conan, would be closed. The Fifth Report concluded with the Charges and Expenses for fees and travelling costs amounting to a total of £1,455 5s 3d.

The Sixth Report Oct 1831

The Commissioners accounted for the grant of £50,000 (plus the interest accruing from the investment of this sum). They built 32 churches with manses, one church without a manse, and ten manses, most of the manses having well-fenced gardens attached to the property. 30 of the churches built by the Commissioners had had galleries added to them at the heritors' expense, increasing sittings up to 500. (See also the drawings at the end of the colour section.)

Each church with galleries cost £750, the single-storey churches cost £700, and the manses £720. The Commissioners believed that ministers had been placed where they were needed, many in the same places where missionaries had officiated, many of them indeed the missionaries themselves. The other costs of implementing the Act included expenditure of £10,000 for general management, in legal conveyances of land, and in the superintendence of the remote and scattered works. The considerable addition to these costs were the stipends of 42 ministers amounting to £5,040 per annum for a perpetual annuity, totalling £120,000, bringing the total cost of implementing the Act for the advancement of Religion in the Highlands and Islands of Scotland to £180,000.

The offices in London from which the Commissioners operated had closed. One continuing cost under the provisions of the Act would be for a surveyor, at a cost of £250 per annum for two or three years, to ensure that due care and maintenance of the churches and manses would continue.

The Seventh Report May 1835

It was the hope of the Commissioners that, by retaining a surveyor for the first two or three years after completion, this would spur the heritors and ministers into planning ahead to undertake any required maintenance. The Surveyor accordingly visited most of the additional churches as frequently as opportunity occurred in his other office under the Commissioner of Highland Roads and Bridges; nor did he fail to visit, once at least, the most remote of the new churches, those in the Northern and Western Islands. His final Report forms a valuable summary. A small map, showing the situation of all the new establishments, was added for clarity and information, and the Commissioners pointed out its unusual character as being perhaps the only map which exhibited in due proportion the Orkney and

Shetland Islands, and their distance from the Northern counties of Scotland. They usually appeared on a reduced scale, and thrust into a corner, thereby failing to demonstrate the full extent of the country.

Joseph Mitchell, the Chief Surveyor to the project, wrote a closing letter in this Report:

> With the exception of the Churches in Skye, two of those in Islay, and two or three others where the Repairs are either in progress or deferred until next Spring, all the Churches and Manses built by the Commissioners are in a complete and satisfactory state of repair. Almost all the Buildings are in situations greatly exposed to the storms of wind and rain, which are frequent and severe in these remote districts; and experience has shown, not only in those buildings, but in all others so situated, that constant attention is necessary to preserve them from the effects of the climate. I was minute in detailing the defects which I have noticed during my inspections, more than may seem proper; but I deemed it advisable to go into this detail for the purpose of proving to those interested in the preservation of the buildings, that, although minor defects may not create much present inconvenience, it is absolutely necessary, with a view to prevent more serious dilapidation, that they should be promptly and readily attended to.
>
> I regret to have to state, that it was not without difficulty I could prevail on some of the parties to carry into effect the Repairs now executed. Although my Circular Letter was forwarded to all the Incumbents in May last, urging speedy attention to any little defects which might appear, it was not in most cases till after I had visited the Buildings that the repairs were attended to, and then only after detailed instructions and repeated correspondence. It is true that in these remote situations, tradesmen are not always to be procured, and that it is somewhat vexatious to incur, for the rectification of some trifling defect, which may be done in the course of a few hours, the expense of two or three days for tradesmen travelling to the place. That there should be tardiness exhibited by some of the Ministers, where the expense is to be incurred by themselves, is perhaps natural; but that delay should be frequently exhibited where the Seat-Rents were sufficient to defray the expense, has been to me somewhat perplexing.
>
> The Heritors and Ministers interested cannot be too urgently reminded of the importance of speedy attention to the most trifling defects; as in many cases the outlay of a few shillings at the proper time may insure the comfort of the Buildings, and ultimately save a very great expense and trouble. Those acquainted with the climate are well aware that there is no building in the Highlands but occasionally

admits water, however perfectly executed; and this from Taymouth or Armadale Castles to the most common dwelling-houses; and it is only by minute and prompt attention that they are preserved in good and habitable order.

Although Seat-Rents have hitherto been collected at about half the Stations, to an amount sufficiently adequate for the purposes of repair, yet this source of revenue has been gradually decreasing until in some cases it has ceased altogether. The Ministers complain that the exaction of Seat Rents has been to them all along a very unpleasant and unsatisfactory duty. The people generally are so poor that a tax of a sixpence or shilling per sitter is no small burden upon them; and the Ministers rather than prevent them from attending Divine Service, and causing any unpleasant collisions with them, have paused in several instances from collecting Seat Rents altogether. It would therefore be a desirable improvement to relieve the Ministers from this unpleasant duty, not only for the sake of preserving their usefulness and popularity among their congregations, but also to insure a more efficient collection of the funds. The people also attending the new Establishments conceive it a hardship that they should be made to pay for Seat Rents, while persons attending the Parish Churches sit free from any burden of this sort.

It is quite clear, however, that hereafter some more efficient and satisfactory mode of raising funds, and enforcing the necessary repairs, should be introduced than at present exists; and this perhaps may be included in some general arrangement, whenever the existing state of the National Church of Scotland shall be specially brought under the notice of Parliament.

During my visitations and conferences with several Ministers, many of them represented the inadequate accommodation afforded in their respective districts for the purposes of education. In Scotland it is so customary to consider a School-house as an indispensable appendage to a Parish or District Church, that the inconvenience in the present instances is the more felt; and as I observe that active representations are at present being made to the Government on the subject of extending additional means of education to the Highlands, I do not see how this object could be better furthered, (at least in so far as it would go,) than by attaching Schools to all the Parliamentary Church Establishments.

I have the honour to be,
&c. &c. &c.
Joseph Mitchell

Closing Examples and Overview

In his letter Mr Mitchell singles out Skye churches, two on Islay and two or three others where buildings were not in a satisfactory state. One was Hallin in Waternish on Skye, where he declared that no attention had been paid to the church since it was erected. The walls of the manse had been harled, but poorly done. It seemed that the new owner of the property was questioning his liability for the repairs to the church, despite many letters from Mr Mitchell. The other Skye church causing concern was Stensholl in Trotternish. It is likely that the builder who applied the harling at Stensholl had also worked at Hallin: again, it was poorly done. Joseph Mitchell wrote to the minister several times and to Lord Macdonald's chamberlain stressing the urgency of the repairs in view of the tempestuous climate, but without effect. In 1840 the minister simply remarked that the church had as yet no gallery.

The Islay church that was of most cause for concern was Portnahaven. The minister had demitted, and during the vacancy many slates had been blown from the roof of the church and panes of glass broken, and repairs had not been done. Roof and window damage to the manse was just as extensive and the interior in great need of repainting. Mr Mitchell had written to the newly appointed minister, urging him to attend to the repairs. The other Islay church he had been concerned about was at the Oa, but he learned that a new minister had moved into the manse which had been completely repaired. The church too, he noted, was in excellent order. But in 1844 the Rev Archibald Mactavish remarked that the buildings at the Oa were 'insufficiently executed'.

Some other churches had suffered a little neglect, such as Trumisgarry and Keiss, but Mr Mitchell was able to announce that repairs had been done and the buildings were in good order. Typical of these was Duror: the side walls of the church had admitted water in several places during a severe, wet winter, but the joints had been properly picked and re-pointed during the summer, and the whole walls rough-cast. He was encouraged to see regular maintenance being carried out in most of the churches and manses: in summer, buildings needed to be white-washed, slates replaced, doors and windows painted, gates re-hung. A good number of the churches had added one or more galleries: in Tobermory the Minister and Kirk Session built a gallery on the west end, and then contracted for another to be erected in the aisle. The proprietor of Plockton had erected galleries and turned a small church into a commodious building. A number of ministers had built an extra room for the manse as a kitchen, turning the original kitchen into an extra bedroom. The minister at Strontian, at his own expense, had erected a barn and cart-house.

Mr Mitchell was impressed with changes made to the original plans: in North Ballachulish the space intended for a staircase had been converted into a small vestry which was serviceable on sacramental occasions. Several churches had opened casements to improve ventilation to the building. In North Ronaldsay a back wing had been built on the manse, containing two rooms and a closet, constructed at the expense of the Minister. Mr Mitchell found the buildings at Cross in excellent order but noticed that although the proprietor had very liberally attached 6 acres of land as glebe, the minister had only been put in possession of three acres, through some misunderstanding of the Seaforth factor. Joseph Mitchell supplied the minister with a plan of the glebe, and the factor agreed to rectify the mistake.

At the beginning of the programme of work in 1824, the Commissioners had to invite heritors to apply for churches where they wished to erect them. It therefore fell to heritors to supply the land and, under the terms of the Act, undertake future maintenance of the church whose expenditure could be offset by pew rents. Since this was the case, the Commissioners had conceded that the proprietors were in a strong position and had the last word. Often, tardiness in carrying out their obligations sometimes actioned lively correspondence between Commissioner and heritor.

In the reports of ministers to the 1836 Commission on Religious Instruction and in the New Statistical Return in the later 1830s and early 1840s it became clear that in several cases the churches were built in the wrong locations, or even more additional churches were needed. Indeed, the 1836 Commission reported 74 Highland parishes were deficient in opportunities for worship and pastoral superintendence. The problems identified were familiar ones: large distances, scattered communities, difficulties of terrain, eccentric parish divisions, too few ministers, inadequate size of the parish churches and their poor condition, and small stipends. The minister of the church at Store (earlier Rhuistore, later Stoer) remarked that the new church served a population of 1403 'leaving upwards of 1700 scattered over a vast extent of inaccessible surface'.[20] In the same Statistical Account it was stated that the church at Berriedale, was 'of very neat construction,

---

20 *The Statistical Accounts of Scotland 1840*, Assynt, County of Sutherland, vol. XV, 116.

though small in size. In consequence of some of the families having been removed since the church was built, it is now too remote for the more populous districts connected with it, but is, notwithstanding, still very useful; and were a small church to be erected in the eastern quarter, where the minister could preach every alternate Sabbath, it would be still more so'.[21] At Berneray it had been brought to Mr Mitchell's attention that, due to the recent introduction of sheep-farming, many people had been cleared from the land. A response from Kinloch-Luichart to the Commission on Religious Instruction of 1836 stated that nearly all the parishioners were at least two miles from the church, 75% more than four miles and more than a quarter further than six miles from the church. A population of 100 in one area and 18 families in another were prevented from attending in winter owing to flooding. In Kinloch-Bervie the greatest need was improved roads: In the autumn, access to the church was impeded for all – a complete lack of made roads and wet and broken ground. 'Many families face high and rugged hills, small rivers swollen in winter, and long miles to reach church. A couple of small stretches of new road in the making will improve the situation to a small degree.'

At Poolewe, 240 houses were more than six miles from the church. One district with a population of 1547 had no road and two rivers to cross, impassable in winter. Three other districts were in the same position. The minister voluntarily preached every fourth Sabbath in a remote district where attendance was double the parish numbers; he held the view that the district of Laigh on the coast needed a church established there. At Shieldaig, 250 parishioners lived more than six miles from the new church. Sea and rivers impeded access to the church for all but 57 families. It was the minister's opinion that Torridon with 950 parishioners and Kishorn with 600 should both have their own church. The new minister at Trumsigarry Church asserted that the church did not nearly contain sufficient accommodation for the parishioners. The minister of Ullapool claimed that a new church built at Achiltibuie would bring easy access to the 400-600 people living within a mile of that point. A couple of comments to the 1836 Religious Instruction survey stated, 'Loch and mountains impede access to church for some families', and, '30 inhabit an island; another 78 are impeded by arms of the sea'. Some things could not be changed, nor could shifting populations be anticipated due to the Clearances. In

---

21 *The Statistical Accounts of Scotland 1840*, Latheron, County of Caithness, vol. XV, 91.

the relatively short space between initial surveys being drawn up for the new churches and the Religious Instruction Commission, no more than 10 years, the landscape for many had changed considerably with some church buildings almost redundant because of a severe lack of congregational numbers.

A final observation in Joseph Mitchell's closing letter attests to the glaring need for more schools in the Highlands and Islands. The Reformation had established a traditional link between church and school and during his visitations many ministers spoke to him of the inadequate educational facilities. He recommended that the government be urged to attach schools to all the parliamentary churches. That would go some way towards improving the situation. When he visited Quarff, Joseph Mitchell found the Church occupied as a school-house, there being no other accommodation for that purpose in the District. The Revd Dr D. McArthur, minister of Kilninian and Kilmore in Mull (which incorporated the *quoad sacra* parishes of Ulva, Tobermory and part of Salen) declared that the government had 'conferred a lasting and valuable boon to the population, and if to each government church could be added a school, the boon will be a double blessing'.[22]

In the Final Analysis . . .

The achievement of the Commission is almost lost in the minutiae of their Reports to Parliament, their meticulous recording of payments from the fund to the last ha'penny, the formal and dry accounts of the building programme's progress through the seven Reports. There is no mention of the frustration and irritation over the scarcity of materials, and shortage in most areas of skilled workmen – masons, carpenters, men to split timber or slate roofs or even skilled volunteers, the deep reluctance of some of the heritors to rise to the quality of building the Commissioners considered essential due to the exposed areas of the country, the problems and cost of transporting materials across difficult terrain. Bishop Andrew Scott's correspondence alone conveys something of the pain and difficulties encountered by workmen and locals manhandling building materials such as lime and slate by several stages over land and water, in uncooperative weather. With all these problems, it was an amazing feat to complete the building of 33 churches, 32 of them with manses, and 10 other manses for existing churches in the remote areas of the Highlands and Islands between 1824 and 1831. From

---

22 *The Statistical Accounts of Scotland 1845,* Kilninian and Kilmore, County of Argyll, vol. VII, 341.

Joseph Mitchell's comments on revisiting the churches and manses by the end of 1834, from returns to the Parliamentary Commission in 1836 on Religious Instruction in Scotland, and from ministers' reports in the New Statistical Account (1845) it is also clear that until the mid-1840s most churches were being used to their full capacity.

Table 2 (Churches and Manses, from the First Report)

County	Parish or Island	Place	Population	Remarks
Argyll	Appin	Duror	600	In the vicinity, and the minister will be auxiliary at Appin Parish Church
	Ardnamurchan	Strontian	1,350	
	Ditto	Acharacle	700 -	Roman Catholics not included
	Glassary	Lochgilphead	2,000	
	Islay (Island)	Portnahaven	800	
	Ditto	Oe or Oth	2,000	
	Kilmallie	Ardgour	467	Small scale church: served by minister of North Ballachulish Church
	Mull (Island)	Tobermory	2,000	
	Ditto	Kinloch Spelvie	700	
	Ditto	Ulva Island	900	
	Ditto	Iona Island	460	And 300 on the nearest part of mull separated by sound one mile wide
Banff	Kirkmichael	Tomintoul	300	In the village, and as many more within reasonable distance
Caithness	Latheron	Berriedale	1,750	
	Wick	Keiss	1,414	

Inverness	Duthill	Rothiemurchus	1,026	
	Harris	Berneray Isle	500	And as many more in adjacent isles of Pabbay and Killigray
	Kilmallie	N. Ballachulish	656	Besides those who may cross by the ferry
	Skye (Island)	Stensholl in Trotternish	1,800	
	Ditto	Hallin in Waternish	1,312	
	North Uist (Island)	Trumisgarry	1,470	
Ross and Cromarty	Applecross	Shieldaig	1,200	
	Contin	Kinloch Luichart	700	
	Ditto	Carnoch	1,200	
	Kincardine	Brae	900	
	Lewis (Isle)	Cross or Ness	1,180	
	Ditto	Eye	1,150	
	Lochalsh	Plockton	850	
Shetland	Quarff	Quarff	220	The minister will take charge of the Burray Isles with 620 inhabitants
Sutherland	Assynt	Rhuistore	1,100	
	Farr	Strathy	1,078	
	Edrachilles	Kinloch Bervie	550	

Table 3 (from the Fifth Report)

County	Parish/Island	Place	Population	Remarks
Argyll	Appin	Duror	600	Completion certified
	Ardnamurchan	Strontian	1,350	Certified
		Aucharacle	700 -	Certified
	Glassary	Lochgilphead	2,000	Certified
	Iona	Iona	460	Certified
	Islay (Island)	Portnahaven	800	Certified
		Oe or Oth	2,000	Certified
		Kilmeny	2,000	Certified
	Kilmallie	Ardgour	467	Certified. No manse
	Muckairn	Muckairn	2,500	Certified
	Mull Island	Kinloch Spelvie	700	Certified
		Salen	800	Certified
		Tobermory	2,000	Certified
	Ulva	Ulva Island	460	Certified
Banff	Kirkmichael	Tomintoul	300	Certified
Caithness	Latheron	Berriedale	1,750	Certified
	Wick	Keiss	1,414	Certified
Elgin	Kingussie	Inch	800	Certified
Inverness	Rothiemurchus	Rothiemurchus	1,026	Certified
	Harris	Berneray Isle	500	Certified
	Kilmallie	North Ballachulish	656	Certified
	Skye (Island)	Stensholl in Trotternish	1,800	Certified
		Hallin in Waternish	1,312	Certified
	North Uist (Island)	Trumisgarry	1,470	Certified

Perth	Dull	Kirktown of Foss	789	In progress
	Fortingall	Interwick in Glenlyon	1,000	Certified
		Rannoch	1,269	Completed, ready for inspection
Ross and Cromarty	Applecross	Shieldaig	1,200	Certified
	Contin	Kinloch Luichart	700	Certified
		Carnoch Strath Conan	1,200	Not yet commenced
	Gairloch	Poolewe	300	Certified
	Kincardine	Croick	900	Certified
	Lewis (Isle)	Cross or Ness	1,180	Certified
		Eye	1,150	Certified
	Lochalsh	Plockton	850	Certified
	Loch-Broom	Ullapool	800	Certified
Orkney and Shetland	Quarff	Quarff	220	Completed, ready for inspection
	St Andrew and Deerness	Deerness	700	Completed, ready for inspection
	Cross and Burness	North Ronaldsay	467	Completed, ready for inspection
	Dunrossness	Sandwick	649	Completed, ready for inspection
Sutherland	Assynt	Rhuistore	1,100	Certified
	Farr	Strathy	1,078	Certified
	Edrachilles	Kinloch-Bervie	550	Certified

Table 4 (from the Sixth Report)

Name of place	Parish or Island	County	Population in vicinity	Cert. of completion
Loch-Gilphead	Glassary	Argyle	2,500	March 1828
Muckairn (manse only)	Muckairn		830	November 1828
Duror	Appin		650	August 1827
Kilmeny (manse only)	Islay		2,500	November 1828
Portnahaven			1500	November 1828
Oe or Oth			2,500	November 1828
Kinloch Spelvie	Mull		500	March 1828
Salen (manse only)			850	March 1828
Tobermory			2,000	March 1828
Ulva	Ulva		900	March 1828
Iona	Iona		1,000	November 1828
Strontian	Ardnamurchan		1,500	March 1829
Aucharacle			700	March 1829
North Ballachulish	Kilmallie	Inverness	600	April 1829
Ardgour (no manse)	ditto	Argyle	400	April 1829
Rothiemurchus (manse)	Rothiemurchus	Inverness	1,000	July 1830
Tomintoul	Kirkmichael	Banff	600	June 1827
Inch (manse only)	Kingussie	Elgin	600	March 1828
Stensholl in Trotternish	Skye	Inverness	1,700	March 1829
Halen in Waternish			1,000	April 1829
Trumisgarry	North Uist		1,150	March 1829
Berneray Isle	Harris		1,000	March 1829

Essay 9: Planting New Churches

Plockton	Lochalsh	Ross and Cromarty	600	June 1827
Shieldaig	Applecross		800	June 1827
Carnoch, Strath-Conan	Contin		1,200	July 1830
Kinloch-Luichart			700	June 1827
Poolewe	Gairloch		1,500	November 1828
Croich	Kincardine		500	June 1827
Ullapool	Loch-Broom		2,000	April 1829
Cross (Ness district)	Lewis		1,500	March 1829
Knock (Eye district)	ditto		1,450	March 1829
Rhuistore	Assynt	Sutherland	1,400	March 1829
Kinloch-Bervie	Edrachilles		1,000	March 1829
Strathy	Farr		1,000	March 1828
Berriedale	Latheron	Caithness	1,750	August 1827
Keiss	Wick		1,100	August 1827
Deerness (manse only)	St Andrew + Deerness	Orkney and Shetland	700	January 1830
N. Ronaldsay (manse)	Cross and Burness		560	January 1830
Sandwick (manse only)	Dunrossness		650	July 1830
Quarff	Quarff		830	July 1830
Interwick (manse only)	Fortingall	Perth	1,100	November 1828
Rannoch (manse only)			1,650	December 1829
Kirktown of Foss (manse)	Dull		800	December 1829

Essay Ten

The Parliamentary Churches and The Disruption

REPRODUCED WITH KIND PERMISSION OF THE FREE CHURCH OF SCOTLAND

The Revd Dr Patrick MacFarlan (1781-1849) minister of the West Kirk in Greenock is first to sign the Deed of Demission, which commemorated the establishment of the Free Church of Scotland.

He resigned the highest living in the Church of Scotland at the time, said to be £1,000 annually.

The Disruption was a spectacular and tumultuous event, culminating in a walk out from the General Assembly on 18 May 1843; 121 ministers and 73 elders left that day. On 31st May the Scotsman newspaper printed the names of the ministers who associated with the departure from the Church of Scotland, noting their status as minister and a rough indication of parish location. The total number of ministers named in the report was 386, but the paper reported that 444 ministers (including assistants, professors, parliamentary and quoad sacra ministers) left the Kirk. There now seems to be general agreement that a total of 474 ministers gave up their livings in accordance with the Act of Separation and Deed of Demission.

Planning for the Disruption

Although it was a tumultuous event it was not one without planning behind it. The Revd James Wylie wrote in his memoir:[1]

> Three months before the Disruption, that is, in the February of 1843, there was sketched a programme of work to be undertaken by the Church after the Disruption, which was now looked upon as certain. That work was arranged under the four following heads:
>
> (1) The erection of churches.
>
> (2) The providing of Sustentation for the ministry, together with a Theological College.
>
> (3) The extension of the Gospel at home by the planting of new charges.
>
> (4) The evangelisation of the heathen world by means of foreign missions.

This was no light programme on the part of a Church that stood face to face with dis-establishment. The Disruption heralded unprecedented change and upheaval around the parishes of Scotland. It left Scotland with two national churches – the Church of Scotland and the Free Church of Scotland – instead of one. Some ministers left their charge to join the Free Church with some of their congregation; sometimes the majority of the congregation left with the minister; and there were some churches which were left empty: both minister and entire congregation left and joined the Free Church. Ministers who joined the Free Church lost their homes and their income in one fell swoop, and those accompanied by church members were in want of buildings in which to meet and gather a worshipping community.

Not surprisingly, Dr Wylie's list of tasks facing the new Free Church targets first of all the erection of churches and secondly, sustentation to support ministers and their families. In the forward-planning it was assumed that the laity would support a sustentation fund. The Highlands were not in a position to contribute much, although no doubt some sacrificial giving was made, but the urban middle classes in the south provided enough to enable the new church to grow. In an amazingly short time, sufficient new churches appeared to provide for the people. Despite the immediate establishment of a new Scottish denomination, from the very beginning Highland landlords were obstructive in giving over land whereupon these new 'Free' churches

---

1 James A. Wylie, *Disruption Worthies*, Thomas C. Jack, Edinburgh 1881 (chapter 1).

could be built. Landlords had a financial stake in maintaining the rights and privileges accruing to them through the Established Church so there was fierce opposition to acceding to the requests of a rival church.

Some ministers who remained in the Church of Scotland lost members of their congregations, and in some instances the great majority of their members left to join the Free Church. See Appendix 5 for details.

Church of Scotland congregations which had lost their ministers to the Free Church were urgently seeking ministers to replace them, and ministers of the Church of Scotland, left sometimes with only their own family as church members, were looking for charges. Many of those who chose to remain in the Church of Scotland moved within months of the Disruption, presumably to a more viable charge, or perhaps just to make a fresh start. The Revd Donald Jackson, is a typical example (see Table 2 in Appendix 5). He chose to remain in the Church of Scotland but by August 1844 had moved from Lochgilphead to become parish minister in Kilmartin as that minister had moved to another charge. At the same time, ministers who 'came out' were being sought by groups who wanted to form themselves as new Free Church congregations and were seeking leadership.

It was a turbulent, difficult and painful time. In Inverness-shire, Sutherland, Ross and Cromarty, Lewis and Harris, around 50% of ministers left the Church of Scotland. Thomas Brown, writing in *Annals of the Disruption*, sets a scene that must have been enacted in many Highland parishes: 'It was recorded,' he wrote, 'that in one place the Elders in a band came forward to their minister with this message: "Sir, you must now declare to us what your resolution is. Are you to remain in the Establishment or join the faithful band who are about to quit it? For if you are to remain, we, as a body, have come to the resolution of never submitting ourselves from this day to your ministry."'[2]

To focus on ministers, however, is to miss the major impact of the Disruption on the Highlands: the impact on the Highlands and Islands might be assessed as perhaps tenfold that experienced in Scotland generally. It has been estimated that in the northernmost parishes, fully 90% of the worshippers left the Church of Scotland,[3] due to the

---

[2] Thomas Brown, *Annals of the Disruption: with extracts from the narratives of ministers who left the Scottish establishment in 1843*, MacNiven & Wallace, Edinburgh 1884, 649-50.

[3] In Donald Smith's PhD Thesis, *The Failure and Recovery of Social Criticism in the Scottish Church 1830 – 1950.*.

growing Evangelical spirituality of the Highlands and Islands over the preceding fifty years, particularly in the most northern presbyteries and parishes. The arguments had become more focused and bitter during the 'ten years' conflict'. These were years mired in controversy and confusion, a battle for the soul of the Kirk. Two wings were pulling in opposite directions: Moderates still put their trust in strengthening the administrative capabilities of the Kirk to bring about its missionary ambitions and who represented the interests of the landowners, factors and wealthier single tenants; the Evangelical imperative was founded solely upon Reformation principles, the first being the complete surrendering of the self to the claims of the Gospel. Increasingly Evangelicals spoke for the crofters and cottars. Evangelicals put their trust in Almighty God, Moderates appeared to put their trust in improving how the Kirk was organised, by strengthening Presbytery and Synod oversight. The Moderate Party never quite lost its moniker as the 'party of law and order'.

A time of confusion and hardship

For the Highlander and his family, this was truly an era of confusion. But disruption to family life, working habits and land-rights, livelihoods and prospects caused such upheaval that neither the Highlands and Islands, including the Kirk, were ever the same again. In reality, these 'disruptions' had been going on for the century before 1843, unsettling long-held practices which had confirmed for the Highlander who he was and what and where his place was. For generations the Highlander could affirm his place within the clan-family under the protection of the Chief, but the Stuart rebellions of 1715 and especially after 1746 changed all that. The Highlander believed he had ancestral rights to the croft he farmed, but the Clearances changed all that and confirmed for the Highlander two things: his chief had now become a 'landlord' with a keen eye on profit and loss; and, as a crofter and farmer, he was now of less value than the sheep which replaced him.

Yet through these tumultuous changes, it appears that the Highlander had never completely lost his or her sense of self. In a recent interview, the MSP Kate Forbes put it this way: 'You are a Highlander first, before you are Scottish and British. Identity matters to people here'[4] – earlier she had pointed to a sign for Culloden, where the Jacobite uprising was defeated in 1746 – 'and that identity is shaped by memories of emigration and of remote, rural, deprived communities. There is a

---

4 *New Statesman*, 8th December 2023.

strong sense of community, of togetherness – the ceilidh, the church, the Gaelic language.' It appears that for Forbes, and many modern Gaels, the 'glue' which holds Highland communities together today is strong but from the mid-18th century, as we have seen, there had been various attempts to unpick this 'glue' with varying degrees of success.

After the Disruption, the Highlands would go on to face further hardships which again threatened the very lives of Highlanders themselves. Over a 30 year period, beginning in the mid-1830s, the people of the Highlands and Islands were to suffer regular periods of crop failure putting the population on famine-footing. The great famine (as a result of potato blight) of 1846 which lasted through to 1856 had a devastating effect upon the Highland population. Those left starving walked the seashores looking for any kind of nourishment while dysentery, influenza, scurvy, typhus and cholera killed in large numbers. Destitution boards were set up to provide help, however only the most limited amount was provided. Relief rations were confined to a bare subsistence. The privations are thought to have affected around 200,000 people.

Highlanders were made to feel that this was Government charity which could be withdrawn at any time, while they were encouraged to find remedies themselves. A 'destitution test' was administered to ensure that each man worked his required hours. The labour included the creation of 'destitution roads' which pioneered routes in remote parts of the Highlands. A day's work for oatmeal rations involved eight hours of labour, six days a week. Rations for the workers were set at 1.5lbs for men, 12ozs per woman and 8ozs per child. The Government of the time was restricted by the common attitudes of the middle of the 19th century: minimal intervention and a 'hands-off' approach to avoid upsetting free-market conditions. Many in Government rehearsed the old Malthusian solution: reduce the number of the population to 'fit' the amount of food available. Thus planned emigration to the colonies was suggested.

It was the Free Church, now a strong presence in the affected areas, which provided prompt action in raising the alarm and organising relief; it was the only body actively doing so in late 1846 and early 1847; relief was given regardless of denomination. The Free Church also organised transport for over 3,000 men from the famine-struck regions to work in Lowland railways. By the end of 1847, the 'relief committee' comprising the Free Church and voluntary groups set up in Edinburgh and Glasgow, had raised £210,000 to support relief work (a little over £18m in today's terms). The loyalty to the Free Church shown by Highlanders was further cemented by the church's charitable endeavours. Despite this, it is estimated that the crofting areas lost about one-third of their population between 1841 and 1861. Many opted for the new worlds of the Americas and Australia, assisted financially by landlords eager to rid themselves of further responsibilities. Thousands died either on these voyages or soon after having reached landfall.

The Evangelical Thomas Chalmers sided with Government thinking of the time and stated that if people became systematically trained to expect relief as a right this would destroy the connection between economy and independence and between improvidence and want; self-reliance should be encouraged in the people and the relief of genuine destitution should be left to private charity. This was something of a change of heart for Chalmers since his days in St John's 20 years previously, where he had espoused the values of church-financed poor relief. These principles of self-reliance and economic rectitude were thoroughly grounded in the Enlightenment philosophies of Adam Smith and Edmund Burke.

Throughout this period of famine when the Government had to be seen to assist a population in deep distress, questions over the Anglicization of the Gael reared its head yet again. The *Scotsman* newspaper, no friend of the Highlander, advanced the notion that the destitution had been brought on by the Highlanders inherent laziness and reiterated the old trope about Gaelic culture and language being a brake on progress. Gaelic culture was still seen as an obstacle to long-term happiness and prosperity which would only be achieved by making the whole of the north and west English-speaking. The *Scotsman* still thought the Highlander should be 'brought to heel'. Two decades after the famine the *Edinburgh Courant* noted that emigration from the Hebridean Islands, the 'best cure for their ills', was accelerated by education:

> It is startling enough to be asked to establish and maintain a school system for the purpose of depopulating a district, but we would have little doubt this would be the first effect and the best success of the thorough education of the Highlands.[5]

In the hope of consolidating the 'united' kingdom, the 'improvability' of the Highlander remained the ambition for many living south of the Highland line.

---

5 Extract from *Edinburgh Courant* as reprinted in the *John O' Groat Journal*, 10 October 1867.

Hierarchies and Institutions

This was also the era of tense relationships with the competing forces of national and state, civil and ecclesiastical institutions ebbing and flowing across the decades. As we have seen, it was essentially the differences in the attitudes of Moderates and Evangelicals to the question of the primacy of law, civil and ecclesiastical, which was a deciding factor in the Disruption. While the 1820 General Assembly, referred to in Essay Six, had raised the temperature between the two parties, previous arguments had been settled in the Moderates' favour due to their continuing dominance in the courts of the Church. However, events at this General Assembly (a galvanising moment for Highland Evangelicals) and the proposed adoption of the Privy Council's directive to pray for the monarch and his household, set the two parties on divergent paths which led directly to the ten years' conflict and came to a head in 1843.

This matter had implications for the north and south of the country and confirmed for Highland Evangelicals that General Assemblies, while in the control of the Moderates, prioritised politics ahead of all else: to encourage the peoples' loyalty to the crown and constitution, and to reassure the monarchy of the continuing loyalty of the Presbyterian Church. Quite clearly, these were not the priorities of the Evangelical Party.

During the decades leading to the Disruption, a number of contests for dominance were playing out across the nation. As these essays have tried to show, one of the recurring themes was the imposition of authority to control, order and direct by one vested interest group over another. Being 'kept in one's place' or simply 'knowing one's place' seemed to be paramount. First, as we have already seen, Parliament and the Kirk were embroiled in discussions over the level of financial assistance the state was prepared to give in order that the Kirk might fully fund an effective ministry, especially across the Highlands and Islands, the area of Scotland which never quite threw off its reputation as being 'other', 'awkward' and 'troublesome'. In the end, Parliament got its way unconvinced by the Kirk's pleadings for a national endowment. The Kirk was 'kept in its place'. Yet, correspondingly, Parliament had high expectations of the Kirk, again especially across the north and west, that the Kirk would utilise its undoubted historic authority to impose law and order, almost as an adjunct of the state and do its bidding. It was an 'agreement' which undoubtedly favoured Governments with Parliament establishing a measure of proprietorial rights.

Second, the two opposing wings of the Church were locked head-to-head over the nature of what constituted the essence of 'being Christian', the nature of the sacraments of baptism and communion or the route-map to salvation. While Moderate sermons prioritised the pursuit of good behaviour and better manners to save the nation, Evangelicals looked to a recovery of Reformation principles to save the Kirk. The Moderates managed to keep the Evangelicals 'in their place' until the mid to late 1820s.

Third, the Irish/Catholic question still commandeered much Parliamentary time and both Evangelicals and Moderates were on guard for any possible Catholic incursion: for Moderates, Catholics posed a continuing threat to the Crown and Parliament; for the Evangelicals, the dangers of a resurgent popery diluting the 'true' faith were never far away. It was essential therefore that Catholics 'knew their place'.

Fourth, with the power of the civil law behind them, landowners especially across the north and west were emboldened to hold out against the Kirk's own candidates for certain pulpits, by installing their own. They regarded this as their right. Landowners and heritors wielded such control over large swathes of the Highland and Islands that, in most cases, they acted with impunity. Patronage would remain in place until Parliament abolished it in 1874. Landowners, at the height of the Clearances, were determined to rid themselves of pesky irritations, and looked to the Established Church for support. Further Highland turmoil was to come, however, in the later years of the century with what became known as the Crofters' War. From 1880 to the culmination of the Crofters' Act of 1886, these years witnessed a renewed sense of self-awareness, solidarity and confidence among ordinary people, and created an active association of the crofting population throughout the Highlands in a very short space of time. It proposed changes which called in question the very basis of the Highland landlord – the right in law to own and dispose of land without reference to those who lived and worked upon it. Here, there were echoes from the time of the Clearances but now there was more organised resistance, and there were some violent clashes between crofters and law-officers, confrontations involving gunboats, marine task-forces and military occupations, but in the end the popular will of the people could not to be thwarted and landowners were forced to retreat and capitulate. The Napier Commission, finding in favour of crofters' claims, essentially redrew the Highland map. Again it was the Free Church, with its mass following in the Highlands and considerable authority among the crofters, which spoke out in support of the crofters' actions, but the appeal was limited in its call to arms due to doctrinal considerations over disobedience to the law.

The 150 years which spanned the mid-18th century to the end of the next saw an unprecedented upheaval in the lives of most Gaels living across the north and west: the Clearances, the Disruption, famine and the Crofters' War. As far as the Church of Scotland was concerned, the majority in the north and west no longer felt able to maintain and support the Established Church or ministry which appeared to be at the beck and call of landowners and whose ecclesiastical laws were undermined by the civil authorities. These ministers and congregations with a different outlook found a new home in the Free Church of Scotland. However, it must be stated that at the time when the Kirk appeared to be tearing itself apart over a period of 25 years leading to The Disruption, the Kirk's presence across the north and west provided a measure of social stability to communities caught up in the maelstrom of upheaval, change and dislocation. The Highlander, in the main, was law-abiding, compliant and uncomplaining.

The 32 Parliamentary Churches, in their initial iteration, lasted less than 15 years but brought the Kirk's mission-presence into areas of the Highlands and Islands where previously there had been little. As a project, the establishing of Telford's Churches was a success by any measure and might have provided a blueprint for further extension across the Highlands had funds, with or without political will, been evident. The Kirk's church extension energies, with its capacity for fund-raising, were mainly directed at the urban situation.

Filled in the main by energised, young Evangelicals, many of these men would lead their Highland and Island congregations out of the Kirk and into the Free Church. The Evangelical imperative was based upon a strict adherence to the laws of God, Reformation principles and the claims of the gospel, impervious to the social upheavals occurring at the time. It was the Evangelical ministers who asserted the primacy and claims of God above all else, above the actions and ambitions of landowners, above complicit and compliant Moderate ministers and Presbyteries and crucially, above the civil law. These ministers galvanised their congregations to reclaim and reassert their identity as proud people of God and beholden to no other authority. And it was this community of faith which provided them with solace and succour in times of need, confusion and hardship.

Epilogue

The Highland Churches Bill of 1824 was enacted to facilitate the building of additional churches across the north and west of Scotland. Prior to the establishing of the Parliamentary Churches, the Kirk had recognised that there were many areas which remained unserved, despite the entire nation being covered by the parish system. That the Established Church of Scotland is now, some 200 years or more later, reverting to the situation it found itself throughout the 18th century and into the first decades of the 19th admits of a general decline. Despite the parish system remaining in place, some people of faith, especially in the remotest areas, now find themselves unserved by the Kirk because of the wholesale changes which it is currently being forced to make.

Historically and contemporaneously, the Kirk has failed, and is failing, to be the Church it has always wanted to be and needed to be. The legacy issues of the unions, first of 1900 and then 1929 to reunite the United Free Church of Scotland (which in itself was a union of the United Presbyterian Church and the Free Church of Scotland) with the Auld Kirk, those who never left the Established Church of Scotland, have now come home to roost. These historic unions effectively tripled the number of buildings the Kirk had to finance and also fund a ministry substantially increased in size. Now the Kirk is in financially straitened circumstances with many calls upon its dwindling income. For many, there is no longer any 'crisis of faith': people now simply do not 'believe'.

It is easier to offer a diagnosis than to provide a cure, or at least a treatment. This series of essays has attempted the former but has demurred from offering a cure suitable for the 21st century. If there ever was a time for treatment for its ills, perhaps history shows that the Kirk has been in constant pain and turmoil since 1560. The optimistic view declares that the Church is ever reforming and new growth will yet emerge from the current travails. The coming of Parliamentary Churches, in its own way, was a bold initiative to treat a specific 'Highland Problem' and offer a way forward. Matters might have turned out differently had Governments of the day viewed further expenditure as an investment by the Crown rather than a cost to the Exchequer.

During his Highland tour, Dr Johnson declared 'of the destruction of churches, the decay of religion must in time be the consequence'. Time will tell if Dr Johnson is correct.

Appendix 1: Glossary of Terms

Boll is a Scottish measure equal to four imperial bushels of meal and nearly six imperial bushels of barley, oats etc

Erse, or Irish language – used to mean Scottish Gaelic

Glebe – land, arable and pasture, for the minister's use; ideally at least 4 acres

Heritor - landowner owning land in the parish

Manse and Offices – house for minister and subsidiary buildings such as stables, coal sheds, wash houses, and earth closets

Scotch or Scots pound and merks – Both the English and the Scottish pound were made up of 20 shillings, each of 12 pence. Thus there were 240 pence in a pound. But there were 12 Scots pounds to the English pound. The merk was two thirds of a Scottish pound, or 13 shillings and 4 pence.

Scottish value	Scottish name and value	Sterling value
3 shillings and 4 pennies	1 merk or mark	13 pence
18 merks or marks	12 pounds Scots	£1

Teinds - a portion of land value dedicated to the maintenance of the clergy

The Statistical Account of Scotland 1791-1799

The New Statistical Account of Scotland 1834-1845

The Statistical Accounts of Scotland

A major contribution to our knowledge and understanding of Scotland in the last decade of the 18th century and 45 years into the 19th century was made by the Statistical Accounts of Scotland. The first edition was finalised in 1799 and the second – the New Statistical Accounts of Scotland – in 1845. Sir John Sinclair was the compiler of the first edition, and the originator of the idea: his purpose to 'elucidate the Natural History and Political State of North Britain.' In order to collate the information that he wanted, he decided that parish ministers would be best placed to provide detailed, local intelligence.

He admits in the Preface to his Statistical Accounts that the replies he received from ministers provided 'such merit and ability, and so many useful facts and important observations [that] I was thence induced to give the Work to the Public in its present Shape.' When printed and published, it amounted to 21 volumes. In 1832, the General Assembly asked the Society for the Sons and Daughters of the Clergy to undertake the task

App. 1: Glossary of Terms

of producing a New Statistical Account of Scotland. A Superintending Committee was formed for the task, and it presented 15 volumes to the General Assembly in 1845.

Sir John provided a list of topics 'as a key to inquiry' rather than a questionnaire, allowing the clergy to convey the particularities of their areas. He expressed his gratitude to the spirit in which they approached this laborious undertaking; some of the submissions were more than 40 pages in length. The preface closes with a quotation from 'a respectable citizen of this country', George Dempster of Dunnichen, commending the work: 'No publication of equal information and curiosity has appeared in Great Britain since Dooms-day Book; and from the ample and authentic facts which it records, it must be resorted to by every future Statesman, Philosopher, and Divine, as the best basis that has ever yet appeared for political speculation.'

The 'Key to Inquiry'

The name of the parish, and its origin
    Situation and extent of the parish
Description of the soil and surface
    Number of acres
Nature and extent of the sea coast
Lakes, rivers, islands, hills, rocks, caves, woods, orchards, etc.
Climate and diseases
    Instances of longevity
State of property
    Number of proprietors
    Number of residing proprietors
Mode of cultivation
    Implements of husbandry
    Manures
    Seed-time and harvest
    Remarkable instances of good and bad seasons
Quantities and value of each species of crop
    Total value of the whole produce of the district
Total real and valued rent
Price of grain and provisions
Total quantity of grain and other articles consumed in the parish
Wages and price of labour
Services, whether exacted or abolished
Commerce
Manufactures
Manufacture of kelp, its amount, and the number of people employed in it
Fisheries

Towns and villages
Police
Inns and alehouses
Roads and bridges
Harbours
Ferries, and their state
Number of ships and vessels
Number of seamen
State of the church
    Stipend, manse, glebe and patron
    Parochial funds, and the management of them
Number of poor
State of the schools, and number of scholars
State of population
    Causes of its increase or decrease
Exact amount of the numbers now living
    Number of families
Division of the inhabitants
    1. By the place of their birth
    2. By their ages
    3. By their religious persuasions
    4. By their occupations and situation in life
    5. By their residence, whether in town, village, or in the country
Number of houses
    Number of uninhabited houses
Number of dovecots (and the extent to which they are destructive of the crops)
Number of horses, their nature and value
Number of cattle and ditto
Number of sheep and ditto
Number of swine and ditto
Minerals in general
    Mineral springs
Coal and fuel
Eminent men
Antiquities
Parochial records
Miscellaneous Observations
Character of the people
    Their manners, customs, stature, etc.
    Advantages and disadvantages
    Means by which their situation could be meliorated.

Spelling

It is commonly accepted that for the printed word, the spelling system became standardised by the end of the 17th century. This was due in no small way to the advent of the printing press and the publication of dictionaries. However, the Statistical Accounts of Scotland which covered the period 1791 to 1845 were, of course, all hand written by ministers, and on occasions, aided by schoolmasters. Where Highland place names are recorded and have been quoted in this volume, either from the Statistical Accounts or from contemporary sources, the reader may find multiple variants of the same location, or same surname, eg Kinloch-Luichart *or* Kinloch-luichart *or* Kinlochluichart *or* Kinloch Luichart. 'Interwick' and 'Innerwick' appeared to be interchangeable. Similarly with surnames eg MacKenzie *or* Mackenzie *or* McKenzie *or* Mckenzie. The Borders' surnames of Kerr and Hogg suffered in a similar way with members of the same family known as Kerr or Ker, Hogg or Hog.

Appendix 2: Current Status of Parliamentary Churches

...when the buildings are seen well-maintained and whitewashed in their Highland settings, they are not without charm.

Sonia Hackett and Neil Livingston, essay in *Studies in Scottish Antiquity*

The situation across Scotland is still fluid in terms of the final settlement of congregations and buildings. Readers are advised to consult websites to ascertain up-to-date information.

The following list gives the current status of the Parliamentary Churches as at the time of writing:

LOCHGILPHEAD: Original church demolished and replaced in 1885. Under the current Presbytery Plan for Argyll there are plans to close this building no later than 2026.

MUCKAIRN (Manse only): Under the new Presbytery's proposals, the church will remain in use for the foreseeable future.

DUROR: The church is still in use holding twice-monthly services. It forms part of South Lochaber Parish Church.

KILMENY (Manse only): Under the Presbytery Plan for Argyll, the Kilmeny building hosts a monthly service for the newly-united congregation of Islay North and West Parish.

PORTNAHAVEN: As with Kilmeny, the Portnahaven building hosts a monthly service for the newly- united congregation of Islay North and West Parish.

OA ISLAY: The church is now a roofless ruin, standing as a memorial to the ministers who served there. It was set on fire in 1915 and closed after the final service in 1930.

KINLOCHSPELVIE : The church was converted to private house.

SALEN (Manse only) : The manse is now a private house.

TOBERMORY : The original Telford church was replaced by a fine new building in the Victorian Gothic style in 1897. Along with Salen, Dervaig and Craignure, Tobermory forms part of North Mull Parish.

ULVA: The original Telford church was replaced in 1899 and is now used as a community resource with occasional services held.

App. 2: Current Status of Parliamentary Churches

IONA: The interior was reordered and turned through 90 degrees in 1924. The building remains in use, holding services on the first and third Sundays in the month. Iona is linked with the congregations of Kilfinichen, Kilvickeon and the Ross of Mull.

STRONTIAN: The original church was remodelled in 1924 and is now unrecognisable as a Telford church. Now part of the Peninsula Churches, services are still held here on the second and fourth Sundays of the month. The Peninsula Churches consist of the former congregations of Acharacle and Ardnamurchan and Ardgour, Morvern and Strontian.

ACHARACLE: The interior was reordered and turned through 90 degrees in the 1930s. Now part of the Peninsula Churches, services are still held in the original building.

NORTH BALLACHULISH / ARDGOUR: North Ballachulish church replaced in 1900. Ardgour was created a distinctive parish in 1899 and now forms part of the Peninsula Churches. The church is still in use.

ROTHIEMURCHUS (Manse only): In private hands

TOMINTOUL: Unrecognisable now as a Telford church with many Victorian accretions.

INSH (Manse only) : Now a private dwelling.

STENSCHOLL : Now linked with Kilmuir Parish Church, services are still held.

HALLIN IN WATERNISH : Now redeveloped as a self-catering unit.

TRUMISGARRY : Now a roofless ruin.

BERNERAY : A roofless ruin until 2011 when it was rescued and transformed into a creative studio for artists, actors and musicians, as seen in Channel Four's programme 'The Restoration Man'.

PLOCKTON : The building was renovated and rededicated in 1961. It is now used by both the Free Church and the Church of Scotland as a popular place of worship.

SHIELDAIG : Original church demolished and rebuilt on Telford's foundations and footings. Now linked with Applecross, Lochcarron and Torridon parishes, services are held twice a month.

STRATHCONAN AND GARVE (Carnoch) : Fell into disuse and converted to a domestic dwelling in 2017. The conversion was featured in the programme 'Scotland's Home of the Year' 2022.

KINLOCHLUICHART : At present, the church remains in use.

POOLEWE : According to Highland Historic Environment records, the church was made redundant.

CROICK : The church is temporarily closed due to an unsafe gable end. Services were conducted once a month during the summer. The congregation is now part of Dornoch Firth Churches centred on Dornoch Cathedral.

ULLAPOOL : Last used as a church in 1935 and was sold to Ullapool Museum Trust who completed renovations, opening as Ullapool Museum in 1995.

CROSS (or NESS) : The church was in use until 1905 but has since been demolished.

KNOCK : The original church was demolished.

STOER : The church was in use until 1963 and has been derelict since 1970. Planning application was lodged in January 2024 to turn the church into a private dwelling.

KINLOCHBERVIE : The original church now hosts the Free Presbyterian congregation.

STRATHY : Now a private dwelling.

BERRIEDALE : The building ceased as a parish church in 2008. Now under the auspices of the Berriedale Church and Cemetery Association, the church is available for weddings, talks, musical events and exhibitions.

KEISS : The church is still in use as part of Pentland Parish, a union with Canisbay, Olrig and Dunnet churches.

DEERNESS (Manse only) : Now a private dwelling.

RONALDSAY : Current status unknown.

SANDWICK : The church is still in use, hosting weekly services.

QUARFF : The church is currently on the 'Buildings at Risk' register with the latest inspection being on October 2022. There had previously been a planning application submitted in 1993 to convert it to a dwelling but this was refused. It is now in the hands of Quarff Church Trust.

INNERWICK - GLENLYON (Manse only) : Manse now demolished although the heritor paid for the erection of a rectangular sanctuary bearing many of the features of a Telford Church.

(KINLOCH) RANNOCH (Manse only) : current status unknown. As with Innerwick, the heritor paid for the erection of a rectangular sanctuary bearing many of the features of a Telford Church.

KIRKTOWN OF FOSS (Manse only) : Manse now a private dwelling.

Appendix 3: Proprietors

LOCHGILPHEAD: *John McNeill of Oakfield* owner of Auchendarroch Estate, situated west of Lochgilphead and bordering the Crinan Canal. Acquired in the late 18th century from a bankrupt Campbell family. He played a key role in developing Lochgilphead and supported the building of the canal. Bad investments ruined him and, by way of paying a debt, passed the 7,000 acre estate to Alexander Campbell of Inverawe in 1837.

MUCKAIRN (Manse only): *General Duncan Campbell of Lochnell and Barbreck (1763-1837)* was a Scottish soldier and Whig politician representing Ayr Burghs as MP.

DUROR: *Robert Downie of Appin (1771-1841)* was the chairman of the Edinburgh and Glasgow Union Canal Company. He acquired 35,000 acres on Loch Linnhe from trustees on behalf of 8th Marquis of Tweeddale. MP for Stirling Burghs. He was stoutly anti-Catholic and called his constituents 'damned scoondrels'. He was vice-president for SPCK. Raised Presbyterian he latterly embraced Episcopalianism and was an important investor in the construction of St John's Episcopal Church in Edinburgh.

KILMENY, PORTNAHAVEN AND OA: *Walter F Campbell of Shawfield and Islay (1798-1855)* was MP for Argyllshire 1822-1832 and again 1835-1841. He was a committed improver of drainage, planting and conservation.

KINLOCHSPELVIE, MULL: *Murdoch Maclaine, Chief Lochbuie Maclaine (1791-1844)* converted to Presbyterianism after the 1745. He held lands on Mull, Jura, Morvern and Tiree. He fought in the Peninsula War gaining the rank of lieutenant in the 42nd Highlanders (Black Watch).

SALEN: *Rt Hon James Drummond, Viscount Strathallan (1767-1851)* was a son-in-law of the Duke of Argyll who sponsored him into parliament as MP for Perthshire, in 1812 and again in 1820. Elevated to the Lords in 1825. He was a staunch anti-reformer and protectionist.

TOBERMORY: Held by the British Society for Extending the Fisheries.

ULVA: *Charles MacQuarrie of Ulva 1771-1835* was the son of Lachlan who sold their lands to pay off creditors. Charles was close to Maclaine (above) but they fell out over a business deal.

IONA: *George William, Duke of Argyll 1768-1835* was MP for St Germans, one of the English 'rotten boroughs'. He was Keeper of the Great Seal of Scotland and an enthusiastic improver.

STRONTIAN/ACHARACLE: *Sir James M Riddell of Ardnamurchan 1787-1861* was a landowner and committed improver of his lands at Sunart. The family estate was at Strontian. Riddell publicly and bitterly denounced those who had broken away from the Established Church fearing this would lead to a general uprising.

NORTH BALLACHULISH: *Donald, Cameron of Locheil 1769-1832* was an absentee for most of these years, although pushed ahead with the Cameron Clearances. Deemed unfit to run the estate, trustees were appointed but Locheil regained control in 1819.

ARDGOUR: *Alexander McLean of Ardgour 1764-1855* was the 13th laird. A professional soldier he achieved the rank of major. In 1805 he was appointed Receiver General of Land Rents, Paymaster of the Civil Establishments and Receiver General of Land Tax.

ROTHIEMURCHAS (Manse only): *Sir John Peter Grant of Rothiemurchas 1774-1848* was one of many who squandered an inheritance and he also fell short in his aspirations in politics and law. Served as MP for Great Grimsby and Tavistock. Financially irresponsible, he abandoned his Edinburgh home and relocated to his Highland estate now some £60,000 in debt. He was hounded by his creditors and went on to serve as a judge in Bombay (Mumbai) and Bengal.

TOMINTOUL: *Alexander, 4th Duke of Gordon (1743-1827)* raised the Gordon Highlanders. He was Keeper of the Great Seal of Scotland, Chancellor of King's College and Lord Lieutenant of Aberdeenshire. He was responsible for establishing the villages of Fochabers, Tomintoul and Portgordon.

INSH (Manse only): *Sir George McPherson Grant of Ballindalloch (1781-1846)* was MP for Sutherland from 1809 to 1812, and again from 1816 to 1826. He was a devoted farmer and conscientious improver of his estate.

STENSCHOLL: *Sir Godfrey Macdonald, Lord Macdonald (1775-1832)*, a professional soldier he gained the rank of Major-General fighting in the Peninsula War. He inherited his uncle's fortune and Yorkshire estate, Gunthwaite.

HALLIN: *Rt. Hon. Charles Grant of Glenelg (1778-1866)* was MP for Inverness Burghs, later Invernessshire. He was appointed Lord of the Treasury, Chief Secretary for Northern Ireland, and Vice-President of the Board of Trade. A humanitarian evangelical Anglican he staunchly supported Catholic emancipation. He was a commissioner of the Caledonian Canal and of the Highland Churches.

TRUMISGARRY: Lord Macdonald (see above)

BERNERAY: *Alexander Norman McLeod of Harris (?-1834)* inherited his grandfather's fortune who had improved harbours and established fishing stations. When the kelp industry collapsed he lost 75% of his income and became a ruthless clearer of his Harris estate to recoup his loses. However, he was profligate and, with debts mounting, his appointed trustees sold the estate to Lord Dunmore.

PLOCKTON: *Sir Hugh Innes of Lochalsh (1764-1831)* was MP for Ross-shire and then Sutherland. Created a Baron in recognition of his services to the countryside despite having cleared the whole of Kintail. He financed the building of churches at Plockton in 1794 and at Kirkton in 1807. Plockton boomed during the fat herring years, but due to changes in fish migration, went bust and became the 'village of the poor'.

SHIELDAIG: *Thomas Mackenzie of Applecross, 8th Laird (1789-1827)* was MP for the county of Ross. Enthusiastic 'improver', Mackenzie removed his tenants to the unproductive shoreline while establishing a large sheep run. Robert Burns wrote his poem 'Address to Beelzebub' with the criticism of Mackenzie in mind.

STRATHCONIN: *James Stuart of Dunearn (1775-1849)* was a Whig politician, controversial, quarrelsome and attracted lawsuits. In 1821, the entire Strathconin estate was for sale and Stuart appears as a 'heritor' in 1825 when the application was made for a new Parliamentary Church. Stuart was already bankrupt and left the country in 1828 and the estate in the hands of trustees.

KINLOCHLUICHART: *Sir James Mackenzie of Scatwell (1770-1843)* was MP for Ross-shire and Lord Lieutenant of the county.

POOLEWE: *Sir Francis A Mackenzie of Gairloch (1798-1843)* was 5th Baronet. Known as a 'well-informed, enthusiastic agricultural improver' he was a benevolent landlord who opposed the Clearances and planned new townships for his crofters to give them more land, security of tenure and better living conditions.

CROICK: *Sir Charles Ross of Balnagowan (1812-1883), 7th Baronet.*

ULLAPOOL: Held by the British Society for Extending the Fisheries.

CROSS (or NESS): *Sir James A Stewart-Mackenzie of Glasserton and Seaforth (1783-1862)* was MP for Ross-shire 1831-1832 and then for Ross and Cromarty 1832-1837. Became Governor of Ceylon and then Lord High Commissioner of the Ionian Islands.

KNOCK: *Hon Mrs Mary Elizabeth Frederica Stewart-Mackenzie (1783-1862)* married Sir James (above) and was the subject of the Brahan Seer's most famous prophecy that not a male heir to the Seaforth dynasty would remain and that the extensive land-holdings would be dispersed. This all came to pass.

RHUISTORE (or STOER or STORR): *Countess of Sutherland (Stafford) (1765-1839)* b. Elizabeth Sutherland Leveson-Gower. At the age of one, she succeeded to her father's titles and estates which were heavily mortgaged, on her parents' deaths. Married George Levison-Gower who succeeded his father's title of Marquess of Stafford, later Duke of Sutherland. GLG's huge inheritance facilitated the purchase of their subsequent estates. By 1816, the Staffords owned two-thirds of Sutherland but it was the Countess who actively managed the 1.5 million acres. An entry in Telford's first report states: 'The site of the church is remarkably well-selected. The noble proprietors Marquis and Marchioness of Stafford have, with their accustomed liberality, granted 9 acres as garden glebe, with liberty to cut peats in the moss.'

KINLOCHBERVIE: *Eric, Lord Reay 7th Baronet (1773-1847)* sold the Reay lands to the Staffords in 1829, from whom he had borrowed £100,000 in 1825 (the equivalent of £7.6m today). He bought a plantation in Guyana and in 1835 received £17,205 compensation for the emancipation of 331 slaves. Telford, as with Rhuistore, reports with fulsome praise for the Staffords: 'As this portion of the country has lately become the property of the Marquis of Stafford, to whom the Highlands of Scotland are so much indebted, great improvement may reasonably be expected in the means of internal communications, in the promotion of fisheries and consequent improvement of the people'.

STRATHY: *Duke of Sutherland (see above)*

BERRIEDALE: *James Horne of Langwell (1754-1831)* was a successful lawyer at the heart of the Edinburgh establishment and purchased Langwell in 1813 from Sir John Sinclair of Ulbster for £40,000. Sir John had made significant improvements as a benevolent landowner but Horne reversed much of these by introducing clearance on a widespread scale.

KEISS: *Kenneth Macleay of Newmore (1765-1825)*. By the time of his death, the family was already in financial crisis, one of the sons having to give up medical studies at Edinburgh University. Barbaraville was originally a planned village on Macleay land. Along with Lords Reay and Seaforth and Hugh Innes, Macleay were original subscribers to the building of Tain Academy in 1810.

App. 3: Proprietors

DEERNESS (Manse only): *John Balfour (1750-1842)* made his fortune with the East India Company, returning in 1790. He was MP for Orkney and Shetland 1790-1796 and again 1820-1826. An absentee landlord he lived chiefly in Edinburgh and London.

RONALDSAY: *William Traill of Woodwick (1797-1858)* was a Justice of the Peace and made Burgess and guild brother of Kirkwall, by order of the council, in 1818.

SANDWICK: *John Bruce of Sunburgh aka Bruce of Symbister (1798-1885)* served in the Royal Navy after education at the Royal Naval College in Portsmouth. He was known as a 'merchant-laird' deriving much of his income from his tenant farmers. Father of 13 children.

QUARFF: *John Ogilvie of Quarff 1800-1840* established The Shetland Bank in 1821 and for many years was Convener of Shetland.

INNERWICK (INTERWICK): *Ronald (Stewart) Menzies of Culdares (1790-1829)*. The family had split loyalties with sympathisers both of the Stuart claim to the throne and supporters of the Crown.

RANNOCH: *Allan Stewart, 4th of Innerhadden (1758-????)*.

FOSS: Major-General Stewart of Garth ((1772-1829) was a professional soldier in the Black Watch. Published two volumes which laid the foundation for the modern image of the Highlander, clans and regimental system. Moved in rarified circles in Edinburgh and became Governor of St Lucia.

Appendix 4: First Ministers of Parliamentary Churches

Names of first ministers of the Parliamentary Churches presented either by George 1V or William 1V, either ordained (ord.) into first parishes or 'admitted' (adm.) having been ordained elsewhere previously (prev.), usually as a missionary (miss.)

Lochgilphead	Peter MacKitchan	ord. 25 Sept 1828
Muckairn	Peter McVean	ord. 14 May 1829
Duror	Donald MacNaughton	ord. 7 May 1828 prev. miss. Glencoe
Kilmeny	James Pearson	ord. 6 May 1829 at Bowmore
Portnahaven	Alexander Campbell	ord. 6 May 1829 at Bowmore
Oa/Oth	Alexander MacNab	adm. 6 May 1829 at Bowmore, prev. ord. miss. Lochfyneside 1827
Berriedale	Donald MacLachlan	ord. 27 Dec 1827 SPCK Mission maintained
Plockton	Alexander MacDonald	ord. 29 Nov 1829 prev. Royal Bounty miss. at Strath
Sheildaig	Roderick Macrae	adm. 21 Aug 1827 ord. miss. Applecross 1793
Ullapool	Alexander Ross	adm. 16 Sept 1829 ord. miss. Ullapool 1819
Hallin (Waternish)	Roderick Reid	adm. 28 Sept 1829 ord. miss. Lyndale, Skye
Stenscholl	John Nicolson	adm. 23 Sept 1829 ord. miss. Minginish 1817
Trumisgarry	William MacQueen	adm. 22 Sept 1829 ord. by Pres. Uist 1824

APP. 4: FIRST MINISTERS OF PARLIAMENTARY CHURCHES

Cross (Old Ness)	Finlay Cook	adm. 29 July 1829
	ord. miss. Halsay and Halladay, catechist New Lanark 1816	
Deerness	Thomas Waugh	adm. 6 May 1830
	ord. Thornleyford, Northumberland 1807	
Quarff	James Gardner	ord. 10 Sept 1830
	assistant at Bressay	
Kinloch-Spelvie	David Stewart	ord. 11 Sept 1828
Salen	Duncan Maclean	adm. 4 Sept 1828
	ord. miss. Benbecula 1823	
Ulva	Neil Maclean	adm. 28 Aug 1828
	ord. Assistant Coll 1809	
Ballachuilish	John McMillan	adm. 28 Sept 1828
	ord. Pres. Abertarff.	
Strontian	Alexander Mackenzie	ord. 25 Sept 1829
Iona	Duguld Neil Campbell	ord. 7 May 1829
Tomintoul	Charles McPherson	ord. 25 Sept 1827
	schoolmaster	
Kinloch-Rannoch	John MacDonald	ord. 20 May 1830
Berneray	John Bethune	adm. 4 Sept 1829
	ord. miss Rhum and Canna 1821	
Croick	Robert Williamson	ord. 25 Sept 1828
	to Picton, Nova Scotia 1840	
Carnoch	John MacKenzie	adm. 28 Sept 1830
	schoolmaster Kiltearn ord. miss. Strathconin 1829	
Kinlochbervie	David MacKenzie	ord. 29 Aug 1829
Kinlochluichart	David Tulloch	ord. 27 Sept 1829
	schoolmaster Killearnan 1816	
Strathy	Angus MacIntosh McGillivray	ord. 25 Sept 1828
Keiss	Thomas Jolly	ord. 31 Dec 1827
Poolewe	Donald Macrae	adm. 13 May 1830
	schoolmaster Applecross, ord. miss. Benbecula 1824	
Stoer	Donald Gordon	adm. 2 Feb 1829
	ord. assistant Eddrachillis 1822	

North Ronaldsay	Patrick Fairbairn	ord. 28 July 1830
Knock	Robert Finlayson	ord. 23 Sept 1829
Glenlyon (now Innerwick)	John Macalister	ord. 9 Sept 1824 Parl. Church consecrated 1829
Rannoch	John MacDonald	ord. 13 May 1830 adm. miss. Berriedale 1807 Parl. Church consecrated 1826
Foss	Alexander Robertson Irvine	ord. 14 May 1830 Lochfyneside 1827
Berriedale	Donald MacLachlan	ord. 27 Dec 1827 SPCK Mission maintained
Plockton	Alexander MacDonald	ord. 29 Nov 1829 prev. Royal Bounty miss. at Strath
Sheildaig	Roderick Macrae	adm. 21 Aug 1827 ord. miss. Applecross 1793
Ullapool	Alexander Ross	adm. 16 Sept 1829 ord. miss. Ullapool 1819

Appendix 5 shows ministers who were in the Parliamentary Churches after the Disruption.

Churches whose first ministers were former missionaries and who remained within the Church of Scotland were Hallin-in-Waternish, Berneray, Ullapool and Kinlochbervie.

Those churches whose first ministers were former missionaries and who left to join the Free Church of Scotland were Kilmeny, Trumisgarry, Plockton, Shieldaig, Strathconon, Poolewe, Stoer and Berriedale.

Appendix 5: Post-Disruption Ministers

What happened in the parliamentary churches? By focusing on the Parliamentary Churches in the Highlands and Islands, we can account for the ministers of all but two charges vacant at the time of the Disruption.

Table One – 22 ministers remained and 18 left (i.e. 55% remained)

Parliamentary Church	Minister remained	Minister joined Free Ch.
Acharacle	Hugh Macdiarmid	
Berneray Isle	John Bethune	
Berriedale		Samuel Campbell
Croick		Gustavus Aird
Cross		John Finlayson
Deerness	Thomas Waugh	
Duror	Donald Macnaughton	
Foss (Kirktown of)	James Armstrong	
Hallin	Roderick Reid	
Insh	Lewis Macpherson	
Innerwick	(vacancy)	(vacancy)
Iona		Donald M'Vean
Keiss		Thomas Gunn
Kilmeny		James Pearson
Kinlochbervie	Robert Clark	
Kinlochluichart		Alexander Anderson
Kinlochspelvie	David Stewart	
Knock		Duncan Matheson
Lochgilphead	Donald Jackson	
Muckairn	(vacancy)	(vacancy)
N. Ballachulish+Ardgour		John Macmillan
Oa	Alexander Macnab	
Plockton		Alexander Macdonald
Portnahaven	Colin Hunter	
Poolewe		Donald McRae
Quarff		James Gardner
(Kinloch) Rannoch	John Macdonald	
Ronaldshay (North)		Adam White
Rothiemurchus	Charles Grant	
Salen	James Dewar	
Sandwick		Alexander Stark
Shieldaig		Colin Mackenzie
Stenscholl in Trotternish	Henry Beatson	
Stoer		Peter Davidson
Strathconan		John Mackenzie
Strathy	David Sutherland	
Strontian	Alexander Mackenzie	
Tobermory	Donald Stewart	
Tomintoul	Charles Macpherson	
Trumisgarry		Norman MacLeod
Ullapool	Alexander Ross	
Ulva	Neil Maclean	

Table Two: Parliamentary Churches listed by Counties

Parliamentary Church	Parish/Island/County
Lochgilphead	Glassry, Argyle
Muckairn	Muckairn, Argyle
Duror	Appin, Argyle
Kilmeny	Islay, Argyle
Portnahaven	Islay, Argyle
Oa	Islay, Argyle
Kinlochspelvie	Mull, Argyle
Salen	Mull, Argyle
Tobermory	Mull, Argyle
Ulva	Ulva, Argyle
Iona	Iona, Argyle
Strontian	Ardnamurchan, Argyle
Acharacle	Ardnamurchan, Argyle
NorthBallachulish and Ardgour	Kilmalie, Inverness/Argyle
Rothiemurchus	Rothiemurchus, Inverness
Tomintoul	Kirkmichael, Banff
Insh	Kingussie, Elgin
Stenscholl in Trotternish	Skye, Inverness
Halin in Waternish	Skye, Inverness
Trumisgarry	North Uist, Inverness
Berneray Isle	Harris, Inverness
Plockton	Lochalsh, Ross& Cromarty
Shieldaig	Applecross, ditto
Strathconan/Carnoch	Contin, ditto
Kinlochluichart	Contin, ditto
Poolewe	Gairloch, ditto
Croick	Kincardine, ditto
Ullapool	Loch Broom, ditto
Cross	Lewis, ditto
Knock	Lewis, ditto
Stoer (Rhuistore)	Assynt, Sutherland
Kinlochbervie	Edrachillis, Sutherland
Strathy	Farr, Sutherland
Berriedale	Latheron, Caithness
Keiss	Wick, Caithness
Deerness	Orkney & Shetland
Nth Ronaldshay	Orkney & Shetland
Sandwick	Orkney & Shetland
Quarff	Quarff, Orkney &Shetland
Innerwick	Fortingall, Perth
Rannoch (Kinloch)	Fortingall, Perth
Kirktown of Foss	Dull, Perth

Note: It is hard to be confident in the arithmetic of the whole Disruption event across Scotland.

Bibliography

Primary Sources

Acts and Proceedings of the General Assembly of the Church of Scotland, 1814-1820 (Special Collections, Glasgow)

An Act for building Additional Places of Worship in the Highlands and Islands of Scotland (London, 1823)

An Act to amend an Act for building Additional Places of Worship in the Highlands and Islands of Scotland (London, 1824)

Church of Scotland Records: Acts of the General Assembly of the Church of Scotland 1638-1842 (British History Online)

Ewing's Annals of the Free Church of Scotland

General Index to the First and Second Series of Hansard's Parliamentary Debates ed. Sir John Philippart, 1834

Highland and Island Emigration Society Records

Minutes of the Synod of Argyle, 1690 (NRS CH2/557/3)

Records of the Parliament of Scotland 1696

Register of the Actings and Proceedings of the General Assembly of the Church of Scotland 1814-1820 (Special Collections, Glasgow University Library)

Register of the Actings and Proceedings of the General Assembly of the Church of Scotland 1821-1823 (Special Collections, Glasgow University Library)

Reports (1-7) of the Commissioners for Building Churches in the Highlands and Islands of Scotland (London, The House of Commons, 1825-1835)

Royal Commission for inquiring into the Opportunities of Public Religious Worship and Means of Religious Instruction and the Pastoral Superintendence afforded to the people of Scotland 1835

Statutes of the Scottish Church 1225-1559, Scottish History Society Vol. LIV (Edinburgh, Scottish History Society 1907)

A Survey and Report of the Coasts and Central Highlands of Scotland; Made by the Command of The Right Honourable The Lords Commissioners of His Majesty's Treasury, Thomas Telford F.R.S. (London, The House of Commons, 1802-5)

To the Commissioners for Building additional Churches in the Highlands and Islands of Scotland under Statutes 4th Geo. IV. c. 79, and 5th Geo. IV. c. 75, so far as regards the Nomination of Ministers by Appointments from the Crown.

A Letter respectfully submitted by the Reverend Dr G. Baird, one of the Ministers, and Principal of the University, of Edinburgh, 1828 (published in The Fourth Report of the Commissioners for Building Churches in the Highlands and Islands of Scotland)

Contemporary books, pamphlets and articles

Aberdeen Press and Journal

Auld, Alexander, *Ministers and Men in the Far North* (John Menzies & Co, 1891)

Brown, Thomas, *Annals of the Disruption: with extracts from the narratives of ministers who left the Scottish establishment in 1843* (Edinburgh: MacNiven & Wallace, 1884)

Burns, Robert, *Winter; A Dirge* (Facsimile Edition, Lomond Books, 1991)

Duncan, Mary G.L., *History of the Revivals of Religion in the British Isles, Especially in Scotland* (Edinburgh, William Oliphant, 1t, 11 August 1792

Engels, Friedrich, *The Condition of the Working Class in England in 1844* (Oxford University Press, 1993, first published 1844)

The Free Church of Scotland Monthly Record, October 1, 1864, 1874

Inverness Courier

Johnson, Samuel, *A Journey to the Western Isles of Scotland* (a new edition printed for A. Strachan and T. Cadell, London 1791)

Kinloch, James, *An Account of the Improvements on the Estates of the Marquis of Stafford, by James Kinloch, General Agent of the Sutherland Estates* (London, printed for Longman, Hurst, Rees, Ovine & Brown,1820)

Lauder, Thomas, *The Great Floods of August 1829* (Elgin, R. Stewart, 1873)

London Gazette

Martin, Martin, *A Description of the Western Isles of Scotland (*London, Andrew Bell, 1703

Mackenzie, Sir George Steuart, *General View of the Agriculture of the Counties of Ross & Cromarty* (London, Richard Phillips, 1810)

McCosh, James, *The wheat and the chaff gathered into bundles : a statistical contribution towards the history of the recent disruption of the Scottish ecclesiastical establishment* (Perth, J. Dewar, 1843)

Miller, Hugh, *My Schools and Schoolmasters or The Story of My Education*, (Edinburgh, B&W Publishing, 1993, first published 1860)

Mitchell, Joseph, *Reminiscences of my Life in the Highlands, Vols 1 and 2* (Devon, Lewis Reprints, 1971, originally published 1884)

More, Thomas, *Utopia* (London, Penguin Classics, 2012)

Northern Times

Pope, Alexander, *An Essay on Criticism* (Project Gutenberg EBook of *An Essay on Criticism*, first published 1811)

Sage, Donald, *Memorabilia Domestica or Parish Life in the North of Scotland* (Wick, William Rae. Edinburgh: John Menzies & Co. 1899)

Southey, Robert, *Journal of a Tour of Scotland in 1819* (London, John Murray, 1929)

Telford, Thomas, *A survey and report of the coasts and central highlands of Scotland; made by the command of the right honourable the lords commissioners of his Majesty's treasury in the Autumn of 1802* (Philosophical Magazine Series 1, 15:60, 300-311, DOI)

The Scotsman

Weir, Daniel, *A History of the Town of Greenock* (D. Weir, 1829)

Wylie, James A., *Disruption Worthies* (Edinburgh, Thomas C Jack, 1881)

Secondary Sources: Books

Ansdell, Douglas, *The People of the Great Faith: The Highland Church 1690-1900* (Stornoway, Acair, 1998)

Atkinson, Tom, *The Empty Lands: The Northern Highlands of Scotland, lands of endless natural beauty, including Western Ross, Caithness and Sutherland* (Edinburgh, Luath Press 1999)

Blackie, John Stuart, *The Scottish Highlanders and the Land Laws* (London, Chapman and Hald, 1885)

Bradley, Ian, *The Coffin Roads – Journeys to the West* (Edinburgh, Birlinn, 2022)

Breeze, David, ed. *Studies in Scottish Antiquity* (John Donald, Edinburgh, 1984)

Brown, Stewart J., *Thomas Chalmers and the Godly Commonwealth* (Oxford University Press, 1992)

Burleigh, J.H.S., *A Church History of Scotland* (Oxford University Press, 1960)

Burns, Thomas, *Church Property: The Benefice Lectures 1905* (Edinburgh, George E. Morton, 1906)

Carmichael, Alexander, *Carmina Gadelica: Hymns and Incantations* (Edinburgh, Floris Books 1992)

Cooper, Derek, *Road to the Isles* (Routledge & Kegan Paul Ltd, 1979)

Cooper, Derek, Skye (Edinburgh, Birlinn, 1995)

Cheyne, A.C., *The Transforming of the Kirk* (Edinburgh, St Andrew Press, 1983)

Dawson, Jane A.E., *The Origin of the "Road to the Isles": Trade, Communications and Campbell Power,* in Mason & Macdougall, eds., *People and Power in Scotland,* (Edinburgh, John Donald Publishers, 1992)

Devine, T.M., 'The Making of Industrial and Urban Society: Scotland 1780-1840' in Mitchison, Rosalind ed., *Why Scottish History Matters* (Edinburgh, The Saltire Society, 1991)

Devine, T.M., *The Scottish Clearances: a History of the Dispossessed* (Allen Lane, 2018)

Dodgshon, Robert A., *From Chiefs to Landlords: Social and Economic Change in the Western Highlands and Islands, c.1493-1820* (Edinburgh, Edinburgh University Press, 1998)

Donaldson, Gordon, *The Faith of the Scots* (London, B.T. Batsford Ltd, 1990)

Donaldson, Gordon, *Scotland: The Making of the Kingdom James V-James VII* (Edinburgh, Mercat Press, 1994)

Fagan, Brian, *The Little Ice Age* (USA, Basic Books, 2000)

Fulton, Graham, *The Paisley Civil War* (Controlled Explosion Press, Paisley, 2018)

Gibb, Alexander, *The Story of Telford: The Rise of Civil Engineering* (London, Alexander MacLehose, 1935)

Gray, Daniel, *A Life of Industry: the photograph of John R. Hume* (Edinburgh, Historic Environment Scotland, 2021)

Grigor, Iain Murray, *Mightier than a Lord* (Stornoway, Acair Limited, 1979)

Haldane, A.R.B., *New Ways Through The Glens* (Newton Abbot, David & Charles, 1962)

Hamilton, T.W., *How Greenock Grew: A Civic Survey – Housing and Town Planning* (Greenock, James McKelvie & Sons, 1946, revised 1947)

Hanna, W., *Life of Thomas Chalmers* (Hardpress, 2020)

Hunter, James, *The Making of the Crofting Community* (Edinburgh, Birlinn, 2000)

Hunter, James, *Set Adrift Upon the World – The Sutherland Clearances* (Edinburgh, Birlinn, 2015)

Hutchinson, Roger, *Martyrs: Glendale and the Revolution in Skye*, (Edinburgh, Birlinn, 2015)

Johnson, J.T., *The Rev Patrick Brewster: His Chartist Socialist Sermons* (Glasgow, Forward Printing, 1839)

Kennedy, John, *The Days of the Fathers in Ross-shire* (Inverness, Northern Chronicle Office, 1927)

Kennedy, John, *'The Apostle of the North' – Rev Dr John Macdonald*, (Thomas Nelson and Sons, London 1867)

Lockhart, John Gibson, *Memoirs of the Life of Sir Walter Scott* (Edinburgh, Adam and Charles Black, 1872)

Lynch, Michael, *Scotland: A New History* (London, Pimlico, 1991)

MacAskill, John, ed. *The Highland Destitution of 1837: Government Aid and Public Subscription* (Scottish History Society, 2012)

Macaulay, Murdo, *Aspects of the Religious History of Lewis – Up to the Disruption of 1843* (Inverness, John G. Eccles Printer, 1980)

MacColl, Allan W., *Land, Faith and the Crofting Community* (Edinburgh University Press, 2006)

Macdonald, Finlay, *From Reform to Renewal* (Edinburgh, St Andrew Press, 2017)

MacGillivray, Angus, *Revivals in the Highlands* (Reformation Press, 2016)

MacInnes, Alan I., Jacobitism, Wormald, Jenny *Scotland Revisited*, Chapter XI (London, Collins & Brown, 1991)

MacInnes, J., *The Evangelical Movement in the Highlands of Scotland* (Aberdeen, 1951)

MacKenzie, Alexander, *History of the Highland Clearances* (A. & W. MacKenzie Inverness, 1883; reprinted by Mercat Press, Edinburgh 1991)

MacLean, Allan, *Telford's Highland Churches*, (Society of West Highland and Island Historical Research 1989 – and see under 'Theses' below)

Maclennan, Iain, *Applecross and Its Hinterland: A Historical Miscellany* (A'Chomraich Publishing 2013)

Macnaughton, Colin, *Church Life in Ross and Sutherland from the Revolution 1688 to the Present Time* (Inverness, The Northern Counties Newspaper and Printing and Publishing Company, 1915)

Macrae, Alexander, *Revivals in the Highlands and Islands in the 19th Century* (Tentmaker Publications 1998)

MacSillar, Donald, *St Michael and the Preacher: A Tale of Skye* (Inverness, Law, Justice & Co, 1883)

Magnusson, Sally, *Music in the Dark* (John Murray/Hachette, 2023)

McCormack, Rachel, *Chasing the Dram, Finding the Spirit of Whisky* (Simon and Schuster, 2017)

McKay, Johnston, *The Kirk and the Kingdom* (Edinburgh University Press, 2012)

Minto, Jenni and Wilson, Les, *Islay Voices* (Edinburgh, Birlinn, 2016)

Mitchison, Rosalind, *A History of Scotland* (London and New York: Routledge, 2nd edn 1982)

Moffat, Alistair, *Scotland's Last Frontier – A Journey Along The Highland Line* (Edinburgh, Birlinn, 2012)

Morris, Chris, *On Tour with Thomas Telford* (Longhope, Tanners Yard Press, 2nd edn, 2006)

Morris, Chris, *Thomas Telford's Scotland*

Newell, John Philip, *Sacred Earth Sacred Soul* (William Collins 2021)

Newell, John Philip, *A.J. Scott and his Circle*

Niebuhr, Reinhold, *The Children of Light and the Children of Darkness*, (University of Chicago Press, edition 2011)

Noble, John, *Religious Life in Ross*, (Inverness, The Northern Counties Newspaper and Printing and Publishing Company, 1909)

Paton, David, *The Clergy and the Clearances* (Edinburgh, John Donald, 2006)

Pearce, Rhoda M., *Thomas Telford* (Princes Risborough, Shire Publications Ltd, 2nd edn, 1992)

Phillipson, N.T. and Mitchison, Rosalind, eds, *Scotland in the Age of Improvement* (Edinburgh University Press, 1970)

Prebble, John, *John Prebble's Scotland* (London, Secker and Warburg, 1984 (and Penguin 1986)

Rahner, Karl, *On the Theology of Death* (New York, Herder and Herder 1965)

Rait, Sir Robert and Pryde, George, *Scotland* (London, Ernest Benn Limited, 1934)

Roberts, Alasdair, *Chapels of the Rough Bounds: Morar, Knoydart, Arisaig, Moidart* (Mallaig, 2015)

Roberts, Alasdair and Dean, Ann, *Northern Catholic History Notes,* (Mallaig, Mallaig Heritage Centre, 2015)

Robertson, C.J.A., *Railway Mania in the Highlands,* from Mason and Macdougall, Eds., *People and Power in Scotland* (Edinburgh, John Donald Publishers, 1992)

Rolt, L.T.C., *Thomas Telford (London, The Scientific Book Club, 1958)*

Smith, Donald, *God, the Poet and the Devil: Robert Burns and Religion* (St Andrew Press, 2008)

Stein, Jock, *Temple and Tartan, Psalms, Poetry and Scotland* (Haddington: Handsel Press 2022)

Taylor, William Harrison and Messer, Peter C., eds, *Faith and Slavery in the Presbyterian Diaspora* (Bethlehem PA, Lehigh University Press, 2016)

Watts, John, *A Record of Generous People: a History of the Catholic Church in Argyll & the Isles* (Glasgow, Ovada Books, 2013)

Whyte, Iain, *'Send Back the Money: the Free Church of Scotland and American Slavery',* (Cambridge, James Clarke & Co, 2012)

Wormald, Jenny, ed., *Scotland Revisited* (London, Collins and Brown, 1991)

Secondary Sources: Articles in Journals, lectures etc.

Bangor-Jones, Malcolm, *From Clanship to Crofting: Landownership, Economy and the Church in the Province of Strathnaver* (Scottish Society for Northern Studies)

Brown, Stewart J. (1997). *Religion and the Rise of Liberalism: The First Disestablishment Campaign in Scotland, 1829–1843* (The Journal of Ecclesiastical History, Vol. 48, 682-704 doi:10.1017/S0022046900013464)

Campbell, Donald John, *Waternish Churches Facebook,* 2020

Ferguson, William, *The Problems of the Established Church in the West Highlands and Islands in the Eighteenth Century* (Records of the Scottish Church History Society, Vol. XVII, part I, 1969)

Hacket, Sonia and Livingston, Neil, in Breeze, David (ed.), *Studies in Scottish Antiquities* (John Donald, Edinburgh)

Jack, Ian, *Chasing Steel*, an article in the London Review of Books, 22 September 2022.

Kelly, Jamie, *The Mission at Home: The Origins and Development of the Society in Scotland for Propagating Christian Knowledge, 1709-1767* (University of Glasgow eSharp Issue 24: Belonging and Inclusion, Spring 2016)

Lennie, Thomas, a lecture: *Revivals in the Highlands and Islands*, (Highland Theological College, University of the Highlands and Islands, March 2017)

Macdonald, Michael, *Priests of South Uist* (Public Lecture 2010)

Macinnes, Allan, 'Lochaber: Bandit Country or Jacobite Heartland?' Lecture, May 2013, The Sunart Centre, Strontian Report by Kate Kennedy

Mearns, Alexander B., *The Minister and the Bailiff: A Study of Presbyterian Clergy in the Northern Highlands during the Clearances* (Records of The Scottish Church History Society, 1990, 53-75)

Sawkins, John W., *The Financing of Ministerial Stipends in the Established Church of Scotland: the Rural Parish* (The Journal of Ecclesiastical History, Vol. 76 Issue 3 July 2023, 535-570 doi:10.1017/S0022046922002007)

Theses

Currie, David Alan, *The Growth of Evangelicalism in the Church of Scotland 1793 – 1943* (PhD thesis University of St Andrews 1991)

Lodge, Christine, *The Clearers and the Cleared; Women, Economy and Land in the Scottish Highlands 1800 – 1900* (PhD thesis University of Glasgow 1996)

Maclean, A.M., *Scottish Architecture, Parliamentary Churches* (Diploma thesis University of Edinburgh Scottish History Department 1972)

Smith, Donald C., *The Failure and Recovery of Social Criticism in the Scottish Church 1830 – 1950* (PhD thesis University of Edinburgh 1963)

Stephen, John R., *The Impact of Geography on Ecclesiastical Endeavour in the Highlands'* (PhD thesis University of Glasgow 2004)